BIG BABIES

Big Babies

Michael Kinsley

William Morrow
and Company, Inc.
New York

It is the policy of William Morrow and Company, Inc., and its imprints and affiliates, recognizing the importance of preserving what has been written, to print the books we publish on acid-free paper, and we exert our best efforts to that end.

Library of Congress Cataloging-in-Publication Data

Kinsley, Michael E.
    Big babies / by Michael Kinsley.—1st ed.
        p.   cm.
    ISBN 0-688-12452-6 (alk. paper)
    1. United States—Politics and government—1981–1989. 2. United
States—Politics and government—1989–1993. 3. United States—
Politics and government—1993– I. Title.
E876.K53   1995
973.92—dc20   95–14364
                                                                      CIP

Printed in the United States of America

First Edition

1 2 3 4 5 6 7 8 9 10

BOOK DESIGN BY DEBORAH KERNER

ONTENTS

INTRODUCTION

As a magazine editor, I tried to forbid quotations from Tocqueville. But as a writer, I cannot resist: "The French under the old monarchy held it for a maxim that the king could do no wrong; and if he did do wrong, the blame was imputed to his advisors. . . . The Americans entertain the same opinion with respect to the majority."

Tocqueville calls this "the courtier spirit in America." He goes on:

> It is true that American courtiers do not say "Sire" or "Your Majesty," a distinction without a difference. They are forever talking of the natural intelligence of the people whom they serve; they do not debate the question which of the virtues of their master is pre-eminently worthy of admiration, for they assure him that he possesses all the virtues without having acquired them, or without caring to acquire them; they do not give him their daughters and their wives to be raised at his pleasure to the rank of his concubines; but by sacrificing their opinions they prostitute themselves. Moralists and philosophers in America are not obliged to conceal their opinions under the veil of allegory; but before they venture upon a harsh truth, they say, "We are aware that the people whom we are addressing are too superior to the weaknesses of human nature to lose the command of their temper for an instant. We should not hold this language if we were not speaking to men whom their virtues and their intelligence render more worthy of freedom than all the rest of the world." The sycophants of Louis XIV could not flatter more dexterously.

I hope no one can accuse me of displaying the "courtier spirit" in this book. Indeed, if there is a theme running through these pieces from the past decade—and there is, sort of—it is one of annoyance at the fatuous populism that dominates American politics. This may be summarized as, "The politicians are awful, but the people are wonderful." That is at least half-wrong. The politicians, most of them, may deserve no prize. But in a democracy, the people cannot duck responsibility by blaming the politicians.

And, although various procedural explanations are available to explain why the results of democracy leave most voters noisily dissatisfied (special-interest gridlock, constitutional defects of the separation of powers, etc.), at bottom the citizens as individuals *are* to blame for American democracy's current discontents. They make flagrantly incompatible demands—cut my taxes, preserve my benefits, balance the budget—then explode in self-righteous outrage when the politicians fail to deliver. As we go to press in mid-1995, the Republicans claim to have proved me wrong on this point. We shall see. They demand "change," but really want everything to stay exactly the same. Their attention wanders from issue to issue, with duration of interest seemingly in inverse relation to its intensity. They are, in short, big babies.

As I maintain, somewhat defensively, throughout this collection, I don't think this argument is elitist. It is holding your fellow citizens to the same standard to which you would hold a respected friend. Nevertheless, let me absolve my fellow liberals of any guilt by association. The big-babies argument has no particular political coloration, and most Democratic politicians indulge in the "courtier spirit" just as assiduously as most Republicans do.

In fact, the big-babies critique is really just the political version of a broader critique of American society that is more often heard from conservatives. Americans, it is said, are wallowing in debilitating self-pity, and imprisoned in a "cult of victimization." Manifestations include the ubiquitous twelve-step programs of the misnamed "self-help" movement; the explosion of tort lawsuits over trivial or imagined abuses; and the "political correctness" epidemic on college campuses. I think there's a lot to this, though there is also some exaggeration (especially about political correctness). But in the political arena it is conservatives, more than liberals, who stoke the fires of resentment and encourage vast swaths of the electorate to indulge in fantasies of victimization by others.

Not every piece in this collection is a variation on the big-babies theme. The articles cover three presidencies and a wide variety of topics, some not political at all. And some of the pieces are humorous, or at least are supposed to be. This is another matter on which I'm a bit defensive, since—like any pundit, especially a pundit seeking the prestige of hard covers—I wish to be taken seriously. But it does seem to me that humor is not only valuable for its own sake. It also efficiently makes the point that much of what goes on is perfectly ridiculous. This is a point that serious political punditry often suppresses. If that's not too pompous.

The articles in this collection come from *The New Republic*, *Time* magazine, *The New Yorker*, *The Washington Post*, *The Wall Street Journal*, and *The New York Times*. Thanks to editors too numerous to mention at all these places, but especially to Dorothy Wickenden, Rick Hertzberg, Andrew Sullivan, and David Shipley at *TNR;* Henry Muller, Jim Gaines, and Dick Duncan at *Time;* Tina Brown, Henry Finder, Deborah Garrison, and Rick Hertzberg (again) at *The New Yorker;* Meg Greenfield and Ken Ikenberry at the *Post;* Bob Bartley and Tim Ferguson at the *Journal;* and Mike Levitas at the *Times*.

Professor Paul Gewirtz of Yale Law School, whom I had never met at that point, sent me a letter out of the blue several years ago, suggesting (based on his reading of my columns) a book on the big-babies theme. This is the closest I'll ever come, so many thanks to him. And thanks to my patient and tolerant agent, Raphael Sagalyn. Thanks as well to all my colleagues at CNN's "Crossfire," who have taught me much over the years.

This book is dedicated to *The New Republic*, as an institution and as a collection of remarkable people. It is dedicated especially to Marty and Anne Peretz, who have sustained it—and me—for two decades.

BIG BABIES

LITTLE NOTE

(*The New Republic*, JANUARY 20, 1986)

The list of people I personally despise is very short, and the man at the top of it (a former boss) sent me a nice note the other day, complimenting something I'd written. My correspondent and I haven't crossed paths for several years, but he is a man of no largeness of soul whatsoever, and I'm pretty sure that he still holds up his end of our mutual contempt. Nevertheless, his note made my day. This demonstrates Kinsley's law of flattery, which holds that insincere flattery is more flattering than sincere flattery. After all, what do I care what this philistine oaf actually thinks about my article? On the other hand, there is a genuine if unintended compliment in the fact that he troubled to write—and the less he meant what he said, the greater that compliment is.

The "little note" is a great social institution about which little has been written, apart from a passing reference in the Gettysburg Address ("The world will little note nor long remember . . ."). Kinsley's law is really just a corollary of the general proposition that all flattery is flattering. The wonderful thing about the "little note" is that, however cynical or stupid, it cannot fail to achieve its purpose of pleasing the recipient. Every New Year I resolve to write more of them. Only sincere ones, of course. But I'm sure I speak for every journalist in America in saying that if you were to program a computer to send me a letter once a month saying simply, "Dear Mike: Superb piece! All best," I would gratefully fill in the details, and come to respect your discernment. A friend suggests the same technique might also work with politicians, as in, "Dear Senator: That was a tremendous act of statesmanship last week." But the typical pol might find such a vague compliment more frightening than flattering. My God, what had he done?

Hostage to Hypocrisy

(*The New Republic*, DECEMBER 8, 1986)

These are trying times for the loyal Reaganite. Not since that poignant moment in 1939 when American Communists learned about the Hitler-Stalin pact has a sudden policy reversal put devoted ideologues to such a severe test of their devotion. A party line of stark moral simplicity—no dealing with terrorist states—has suddenly gone all gooey and geopolitical. Reagan cultists had a couple of years to readjust their thinking about deficits. No such luxury this time.

As in 1939, many are falling off the train as it rounds this sharp bend. But a tenacious few hold on. Jeane Kirkpatrick, for example. Just last summer, she was writing with scorn about our craven allies who refuse to isolate terrorist nations. Now she writes with equal scorn of those who refuse to recognize "the hard realities with which governments must deal. . . . Governments, including those of our best friends, normally maintain open channels and working relationships with as many other governments as possible. . . . This is the way the world is." Dealing with terror even "may, occasionally, mean paying blackmail." Who'da thunk it?

And the gooeyist geopolitician of all is our president. Just last year Iran was part of "a new international version of Murder Incorporated." Now it "encompasses some of the most critical geography in the world . . . a critical position . . . oil flows . . . an absence of dialogue. . . ." Parts of Reagan's November 13 speech read like an application essay for the Trilateral Commission.

It's widely considered boring and juvenile to complain that an important national policy is hypocritical. Around my office, you get bopped on the head with quotations from Machiavelli if you try. The preferred complaints about Reagan's dealings with Iran analyze them in terms of ineptitude ("blunders"), decision-making disarray, or—ironically—geopolitical naïveté (we really should be tilting toward Iraq). Next in order of prestige come moral qualms about trading weapons for hostages. The simple objection that our president was saying one thing and doing another ranks very low.

Even when the focus is on the gap between Reagan's words and his deeds, the sophisticated term of abuse is "credibility," an interesting word. The implication is that the president doesn't actually have to be sincere, he just has to be believable.

It's true that in international diplomacy, as in personal relations, some hypocrisy is essential. But on the level of politics it is, or ought to be, less acceptable. Democracy can't function if leaders are allowed to say one thing and do another. The question of how to deal with terrorism has been one of the major foreign policy debates of the past few years. The perception that Reagan had very different ideas from President Carter about terrorism in general, and Iran in particular, was a key factor in his election. Imagine what would have happened in the last election if some Democratic candidate had tried to make a campaign issue out of the need to reach out and open a dialogue with Iran, because of its key strategic position and to free American hostages. Yet what is the point of elections if the winners can hide the fact that they aren't doing what they say?

There are laws—derived from bitter experience—that are designed to assure democratic review of official actions. In order to justify operations like the secret Iran dealings, and funding of the Nicaraguan contras, and the Libyan disinformation campaign, Reagan administration lawyers have worked overtime to produce highly creative (though inadequate) explanations of how these laws don't apply on alternate Thursdays when the moon is full, and so on. Contrast this enthusiasm for legal sophistry with the administration's supposed devotion to "original intent" in the case of constitutional interpretation. It seems that reverence for the wishes of democratically elected representatives only applies if they've been dead for two centuries.

Reagan's new approach to Iran may even be the correct one. It's more geopolitically sophisticated and more compassionate toward the hostages than his previous tough-guy stance. (And there's been no little hypocrisy among Reagan's liberal critics who now criticize him for selling out.) But Reagan is the one who's made his reputation by seeming to reject both this sort of decadent geopolitical sophistication and this potentially paralyzing sentimentality.

Most agonizing foreign policy questions usually boil down to the trade-off between innocent lives and long-term national interests. War, for example. If Reagan's alleged "standing tall" means anything at all, it means that he is more prepared than others to sacrifice the few for the good of the many.

In fact, he has been spectacularly successful in having it both ways: taking "tough" actions that only cost the blood of foreigners—albeit including innocent foreigners—such as the contra war and the Libya bombing. (Oh, sure, there's Grenada, too: the toy war that was over before people knew it had happened.)

The reason Reagan gets away with this, of course, is that his hypocrisy mirrors the hypocrisy of the voters, who also want to be hard-nosed and sentimental at the same time. In that sense, unfortunately, the president's duplicity is a fulfillment of democracy more than its betrayal. We like being lied to.

Fifth Amendment Patriots

(*The New Republic*, JANUARY 5, 1987)

Five men, including two active-duty military officers, have now taken the Fifth Amendment rather than tell a congressional committee about their role in Iranamok.* Moist-eyed Lieutenant Colonel Oliver North says there's nothing he'd like better than to reveal all about the activities he went to such lengths to keep secret. Then he declines, with a tragic sigh, to say anything. Strong congressmen swoon.

Historically, the privilege against self-incrimination evolved as a protection for political dissenters. Nevertheless, the Fifth Amendment applies to government officials just like anyone else. Oliver North has a perfect right to take the Fifth. What he has no right to do is to strike a pose of heroic innocence, prattle on about upholding the Constitution, and expect anyone to believe him.

The Fifth Amendment right against self-incrimination is one of the many rules that make the criminal justice system a highly stylized fact-finding process, quite different from the way people go about gathering information and drawing conclusions in their everyday lives. Other examples include the rules of evidence and the burden of proof "beyond a reasonable doubt." These protections are rightly cherished. But outside the courtroom, people are entitled to use their common sense. They are

---

*"*Iranamok*" was The New Republic's *attempt to christen the arms-for-hostages-cum-aid-to-the-contras scandal. It didn't take.*

not bound by the court rules, they are not bound by any court's conclusion, and they are not bound to wait until the wheels of justice have turned before reaching their own conclusions.

Under the Fifth Amendment, you can't be compelled to offer testimony against yourself. As a necessary corollary, judges and juries in criminal trials are not supposed to infer anything one way or another from an accused person's refusal to testify. But others are free to infer whatever they wish. And, of course, the logical inference is overwhelming: People who take the Fifth have something to hide.

Liberals are understandably but needlessly squeamish on this point because of the experience of the McCarthy period. Between 1950 and 1956, about five hundred people took the Fifth rather than testify about their Communist connections. Those who didn't, such as the Hollywood Ten, often went to jail. Even those who did—"Fifth Amendment Communists," as Senator McCarthy called them—generally lost their jobs. As president of the Screen Actors Guild, Ronald Reagan endorsed the motion picture industry's policy of firing "uncooperative witnesses."

This history is what leads the great civil rights lawyer Joe Rauh to say, as he did recently on ABC News's *Nightline:* "The Fifth Amendment plea has nothing, really, to do with guilt or innocence." That's noble, but absurd. Rauh's famous client, Lillian Hellman, took the Fifth and then swore until her death years later that she had not been a Communist. Her purpose, she said, was to protect her friends. If that's true (and Hellman's reputation for veracity has not outlived her), she had no right to plead the Fifth. She was in contempt of Congress and possibly guilty of perjury.

The injustice done to those who took the Fifth during the McCarthy period was not the widespread assumption that they were or had been Communists. That assumption was correct. The injustice was penalizing them for their political beliefs and associations. Today, laws against membership in the Communist party are recognized as unconstitutional. The laws Ollie North is refusing to reveal whether he broke, for fear of revealing that he broke them, are not unconstitutional. Yes, he's still entitled not to testify. But White House communications director Patrick Buchanan is not entitled to get all blustery ("that creature," he called Representative Michael Barnes on CBS's *Face the Nation*) when people draw the obvious conclusion.

But anyway, Buchanan does not mind if "some technical laws" were broken in the far more important effort to "stop communism in Central

America." (And if the president's communications director is not communicating on behalf of the president, the president hasn't said so.) Buchanan's argument boils down to the proposition that it's okay to break the law provided that, first, your motives are high-minded and, second, you're willing to take your punishment like a man.

In the case of Ollie North, both of Buchanan's factual premises are at least open to dispute. You do not hire Edward Bennett Williams's law firm to make sure you get the punishment you deserve. Nor do you take the Fifth Amendment if your goal is purity through suffering. As for North's motives, I suppose they were similar to those of the Hollywood Communists: a combustible blend of misplaced idealism and swollen self-importance. It's clear from the facts that have already come out that North relished his role and wasn't averse to exaggerating it. Like all amateur totalitarians, he's a power-tripper.

On the theoretical level, Buchanan's list of historical examples of people who broke the law for a higher cause gets longer and sillier by the day. He has been ridiculed out of his analogy between public acts of civil disobedience and secret lawbreaking by government officials. His latest gambit is: "Look, friend, this country was founded by moral men in an act of treason against the Crown." And so, once again, the Founding Fathers are called upon to bail out the Reagan administration's Central America policy. (The first time was when Reagan himself said the contras were "the moral equivalent of our Founding Fathers.")

This example is wonderfully revealing. The point about the Founding Fathers is that they regarded the authority of the British Crown as illegitimate. I can refer Buchanan to a document that explains all this rather clearly. Said document also makes clear that the Founding Fathers regarded a challenge to established law—even law they thought not merely mistaken but actually illegitimate—as a serious step, and certainly nothing to be done on the sly. Based on this example, the question for Buchanan—and for the President he communicates for—is whether they regard the authority of American law as illegitimate. Of course they may remain silent if the answer is incriminating.

GETTING CLUBBED

(*The New Republic*, MARCH 16, 1987)

The top court of New York State has upheld a city ordinance requiring the snooty gentlemen's clubs of Manhattan to admit women as members, thus reopening one of the more tedious hardy perennials among civil rights controversies. It's tempting to say that the women who engineered this legal triumph should be condemned, as punishment, to spend every lunch hour for the rest of their natural lives eating overcooked beef in surroundings of stifling gloom while listening to some half-stewed, self-important old bore recount the exploits of the 1937 Princeton football squad.

But of course the activists on this issue claim that men's clubs are not solely devoted to pleasures such as these. They assert—and, for all I know, they're right—that these institutions are caldrons of freemasonry (or "networking," as we now call it) among the power elite, where deals are done, connections are made, and earthly achievements are recognized and rewarded. Therefore, the men-only policies of these places are keeping successful women from reaching the pinnacles of American society. They are "the last bastion," one legal commentator asserts. Perhaps. But even so— or especially if so—this campaign strikes me as an exercise in missing the point.

The usual argument against using the civil rights battering ram to break down this particular barricade is threefold. First is the constitutional right to freedom of association (one of those so-called "penumbra" rights that conservatives usually have no tolerance for because they're not written down in so many words). If white male Protestants wish to eat lunch only with one another, up to a point that is their privilege. Second, rights aside, there is a limit to what government can achieve or ought to attempt in the way of restructuring society. You can't "legislate morality," as they say. Third, how can you dismantle these bastions of cultural supremacy without incidentally destroying the institutions where other groups—women, blacks, Jews—gather for mutual succor and support? Surely the vision of a just society does not preclude all opportunities for like to mix with like.

On the other hand, it's certainly true that harmless male bonhomie does not describe the complete agenda at these locales. During my brief career as editor of *Harper's* magazine in New York, I was hired over lunch at the Century Club, survived an attempt to fire me during a board meeting at the University Club, and was gently informed that I might be happier elsewhere over drinks back at the Century. So civilized.

The 1964 Civil Rights Act specifically exempts private clubs, and its public accommodations provision doesn't even cover discrimination on the basis of sex (an omission derived, in part, from a desire to protect women-only hotels). But the Supreme Court held three years ago that the Jaycees could be required to admit women under a state civil rights act, and it is hearing a similar case next month involving the Rotary Club. Another legal tactic is to deny various government privileges to these clubs, on the theory that society has the right not to be implicated in their discriminatory practices. The all-male Burning Tree Country Club outside Washington has lost its special "green space" property tax abatement, and there is a campaign to deny the Cosmos Club here in D.C. its liquor license, without which it would not long survive.

Ironically, the more genuinely elite a club is, the more protected it is from the law. The Supreme Court emphasized in the Jaycees case that the Jaycees weren't really exclusive at all, except for excluding women. That made them more like a public accommodation and less like a private association. Yet the truly exclusive clubs are the ones that excite the most ire from women who want in, and this is where I get doubtful. What kind of constipated egalitarian vision is it that dreams of private clubs just as influential in society as these critics imagine them to be, and just as exclusive—with one exception?

The women's movement always has been torn about whether the proper goal is to remake society or to get an equal share in society as it now exists. It's not an easy question. But this campaign to open up private clubs seems like a particularly egregious example of a civil rights effort designed to redistribute inequality rather than reduce it. (Federal contract set-asides for millionaire black businessmen are another example.)

Surely the utterly gratuitous elitism of these absurd institutions that sift and sort people according to some pompous standards of clubbability ought to be easy enough to reject completely, not just to the extent it discriminates on the basis of sex. The campaign against these clubs ends up actually reinforcing their own preposterous idea of themselves as noble elites. In real life, a law of entropy usually assures that clubs ostensibly devoted to high artistic or intellectual attainment—just like neighborhoods of the same coloration—end up full of lawyers.

Why should country clubs get a property tax abatement for preserving green space accessible to only a privileged few, even if those few *do* include some women? Why should social club dues be deductible at all? There's no need for a vendetta. Beyond eliminating these special favors (and I don't count a liquor license as a special favor), I wouldn't join a campaign against a club that wouldn't have me as a member. Who cares?

As women advance in the world, many remaining sexual barriers among the elites are going to collapse of their own sheer anomalousness. I recently was taken for a drink at the Carlton Club in London, which is associated with the British Conservative party and decorated like a religious shrine to the Goddess Thatcher (huge oil painting over the stairway, bust on the way to the men's room, and so on), yet not open to women. This sort of thing probably won't last. The question is whether the world will really be a better place when self-defined "top" women can sit around exclusive clubs eating rare breast of squab in raspberry vinegar, drinking Perrier, and swapping stories about the Yale field hockey team of 1983.

D OUBLE IDENTITY

(*The New Republic*, APRIL 6, 1987)

Why should the conviction of two Americans caught spying for Israel* revive old talk about the "dual loyalty" of five million patriotic American Jews? In part because that is the fate of Jews on this earth, even in America. In part because Jews (including this one) are characteristically among the first to worry a bone like this in public. And in part because the special relationship of Jews outside Israel to the Jewish state does require a bit of explanation. "Special relationship" doesn't mean treason: There's no decent explanation for that.

Until World War II, Zionism—the belief in a Jewish national homeland—was a minority taste among Jews. Most American Jews rejected the idea that Jews were a nation. America was a nation. Judaism was a religion. The founders of Zionism, by contrast, were resolutely secular. The Holo-

*Jonathan and Anne Pollard

caust ended this interesting theoretical argument. But it didn't solve the seeming contradiction for American Jews who cherish Israel but have no desire to emigrate. Zionist zealots and anti-Zionist zealots both ask the same good question: How can you believe in the Jewish state and also believe that Jews can be full, normal citizens of other states?

The widely accepted answer is that America is a nation of nations. There is no one type of American and no one American interest. Our people are an ethnic melting pot and our politics are pluralistic. As Professor Oscar Handlin put it in the early days of this debate four decades ago: "The position of Israel with regard to Jewish Americans is . . . entirely similar to the position of Italy and Ireland with regard to Italian and Irish Americans."

This comforting theory doesn't really describe Israel's importance to many American Jews or America's importance to Israel. There are theoretical problems, too. Most nations are not ethnic melting pots, though they have ethnic minorities. Is "dual loyalty" a more legitimate question for Jews in Britain or France? Ironically, while a theory of ethnic pluralism makes it easier to explain American Jewish support for Israel, it makes it harder to explain Israel itself: a nation based, like the old nations of Europe and elsewhere, primarily on ethnic principles.

A second answer to the dual-loyalty question is that there is only a single loyalty, to values that Israel and America share: democracy, freedom, and so on. American nationalism, unlike most other kinds, is primarily about such values, and protecting Israel is one way to serve them. If America and Israel ever came into fundamental conflict—which is almost impossible to imagine—it would have to be because one or the other had betrayed its most fundamental values, which would make the choice between them easy.

This argument is also comforting but a bit facile. Shared political values strengthen the bond between Israel and all Americans. But American patriotism is not really so bloodless and analytical, nor is the Jewish love of Israel, nor is American Jews' passion for both nations.

A third, less comforting, answer to the dual-loyalty question is that we are all guilty of not just dual but multiple loyalties. What's more, these loyalties do in fact conflict with and detract from one another. But only a totalitarian or a vulgarian would insist that the loyalty of citizenship must always "come first," whatever that means.

E. M. Forster is held in contempt for saying he would betray his country before he would betray a friend. This is considered the epitome of effete intellectual decadence. But suppose Forster had said "wife" or "child" (he had neither, of course) instead of "friend." Perhaps a man should be prepared to betray his family before his country, but no one would claim it's an easy question.

And in everyday life, where the melodramatic question of "betrayal" does not arise, all of us constantly make choices that subordinate the interests of the state to other loyalties: religious, ethnic, local, familial. And why not? That's one of the things America is about.

Nevertheless, the emotional attachment of American Jews to Israel undeniably complicates their attachment to their own country. That's okay. Life is complicated. American Quakers refuse to serve their country in the military. Jehovah's Witnesses refuse to salute the flag. This puts them outside the mainstream in ways they just have to live with. Some nations try to make this hard. America, God bless it, tries to make this easy. But it will never be painless.

As many have noted, in some ways it is America that has become the Jewish promised land. By any objective standard, sadly, Jews are physically safer and freer to thrive here than in Israel. But sneery Israelis are right that Jewish Americans will always bear a burden of outsiderness that citizens of the Jewish state don't. They will always be taking the temperature of anti-Semitism like a worried parent, and always be finding a slight fever (though never, I suspect, a severe one). They will always cringe when an Ivan Boesky or a Martin Siegel gets arrested.

The challenge of outsiderness can be ennobling. It drives many Jews to be better Americans—harder working, more generous to charities, more civically involved than the average citizen. It also can be emotionally degrading, as when Jews worry about being "too obvious" in social behavior or political life, and when they feel they must prove themselves by being the loudest to denounce the Pollards or the Rosenbergs. If any American Jew claims to be free of such anguishes, don't believe it.

On the other hand, there are worse fates.

The American Dream

(*The Wall Street Journal,* MAY 7, 1987)

For months now I have been brooding about a survey released in February by Dow Jones, the company that publishes *The Wall Street Journal,* on the subject of "The American Dream." The survey is part of an elaborate promotion keyed to the *Journal*'s advertising slogan that it is "the daily diary of the American Dream." Conducted by the Roper Organization, the poll purports to find that the American Dream "is still alive." Like all such mock-scientific explorations of the national psyche by opinion pollsters, however, the "data" can be used to reach the opposite conclusion, or almost anything in between.

The upbeat determination that the dream is still alive derives from findings that most of the public believes the dream is either "very much alive" or "somewhat alive"; that the average person thinks he or she will get to 8.2 on a scale of 10; and so on. On the other hand, less was made of findings that a majority think the dream will be harder to achieve in the next generation, and that the desire to do better than one's parents is actually leaching out of the American Dream as that prospect becomes less and less likely. (Sixty-nine percent of those over forty-five say this is part of their dream, but only 52 percent of those under thirty.)

The most interesting question in the poll was, "How much income per year would you say you and your family would need to fulfill all your dreams?" The median income of respondents was $23,000 and the median answer was $50,000. "These modest expectations," says the Roper Organization, "help to explain vividly why so many Americans feel that The American Dream, as they define it, is within reach."

In fact, if you take this poll seriously (which I don't), the American Dream is a confidence trick. As the magic $50,000 is approached, the dream recedes. People making $25,000 to $50,000 (median income $36,000) want $60,000 to fulfill all their dreams. People making over $50,000 (median income $69,000) want $100,000—or, "a modest $100,000," as a press release accompanying the survey charmingly describes this round figure. I daresay a poll of John Kluge, Sam Walton,

Warren Buffett, and so on would show that those with assets of more than a billion dollars feel that a modest $7.3 billion or so would be the dream-fulfilling amount.

These results, in short, provide almost clinical confirmation of one Marxist critique of capitalism: that it stimulates crude financial appetites as fast as it sates them, thus leaving everybody perpetually unsatisfied. The people making $23,000 a year are just $27,000 away from their dream. Having lifted themselves by their bootstraps in the approved manner all the way to $69,000, they find they are now $31,000 from their dream. What's the point?

It's fortunate for *The Wall Street Journal* that its readers don't believe this survey, since they have already attained and surpassed the magic $50,000. If the American Dream were really so easily fulfilled—or, alternatively, if people became convinced that it was an ever-receding mirage—this newspaper's marketing strategy of presenting itself as a vital tool in pursuit of that dream would collapse.

Probably the most famous and successful "package" in the history of the direct-mail marketing business is a solicitation letter the *Journal* has been using for many years. You've probably gotten it. "On a beautiful late spring afternoon, twenty-five years ago," it poetically begins, "two young men graduated from the same college. They were very much alike, these two young men." The letter (currently signed by Associate Publisher Peter Kann) goes on to say that these two similar young men now work for the same company, except that one is "manager of a small department" and the other is president. The explanation? Well, it seems that the second man's family owns the company. No, actually, the difference is that the second man subscribed to *The Wall Street Journal*! Amazing.

Year after year the letter goes out by the millions, the two men—forever young—keep graduating from college, keep returning for their twenty-fifth reunion, and the one who reads the *Journal* keeps becoming president of the company.

But the direct-mail letter fails to address the question whether the company president is happier than the fellow who only manages a small division. Is he closer to the American Dream? Of course, he gets to read *The Wall Street Journal* every day. But can that alone bring happiness?

Despite the results of the *Journal*'s own survey (which also concludes that a happy family life is more important to success than more-material achievements), people cling to the suspicion that it can. Or at least that material success—the inevitable result of reading *The Wall Street Journal*—can do so. I think people are on to something.

Nice Young Man

(*The New Republic*, JUNE 1, 1987)

Surveying the Democratic field, I'm already starting to miss that hint of insanity that disturbed so many people about Gary Hart. Not everyone will agree, of course, that a touch of madness is a desirable qualification for a presidential candidate. Sanity buffs will be increasingly attracted in the next few weeks to Senator Albert Gore, Jr., a self-described "raging moderate" who nevertheless does a good Hart-style generational-future routine. Thoughtful, sincere, responsible to a fault, handsome in a reassuringly unglamorous way, Gore is not the type who would ever change his name, alter his signature, or sail away on the good ship *Monkey Business.*＊

Gore's presidential qualities already have attracted "IMPAC '88," several dozen rich Democratic fund-raisers who hope to maximize their leverage in the party by acting in concert. Gore had decided not to run in 1988, but importuning and promises of financial support from this group persuaded him to change his mind. The IMPAC people like Gore's freshness and his moderation. The standard poop holds that, as a thirty-nine-year-old Tennessean, Gore will also exert a special appeal for southerners and young people.

Gore, though, is not really a southerner. What he is is the presidential candidate from Washington. He was born here, the son of Representative, later Senator, Albert Gore, Sr. The elder Gore, famous as a progressive populist, sent his son to St. Alban's, Washington's leading prep school, where Al was captain of the football team, and on to Harvard, where he graduated with honors. After marrying a Washington girl and serving in Vietnam, young Al settled in Nashville, where he worked on the local

---

＊Monkey Business *was the name of the boat on which Gary spent a famous dirty weekend with Donna Rice.*

newspaper and attended law and divinity schools before running for Congress in 1976, at age twenty-eight, and moving up to the Senate in 1984, at age thirty-six.

There is nothing wrong with this history. In fact, it's admirable. But the career path it describes would be more familiar to British politics than to American. There, distinguished left-wing politicians see no irony in breeding their kids for politics by raising them in the capital and sending them to the best schools. Gore is a dynastic candidate in a way even the Kennedys have not yet become. Kennedys are messier; none has buffed his résumé to quite such a high gloss. And no Washington-bred Kennedy has yet run for president. Gore tediously insists that he wasn't interested in a political career until his newspaper work exposing corruption in local government made him realize that politics could be a positive force for change. That is a bow to the American convention that politics should not be a life's ambition.

As for his youth, Gore is an old person's idea of a young person. That also is admirable. Some people, like Ronald Reagan, go into politics out of genuine ideological passion. Some, like most of the presidential candidates of both parties, are motivated by naked ambition, which leaves them twisted in various ways. Gore is ambitious, to be sure, but his ambition is overlaid with calm dynastic self-assurance. It's easy to imagine those wealthy fund-raisers interviewing Al Gore, comparing him mentally to the sweaty pack of middle-aged rivals, and thinking, What a nice young man! Whether a nice young man is what the youth of America hungers to rally around is more problematic.

Gore has got moderation down to a science. "Some observers," he says, "have concluded that government itself is the problem. . . . Others argue that government is all that keeps matters from getting still worse. Both sides are right—to a point." He opened his campaign with a call for "international cooperation to combat AIDS and Alzheimer's disease." He recently introduced legislation to establish "International Greenhouse Effect Year" and also has been in the forefront of concern about the ozone layer. Last year he sponsored the "Supercomputer Network Study Act," intended "to explore the potential of fiberoptic networks to link the nation's supercomputers. . . . "

The focus on "study" is a characteristic Gore touch. Asked his opinion of the Baby M (surrogate mother) case by *The New York Times*, he said: "We need to accelerate the development of a consensus. But it must emerge from a broad discussion. It would be important and helpful to all if the Congressional Biomedical Ethics Board would designate these issues as topics for priority study and action." And have I mentioned Gore's proposal for an International Copyright Tribunal? His bill to create a computerized link between organ transplant donors and recipients? His hearings on the release of genetically engineered organisms?

All this is admirable, admirable, admirable. Decades from now, if we are all frying for lack of ozone or roasting in a global carbon dioxide greenhouse, if our supercomputers are lonely and unlinked, if genetic mutants have seized control of the Congressional Biomedical Ethics Board, the concerns of today's other politicians will seem criminally petty. But the "pragmatic," "visionary," "problem-solving" approach to politics that Gore has perfected is in some ways an evasion of politics.

Politics is about disagreement, and disagreement is not usually due to a lack of foresight, planning, study. The important political disagreements involve the clash of material interests. "Instead of telling people what to do," Gore says, "we should listen and learn how to give them the tools to do what they want." But true leadership consists of telling people things they don't want to hear sometimes, making them mad, changing their minds. Gore's style of moderation is to go instead for issues that are "difficult" in the sense of being obscure or complicated, but not contentious.

Making friends is easy in politics. Al Gore needs to prove himself by making some serious enemies.

TELL ME ANOTHER ONE

(The New Republic, JUNE 19, 1987)

Have you heard the one about the new movie called *Jews?* It's the story of a small resort town terrorized by a loan shark.

Now, I think that's pretty funny. And, I'm sorry, I just can't find enough high-mindedness within me to wish that this sort of joke didn't exist.

President Reagan told a good one in Venice the other day. As per usual, he thought the microphone was off. It seems there was this gondolier singing "O Sole Mio" and the Lord wondered what would happen if he lost 25 percent of his brainpower. Result: He sang, "O sole, O sole."

So the Lord took away half his brains and he sang, "O so, O so." Finally, the Lord took away all his brains and he sang "When Irish Eyes Are Smiling." Reagan noted, "See, I can tell that, being Irish."

In fact, it's amazing he got away with it. In other circumstances, it easily could have become a political life-threatening gaffe. Imagine if George Bush had said it in New Hampshire. Yet there's been no fuss at all. Reagan being Irish had less to do with this than Reagan being Reagan. He has uttered so many boners, faux pas, and non sequiturs over the past seven years that people have become numb and the media have wearied of trying to stir up trouble. In the 1980 campaign he told a joke about a Pole and an Italian at a cockfight. Confronted at a press conference, he explained that he was just illustrating the kind of joke politicians shouldn't tell. Now he doesn't bother to explain because no one asks.

But maybe Reagan's bizarre immunity on matters of this sort will help to set a new standard, and we will be spared episodes like the one in the 1984 campaign when Walter Mondale made Gary Hart apologize repeatedly for making a little joke about New Jersey. After all, it's not as if there's a surfeit of good jokes in the world. We don't need more reasons not to laugh.

Of course, it's undeniably true that ethnic jokes affront the brotherhood and sisterhood of all humankind, as well as the individuality of each person. In America, we have a special need to minimize ethnic friction and resentment. But a world of universal and constant respect for these ideals might be hard to live in—and, in any event, is not on the horizon.

There are those, no doubt, who can refrain from telling ethnic jokes. And there may even be some—a much smaller group, and one you probably wouldn't care to share a long cruise or jail term with—who can refrain from laughing at any of them. As for the rest of us, what we need are some etiquette guidelines aimed at providing maximum gaiety with minimum offense. Pending congressional hearings, here are a few suggestions.

Rule 1. As Reagan noted, it's better to tell jokes on your own ethnic group. He's Irish, I'm Jewish. Of course Reagan doesn't really believe that the Irish are inordinately stupid, and I don't really believe that Jews are inordinately avaricious. But an ethnic joke told on oneself can become a way of laughing at the stereotype, thereby undermining it, rather than promoting it.

Rule 2. If the joke is about some other ethnic group, a good seat-of-the-pants test is whether you would tell it in the presence of a friend from that group. If you'd be embarrassed to tell the joke in front of your friend, maybe you shouldn't tell it elsewhere. If you don't even have a friend from this particular group, that's an even better signal to stay away.

Rule 3. Jokes about some groups are less offensive than jokes about others. This is a double standard, but a valid one. Black Americans are still everyday victims of oppression and discrimination based on ethnic stereotypes; Italian, Irish, and Jewish Americans far, far less so. Of the common subjects of ethnic jokes, I would rank them in order of legitimate sensitivity as: blacks, Hispanics, Poles, Jews, Italians, Irish, WASPs.

Unfortunately, most WASP jokes just aren't very funny. (From *Truly Tasteless Jokes* by Blanche Knott: "How can you tell the only WASP in a sauna? He's the one with the *Wall Street Journal* on his lap." Not terribly tasteless.) WASP jokes have a sense of strain, almost a sense of duty about them, not a sense of natural vicious inspiration. Many are actually jokes at the expense of other groups—variations on "What do you get when you mix a WASP and a Puerto Rican?" and so on. This illustrates the unavoidable truth that a good ethnic joke must contain an element of gloating superiority. It can be vestigial, but it must be there. A well-meaning naïf once suggested that we should invent an all-purpose imaginary group to be the butt of ethnic humor. Unfortunately, it wouldn't work.

Rule 4. Jokes about certain alleged traits are more offensive than jokes about others. This has nothing in particular to do with the validity of the stereotype involved. For example, it is not true that certain ethnic groups inherently smell bad and/or attract insects, and jokes based on this premise are pointless and disgusting. On the other hand, a whole genre of jokes has surfaced in recent years based on the equally absurd premise that all Jewish women are frigid (exactly the opposite of the historical stereotype). In that case, it seems to me, the patent falsity of the premise turns it into a harmless convention. Meanwhile, jokes that turn on blacks having curly hair are stupid and offensive even though—or actually because—it's true. Where's the joke?

Of course all ethnic stereotypes are invalid generalizations. But jokes about drunkenness, laziness, greed, are more tolerable than jokes about physical characteristics or personal habits. The tough call is stupidity, since (unlike, say, bad table manners) it implies genuine and immutable inferiority, and yet is the basis of probably half of all ethnic jokes, including some good ones. One comfort here is that the literature lacks any clear consensus about which groups are ostensibly dumber than others. Reagan's joke turned on the Irish being dumber than Italians. *Totally Gross Jokes*, Volume II, has a similar joke about progressive loss of brainpower whose punch line is "Oh, mama mia!"

Rule 5. If you tell an ethnic joke, make sure it's funny. Most ethnic humor in the recent rash of paperbacks and on those gross-out radio talk shows is witless. Wittiness is important not only for its own sake—to compensate for any offense—but as a test of motive. An unfunny ethnic joke is merely an expression of contempt. A funny one need not be.

Rule 6. If you hear one you think is good, feel free to laugh. Examine your conscience later. It's healthier that way.

T HE G REAT C OMMUNICATOR

(The New Republic, SEPTEMBER 7, 1987)*

J ust 3,359 years since his most recent press conference, Pharaoh Amenhotep III welcomed me into his tomb for an exclusive interview to discuss his impressive plans for the remaining millennia of his rule. The sharks and cynics who count Amenhotep out just because he has been dead for close to thirty-four centuries characteristically underestimate this man of rare vision and courage.

Amenhotep's tomb is an island of calm and quiet amid the hurly-burly of the modern world. Undisturbed now for most of recorded history, the pharaoh has been able to lie entirely motionless, amid foot-thick layers of dust and dead insects, and take the opportunity to reflect on the larger issues of world peace and prosperity that far override the petty quotidian concerns of his critics.

In the early part of his reign, circa 1400 B.C., Amenhotep was widely acknowledged as the leader who had brought Egypt into its period of greatest splendor. More recently, there are those who charge that he has lost some of his old effectiveness, just because he is embalmed, wrapped in sheets from top to toe, and encased in a jewel-bedecked sarcophagus. I can testify, however, as the only journalist who has been let anywhere

---

This piece was inspired, if that's the word, by an interview with President Reagan by Hugh Sidey of Time magazine. It was Reagan's first interview after several months of withdrawal due to Iran-contra and a good example of high-camp Reaganism in its decadent late phase.

near him in more than a millennium, that this is a vile slander. Oh, perhaps the wrapping has frayed a bit, and mischief-makers seem to have made off with his head. But in all important respects, he is the same Amenhotep whom I first had the privilege of interviewing five hundred years ago. (Who needs a head? I don't.)

And yet the constant braying of the jackals has taken its toll. The pharaoh from whom words of inspiration once flowed like the Nile itself has grown hesitant, knowing that anything he says will be viciously misinterpreted. Indeed, during the course of our hour-and-a-half-long interview, he failed to utter a single syllable. And yet his powers of communication remain so great, albeit not in words, that he still can deliver a more powerful message with the impassive face painted on the top of his coffin than anything contained in the endless verbiage of lesser politicians.

As always, Amenhotep is a stoic, unbowed by time or care. His confident belief in the rightness of his own course allows him to accept the calumnies of his enemies without feeling the need to respond. There was no hint of bitterness or anger in his voice as he graciously declined to answer all my questions.

"Tell me, O Great One," I asked the pharaoh, clinging to his knees in my customary posture of reverence, "are the dark days of inquisition over? Have the people at long last put behind them the bilious charges of your persecutors? Don't debase yourself by answering in words, O God-King. Just knock three times on the top of your sarcophagus if you disagree that, at this extraordinary moment in the history of your reign, it's time to move on to the agenda of the future."

The silence was eloquent.

Some observers have contended that in light of the destruction of Egyptian civilization and the growing criticism of practices such as slavery, polytheism, and human sacrifice, it was a failure of vision and leadership for Amenhotep to have spent the past three thousand years buried under hundreds of feet of solid rock with his eyes covered by precious stones. Does he not have an obligation to answer the charges of his critics? Did he, for that matter, even listen to some of the recent inquiries into the practices of his reign? Amenhotep's wise open-eyed smile made the obvious response to such carping: Although he was aware of complaints, as earthly representative of the sun-god Ra he could not allow such matters to distract him from his essential pharaonic responsibilities. He therefore has been determined throughout this crisis to maintain his daily schedule of lying perfectly still and doing absolutely nothing.

As my audience drew to a close, I decided I had subjected the pharaoh to enough interrogation about affairs of state. So, during the last three quarters of the interview, Amenhotep and I reminisced together about some of his earlier lives: as a slave girl in the dynasty of Amenemhet I, and as a camel during the early Hittite period. I myself was a serious journalist about the same time. How we laughed and reminisced! But Amenhotep made clear that, for him, nothing compares with being pharaoh. "Don't let on, but it's the easiest job in the world," his eyes said, with what I could have sworn was a wink.

After the trauma of the past few centuries, Amenhotep is planning a well-deserved rest for the next ten thousand years or so. He will loll around his tomb and pursue his favorite hobby of staring blankly ahead. Even at age 3,398, he can do this for hours at a time, outlasting far younger men such as the members of his entourage. Then, long after today's malcontents have dried into dust, or been reborn as desert beetles, he will inspire us once again with his calm invincibility, his unfashionable determination to pursue the same course century after century, and—above all—his sheer ability to survive.

THE CASE AGAINST BORK

(The New Republic, OCTOBER 5, 1987)*

The controversy over President Reagan's nomination of Robert Bork for the Supreme Court is a rebuke to those—including this journal—who are wont to complain that the American political dialogue is cheesy and trivial. In the bicentennial year of the Constitution, we are enjoying an astringent debate over first principles: the allocation of power among branches of government, the meaning of the Bill of Rights, the tension between majority rule and individual freedom.

Robert Bork is a victim of this development. Few any longer maintain that such philosophical questions are irrelevant to his confirmation by the Senate—that he should be judged on "competence" alone, a test he would

*This was TNR's editorial against the nomination of Robert Bork for the Supreme Court.

pass with ease. Bork is a victim, as well, of his own intellectual exertions: a lifetime of earnest and honest reflection on basic questions, expressed with admirable provocative swash. As a result, he is being judged by standards that did not apply to Sandra Day O'Connor or Antonin Scalia.

But the Equal Protection Clause of the Fourteenth Amendment (as Judge Bork would surely agree) doesn't guarantee equal treatment of Supreme Court nominees. "More than any nominee in recent decades," writes Stuart Taylor in *The New York Times*, "Judge Bork is the representative and leader of a school of thought. He has worked out an overarching legal and constitutional philosophy that he says should govern all judicial decision-making." Reagan nominated Bork because of this philosophy, and senators have the right and duty to decide whether they share this philosophy in voting on his confirmation.

In contrast to the demeaning White House campaign to portray its nominee as "open-minded' and "unpredictable," *TNR* wishes to pay Bork the compliment of taking his philosophy seriously. While we admire Robert Bork as a man and as a thinker, we do not share his judicial philosophy and do not wish to see him on the Supreme Court. This is true although we ourselves have had occasion to complain about the liberal fixation with "rights" and the overreliance on courts to invent and enforce them. We agree with Bork's critique of some judicial excesses, especially the *Roe* v. *Wade* abortion decision. But we do not agree that intellectual consistency therefore requires us to renounce much of postwar constitutional jurisprudence.

The development of Robert Bork's thought can be traced in a series of now thoroughly pawed writings, beginning with a 1963 article in these very pages. In that *TNR* essay (later recanted), Bork denounced the public accommodations provision of the incipient Civil Rights Act—outlawing racial discrimination by commercial establishments—as "legislation by which the morals of the majority are self-righteously imposed upon a minority." The notion that "a majority may impose upon a minority its scale of preferences," Bork wrote, is "a principle of unsurpassed ugliness."

Unsurpassed ugliness, perhaps, but not unconstitutional. In 1971, in the *Indiana Law Review*, Bork used the moral relativist's credo as the foundation for his philosophy of judicial restraint. "Every clash between a minority claiming freedom and a majority claiming power to regulate involves a choice between the gratifications of the two groups." Since "there is no principled way to decide that one man's gratifications are more deserving of respect than another's," the majority's wishes must prevail unless "constitutional materials . . . clearly specify" otherwise. A married couple's wish to use contraception has no greater claim against the majority will than a utility company's wish to pollute the atmosphere. Constitutionally, "the cases are identical."

By this basic reasoning, Bork has written in 1971 and since that the Supreme Court was wrong to prevent states from enforcing racial restrictions in real estate deeds; wrong to invalidate the poll tax; wrong to require "one-man-one-vote" for state legislatures; wrong to apply the Fourteenth Amendment to discrimination against women or any other nonracial group; wrong to ban sterilization of criminals and prayers in schools; wrong to find any right of privacy in the Constitution; and so on.

The 1971 article also focused on freedom of speech. Constitutional rights, Bork argued, are of two sorts: those explicitly mentioned in the text and those that "derive . . . from governmental processes" in the Constitution. Free speech, he said, is of the second sort. "The Framers seem to have had no coherent theory of free speech," and judges therefore "are forced to construct our own theory." Bork's theory was that "governmental processes" only require protection of political speech. Speech on nonpolitical subjects and speech advocating violation of the law, he argued, can be censored or punished without constitutional constraint.

Despite its professed view that one moral value is as good as another—the premise of its narrow reading of the Constitution—Bork's 1971 article took special aim at pornography, noting that it could be seen as "a problem of pollution of the moral and aesthetic atmosphere precisely analogous to smoke pollution." By 1978, in a speech on the First Amendment at the University of Michigan, Bork had decided that "the consequences of such 'private' indulgence may have public consequences far more unpleasant than industrial pollution." He criticized "the shopworn slogan that the individual should be free to do as he sees fit so long as he does no harm to others" because advocates of this formula recognize only "physical or material injury" and not moral harm to the community. In 1984, in a Washington speech on "Tradition and Morality in Constitutional Law," Bork argued that the "community is entitled to suppress . . . moral harms" in general. He condemned the "privatization of morality which requires the law of the community to practice moral relativism."

Two other Bork writings of recent years amplified and/or modified his views on strict constructionism and judicial restraint. In 1984, as a circuit judge, he concurred in the First Amendment dismissal of a libel action against the columnists Evans and Novak. Even though there's no evidence that the Framers intended to restrict libel suits, he argued, a broader interpretation of their design is needed: "There would be little need for judges . . . if the boundaries of every constitutional provision were self-evident. They are not. . . . It is the task of the judge in this generation to discern how the Framers' values, defined in the context of the world they knew, apply to the world we know." In a 1985 pamphlet published by the conservative Center for the Study of the Judiciary, Bork contended that there is a principled middle ground between blind literalism—which would doom the Constitution to irrelevance as times change—and irresponsible freelancing.

No one, of course, admits to making up rights and blithely sticking them in the Constitution. Everyone in this debate claims to be honoring the intentions of its authors, if only their intention to be broadly interpreted. Is Bork's analysis so compelling that less stinting views must shudder and give way? We think not.

Bork's intellectual progress, surveyed above, contains more than one anomaly. For example, moral relativism led him to conclude that the principled derivation of broad individual rights from the language of the Constitution was a hopeless task. Since then, he has abandoned moral relativism with a vengeance. Yet he clings to the belief that the task is hopeless. Now that he has concluded that his own moral values can be more than just a series of random "gratifications," why won't he extend the same courtesy to the authors of the Bill of Rights?

Bork defends his narrow reading of the First Amendment's freedom of speech on the contradictory grounds that the purpose of free speech is to facilitate the political debate, and that society has the right to protect its own moral values. Moral values are a central political question. But Bork apparently believes that current moral values are beyond permissible challenge. Remember, we are not talking about public displays here. The "moral harm" society is entitled to "suppress"—a harm Bork analogizes to pollution—derives entirely from the effect on individuals of their own voluntary private decisions about what to read, see, and hear. The same logic could apply just as easily in many areas other than speech. This may not be "a principle of unsurpassed ugliness," as Bork once described the imposition of majority values on minorities, but it is rather unattractive—and ominous.

Bork's paradigm of legitimate judicial creativity is the 1967 Supreme Court decision defining electronic surveillance as a "search and seizure" under the Fourth Amendment. The Framers didn't know about electricity.

If they had, they probably would have wanted the people to be protected from bugging as well as from physical police intrusion. Well, sure. That one's easy. But Bork himself realizes it's not always so easy. In his Evans and Novak opinion, he struggles to explain why it's okay for the Supreme Court to read restriction on libel suits and segregated schools into the Constitution, even though both of these practices were known to the Framers and apparently not disapproved of. It seems that in these cases the Court was "applying an old principle according to a new understanding of a social situation." A new understanding? That gives the game away. Bork is entitled to claim that his new understanding is superior to others', of course. But he is not entitled to assert that he has discovered the philosophers' stone that converts original intent into modern meaning, and that broader "understandings" than his own are inherently unprincipled.

Bork's intellectual history is a series of wild ideological fusillades followed by mid-course corrections. This, in itself, is unobjectionable. Foolish consistency and all that. Still, there is something unnerving about Bork's pattern of conveniently mellowing his harsh principles. He has never satisfactorily explained how he, the strictest of strict constructionists, can defend *Brown* v. *Board of Education*, the great school desegregation decision. In his 1971 law review article, he babbled about "psychological equality" in a way that would do any liberal sociologist proud.

Bork now says he would define "political speech"—protected by the First Amendment—to include a broad "spectrum" of moral, scientific, and literary expression. He now says his exclusion of speech advocating illegality might not apply to advocacy of civil disobedience such as the civil rights sit-ins. In recent years he has been complicating his views on original intent, and has argued for expanded First Amendment protection of the press. His views on when to overrule precedents have noticeably softened in just the past few weeks. According to Michael Kramer in *U.S. News & World Report*, Bork has even told senators in his preconfirmation rounds that he is willing to reconsider whether there is a constitutional right to abortion, "that just because he hasn't found it doesn't mean it's not there"—as if constitutional law were an Easter egg hunt and there might be some obscure provision he's overlooked in his years of scholarly searching. Is this "open-mindedness" reassuring? Or is it all a bit too facile for someone hungry for a lifetime appointment that would put his views beyond the need for further calibration?

After the *Roe* decision in 1973, this journal commented (in an editorial written by Robert Bork's mentor, Alexander Bickel): "There is no answer that moral philosophy, logic, reason, or other materials of law can give to this question of abortion. That is why the question is not for courts, but should have been left to the political process." *Roe* implausibly found in the Constitution a detailed regulatory scheme dividing pregnancy into trimesters, with illogical and hypocritical rules for when and how the state could interfere during each period. *TNR* has long maintained that *Roe* was actually a disaster for liberals. It cast a retrospective shadow of illegitimacy over all the important cases of the Warren era. It short-circuited a political process that was rapidly legalizing abortion anyway. It reinforced the liberal addiction to court-imposed rather than democratic solutions to social problems. Meanwhile, as liberals grew complacent, *Roe* politicized a generation of social-issue conservatives. The right-to-life movement became a major building block of the "New Right," now a powerful reactionary political force.

But if some liberals fail to see the difference between finding a ban on abortion in the Constitution and finding a ban on real estate racial covenants, Judge Bork suffers from the same astigmatism. He believes that—with the exception of *Brown*—virtually all the most prominent postwar Supreme Court cases expanding individual rights against the state were wrongly decided.

Bork's views on freedom of speech are the scariest and least supportable, in our view. Although a "strict construction" of the First Amendment ("Congress shall make no law . . . abridging the freedom of speech.") would seem to invite a fairly active judicial role in preventing state censorship, Bork characteristically sees that role as quite limited. And yet the limits he draws would give judges far more leeway to impose their own personal "gratifications" than the simple, broad right of free speech we enjoy today. Is this play politically relevant? Will this book undermine the reader's moral values? Has this protester crossed the line between acceptably challenging the law and unacceptably advocating its violation?

Bork's professed radical majoritarianism has some peculiar exceptions. He believes that congressional limits on presidential power such as the War Powers Act and the special prosecutor law—laws passed by a majority of both houses and signed by the president himself—are unconstitutional. He has criticized the line of Supreme Court cases, beginning with *Bakke,* that permit some forms of governmental affirmative action—every conservative's least favorite exercise of judicial restraint.

Liberal interest groups stand accused, justly, of spreading hysteria about Robert Bork. Even if he got his way and all the Supreme Court precedents he objects to were overturned, we would not return immediately to a land of back-alley abortions, forbidden contraceptives, and racially restricted neighborhoods, because the majority view on these issues has changed and the laws the Court overturned would not be put back on the books. But the telling point is that laws banning contraceptives and upholding racial deeds, now so unthinkable, existed and were enforced only twenty or thirty years ago. Who's to say for sure they won't return? More fundamentally, who knows what manifestations of the majority will today will seem similarly unthinkable twenty or thirty years from now?

The Bill of Rights and the institution of judicial review are frankly antimajoritarian. If we did not want to have unelected judges overruling democratically enacted laws, we would not need a Constitution. It's an odd arrangement. Yet every time the Senate votes on a Supreme Court nominee, the majority through its elected representatives is repeating the remarkable act of democratic self-abnegation that created the Constitution in the first place. Why? Partly because every member of the majority knows he or she is also a potential minority. The power we therefore give to judges is easy to abuse. Judges need enormous intellectual integrity. But they also need vision. By the definition of their constitutional role, they must see things the majority doesn't see. In 1971, Robert Bork saw the wisdom of *Brown* v. *Board of Education*. By then, so did most people. Would he have seen it in 1954?

For decades Ronald Reagan has been inveighing against the Supreme Court and demanding a sea change in constitutional law. Now, preposterously, the administration insists that its nominee would actually have very little impact. But the tedious statistical debate about how often Bork's lower-court opinions have or have not been reversed by the Supreme Court is beside the point. So is the fact that this or that distinguished jurist may have shared Bork's disagreement with this or that Supreme Court ruling. The president and his present nominee could not be clearer about the kind of Supreme Court they want. It is up to the Senate—which, unlike the president, was elected by majorities in all fifty states—to decide whether it wants the same thing.

THE TYRANNY OF BEAUTY

(*The New Republic*, OCTOBER 12, 1987)

So this gorilla shows up at the personnel office and asks for a job. The personnel director says, "Are you kidding? We can't hire you. You look like a gorilla." To which the gorilla replies, "Watch out, buddy, I'm gonna sue you for employment discrimination under the Rehabilitation Act of 1973."

Okay, so it's not much of a punch line. What do you expect? I got it from the *Harvard Law Review,* America's most prestigious legal journal, which recently published an essay arguing that it should be illegal to discriminate on the basis of physical attractiveness. In fact, says the author, "facial discrimination," as he wittily calls it, may already be illegal under laws forbidding discrimination against the handicapped. "It . . . seems an arbitrary distinction to say that an employer cannot refuse to hire a person who has a disfiguring scar on his chin, for example, but can refuse to hire someone whose chin is jutting or unusually shaped."

By tradition, these law review notes are unsigned. But with no particular exertion, I tracked down the author. As a naysayer in the current debate over Robert Bork, I hesitate to say where. Yes, it was in the chambers of Judge Abner Mikva, Bork's most liberal colleague on the influential D.C. Circuit Court of Appeals, where this recent *Harvard Law Review* editor in chief now serves as a clerk. Thus the worst fears of Bork's supporters are confirmed: Even as they labor to dam the flood of "rights" pouring out of the courts, liberals are busy drilling new holes in the dike. Jutting-chin liberation? As Bork can testify, young Adam Cohen may come to regret this display of youthful intellectual exuberance if he should find himself up before the Senate Judiciary Committee in his sober middle years.

But he swears he's serious. And why not? The logic is impeccable. Appearance, like race and sex and physical handicap, is an immutable characteristic. Like these other disadvantages, an unattractive appearance usually has no connection to your ability to do the job. Therefore, discrimination on this basis is just as unfair and should be outlawed. Conservative opponents of the general trend in civil rights would have no trouble agreeing that this is, indeed, the logical extension of that trend.

That, they would say, is a comment on the trend.

Even these conservatives, though, would have to concede that beauty is a great advantage in the world. In good law review style, Cohen cites an array of studies proving the obvious: People automatically assign favorable non-physical characteristics to other people who are good-looking; strangers are more likely to do favors for physically attractive people; ugly people get higher sentences in criminal cases and lower damage awards in civil lawsuits.

Of course many rise above the handicap of appearance to become distinguished professors at Harvard Law School and other successes in life. Nevertheless, no one would choose to be ugly. We are all traumatized to varying degrees about our appearance. Facial discrimination is far more overt and shameless than racial discrimination: Our culture doesn't even attempt to hide its preference for certain arrangements of facial and bodily parts over others. In our personal lives, few of us even pay lip service to the ideal of indifference to physical beauty   if, indeed, there is such an ideal.

Life will never deal an equal hand to the physically unattractive (or the "aesthetically challenged," as one tart conservative predicts the approved term will inevitably become). But is that any reason that they shouldn't at least be protected against discrimination in employment, housing, and college admissions?

Conservatives would argue (as some do in the case of blacks and women) that the market will punish any employer who is stupid enough to discriminate against a better-qualified applicant on the basis of an irrelevant criterion such as looks. And in many cases, looks may not be irrelevant at all. Cohen is prepared to make a few narrow exceptions for jobs like acting. But he takes a hard line against exceptions for salespeople, stewardesses, and so on. If looks are an advantage in these fields (which of course they are), it is only because of prejudice in society as a whole, if not in the particular employer. We don't permit employers to pander to the racism of their customers. Why should we permit pandering to what might be called "looksism"?

No, the justice of the cause is beyond doubt. The question is whether we can afford to expand the awesome machinery of civil rights litigation into this vast new area. Of course there is a natural restraint operating here, which Adam Cohen unintentionally reveals as he describes how an ugly-rights lawsuit might work: "An applicant will be able to point to some 'objective' aspect of his appearance—such as obesity, shortness, an unusual-looking nose, or protruding ears or an applicant may . . . be able to demonstrate that in some general way, given the totality of his appearance, he is considered unattractive." Cohen also suggests the use of expert witnesses. But it will be an exceptionally greedy or bitter person who would wish to pay an expert on beauty to describe in a public courtroom how ugly he is.

Yet conservatives have a point when they ask where it will all end. Cohen suggests that job interviews be conducted over the telephone, to avoid looks bias. But doesn't this leave open the possibility of prejudice on the basis of a whiny voice? Or, he says, job applicants could be interviewed behind a screen—a system already used for symphony orchestra auditions—so that an unpleasant face doesn't obscure an applicant's "pleasant personality." But parents of newborns will tell you that personality is also largely innate and immutable. What about "grouch liberation"?

Well, the one citadel of prejudice we may be sure is free from storming by the battalions of Harvard Law School is our society's overwhelming bias in favor of smart people. They may be short, fat, and ugly up there, with protruding ears, unusual noses, jutting chins, and dyspeptic personalities. But they're not dumb.

Two Deal-Makers

(*The New Republic*, DECEMBER 28, 1987)

he Party acts as the initiator and generator of ideas, the organizer and guiding force and, I would say, the guarantor of perestroika in the interests of consolidating socialism, in the interests of the working people. The Party has assumed a truly historic responsibility. In 1917, Lenin said: "Having started a revolution we must go all the way." The same is true for perestroika: the Party will go all the way.

—PERESTROIKA BY MIKHAIL GORBACHEV

Frankly, I'm not too big on parties, because I can't stand small talk. Unfortunately, they're part of doing business, so I find myself going to more than I'd like—and then trying hard to leave early.

—*TRUMP* BY DONALD TRUMP

As human beings, they couldn't be more different. One is a power-mad egomaniac. The other is modest and philosophical. One loves glitz and escorts a vulgar, social-climbing wife. The other is a natty but tasteful dresser with an elegant, witty spouse. One claims to be a Republican, but is courted by Democrats. The other claims to be a Socialist, but is courted by Republicans. One makes no secret of his hunger for world domination. The other aspires only to universal peace and the betterment of mankind. One is a great New York real estate developer, the other merely leader of the Soviet Union. But Donald Trump and Mikhail Gorbachev have something in common this Christmas season: a book to peddle.

In fact, *Perestroika: The Art of the Deal* and *Trump: New Thinking for Our Country and the World* (or is it the other way around?) have a lot in common. Both are written, or ghostwritten, in that chatty, ostensibly confessional mode so popular these days, full of personal revelation and cracker-barrel philosophy. Trump: "I've always had a personal thing about cleanliness, but I also believe it's a very good investment." Gorbachev: "To do something better, you must work an extra bit harder. I like this phrase: working an extra bit harder. For me it is not just a slogan, but a habitual state of mind."

Both authors draw on their own past to illustrate their philosophies of life. Trump describes borrowing his younger brother's building blocks, promising to return them, and then not doing it. He nostalgically recalls youthful hours spent poring over "listings of FHA foreclosures."

Gorbachev, discussing the wisdom of Lenin, says: "I shall adduce my own experience to corroborate this point," and goes on to describe a "gala session" at which "I referred to Lenin's tenets on the need for taking into account the requirements of objective economic laws, on planning and cost accounting," and so on. "The audience enthusiastically supported this reference to Lenin's ideas," he reports modestly. Lenin is undoubtedly the inspiration for a later chapter heading: "On to Full Cost Accounting!"

Both books, naturally, are of special interest on the subject of negotiations. Trump says: "My style of deal-making is quite simple and straightforward. I aim very high, and then I just keep pushing and pushing and pushing to get what I'm after." Gorbachev's philosophy is quite the reverse. "We must tackle problems in a spirit of cooperation rather than animosity," he recommends. He notes, however—rather patronizingly, I thought—that "emotional outbursts are an inevitable part of any complicated endeavor."

Although Trump is eager to appear tough and Gorbachev is eager to appear sweet, both are vain enough to temper these images with contrary anecdotes. "I always take calls from my kids," Trump reveals, "no matter what I'm doing." What's more, in 1986 he went to pay his last respects to an elderly fellow zillionaire, even though "I happened to have an extremely important business meeting in my office on the day of his funeral in Chicago." Tragically, the meeting could never be rescheduled. But "I have no regrets."

By sheer coincidence, a dramatic highlight of Gorbachev's book was occurring about the same time. It seems that certain elements were pressuring our hero to cancel the Twenty-seventh Party Congress. "Of course, the Congress could have been postponed," he concedes. "This opinion was persistently expressed. . . . But the approaches of the stagnation period that had affected all of us were felt to be behind that. A point of view which, in my opinion, most accorded with the situation—that we should hold the Congress on schedule and draw all healthy forces of society into the preparation for it—ultimately prevailed." Plucky Mikhail!

When it comes to bitchiness—a key ingredient of any best-selling memoir, as their publishers surely told them—Gorbachev goes for the hammer while Trump wields a delicate sickle. Trump on a fellow developer: "Abe has always been considered difficult. But I like him and his family a lot." Gorbo, by contrast, on Khrushchev's "We will bury you" speech: "Probably the most hackneyed statement by a Soviet leader in the West."

On the other hand, Gorbachev's book offers far better value in that other essential ingredient of the tell-all best-seller: total-recall transcripts of conversations with other celebs. My favorite is a surrealistic discussion with West German president Richard von Weizsäcker about the concept of a "common European home," in which Weizsäcker remarks that he doesn't care for the lack of visitation rights between the apartments of this home, or for the trench running through the living room. The author explains helpfully: "He is referring to the fact that the FRG and the GDR [the two Germanys] are divided by an international border passing, in particular, through Berlin."

Then there's this:

> *Mikhail Gorbachev* [to an American tourist]: Have you encountered even one instance of a disrespectful attitude toward Americans during your stay?
>
> *D. Padula:* No, though a man in the street once asked me, when

would there be peace? I told him I hoped peace would come soon.
Mikhail Gorbachev: This is very interesting information.

Well, maybe David Mamet can work on it for the screenplay.

Ironically, though, it is Trump who gets the last word in both books. "I . . . plan to keep making deals, big deals, and right around the clock," his own book concludes. Gorbachev says, in a pun the American Right will sadly concur with: "The past two-and-a-half years have given us a great deal." He goes on to opine: "Now the whole world needs restructuring, i.e., progessive development. . . . " *Perestroika*—restructuring—and development are one and the same thing! Developer Trump for party chairman! On to full cost accounting!

Mr. Democrat

(*The New Republic*, MARCH 21, 1988)

Yes, *that was Mr. Democrat, Robert Strauss, having a quiet lunch yesterday at the Jockey Club with First Lady Nancy Reagan.*

—*THE WASHINGTON POST*

Did I miss the primary where they elected Bob Strauss Mr. Democrat? Can we petition for a recall? Are Democrats allowed to vote, or is it entirely up to the likes of William Buckley and George Will?

Buckley selected Strauss as his Democratic coquestioner in last year's candidate debates. Will has touted Strauss twice for president and once for secretary of state in the past few months.

When he's not being called "Mr. Democrat," Strauss, aged sixty-nine, is labeled an "elder statesman" or "wise man." In fact, he's "the Capital's Leading Wise Man," according to the headline on a recent *New York Times* puffer that was worth a pile to his influence-peddling operation. Strauss, oozed the *Times,* is "a senior statesman who bridges partisan rivalry and ideological factionalism. The capital needs such elders, people known for their straight talk and sound advice."

Strauss is being touted, not least by Strauss, as the potential broker of a deadlocked Democratic nomination fight. Even in the course of dismissing that idea, Albert Hunt of *The Wall Street Journal* says that the next Democratic president would "be a fool not to put Mr. Strauss in his Cabinet."

Why? Wherein, exactly, lies the greatness of Robert Strauss? Is it his devotion to liberal values? His deep insight into the issues facing our nation? Hardly. Strauss's rare public remarks on public issues are embarrassingly banal. For depth and passion, they make his pal Bob Dole (with whom he shares a Florida winter retreat) seem like Henry Kissinger. Writing on trade recently in the *Post*, Strauss opined: "The American people want something done about it. . . . There is no time like the present to get the job done, and the key players all know it. . . . There is nothing to prevent a good, sound bill from being worked out . . ." etc., etc. This is best translated as: "Goddammit, I want Bob Strauss's name in the paper tomorrow."

Strauss is not the sort to maintain a principled disagreement with anyone. I was astonished to read him quoted in the *Times* a few months ago saying that Ann Lewis, a far-left Democratic activist, was unfit to be party chairman. Not that he doesn't think this—he surely does—but why would he say it? Sure enough, the next day's paper carried an "Editor's Note" explaining that the quotation from Strauss "omitted the context" and should have added, "I think she is one of the very credible and sensible political voices in this town and country." It's a testament to Strauss's clout that he got the *Times* to print such a ridiculous correction, and a hint of how he got that clout that he wanted one.

Ordinarily, of course, Strauss's splendid ideological agnosticism tilts him to the right, not the left. It's not that Strauss has conservative beliefs. He has no beliefs, except for his cardinal principle that all the key players ought to sit down and work this sucker out, goddammit.

So what's the secret? Is it his record of devoted public service? Strauss was a successful fund-raiser and party chairman in the early 1970s. During the Carter years, he built up his résumé on the George Bush model: a few months each as special trade representative, President's counselor on inflation, Middle East negotiator, and chairman of the reelection campaign. His achievements in any of these posts were not remarkable (or even, regarding inflation and the Middle East, noticeable). But they got him the title of ambassador and lots of new clients when he returned to his law firm in 1981. Since then the firm has become one of Washington's largest and most profitable.

But, as the *Times* says, "his real influence in Washington derives not from his past titles, but from the force of his personality and the quality of his judgment." "Judgment" has become the preferred euphemism these days for what Washington fixers offer, now that Michael Deaver (another Strauss pal) has discredited the formerly favored "access."

The idea that someone like Strauss is a great fount of "judgment" is about one-third humbug directed at potential critics, about one-third humbug directed at his customers themselves—business clients, presidents, journalists—and about one-third true. But it's judgment of a particular kind. As Carter's chief of staff, Hamilton Jordan, put it in his memoir: "It was always helpful for me to hear what Strauss was saying, because I knew that his 'ideas' were more accurately an amalgam of the collective thoughts and opinions of the Washington political and media establishments." What Strauss really sells to outsider presidents like Carter and Reagan (payment in ego) and to corporate clients (payment in cash) is Washington's blessing.

What he sells to journalists is more subtle. Strauss "gives good quote," as they say, and leaks when he's got something to leak. But it's not as a source that reporters value Strauss. They generally know blarney when they hear it. Jordan describes Strauss's technique of inventing a reason to talk to Carter, however briefly, so he could lunch out on "As I was saying to the president." What seduces journalists into Strauss's conspiracy of hype is more Strauss's mastery of the peculiar Washington style of flattery-by-insult ("How the hell are you, you old pigfucker?"); his genuine interest in their view of things (always a sure sign of wisdom in others), which he can recycle; in short, his warm embrace—his reassurance that there is a Washington establishment and they're in it.

Virtually everyone in Washington recognizes that Bob Strauss is 99 percent hot air, yet they all maintain this "elder statesman" and "Mr. Democrat" routine like some sort of elaborate prank on the rest of the world. Is it unsporting not to play along? I don't think so. It's a little too convenient for conservatives and Republicans that "Mr. Democrat" should be a man so obviously more interested in being seen as a friend of the president than in who the president happens to be. It's an insult to the Democratic party—partly self-inflicted, to be sure—that its symbolic head should be a man whose political influence is out for hire to the highest bidder. And it's a telling comment on the Washington establishment that so laughably shallow a figure should be considered one of its "wise men."

Of course Strauss may be no different from the Democratic elder statesmen of the past. Someone like Clark Clifford worked harder to keep a patina of "law office" on his lobbying business, and came on like a Brahmin, in contrast to Strauss's po'boy routine. But basically the scam was the same.*

In fact, every great capital probably has a Mr. Fixit, a self-promoting middleman who is a friend of all sides no matter how mutually opposed they may be. In Tehran, when you're in need of "judgment," you look up the elder statesman and wise man Manucher Ghorbanifar. He doesn't have much in common, spiritually, with the ruling ayatollahs. They let him make his millions and keep his body parts in one place because he's useful to them. But at least no one calls him "Mr. Shiite."

Skyway Robbery

(*The New Republic*, APRIL 25, 1988)

March 31 was the busiest day ever at O'Hare International Airport. The reason was not masses of people rushing to spend April Fools' Day with their loved ones. The reason was masses of people rushing to qualify for the largest and most brazen commercial bribe in the history of capitalism—triple mileage in airline frequent flier programs. In this latest baroque twist, travelers who flew one round-trip on most airlines before March 31 will get triple-mileage credits on future flights for the rest of the year. Then, under the befuddlingly complex rules, as few as two paid trips may qualify you for a free third one.

Since their invention by American Airlines in 1981, frequent flier programs have become an established part of upper-middle-class culture. Eight million people belong to an average of three or four programs each, and they will have over a billion dollars of free travel coming to them by the end of 1988. People collect mileage like baseball cards, pore over the massive documents the airlines send them, and weigh the value of three first-class upgrades versus a domestic round-trip companion ticket (Ha-

---

Clark Clifford later lost his status as the gold standard of Washington lobbyists. See page 156.

waii not included, certain holidays blacked out) versus off-season round trip to Amsterdam (plus extra weekend day at participating Marriott with changeover in St. Louis), and so on. As the blight spreads to rent-a-car companies, hotels, and credit cards, mileage has turned into a sort of black-market currency operating beside the dollar.

For the airlines, frequent flier programs have two purposes, one they admit to and one they don't. The first is to build brand loyalty in a business where the products are pretty indistinguishable. The second is to deal with the reality that for business travel—about half of all air travel, and by far the most profitable half—the person deciding which airline to fly is not usually the person who is paying for the ticket. This makes straightforward price competition fairly pointless. Frequent flier programs are in essence a bribe to employees deciding how to spend the boss's money. When amounts smaller than a billion dollars are involved, people have gone to jail for this sort of thing.

Frequent flier programs are specifically designed to prevent the boss from reclaiming the kickback. That's one reason they're so complex. American's original program simply distributed coupons on each flight that could be saved up and used for free travel. When companies demanded that employees turn in the coupons, coupons were replaced by today's elaborate computerized accounting systems and various rules were added making the mileage credits hard to transfer.

Frequent flier programs are a rip-off in four ways. First, ticket prices are higher than they otherwise would be, in order to pay for the free travel and because the programs replace true price competition. The airlines have just raised a full coach fare about 15 percent, and tightened restrictions on discount fares, even as the mileage giveaway explodes. The connection is obvious. The American Institute of Certified Public Accountants is thinking of requiring airlines to set aside 10 percent of all revenues—that would be $4 billion a year—to pay for future free travel. Since most travelers aren't yet in frequent flier programs, the "kickback" element in each frequent flier's ticket is clearly far higher than 10 percent.

Second, the programs encourage travelers to go for the airline they belong to, rather than the one with the cheapest fare. That's the main idea, of course. If frequent fliers were paying for their own tickets, this wouldn't matter. But generally they're not. Third, a more egregious form of the same abuse: People take entirely needless trips in order to run up their mileage. Everyone has stories about this sort of thing in his or her own office, and the statistics bear them out. Is it just a coincidence that American Airlines passenger miles during triple-mileage February were up 25 percent over last year, despite higher prices and a slower economy?

Fourth, frequent flier programs protect the established airlines from upstart competition, thereby raising prices. The decade of airline deregulation has seen airline prices drop, in real terms, by about a quarter. But critics have predicted that this is just temporary. After a shakeout, they say, a few large carriers will dominate the market and be able to raise prices. Recent developments are starting to bear them out.

Yet by its nature, the airline industry should be one of the easiest to break into. All you need is a couple of leased airplanes, an unemployed pilot or two, and a bucket of paint for your logo. It's not like having to build a factory. Inept government policy regarding takeoff and landing slots at airports has helped to make fresh airline competition harder than it needs to be, but another vital factor is frequent flier programs. If a business executive has 100,000 miles racked up with United, and is aiming for that first-class round trip for two to the Caribbean next winter, she's not going to switch to Upstart Airlines no matter how cheap or convenient its flights may be.

That's why the best thing the federal government could do to protect the success of airline deregulation would be to prick the frequent flier bubble by starting to tax frequent flier awards taken by business travelers. This is only reasonable, since the companies have already deducted the cost of the ticket. As, in effect, in-kind compensation, frequent flier awards are probably taxable now, though no one has ever pressed the point and no one I know of has ever been saintly enough to declare a free trip as income.

The airlines are said to be secretly hoping the IRS will step in and help to cool frequent flier fever. They fear they have created a monster that will swallow all their profits when people start cashing in their mileage. This is what happens when you get carried away in massaging the great American g-spot (g, in this case, for greed). As corrupters of millions of middle-class innocents, it will serve the airlines right.

Nancy's Star Signs

(The New Republic, MAY 23, 1988)*

What do the stars hold in store for you? Write to Nancy's Star Signs, 1600 Pennsylvania Avenue, Washington, D.C.)

Dear Nancy:

Lately I've been overcome by the feeling that I'm not wanted. I'm just a regular guy who runs a large Justice Department here in town, yet many people treat me like an ogre. Past acts of generosity to old friends keep coming back to haunt me. Trusted associates are denouncing me in public and my boss's wife is trying to get me fired. I honestly think I've done nothing wrong, but it's been said that I'm not very bright. Should I quit my job, or should I stick it out?

E.M. III, Washington, D.C.

Dear E.M. III:

I sense you were born under the sign of Incompetus. Incompetans are noted for their eagerness to do and receive favors, their ethical obtuseness, and their general inability to take a hint. Your Saturn is in Aries, the Moon is the Leo (rising), and your head will continue to be up Uranus for the foreseeable future. This is a good moment to heed the counsel of advisers recommending an immediate change of scene. A new chapter of your life is about to open. Seize the opportunity, but proceed with great caution. Your freedom of movement may be curtailed for five to seven years, with time off for good behavior.

Dear Nancy:

I consider myself an easy person to get along with, yet my husband's career requires me to socialize with one woman I find it very difficult to relate to. Could this be because she is an Anorexian and I am a Marxist-

---

*The occasion for this piece was the publication of Donald Regan's White House memoirs. Regan, who served as chief of staff, revealed that, in making important policy decisions, President Reagan often relied on the First Lady and the First Lady, in turn, often relied on an astrologer. The letter writers are supposed to be Ed Meese, Raisa Gorbachev, Michael Dukakis, and Ronald Reagan, all well-known figures at the time.

Leninist? This woman and her husband are coming to visit later this month. I dread another round of her mindless nattering about furniture and clothes and children, not to mention her catty put-downs of Soviet society. How can I minimize tension, while at the same time making it clear that I think she is a desiccated symbol of oppressed womanhood under capitalism, and a bitch to boot?

(Ms.) R.G., Moscow

Dear R.G.:

Fortunately, in late May, Glasnost will be in the House of Stalin and Mars will be receding from Afghanistan. This is an auspicious moment for reaching out and establishing new relationships. Also for redecorating the guest room, especially in soothing shades of blue-gray and off-white. Fido, the dog star, will be rising through the constellation of Herpes. During this period, special effort must be made to avoid topics of discord such as international relations and comparative economic systems. Reflect on whether past tensions may not have been your own fault, and watch who you're calling a bitch, you overdressed, overeducated, defeminized Communist excuse for a woman.

Dear Nancy:

I would like to become more charismatic. Although my ethnic heritage entitles me to an earthy, raucous, fun-loving personality, I am widely regarded as unexciting and bland. Do the stars foretell any change in my personality between now and, say, November? Please answer within ten days in triplicate on the enclosed form, #117-D-2302.

M.D., Brookline, Massachusetts

Dear M.D.:

I'm afraid the stars offer little consolation. You were born under the sign of Humorlus (the Bore), with Earnest rising through the constellation of Monotone and Nerd in alignment with Uptight. There could be good news in your future, however. The stars indicate a giant forthcoming battle in which a boring nerd will enjoy a great triumph in early November. Unfortunately, the stars indicate that the loser will also be a boring nerd.

Dear Nancy:

My White House memoirs are going to be the last to come out, but I want them to be the best. Unfortunately, the others are getting harder and harder to top. Dave Stockman told about the lying, Larry Speakes revealed that quotes of historic importance were made up by minions, and Don Regan claimed that important decisions were affected by advice from the First Lady's astrologer. My publisher says I really need some killer anecdotes to top this one. Can the stars supply some for me?

R.R., Washington, D.C.

Dear R.R.:

What's left? Voodoo cults? Extortion plots? Cannibalism? Give up. As someone born under the sign of Ignoramus, with Blindeye rising through the constellation of Rosyscenario, you are not well suited to a career as a memoirist. The stars say you should delegate the task of history-writing to others. Avoid strenuous legislative and diplomatic initiatives in the near and middle future. The coming months will be a good time for a nap, especially in the morning, afternoon, and early evening.

THE SUPERRICH ARE DIFFERENT

(*Time*, MAY 23, 1988)

You can understand why Leona Helmsley might want a $45,000 silver clock modeled after a building owned by her billionaire husband, even if you wouldn't want one yourself. What's harder to understand is why she would bother breaking the law to get it. That, in fact, is part of her lawyer's answer to official charges that the Helmsleys cheated the government of $4 million in taxes by wrongly charging off sundry personal gewgaws as business expenses: Would people so rich risk jail for an amount so (relatively) small?

Maybe Mrs. Helmsley did it as a public service. After all, her calamity has brought pleasure to millions. The sacrifice of plutocrats on the altar of public scandal is a treasured ritual of the American civil religion. And the Helmsleys were already among the least sympathetic of the wealth celebrities coughed up by the Reagan era. He is a landlord: fifty thousand apartments, along with other real estate. She is the self-proclaimed "queen" of his hotel chain, famous for being nasty to the help, and a walking exaggeration of every cliché about the second wife as a social type.

The obvious diagnosis of what ails the Helmsleys—greed—doesn't explain much, either morally or practically. Few of us lack greed. And, in our economic system, there is nothing wrong with greed. A variety of diagrams and mathematical formulas is available to show how capitalism usually channels individual greed into productive activity that's good for society as a whole. But, if anything, the Helmsleys ought to be exempt from the forces that stimulate greed in the rest of us. They're already worth an estimated $1.4 billion. They're sixty-seven and seventy-nine years old, with no children. They give to charity generously, but not obsessively. Although the Helmsleys try harder than most other superrich, there's no way they're going to spend what they've already got. So why cheat the government to get more?

Indeed, the question of what may have motivated one superrich couple to break the law is less interesting than the question of what motivates all of them to keep on accumulating, legally or otherwise. A central assumption of supply-side economics—the dominant economic theology of the past decade, which produced large tax-rate cuts for the wealthy—is that people are motivated by rather fine calculations about the reward for further effort. Supply-siders are the chiropractors of capitalism, believing that small manipulations of the incentive structure can produce enormous changes in economic behavior. That may be true for those of us who have some use—if not real need—for everything we earn. But is it true of those at the very top of the economy?

The classic work on the motivations of the rich is Thorstein Veblen's *The Theory of the Leisure Class* (1899). Veblen, who invented the term conspicuous consumption, argued that the rich don't accumulate wealth in order to consume goods. Just the opposite: They consume in order to display their accumulation. "The possession of wealth confers honour; it is an invidious distinction. Nothing equally cogent can be said for the consumption of goods, nor for any other conceivable incentive to acquisition." The rich also display their wealth, Veblen argued, by not working: "conspicuous leisure." In all societies, he wrote, "the upper classes are exempt from industrial employments, and this exemption is the economic expression of their superior rank."

But Veblen may need updating. How to explain people who accumulate more than they could ever possibly consume, and keep on working anyway? Many of the superrich (including Sam Walton, at $8.7 billion the richest man in America) pride themselves on living simply and expecting their heirs to do the same. They have no possible use for more money. Some have businesses to which they bring a missionary zeal, but can missionary zeal be brought to real estate syndications and leveraged buyouts—the prototypical new fortunes of the 1980s? Although some may plead force of habit or lack of imagination, most would deny any explanation that mundane. Why do they keep it up?

Well, Veblen could not have anticipated the cult of commerce, which has made working more chic than idleness. The way you put your billions on display is to bustle like a billionaire businessman, not in a futile attempt to spend them. It is her job as queen of the Helmsley hotel empire, not the spending power of her accumulated wealth, that Leona Helmsley has skillfully converted into today's favorite currency of fame.

What's more, the wealth tabulations that are now a running feature of publications like *Fortune* and *Forbes* have made it possible to display accumulated wealth beyond the natural limits of conspicuous consumption. Veblen would feel vindicated to know that after some initial resistance, many rich people now happily supply the details of their fortunes to the staffs compiling these lists. Harry Helmsley ranks sixty-fifth in the world according to *Fortune*. And—who knows?—another $4 million here and there could make all the difference between sixty-fifth and sixty-fourth.

But surely, if competitive accumulation for its own sake is the point for the very rich, then we needn't worry too much that their productive energies might be sapped by higher tax rates. To take an extreme example, if every billionaire's fortune were cut by half overnight, their relative rankings would be exactly the same, and they'd still have more money than they could ever spend.

One Reagan tax cut that got little attention was a major 1981 reduction in the estate tax. Veblen would say this is the wrong approach to encouraging the greed of the superwealthy. Instead, when a very rich individual (say, $100 million plus) dies, the government should audit the fortune and announce its relative ranking at a special press conference, as a service to "invidious distinction." Then it could, in good conscience, take a large chunk as a service charge.

Japan Handling

(*The New Republic,* JUNE 27, 1988)

I n Hollywood, you know an actress has arrived when she's seen on the arm of a big-shot producer at a trendy restaurant. In Washington, you know a policy idea has arrived when it's endorsed by Henry Kissinger in *Foreign Affairs.* In the current issue, Kissinger and Cyrus Vance offer "Bipartisan Objectives for American Foreign Policy," in which they resolve all outstanding foreign policy problems in a miraculous twenty-three pages—must reading for anyone who would like an excuse not to read *Foreign Affairs* anymore.

On the subject of trade with Japan, Kissinger and Vance write: "The American-Japanese dialogue must not be confined to mutual harassment and recrimination on an industry-by-industry basis. . . . The two countries should . . . establish an overall trade balance the United States would find tolerable; within that balance, Japan would have the choice of either reducing its exports or increasing its imports."

Advocates of this arrangement call it "managed trade." The idea is that instead of endless, wearisome attempts to open up Japanese markets to this product or that one, and rather than throwing up protectionist trade barriers of our own, let's just cajole or coerce the Japanese into agreeing to reduce their trade surplus (still running at about $60 billion a year with the United States) and let them worry about how to go about it.

This approach to the trade deficit has been building steam for a while. Liberal economist Lester Thurow endorsed it years ago. Last winter it was advocated in a widely discussed article in the *Harvard Business Review.* It is promoted in an influential book published this spring, called *Trading Places: How We Allowed Japan to Take the Lead.* Lee Iacocca casually urges it in his own new book, *Talking Straight.* And now . . . Kissinger and stardom.

The theory behind the idea of managed trade is that the Japanese mentality dooms traditional free-trade thinking to failure. As Clyde Prestowitz, the former Reagan administration trade official who wrote *Trading Places,* puts it: "The United States and Japan have fundamentally different understandings of the purposes and workings of a national economy." The

Japanese concentrate on production, not consumption. They're far less obsessed with increasing their standard of living. They treasure traditional business relationships, even at the cost of missing bargains, which makes their home market hard for foreigners to crack. Meanwhile, they are ruthlessly organized to capture foreign markets, irrespective of short-term profits.

All of this means that traditional solutions to the trade deficit are futile. The Japanese will always sell us more than they buy from us no matter how good or cheap our products, no matter how skilled our managers, no matter how many formal trade barriers we knock down. Far better than babbling about open markets and level playing fields, let's talk to them in terms of national economic destiny—a language they understand.

Prestowitz and the others tend to be ambiguous about whether they think we ought to envy the Japanese their alleged economic mentality. Adam Smith's *The Wealth of Nations* was a specific and rather persuasive rebuttal to the idea that a nation prospers by running a huge trade surplus, a philosophy that used to go by the name of mercantilism. If the Japanese actually are genetically programmed to hand over $60 billion dollars of real stuff every year, indefinitely, in exchange for nothing but little bits of paper and electronic blips, it's tempting to say, "Go ahead. Make my day."

Even if they use their blips to buy up American companies and real estate, what does that get them? Until they decide to spend the profits (that is, run a trade deficit instead of a trade surplus), it just gets them more blips.

If we ordered the Japanese to choose between increasing their imports and cutting their exports, there's not much doubt which they'd pick. As Prestowitz and the others describe Japan's economy, the forces that discourage imports are deeply rooted throughout Japanese society and culture, whereas the forces that propel exports are centrally directed. Clearly, if forced to choose, the Japanese would balance their trade by cutting exports. "Managed trade," in other words, would mean less trade, not more trade. Today's managed traders are Commodore Perrys in reverse, threatening, "Stop selling to us, or else!"

But a restraint on trade has precisely the same effect whether it is imposed by the buying country or by the selling country. Advocates of managed trade emphasize that their proposal is an alternative to tariffs and quotas—because they accept the premise that traditional protectionism is harmful—but there is no practical difference between their proposal and traditional protectionism.

Free trade theory does not assume reciprocity. It holds that you benefit from your own open borders whether or not the other fellow follows suit. No American is forced to buy Japanese products. We buy them because we wish to. "Managed trade," like ordinary protectionism, would simply deny Americans products they want to buy at prices they wish to pay. It would make our economy less efficient and our citizens less prosperous. That, at any rate, is the case for free trade. You can deny it if you wish, but you can't evade it by talking about "managed trade" and pretending you don't mean protectionism.

The danger is not that the Japanese are genetically programmed to produce more than they consume forever. The danger is the opposite: that they'll start calling in their IOUs. Then we'll discover that running a trade surplus is a lot less fun than running a trade deficit. That's why, if we're going to impose any trade rule on the Japanese, we'd be better off requiring them to keep running the $60 billion surplus indefinitely.

The trade deficit is a symptom of our economic dilemma, not a cause. Imagine a family that has run up a huge bill at the grocery store and finally loses patience. "Look," they tell the grocer, "we insist that you stop extending us credit. Either buy something from us that you don't really want, or stop selling us food." There's no mystery which option the grocer would pick. The mystery is why the family would think its problems were the grocer's fault.

Acquired Plumage

(*Time*, AUGUST 29, 1988)

The boys of Vietnam fought a terrible and vicious war. It was the unpampered boys of the working class who picked up the rifles and went on the march. They chose to believe and answer the call of duty.
—PRESIDENT REAGAN, MEMORIAL DAY, 1986

"I did not know in 1969 that I would be in this room today," said Dan Quayle last week about his decision two decades ago to pull strings and get into the National Guard rather than risk serving and dying in

Vietnam. It was the most accidentally revealing remark of the week, out-doing even Ronald Reagan's classic Freudian slip at the convention, "Facts are stupid things." As Fats Waller so aptly put it, "One never knows, do one?" In this day when politicians are created like androids by consultants and pollsters, using off-the-shelf parts for everything from hairstyles to stands on particular issues to deeply held moral beliefs, it seems almost unfair that this small item from the past should gum up the works of a state-of-the-art model like the young conservative senator from Indiana.

Senator Quayle is just one of many so-called war wimps or chicken hawks: prominent, youngish Reagan-era conservatives who, one way or another, ducked the war in Vietnam. Others include such Reagan admin-istration foreign policy hard-liners as Elliott Abrams and Richard Perle, commentator Patrick Buchanan, and even Sylvester Stallone (who taught at a girls' school in Switzerland while the Commies were being beastly to his fantasy alter ego John Rambo). A similar Quayle-like controversy also surrounds the Reverend Pat Robertson, whose father, a senator, may have helped him avoid combat in Korea.

It's wonderful to hear prominent Republicans suddenly discovering the vital role of the National Guard in preserving our freedom. Quayle himself said in his Thursday-night acceptance speech that he is "proud" of his National Guard service, during which he was trained as a welder and then put to work grinding out press releases. The same people who make a big issue of Michael Dukakis's veto of a law requiring people to recite the Pledge of Allegiance—implying, though never saying, that this casts doubt on Dukakis's patriotism—insist that it is somehow a cheap shot to ask what Dan Quayle's evasion of combat service in 1969 says about the boisterous hawkish values he professes to hold today. It's not hard to imagine what Republican hatchet men like Bush campaign man-ager Lee Atwater would do with this issue if the shoe were on the other foot.

Echoing a commonly expressed view during the New Orleans con-vention week, George Bush, Jr., said of Quayle, "The thing that's impor-tant is [that] he didn't go to Canada." That is indeed an important distinction, but not in the way Bush junior seems to think. Those who went to Canada knew they were making a fundamental life choice. They, along with those who chose conscientious objection or outright draft re-sistance and jail, acted because they opposed the war. This may have been right or wrong, but it was a serious moral decision with serious moral consequences. The National Guard, by contrast, was a way to avoid Vietnam and the moral consequences at the same time. There is no evidence that the war Quayle ducked is one he opposed, let alone made any effort to end. Perhaps these days, with no draft and no war, people really do join the National Guard out of patriotism. But the idea that a desire to serve one's country motivated anyone to sign up for press-release duty in Indiana while others were fighting and dying in Vietnam is a conceit that won't fool anyone over the age of about thirty-five.

No one is required to be a hero, of course. If a high draft-lottery number hadn't saved me, I would have been grateful for the opportunity to lay my fingers on the line in the National Guard typing pool. Two things make Quayle's wartime experience on the Indiana front a legitimate embarrassment to him. First is how he got in. It's not absolutely clear that connections were necessary to join the Indiana Guard at that time, but it's clear Quayle and his family didn't leave things to chance. A valid issue on its own, this also compounds the GOP ticket's "silver spoon" problem. Second, it's hard for a politician to strike a martial pose and accuse his opponents of insufficient devotion to American military strength when he passed up his one chance to make a personal contribution to that strength.

As a matter of pure logic, what the war wimps did (or, rather, didn't do) two decades ago says nothing about the merits of aid to the Nicaraguan contras or Star Wars or other issues today. But it does say something important about a person's character if he hasn't lived his life in accordance with his professed values. And it obviously tests his commitment to those values as well. That's why the political-robotics technicians of both parties expend so much energy staging tableaux of loving family life, though strictly speaking the number of one's children, grandchildren, and household pets is irrelevant in evaluating one's views on federal day care.

On the matter of war and peace, voters are especially entitled to feel that leaders have lived their beliefs. War has always been a matter of old men sending young men off to die. Sometimes that's necessary. But who wants to entrust that crucial decision to a person who, when young, apparently thought it was necessary for others to go but not for himself?

Ronald Reagan, who spent World War II in Hollywood and whose family life would win no prizes in a *Leave It to Beaver* look-alike contest, has been spectacularly successful as the political avatar of values he hasn't lived by. His line "Go out there and win one more for the Gipper" got the biggest response of convention week, as he and his party forgot for one last joyous occasion that his life is not a movie. In possibly unintentional but genuine tribute to Reagan's magic, the prosaic Quayle, in his acceptance speech three days later, chose to introduce himself to America with an extended reference to the movie *Hoosiers*—which, in truth, bears comparison to Quayle's life more than *Knute Rockne, All American* bears to Reagan's.

Unfortunately for Quayle and the other chicken hawks, it is only the truly rare politician like Reagan who can get away with writing the movie of his own life.

RALLY ROUND THE FLAG, BOYS

(*Time*, SEPTEMBER 12, 1988)

When Michael Dukakis was asked about news stories casting doubt on George Bush's World War II heroism, he said, "I don't think that kind of thing has any place in the campaign. . . . You don't fly fifty-eight missions without enormous courage and tremendous patriotism." Not long afterward, Bush said of Dukakis, "What is it about the Pledge of Allegiance that upsets him so much?"

There is no mistaking Bush's point. It has nothing to do with the constitutional question of whether Dukakis eleven years ago should have vetoed a bill mandating recital of the pledge in school classrooms every day. Bush is implying that Dukakis is unpatriotic, that he doesn't love America as much as he should or as much as Bush does. "He sees America as another pleasant country on the UN roll call, somewhere between Albania and Zimbabwe," said Bush in his convention acceptance speech. Keynoter Thomas Kean, the New Jersey governor formerly admired for his decency and moderation, accused the Democrats of "pastel patriotism," neatly combining the suggestion of insufficient national ardor with the sexual innuendo of Jeane Kirkpatrick's famous "San Francisco Democrats" phrase of 1984.

Bush praises his running mate Dan Quayle on the peculiar grounds that he "damn sure never burned the American flag," as if Dukakis or Lloyd Bentsen or anyone in mainstream public life ever did. Meanwhile, other Republicans spread the baseless rumor that there are photographs of Kitty Dukakis burning the flag. If Bush thinks that kind of thing has no place in the campaign, he lacks the gallantry to say so. He also lacks the candor to say straight out about his opponent what he suggests by innuendo.

Maybe this confession will just tar me as unpatriotic too, but nothing since I came of political age has depressed me so much about American democracy as the apparent success of Bush's pledge offensive. What, after all, is American patriotism about? It's not about purple mountain majesties—they have those in Switzerland. There was endless babble about "freedom" at the Republican convention. But freedom doesn't mean reciting a loyalty oath on command. They have that kind of freedom in the USSR. American freedom means the right not to recite a loyalty oath if—for reasons of religion, politics, or simple perversity—you don't want to. Bush may reject this vision of American freedom, although it is shared by the Supreme Court. That is his privilege: It's a free country. It is not his privilege to imply that anyone who disagrees with him is unpatriotic.

The Bush campaign claims to be running on "issues," while the Democrats emphasize mere "personalities." But these are issues of a peculiar sort. The two Bush has chosen to stress—reciting the pledge in schools and state prison furlough policy—have nothing to do with the duties of the president of the United States. (Republicans, as federalism enthusiasts, ordinarily would be eager to point this out.) Bush in fact is virtually ignoring real issues. He's running on emotions.

That's fair enough. Emotions are a valid part of a presidential campaign. (So, for that matter, are personalities.) But the emotions Bush is stirring up in the name of American patriotism are ugly and—dare I say it—un-American. What unites the pledge nonsense, the furlough business, the attacks on the American Civil Liberties Union, the scare stories about a race of mythic bogeymen called liberals, is an effort to induce a fever of "us" versus "them" majoritarianism.

Most voters are happy to salute the flag, aren't in prison, aren't members of the unpopular minorities the ACLU looks out for, aren't the social losers for whom Bush's fantasy liberals are plotting expensive new government programs. You can always evoke the emotions of normal people against the great "other" and call it patriotism. Politicians in many countries have used this technique successfully. But American patriotism is supposed to be inclusive and tolerant, not exclusive and invidious.

George Bush knows this, too, or at least his speechwriter does. "I want a kinder, gentler nation," he said. Washington is still debating whether

Bush really is the generous-spirited character he intermittently displayed in his acceptance speech. I'm agnostic on that one. But even Bush's critics don't believe he's really the hate-filled demagogue of his current Mr. Hyde phase. He seems, rather, to have made a Faustian bargain: my soul for the presidency. Several of Bush's campaign advisers are well suited to the role of Mephistopheles.

Bush's patriotism is spurious for another reason. It's no-cost patriotism that demands nothing other than self-satisfaction, emotional and material. The Bush-style patriot may refuse to pay more taxes, in fact may demand new tax breaks, while clinging to every government benefit he now enjoys. The Bush-style patriot may call for an assertion of American power but needn't put his own body on the line; he may be "proud" of service writing press releases in Indiana. And the Bush-style patriot can measure his patriotism by his intolerance of people and opinions he doesn't like.

"My opponent's view of the world sees a long slow decline for our country," says Bush. In truth, Dukakis's campaign weltanschauung is as fatuously sunny as Bush's. And Dukakis, like Bush, asks nothing of voters except to lie back and enjoy it. Those who do fear that American civilization might be on a downward slope think the inability of our leaders to make any demands whatsoever of citizens to protect our freedom and prosperity is both evidence and engine of that decline. They find know-nothing remarks like the vice president's reaction to the shooting down of the Iranian civilian airliner—"I will never apologize for the United States of America, I don't care what the facts are"—a sign of national insecurity, not national self-confidence. To those who love America enough to worry about it, George Bush's ask-not-what-you-can-do-for-your-country flag-waving is the opposite of patriotism.

I Hear America Chatting

(*The New Republic*, OCTOBER 3, 1988)

"If you want to touch something basic in your audience," says the full-page ad in the 1988 edition of the *Directory of Experts, Authorities and Spokespersons* (also known as the "Talk Show Guest Directory"), ". . . move them to action: phone, write, praise, damn, cheer, etc. . . . Then you need to present REAL, LIVE COMMUNISTS ON

YOUR SHOW!" Yes, it's the "public relations/media" office of the
Communist Party of the United States, offering to provide "honest-to-
goodness, dues-paying members of the CPUSA" to the nation's masses of
TV and radio talk show producers.

The talk show industry is enjoying a small crisis of conscience these
days over the revelation that two actors managed to get on the Oprah
Winfrey, Geraldo Rivera, and Sally Jessie Raphael shows by pretending
to be a sex therapist and her "cured" patient. The "Talk Show Guest
Directory"—a fat paperback that looks like the yellow pages of a mid-
dle-sized town—is a delirious illustration of how the hunger for
publicity levels us all. Harvard University and the Communist party, the
National Turkey Federation ("serving the nation's turkey industry") and
the Simon Wiesenthal Center ("Holocaust Education/Human Rights"),
the American Sunbathing Association (nudists), the Prisoner Apprecia-
tion Society (celebrating an old TV show, not the Massachusetts furlough program), UNICEF, the South Central Connecticut Regional
Water Authority, and one Elliot Essman (self-described as "the Cyrano
de Bergerac of the Computer Age") all buy space to beg for a chance to
go on TV.

A few self-promoters attempt poetry (THE EYES HAVE IT headlines
the American Optometric Association), but most simply list the topics on
which they wish to expound. If you'd like, the Center for Home Organization and Interior Space will send someone to talk on the subject "If
You Can't Find It, You Don't Own It." Harvard's Kennedy School of
Government frantically offers experts "on virtually any topic concerning
government and public policy." By contrast, Dr. William Campbell Doug-
lass maintains a bit more dignity, offering to discuss only six specific matters, such as "Are the Soviets Responsible for the AIDS Epidemic?" and
the seemingly contradictory "Was the AIDS Virus Invented at Fort De-
trick, Maryland?"

Many would-be talk show guests offer testimonials. A woman calling
herself Laura X—a professional rape victim who apparently seeks publicity
and anonymity at the same time—claims to be have been "commended
by the Surgeon General, Mademoiselle, and the World Congress of Victimology." Nancy Friedman, "the Telephone Doctor" ("What Doctor
Ruth does for the bedroom," she asserts ambiguously, "the Telephone
Doctor does for the phone"), notes that a local TV station called her
"bubbly and sharp on the air." Washington's own Heritage Foundation

brags that it has been "called the 'brain center' of U.S. conservatism by the Soviet news agency Tass."

The two sex-therapy fakers have only enhanced their talk-show-ability by conning three talk shows. Now those very shows want them back to say how they did it. But in the no-such-thing-as-bad-publicity stakes, these people are no match for the Revolutionary Communist party (a Maoist, anti-Soviet sect not to be confused with the Communist party), which actually trumpets its affiliation with "the 'Shining Path' guerrillas of Peru," possibly the bloodiest group of lunatics currently loose in the world. Carl Dix, the party's spokesperson, has all the necessary talk-show-guest qualifications: He's "an experienced revolutionary leader," he's "an accomplished public speaker" who has debated Patrick Buchanan on CNN's *Crossfire,* and he's the author of a pamphlet with the intriguing title "Jesse Jackson: The Right Stuff for U.S. Imperialism."

The index of the "Talk Show Directory," which lists thousands of available topics in alphabetical order, nicely captures both the diversity of American life and the moral and intellectual agnosticism of the talk show culture. "Bulimia; Bulk Business Mail; Bullwinkle; Bunions and Burning Feet;. . . . Cholesterol Testing; Christ's Return; . . . Show Biz Legends; Shroud of Turin; Sibling Relationships . . ."

Then there are the variations on a theme, capturing not so much the diversity but the fragmentation of our society: "Pregnancy; Pregnancy (Unmarried); Pregnancy in Politics; Pregnant Careerwomen; . . . Suicide; Suicide Epidemic, Teen; Suicide Prevention; Suicide in Elderly; Suicide in Rural America; Suicide, Assisted; Suicide, Grief of; Suicide, Survivors; Summer Day Camp. . . ." Neoconservatives who worry that an over-obsession with "rights" is unraveling the national fabric will not enjoy perusing the "R" section, where groups pushing various rights ("Right to Die; Right to Life") nestle together between "Retreaded Tires" and "Rings of Saturn."

Although the breadth of American obsessions is impressive, there's a marked depth of proffered expertise in two areas: sex and money. Both is best. The first time I saw the infamous *Morton Downey Junior* show I was innocently flipping through the channels and came across this man looming over a woman in a chair, pointing a cigarette in her face, and screaming, "You're a whore! You're a prostitute!" Wondering what this poor woman had done to unleash such metaphorical fury, I kept watching and it turned out she really was a prostitute. That was the whole story. They'd found a prostitute to put on TV in order to denounce her as a prostitute. And she was delighted to be there. Something to tell the grandchildren.

Prostitution is, of course, listed in the "Talk Show Directory," where Nevada's famous Chicken Ranch has bought a half-page ad offering "Russell Reade, owner and 'Mr. Madam,' . . . an articulate speaker and expert information source." Under "Sex" (since you ask) there are eighteen entries ranging from "Sex/Golf" (not an ad for Dan Quayle) and "Sexual Abuse" to "Sexual Function of Nose" and "Sexuality/Sensuality" (followed by "Shakespeare").

"Never turn down a chance to have sex or go on television," Gore Vidal is supposed to have said. At the rate things are going, people will soon be advertising their availability to do both at the same time.

READ MY LIPS, GRANNY

(*The New Republic*, OCTOBER 31, 1988)

In 1980 the Reagan campaign stole a copy of the Carter campaign's briefing book for one of the presidential debates. In 1988 it's rapidly becoming clear that an even more serious crime has been committed. The Bush campaign, involving many of the same people, must have stolen the secret plan for the first one hundred days of the Dukakis administration.

I feared as much when Bush began basing so much of his campaign on matters seemingly unrelated to the responsibilities of the President, such as state prison furlough policy. But my fears were confirmed during the vice presidential debate, when Dan Quayle accidentally revealed his awareness of Dukakis's secret plan for midwestern grandmothers. "Dukakis supporters," he said, "sneer at commonsense advice. Midwestern advice—midwestern advice from a grandmother to a grandson— important advice—something that we ought to talk about. . . . "

Yes, if there's anything we Dukakis supporters can't stand, it's grandmothers, with their insufferable stream of commonsense advice. I had a midwestern grandmother once. Her advice was: "You can do anything you want to in this country, and if you don't feel like doing anything, the government will support you. So don't bother working. Just go on welfare." Of course, she was a Democrat.

Traditionally the regulation of grandmotherly advice is left to the private sector ("Oh, do hesh up, Granny"), or at most to the state and local levels of governments. But now that Quayle has tipped his hand, the truth had better be revealed. The ultraliberal governor of Massachusetts (that's where Harvard is, you know) plans, soon after becoming president, to propose a major new revenue enhancement mechanism: a tax on grandmothers. The tax will be applied on a sliding scale, based on distance from the East or West Coast. Kansans will owe the most.

Midwesterners who don't pay up will have their grandmothers confiscated. The grannies will be taken to reeducation camps, mostly former federal prisons from which all the murderers and rapists and drug dealers have been released. Once incarcerated, they will be force-fed a diet of Belgian endive* and sautéed American flag until they agree to forswear commonsense advice forever. On weekend furlough, they will be sent to ACLU-sponsored halfway houses where they will be put to work erasing "In God We Trust" from one-dollar bills.

And why? Well obviously, because the ultraliberal governor of Massachusetts and his supporters (including, of course, all journalists) have contempt for ordinary people of every stripe, but especially midwesterners and their grandmothers.

The biggest political miracle of this campaign is the way Bush has gotten the monkey of elitism off his own back and onto Dukakis's. It was supposed to be George Herbert Walker Bush of Andover and Yale and Kennebunkport and Skull and Bones versus Michael Dukakis, hard-working barely-off-the-boat ethnic. Instead it's Bush the regular fella versus Dukakis the Harvard snob. The Democrats even have a real issue to back up their class sniping: the Reagan-Bush era's pampering of the rich, squeeze of the middle class, and indifference to the poor. But the Republicans have brilliantly fabricated symbolic issues (flag, furloughs) to supplant this practical one, and given them a powerful invidious spin.

My purpose is not to grab elitism back as an issue for the Democrats. My purpose—although it rightly seems suspicious coming from the side that started the sniping—is to call for a truce in this tiresome parody of a class war. While we're at it, let's purge the whole Washington reverse-snob culture, in which BMW-driving political consultants vie with one

---

Dukakis had made an unfortunate remark urging American farmers to grow Belgian endive as an alternative crop.

another to present their candidates as dirt-between-my-toes yokels and journalists who know more Cabinet members than cabinetmakers go on TV to accuse one another of an "inside-the-beltway" mentality. It's boring and false and patronizing.

During the Pledge of Allegiance flap, former education secretary William Bennett offered the thought that people in "that Brookline-Cambridge world . . . think they're smarter than everybody else." You know what? As a generalization, that's probably true. But you know what else? Bill Bennett, for all his disagreements with them, secretly thinks Boston intellectuals are smarter than most other people, too. He also thinks he's smarter than most other people. Can you doubt it?

Sure, the world of Brookline, Massachusetts, is somewhat insular and out of touch with the rest of America. So is Washington, D.C. (though less so than it's fashionable to insist). But so is Americus, Kansas, and Americus, Georgia, and every other community in this vast nation. And each community—eastern intellectuals, midwestern farmers, southern good old boys—harbors the suspicion that it is morally superior to other communities and potentially resents the airs these other communities sometimes put on. What's patronizing about reverse snobbery is the idea that outside of Brookline and/or Washington all Americans are exactly alike and in tune with one another.

It's not similarity but toleration that enables Americans to share this nation. Ironically, when Republicans charge liberal-Massachusetts-Harvard-ACLU Dukakisites with contempt for the rest of America, their evidence actually illustrates toleration. It's easy enough to misrepresent toleration for the odd duck who doesn't want to salute the flag or a minimum of concern for the rights of prisoners as contempt for the flag and for the majority of law-abiding citizens. But it's false. It seems to me the contempt is really on the other side.

DEMOCRACY CAN GOOF

(*Time*, NOVEMBER 14, 1988)

I t looks as if my candidate for president is going to lose this election. If so, he will be constrained to be graceful about it. Not laboring under any such constraint, I am free to say that the voters—or at least a majority of them—are idiots, betrayers of their country's future, misperceivers of their own best interests, ignorant about the issues, gulled by slick lies. Unless, of course, there's an upset. In that case, the voters have magnificently exercised their ingrained popular wisdom, vindicated the faith of the Founding Fathers, demonstrated the innate genius of democracy, etc., etc., etc. I knew it all along. Regarding my candidate for senator, kindly reverse those two explosions of prejudice.

It's widely considered a breach of democratic etiquette to question the collective wisdom of the electorate. To suggest that the voters are wrong, let alone to characterize their error in more melodramatic terms, opens you up to charges of elitism. The contention that people have been misled or manipulated, wrote one smug supporter of the probable winner shortly before the election, "reveals an extraordinary contempt for the political intelligence of the public."

The electorate's decision is held to be self-validating. However knowledgeable or ignorant, focused or distracted, reflective or scatterbrained they may be individually, the voters collectively are always wise. Political pundits who have been concentrating for months on the shallowest and most mechanistic aspects of the election campaign—tactics, commercials, "likability," and so on—will switch gears on Election Day and begin interpreting the "message" of the election in the most grandiose philosophical terms. Reports of the candidates' strategies for appealing to various groups or regions of the country will be replaced by theories about what an undifferentiated mass called "the people" was trying to say. These theories will often be of such exotic sophistication that no single one of the people, let alone all of the people, could possibly have thought of them before voting.

Foremost among the theorizers will be supporters of the winner, who will reject any notion that their man's victory might be due to their own vigorous exertions of the previous few months. It was, instead, they will argue, a fundamental and clearheaded rejection of the "values" represented by the loser. And the neutral political observers will agree: An election loss is supposed to force losers to reconsider not merely their political strategy but their fundamental beliefs.

Yet why should this be so? As a matter of logic, it makes no sense. Serious beliefs derive from serious reflection, over a long time. A serious thinker should always be open to counterarguments from those who disagree, but the mere fact of disagreement, however widespread, shouldn't count for much.

The real insult to democracy, it seems to me, is to treat it as some sort of tennis game where victory is the definitive judgment on the players. And the real insult to the electorate is the patronizing attitude that it is a sort of lumbering collective beast, immune from error because it reaches its judgments through some mystical process that is beyond rational discourse, rather than an amalgam of individuals, each one fully capable of being right and being wrong.

The commentator who sneers that it shows "contempt for the political intelligence of the public" to suggest that the voters may have been duped is a highbrow intellectual who wouldn't dream of reaching his own political judgments based on the information and level of argument offered to the voters by his candidate. (Or mine, for that matter.) Who is showing real contempt for the public? Those who question the infallible wisdom of the majority, or those who hold the voters to a lower intellectual standard than they hold themselves to? Who is more "elitist"?

I extend every voter who votes differently from me the courtesy of serious disagreement: I think you're wrong. You may well have been misled or underinformed or intellectually lazy, or you may be highly informed and thoughtful but have a faulty analysis, or you may have acted out of narrow, unpatriotic self-interest, or you may just be a fool. But whatever the reason, you blew it. In my opinion. And I take democracy seriously enough that my own decision on how to vote was the result of a lengthy intellectual process that is not going to reverse itself overnight on November 8 just because a majority of voters disagrees with me. Finally, although I am always open to dissuasion about my political beliefs, and more than open to suggestions on how to make those beliefs more salable to others, I have enough respect for the political intelligence of the public that I hope a majority may come to agree with me the next time around.

One problem with American politics is that it is dominated by people—the candidates usually and their advisers almost invariably—who don't hold any belief deeply enough to withstand evidence that the majority believes the opposite. Sincerely holding unpopular beliefs is something you accuse your opponent of, an accusation that is generally false.

The theory of democracy is not that the voters are always right. Nothing about voting magically assures a wise result, and for a citizen to dissent from the majority's choice in an election is no more elitist than for a Supreme Court justice to dissent from his or her colleagues' judgment in some case. The proper form of democratic piety was nicely expressed by Senator Warren Rudman during the Iran-contra hearings (explaining why the illegal secret funding of the contras offended him, although he favored contra aid himself). "The American people," he said, "have the constitutional right to be wrong." You can value and honor that right without cheering every exercise of it.

KKR-AAAZY

(*The New Republic*, NOVEMBER 21, 1988)

Three very different prices have been placed on the RJR Nabisco Corporation in the past few weeks. Each price reflects a widely held theory about American capitalism. Trouble is, those theories, like those prices, can't all be right.

Not long ago, the company's shares were being traded on the New York Stock Exchange for around $55 a share, representing a total value of about $13 billion for the company. Widespread public share ownership is how almost all of America's great companies are structured, and schoolchildren are taught what a wonderful thing this is. The claim rests on two premises: (1) that the stock market works efficiently to set the right price for companies' shares; and (2) more important, that the system of public ownership combined with professional management produces well-run corporations and a prosperous economy.

For decades left-wing critics such as John Kenneth Galbraith have argued that the separation of ownership and control—the distinguishing feature of the modern American corporation—gives managers enormous power to serve their own interests, rather than those of the shareholders or the public, and undermines much of the standard case for free-market capitalism. But Galbraith has found few supporters in corporate America.

On October 20, RJR Nabisco's management offered to buy the company from the shareholders, with mostly borrowed money, for $75 a share or $17 billion—a 30 percent premium over the stock market price. How can that be sensible? Well, it seems that widespread public share ownership is not the most efficient system after all. Managers work better when they own the company. Furthermore, financing a company through debt rather than equity (stock) is good discipline; the prospect of all those mandatory interest payments (rather than voluntary dividends) concentrates the mind.

Many businesspeople endorse this plausible theory, but few endorse its necessary implication: that the New York Stock Exchange is a fraud on those millions of ordinary investors and on America in general. Public trading on the Exchange does not assure a fair price for stocks, and the system of public share ownership does not assure that America's major industries are well managed. Business apologists tend to defend both the stock market and these market-swamping special deals as Adam Smith's invisible hand at work. But clearly one invisible hand doesn't know what the other one is doing.

There are two compelling complaints about management buyouts. First, if a company's managers know how to increase its value 30 percent, why didn't they do so when they were being paid fat salaries by the shareholders? And second, when managers sell the company to themselves, how can the price be fair? The profits on management buyouts have been quick and gargantuan, which suggests that the shareholders got screwed.

As if to demonstrate that management underpays, the Wall Street firm of Kohlberg Kravis Roberts soon came along to top management's offer for RJR Nabisco. KKR offered $90 a share or more than $20 billion—a 50 percent premium over the stock market price. If this company is really worth $20 billion, in private hands and properly run (or broken up), that is an even crueler judgment on the American system of public stock ownership.

But is it worth $20 billion? KKR offered this humongous price before it even had access to the company's books (like bidding on a house without going inside). That adds some weight to the charge that the buyout boom is a classic speculative bubble, fed by bankers hungry for fees and perversely encouraged by the tax system.* When the bubble bursts, the skeptics warn, the whole economy could get soaked.

Who's right? I'm not sure. But either the current buyout wave is dangerously excessive or the entire American corporate structure is a fraud. Take your pick.

Whatever your conclusion, there's no doubt something silly and wasteful is going on. The R. J. Reynolds tobacco company and Nabisco, the food manufacturer, merged just three years ago—at huge expense in fees—on the then-fashionable theory that tobacco companies ought to diversify, and that similar marketing patterns made tobacco and food an efficient mix. Now both parties vying for the combined firm plan to break it up, on the grounds that the food and tobacco operations will be more efficient separately.

In the last buyout war, a few years ago, outside "raiders" like T. Boone Pickens attacked slothful entrenched management and the corporate establishment charged the raiders with "plunder." Now corporate managers do their own raiding, of their own companies and others', and we hear no more talk about either sloth or plunder.

Avis Rent-a-Car has changed hands eleven times since its founding in 1946, in response to every Wall Street fad. In the 1960s it was owned for a while by ITT, at a time when conglomerates were all the rage. In the past decade Avis was swallowed by Norton Simon, which was swallowed by Esmark, which was swallowed by Beatrice Foods, all on the theory that bigger is better. Then Beatrice was taken private by KKR and broken up, on the theory that smaller is better. In 1986, Avis was sold to its managers plus a small group of investors led by former Treasury Secretary William Simon, who said, "Management will do an even better job running the firm as an entrepreneurial situation." Fourteen months later management and the investors sold out to the employees (at a $700 million profit on a $10 million investment, made possible in part by federal tax laws meant to encourage employee ownership). The theory this time was that employees will work harder if they have a stake in the profits. Each change of ownership generated large fees for bankers and lawyers.

*An underremarked cause of the 1980s corporate merger boom was the wildly generous depreciation write-offs in the 1981 tax law, only partly corrected in later reforms. By allowing huge deductions in the early years after an asset was acquired, these rules meant that any company that hadn't changed hands recently was worth more to almost anyone else than to its current owner. It was a recipe for pointless, and expensive, churning of corporate assets.

Both buyout offers for RJR Nabisco are being financed by pension funds, banks, and insurance companies. The managers of these organizations are just as detached from the people whose money they're responsible for as traditional corpocrats are from their shareholders. So the argument that leveraged buyouts are good for the economy because they transfer key decisions from hired managers to real owners rings a bit hollow. There's good reason to wonder if these people know what they're doing. In the days since RJR Nabisco was "put in play," its stock price has shot up, reflecting the anticipated buyout, but the price of its bonds has plummeted, reflecting a fear of default. The 16 percent drop in key RJR Nabisco bonds reflects the market's judgment that there is now something like a one-in-six chance the company will go bankrupt. But then, what does the market know?

Come to Uncle

(The New Republic, DECEMBER 12, 1988)

Whither Canada? That is the question millions of Americans, as usual, have not been asking in recent weeks, as Canadians fought a bitter election campaign over the fate of a free trade agreement with the United States. But at least a few die-hard internationalists have felt guilty about it. Now that Canadians have implicitly approved the agreement by reelecting Prime Minister Brian Mulroney, we can put all thoughts of Canada aside without guilt.

But should we? I think not. Canada needs us. Indeed, it's hard not to suspect that in briefly threatening to reject this obviously sensible treaty, Canada—as is so often the case with stagy suicide attempts—was simply trying to draw attention to itself. The entire election was a cry for help.

It was the conceit of the treaty's opponents that free trade is a nefarious plot by Americans to swallow Canada in our embrace and turn it into a fifty-first state. It was the conceit of the treaty's supporters that this was the last thing any Canadian would wish. In reality, there can't be a hundred Americans from sea to shining sea with the slightest desire to annex Canada as a fifty-first state. So, Doctor, whence this recurrent nightmare about being swallowed up by America? Well, it doesn't take a Ph.D. in psychology to realize that Canadians' mock horror at the thought of becoming part of the United States actually masks a deep desire to do precisely that. They protest too much. Their lips say "no, no," but their eyes say "yes, yes."

Anyone who has ever conversed with Canadians will have witnessed their psychological torment. They combine a deep professed disdain for south-of-the-border culture—our crime, our squalor, our imperial bravado, our skeletal social welfare system—with an ever deeper need for approval from Americans. They write letters to the editor of American publications at the slightest hint of a slight. They're notorious for their inability to take a joke. Clearly they're all torn up inside. They desperately want love, but are unable to supply it in return.

There is only one cure for this complex neurosis. We must purge it once and for all by giving Canadians what they secretly want. We must embrace them, adopt them, love them, annex them. In short, we must make Canada the fifty-first state. Or, perhaps, the fifty-first through fifty-fourth states, depending on the best arrangement of stars in the revised American flag.

I hear you saying, "Not so fast, buster." Why should we share our flag—the very symbol over which dozens of political consultants fought valiantly in our own recent election—with twenty-five million foreigners? Don't we have millions of humorless neurotics of our own, in desperate need of teasing, who won't get the attention they deserve if our society is suddenly overwhelmed by Canadians? "Love thy neighbor" is an admirable injunction, but Americans—selfish beasts that we are—naturally are going to wonder, "What's in this for us?"

Although it never occurred to me that Canada should become the fifty-first state until Canadians began insisting hysterically—and unconvincingly—that they don't want to be one, now that they've brought it up I can see that such an arrangement would have many advantages for the United States as well. Indeed, the idea of annexing Canada could have appeal for Americans across the political spectrum:

- *Woolly left-wing one-worlders* should appreciate the erasure of any international border, no matter how faint or porous it is already. We are all fellow passengers on spaceship earth, are we not? The merging of the United States and Canada would be a great spur to conferences, proclamations, and suchlike activities celebrating the irrelevance of nationalism in the postindustrial age. Oh goody.
- *Right-wing American nativists, white racists, and so on* ought to relish the

prospect of a vast infusion of Anglo-Saxon stock into the American melting pot. There is Quebec to worry about—Americans have always thought of the French as somebody else's problem—and Toronto has become alarmingly multiethnic in recent years. However, the majority of Canadians are still of British descent and have relatively ancient roots in North American soil. In an era when Mexico seems to be annexing itself to the United States one person at a time, and people with names like Dukakis are actually running for president, a merger with Canada would add millions of citizens with sturdy names like Mulroney and Turner, who speak English with hardly a trace of an accent, and whose native cuisine is virtually spice-free. Look for Canadian restaurants as the new food trend in New York.

• *Free traders,* of course, should appreciate the addition of a new market the size of California to the United States economy. Protectionist sentiments would melt away with the border. Floridians and North Dakotans happily do business together without the need for tariffs, quotas, voluntary restraints, or other economic prophylactics. Now they could enjoy similar unprotected capitalist pleasures with Saskatchewanians and Nova Scotians.

• *Ecologists, ZPG-running-out-of-room types, etc.* would love the acquisition of a landmass larger than the continental United States with one tenth of the population. Our ratio of people per acre—a key statistic for the overpopulation-minded—would instantly be cut in half. Those misanthropes who feel that Montana has been spoiled because you can no longer spend a week without running into another human being or three could adjourn to northern Alberta and Manitoba, there to await the inevitable spreading of blight.

From almost any point of view, then, the advantages to the United States of merging with Canada are overwhelming. And the disadvantages? Gordon Lightfoot records are already on sale throughout the United States, and Peter Jennings is thoroughly established at ABC. We've paid the price; now is the time to reap the benefit.

But we must act quickly, before Canadians resolve their neurosis on their own. Anti-U.S. propaganda during the recent election campaign mixed two contradictory themes: fear of U.S. power and a desire not to be seen as rats swimming toward a sinking ship. "Is it forward looking for Canada at this time," asked an influential pamphlet, "to be making trade commitments to the U.S. when all indicators show that the U.S. is declining as the economic world leader?"

We'd better complete this seduction before we go totally bald and paunchy. Right now, though, they still want it. You know they want it. Hey, you great, gorgeous piece of frozen northland. Come to Uncle.

TAKE MY KIDNEY, PLEASE

(*Time*, MARCH 13, 1989)

Even Margaret Thatcher's devotion to the free market has some limits, it seems. Reacting to newspaper reports that poor Turkish peasants are being paid to go to London and give up a kidney for transplant, the British prime minister said that "the sale of kidneys or any organs of the body is utterly repugnant." Emergency legislation is now being prepared for swift approval by Parliament to make sure that capitalism does not perform its celebrated magic in the market for human organs.

Commercial trade in human kidneys does seem grotesque. But it's a bit hard to say why. After all, the moral logic of capitalism does not stop at the epidermis. That logic holds, in a nutshell, that if an exchange is voluntary, it leaves both parties better off. In one case, a Turk sold a kidney for £2,500 ($4,400) because he needed money for an operation for his daughter. Capitalism in action: One person had $4,400, and wanted a kidney, another person had a spare kidney and wanted $4,400, so they did a deal. What's more, it seems like an advantageous deal all around. The buyer avoided a lifetime of dialysis. The seller provided crucial help to his child, at minimum risk to himself. (According to *The Economist*, the chance of a kidney donor's dying as a result of the loss is 1 in 5,000.)

Nevertheless, the conclusion that such trade is abhorrent is not even controversial. Almost everyone agrees. Is almost everyone right? This question of how far we are willing to push the logic of capitalism will be thrust in our faces increasingly in coming years. Medical advances are making it possible to buy things that were previously unobtainable at any price. (The Baby M "womb renting" case is another example.) Meanwhile, the communications and transportation revolutions are breaking down international borders, making new commercial relations possible between the comfortably rich and the desperately poor. On what basis do we say to a would-be kidney seller, "Sorry, this is one deal you just can't make?"

One widely accepted category of forbidden deals involves health and safety regulations: automobile standards, bans on food additives, etc. Although we quarrel about particular instances, only libertarian cranks reject in principle the idea that government sometimes should protect people from themselves. But it is no more dangerous to sell one of your kidneys than it is to give one away to a close relative—a transaction we not only allow but admire. On health grounds alone, you can't ban the sale without banning the gift as well. Furthermore, the sale of a kidney is not necessarily a foolish decision that society ought to protect you from. To pay for a daughter's operation, it seems the opposite.

But maybe there are some things money just shouldn't be allowed to buy, sensibly or otherwise. Socialist philosopher Michael Walzer added flesh to this ancient skeleton of sentiment in his 1983 book, *Spheres of Justice*. Walzer argued that a just society is not necessarily one with complete financial equality—a hopeless and even destructive goal—but one in which the influence of money is not allowed to dominate all aspects of life. By outlawing organ sales, you are keeping the insidious influence of money from leaching into a new sphere and are thereby reducing the power of the rich. Trouble is, you are also reducing opportunity for the poor.

The grim trade in living people's kidneys would not be necessary if more people would voluntarily offer their kidneys (and other organs) when they die. Another socialist philosopher, Richard Titmuss, wrote a famous book two decades ago called *The Gift Relationship*, extolling the virtues of donated blood over purchased blood and, by extension, the superiority of sharing over commerce. Whatever you may think of Titmuss's larger point, the appeal of the blood-donor system as a small testament to our shared humanity is undeniable. Perhaps we should do more to encourage organ donation at death for the same reason. On the other hand, however cozy and egalitarian it might seem, a system that supplied all the kidneys we need through voluntary donation would be no special favor to our Turkish friend, who would be left with no sale and no $4,400. Why not at least let his heirs sell his kidneys when he dies? A commercial market in cadaver organs would wipe out the sale of live people's parts a lot more expeditiously than trying to encourage donations.

The moral logic of capitalism assumes knowledgeable, reasonably intelligent people on both sides of the transaction. Is this where the kidney trade falls short? At $4,400, the poor Turk was probably underpaid for his kidney. But in an open, legal market with protections against exploitation, he might have got more. At some price, the deal would make sense for almost anyone. I have no sentimental attachment to my kidneys. Out of prudence, I'd like to hang on to one of them, but the other is available. My price is $2 million.

Of course, I make this offer safe in the knowledge that there will always be some poor Turk ready to undercut me. So maybe, because of who the sellers inevitably will be, the sale of kidneys is by its very nature exploitation. A father shouldn't have to sacrifice a kidney to get a necessary operation for his daughter. Unfortunately, banning the kidney sale won't solve the problem of paying for the operation. Nor can the world yet afford expensive operations for everyone who needs one. And leaving aside the melodrama of the daughter's operation, we don't stop people from doing things to support their families—working in coal mines, for example— that reduce their life expectancies more than would the loss of a kidney. In fact, there are places in the Third World where even $4,400 can do more for a person's own life expectancy than a spare kidney.

The horror of kidney sales, in short, is a sentimental reaction to the injustice of life—injustice that the transaction highlights but does not increase. This is not a complaint. In fact, it may even be the best reason for a ban on such transactions. That kind of sentiment ought to be encouraged.

THATCHER FOR PRESIDENT

(*Time*, MAY 15, 1989)*

The woman at the Wales Tourist Center in London could rent me a car for three days but not for two days. She doubted it was allowable to pay for three days but return the car after two. And anyway, she didn't have the right kind of vouchers. Could I please come back tomorrow?

To any longtime American Anglophile, everything about this epi-

*In hindsight, this piece is embarrassingly optimistic about the extent to which Margaret Thatcher changed British society. But the comparison between Thatcher and Reagan still holds.

sode—the saleswoman's sweet, bovine unreason, the infinite lack of rush, the commercial hopelessness of a Wales Tourist Center seemingly intent on keeping you out of Wales—dripped with nostalgia for a lost civilization: pre-Thatcher Britain. Life isn't much like that anymore. Ten years after Margaret Thatcher became prime minister, an episode far more characteristic of the present moment, and also true, is seeing a waiter from a fancy restaurant chasing up the street after a pinstripe suit, waving a small object, shouting, "Sir! Sir! You left your telephone on the table."

Is it hypocritical for an American liberal who never cared for Ronald Reagan and thinks George Bush is a bad joke to admire Margaret Thatcher? Her latest biographer dismisses the American reaction to Thatcher as one of "drooling effusion."

The British themselves are more divided. There are few outright swooners. And the complaints resemble familiar complaints against the Republican administration that has ruled America during most of the Thatcher era. She has created, say both the Left and the traditional Right, a vulgar, selfish, money-obsessed society, drained of more humane values. Her prosperity has been selective; the gap between haves and have-nots has increased. She has ignored the environment, allowed the public infrastructure to rot, starved the universities and other worthy institutions and causes that depend on public funds. For all her talk of freedom, she is an authoritarian outside the economic sphere and has shown contempt for civil liberties. The Thatcher boom itself, say some, is a mirage, and they offer statistics to back themselves up.

There is something in all of this. But even the most left-wing journalist would have a hard time saying with a straight face that he misses the days (just three or four years ago) when unions forbade the use of computers at newspapers. Even the opposition Labor party isn't proposing to renationalize all the companies that have been sold off to private shareholders or to take back the formerly state-owned houses that have been sold to their tenants. Even those put off by the glitz and the greed of Thatcherworld wouldn't really like to return to the gloomy, hangdog "British disease" atmosphere of the postwar period.

Reagan never attempted a social transformation of America of this magnitude. That is partly because it wasn't necessary, but partly because he lacked Thatcher's principled determination. Thatcher's biographer Hugo Young says her greatest gift is "inspirational certainty." Reagan had inspirational certainty too, but of a different sort. His inspirational certainty was oblivious to reality, allowing him to call for a balanced budget through eight consecutive years of failing to propose one. Her inspirational certainty is oblivious to popularity, allowing her to produce a government budget that's actually in large surplus. Fiscal policy is one area of governance where the wrong principles are often better than no principles at all. That is one good reason even a Reagan-Bush skeptic can admire Mrs. T.

For all the seeming parallels between the Conservative regime in Britain during the 1980s and the Republican one in America, and for all Thatcher's alleged admiration of Reagan, in an important way the two societies have changed in opposite directions. Thatcher has taught the British people self-discipline. Reagan and Bush have taught Americans self-indulgence. After the past three American presidential elections, it is unthinkable for an ambitious politician to call on the citizenry—or any sizable subset of it—to make the slightest sacrifice for the good of society or its own future prosperity. Thatcher, by contrast, positively delights in delivering bad news and stern sermons. "After almost any major operation, you feel worse before you convalesce. But you do not refuse the operation." That typical bit of Thatcher rhetoric is not the kind of metaphor that comes out of the Peggy Noonan poetical-presidential-puffery machine. Nor is it sheep-in-wolf's-clothing mock toughness on the order of "Read my lips, no new taxes." If leadership means leading people where they don't at first want to go, Margaret Thatcher is a leader; Ronald Reagan was not, nor is George Bush.

Both Reagan and Thatcher nurtured their legends with small yet symbolic military triumphs early in their tenures. But contrast Reagan's famous victory in Grenada with Thatcher's in the Falklands. Grenada was conquered before most Americans even knew Grenada existed. But it was more than a month from the time the British task force sailed to retake the Falklands from Argentina to the time the war was won. Whatever the rights and wrongs of either war, announcing the prospect of a battle is leadership; announcing a victory is not. Whether America will actually defend its freedom with blood and money when called upon is—for all the martial rhetoric and credit-card defense spending of the 1980s—unproved.

Even after ten years and three election victories, Margaret Thatcher is not a beloved or even an especially liked figure in Britain. She never has been. And yet—despite a midterm slump in the polls—she would probably win a fourth election tomorrow, and will probably win one two or three years from now. "Although a populist," writes Young, Thatcher is "the ultimate argument against the contention that a political leader needs, in her person, to be popular." There are many explanations for Thatcher's successful unpopularity that are specific to Britain: the parliamentary system, the weakness of the opposition, the role of the queen as an alternative sump for public adulation, a cultural willingness to be bullied (or, to use the preferred term, nannied).

But surely even the coddled and petted American voter could respond to a politician who did not go whoring after popularity, who offered spinach instead of candy and who asked for respect instead of love. Such a politician would not have to be a conservative—or even a woman.

Morganatic Marriage

(*The New Republic*, JULY 31, 1989)

Even in London, where I just spent a few months, people are talking about Dr. Elizabeth Morgan. She's the prominent Washington plastic surgeon who has been in jail for almost two years because she won't reveal the whereabouts of her daughter, Hilary. She says Hilary was sexually abused by the child's father, Dr. Eric Foretich. She sent Hilary into hiding with her maternal grandparents rather than obey a court order granting Foretich unsupervised visitation rights.

Morgan (whom I know slightly) and her family have staged a brilliant publicity campaign that has turned her into the thinking woman's Tawana Brawley.* That's not to say her story isn't true. There is good, though not definitive, evidence on her side. The zillions of experts who have opined on the matter are split, but a majority say yes, Hilary has been sexually abused. (On the other hand, Foretich has passed two lie detector tests.) A Virginia court, looking at similar evidence, has refused Foretich visitation rights with a daughter from another marriage (he's had four). But a few things bother me about the consensus that Morgan is the martyr-heroine of this saga.

First, there's a plausible alternative scenario. Foretich, clearly a mess

---

*Tawana Brawley was a black teenager whose (false) claim that she was raped by several white men became a cause célèbre.

of a man, seduced, impregnated, and hastily married Morgan before he was even divorced from wife number two. By the time Hilary was born in 1982, their marriage was already over. Morgan, a superachiever who had previously failed at nothing in her life, and also something of a self-dramatizer, was humiliated and bitter. She was trying to deny Foretich visitation rights even before wife number two called in 1983 to say she thought Foretich was molesting both their daughters.

The power of suggestion works on children and grown-ups alike. Last year Elizabeth's father sent me, from hiding, a transcript of several conversations he says took place between Hilary and his wife, a psychologist. The Morgan family apparently believes these are devastating evidence against Foretich.

In the transcripts, Hilary does not merely assert that her father forced her to perform various sex acts. She declares that her paternal grandfather and grandmother did as well, along with Foretich's then-fiancée (now divorced wife number four). She says they would "poke" her in "the ears," among more predictable places. She says that she, her father, her grandfather, her grandmother, her father's fiancée, and her half sister all got in the bathtub together. She says her grandmother used to dress up as a witch and her father and grandfather as warlocks. ("Tell me some more things, darling," says her interrogator.) She says that the legal supervisor appointed by the Washington judge—whom the Morgans hate—told her, "I'm going to kill you if you don't be nice to your daddy," and once kissed Dr. Foretich.

Memory or improvisation? Asked what "things" her father put in her mouth, Hilary says he would "put pee in my mouth." Question: "How would he do that?" Answer: "He'd put it into a wine glass and . . . pour it into a wine bottle and put it into a wine glass and pour it into my mouth." And finally, after eleven sessions of this:

Q. Tell me, how do you feel about your daddy?
A. Terrible, terrible, terrible.
Q. What do you mean terrible?
A. Terrible, terrible, terrible, terrible, terrible, terrible, terrible. . . .
Q. And how do you feel about your mummy?
A. Lots of niceness.
Q. Lots of niceness?
A. Nicey, nicey, nicey.

I bet.

This surely doesn't prove that Hilary's basic story is made up. But it does show the risk of taking a child's word, especially when she's swept up with her mother and her whole overwrought family in a whirlpool of self-feeding paranoia. "Judges don't listen to little girls," a pro-Morgan child psychologist quotes Hilary as telling her (another notion I doubt Hilary thought of by herself). Sometimes they have good reason.

A second troubling aspect of the Morgan case is the casual acceptance, even celebration, of the way she has taken the law into her own hands. How many columns has Anthony Lewis of *The New York Times* written over the years on the theme that America is ruled by laws and not men? Yet he is one of many liberal journalists who have taken up Morgan's cause, brushed aside her contempt of court, and urged Judge Dixon to release her.

Morgan's defenders note correctly that the purpose of jail for contempt of court is to coerce compliance, not to punish. A person who has proved herself adamant is supposed to be released. In a triumph many powerful lobbies must envy, they have even gotten the House of Representatives to pass a bill saying that no one can be jailed more than eighteen months for civil contempt in D.C. But what if it were Foretich, the accused sex abuser, whose parents (also accused) had spirited Hilary away? Would there not be outrage if he were released from jail without producing the child on the grounds that, well, he has shown he'll never change his mind?

For all the voluminous proceedings, the plague of psychologists, the massive publicity, there has never yet been a real opportunity for a court to assess the evidence. In a lawsuit by Morgan, a Virginia jury ruled for Foretich; an appeals court held that vital evidence had been wrongly excluded, but there couldn't be a retrial because Morgan had taken matters into her own hands by then. Both Foretich and Judge Dixon say what they want now is not unsupervised visitations but an opportunity for a neutral ruling, with Hilary in foster care until the case is resolved. Foretich has said he will abide by the result. Morgan says she will not deal with an "incest father" or "a judge hungry for the ruin of a little girl." She will not produce Hilary for a new hearing, and will only abide by the result "if Hilary's safety were in no way compromised."

People understandably would like to resolve this case without forcing Morgan to give in. They argue that Hilary's needs matter more than her father's rights. Whatever the truth about him, they say, she is better off with her grandparents than with foster parents (or, possibly, than with either of her real parents), and she hardly needs more agonizing legal proceedings. What is more, if there is any chance Foretich is guilty, isn't that reason enough to keep Hilary away from him? Wouldn't any mother do the same?

Perhaps. But wouldn't any father—if he is innocent—do what Foretich is doing? Foretich may well be guilty. But if Morgan is allowed to decide this for herself, and becomes a popular heroine for doing so, there will be many innocent fathers victimized by vengeful wives—and innocent mothers victimized by vengeful husbands, too, for that matter. Children in general will not benefit. It is the promise of neutral justice that keeps people from taking the law into their own hands in every field, not just family relations. The courts are not infallible. But when citizens are bitterly irreconcilable, they're all we've got.*

LOOPHOLE PATRIOTISM

(*The New Republic*, AUGUST 7, 1989)

> *Thou shalt not make unto thee any graven image.*
>
> —EXODUS 20:3

Maybe when America's politicians—led by the president—are through amending the Bill of Rights, they'd like to amend the Ten Commandments while they're at it, to provide an exception for flag worship.

Democrats in the Senate, led by Majority Leader George Mitchell and judiciary chairman Joseph Biden, are pushing legislation to ban flag desecration without the necessity of a constitutional amendment. House Speaker Tom Foley also favors this approach. They think they've found a way around the Supreme Court's recent decision to overturn a Texas anti-flag-burning statute.

The Democratic leaders have three motives for their effort, all admirable. First, they want to keep this trivia out of the Constitution, and

---

*As of early 1995, Dr. Morgan, her parents, and Hilary were living in New Zealand, beyond the reach of U.S. law.

forestall the first-ever tampering with the Bill of Rights. Senators have introduced no fewer than thirty-eight proposed flag-protection amendments since the Supreme Court ruling. President Bush's version has fifty-three cosponsors. According to People for the American Way, of fourteen state legislatures still in session as of mid-July, resolutions endorsing a constitutional amendment had passed both houses in six and one house in another six.

Second, these Democrats hope that a hasty bit of legislation will get this ridiculous issue out of the way quickly, before it does any more damage to America's dignity. Third, by "taking the lead" on the legislation option, they hope to make sure that Democrats aren't victimized by Republican flag-waving demagoguery in 1990 as Michael Dukakis was by George Bush in 1988.

Unfortunately, it won't work. There is no way to write a law forbidding desecration of the flag that doesn't violate freedom of speech. Those who are pushing for a constitutional amendment are right: If you can't stand the idea of living in a country where people are free to burn the flag, your only option is to build a gimcrack aluminum-siding addition on the elegant Georgian edifice of the Bill of Rights.

Biden says, "We can protect the American flag—as we must—and the cherished values that the flag embodies" without desecrating the Constitution. How? "Mr. Chairman," he testified, "serious and extensive study has gone into my approach, and each word has been chosen with great care and deliberation." His carefully chosen words are: "Whoever knowingly mutilates, defaces, burns, maintains on the floor or ground, or tramples upon any flag of the United States shall be fined not more than $10,000 or imprisoned for not more than one year, or both."

The gimmick is that by avoiding any reference to the perpetrator's intent in burning the flag, or the message conveyed to those watching, the statute saves itself from being an unconstitutional attempt to suppress communication. It forbids specific forms of behavior instead of vague concepts like "desecration." The Texas law overturned by the Supreme Court, by contrast, used the words "defile, damage or . . . mistreat" and talked about knowingly giving offense to those watching.

But who's kidding whom, Senator Biden? The reason you want to ban flag burning is that it offends people. It offends you, you say, because the flag "embodies cherished values." Burning the flag therefore dissents from those values. You want to ban flag burning because it conveys an offensive message—an offensive political message. Political messages offensive to the majority are the heart of what the First Amendment protects. It doesn't matter how you phrase the law. It doesn't even really matter if some particular form of words might turn a 5–4 Supreme Court loss into a 5–4 victory. You know you're trashing the First Amendment.

Speaker Foley noted the other day that it's illegal to deface a mailbox. He drew an analogy. It's a poor one. There are many sensible reasons for making it illegal to deface a mailbox—protecting government property, preventing interference with the mail—all of which have nothing to do with the message conveyed by the defacing. "Thank God for the Postal Service" flouts the purpose of the law just as much as "Viva Federal Express." The courts rightly allow the incidental suppression of speech—and indulge in all sorts of "balancing tests"—when the government has some legitimate, non-message-related purpose. There is no conceivable such purpose in the case of a ban on flag burning.

The courts also make a narrow exception for speech that risks producing an imminent, violent response. The exception has to be narrow, or this can be an excuse for censoring anything a sizable group doesn't like. There is no reason not to apply this narrow exception to flag burning, as some would like to do. But there's no reason it should apply any more broadly to desecrating the flag physically than to insulting it with words.

By making it illegal to burn the flag for any reason whatsoever, even in private, Biden's bill raises the tricky question of how one would legally dispose of a used flag. Right now, cremation is the official recommended method. Leave it to Governor Mario Cuomo to solve this problem. His proposed New York bill follows the basic Biden technique, but provides that "it shall be an affirmative defense that the destruction or mutilation was for the purpose of disposing of a worn flag."

Cuomo styles himself the philosopher-king of the Democrats, and certainly there is a role in the party for someone who could articulate—and sell—a liberal vision to the country. Is there no one eloquent enough to make people weep with gratitude that we live in a country where people are free enough to burn the flag? And angry at those who exploit patriotic symbols to erode that freedom? Instead, in this case, Cuomo is using his philosophical bent to generate jesuitical distinctions that allow the Democrats to duck a fight on what the smart ones know in their hearts to be a matter of principle.

Suppose the Supreme Court were to fall for this sleight of hand and hold that flag burning can be outlawed simply because the flag is a national symbol, totally apart from what it says (and therefore what burning it says). This really would turn reverence for the flag into empty idol worship, the building of graven images. And in fact, about 90 percent of the flag hysteria that's been generated in the past year, starting with the Bush campaign, is no more than that.

It's a terribly insecure nation that makes such an unholy fuss about some minor nut burning the flag. As an emblem of love for America, the flag—a mere collage of shapes and colors—is far less eloquent than, say, the Statue of Liberty, which speaks directly of both our values and our history. It's hard to see why images of the flag should be protected from desecration but not images of Miss Liberty—although the Democrats now offer the flag's very inarticulateness as a constitutional defense of sanctifying it.*

Fractured Gospel

(*The New Republic*, SEPTEMBER 4, 1989)

Almost no one is honest about affirmative action. Liberals cling to the insistence that minority preference is somehow different from reverse discrimination and that percentage "goals" aren't really quotas. But conservatives also have their own cherished denials of the obvious.

Two weeks ago *TNR* ran a short Notebook item making the obvious point that William Lucas, President Bush's failed nominee to be assistant attorney general for civil rights, was selected in large part because he is black. Lucas thus was the beneficiary of reverse discrimination. (The Senate Judiciary Committee shot down the nomination and Bush appointed Lucas to a lesser Justice Department post not requiring Senate confirmation.)

---

*A constitutional amendment to forbid flag burning, which seemed unstoppable at the time this column was written, miraculously never happened. The national passion over the issue simply melted away. Although this is a relief, it is also a telling comment on the childishness of American politics. Millions of people who were convinced they could not sleep at night with the outrage that someone might be burning the American flag have given the matter no thought for years. Republican politicians who vigorously fanned the flames of this pseudoissue at the time didn't even include it in their Contract with America when they finally took over Congress in 1995.

This mundane observation elicited a hysterical—in both senses—response from the editorial page of *The Wall Street Journal*. In a string of editorials the *Journal* had made a great cause of the Lucas nomination, accusing "the liberal plantation" (that's Congress) of stomping on an uppity black man who doesn't toe the party line. Lucas "does not promise quotas or reverse discrimination; he promises no discrimination," said the *Journal*.

But didn't Lucas's own nomination violate this alleged principle? Oh no, no, no, the *Journal* explained (August 14). "We'd like to help our neoliberal friends get clear in their minds":

> *We oppose coerced affirmative action; we oppose quotas, numerical goals, timetables. . . . We do not and never have opposed affirmative action voluntarily practiced. It is perfectly appropriate for a President, university deans, and private employers to go out of their way to find black and other minority job candidates.*

Sorry, but I'm still a bit unclear in my mind. It now seems that reverse discrimination is okay after all, provided that it is "voluntary" and not "coerced" by the government. But even "voluntary" affirmative action is not "voluntary" at all for the person it really affects. Unlike *The Wall Street Journal*, a white male who loses a job because of his race will not take much comfort that his would-be employer screwed him voluntarily. Furthermore, in the case of a job as assistant attorney general for civil rights, the employer is the government. When President Bush appoints a black man because of his race, he is coercing the taxpayers into an act of racial discrimination, just as he would be if he chose a white for racial reasons.

I thought the conservative position was that the law and the Constitution are supposed to be "color-blind." (Indeed, "The Color-blind Vision" was the magisterial title of an earlier *Journal* sermon on this subject.) But the Civil Rights Act clearly forbids public and private employers to "voluntarily . . . go out of their way" to discriminate against black people. The Fifth and Fourteenth amendments are generally interpreted to impose a similar constitutional duty on government officials. The *Journal* claims to believe in the Civil Rights Act of 1964—in its "original meaning," of course, before affirmative action. So do most conservatives, although many, including President Bush, opposed it at the time. Is the *Journal* now saying that the Civil Rights Act does not apply equally to discrimination against white people, that the law is not color-blind? That—perhaps—it's not quite so simple? If so, this is quite a concession.

As it happens, that was precisely the issue in one of this year's big Supreme Court cases, *Richmond* v. *Croson,* which held that the city of Richmond could not "voluntarily" reserve 30 percent of its public works contracts for minority firms. The *Journal* applauded this decision, quoting with approval from Justice Scalia: It would be "fatal to a nation such as ours . . . to judge men and women on the basis of . . . the color of their skin." A fine sentiment, but where does that leave Mr. Lucas, who also endorsed both the sentiment and the ruling? (There is a technical argument that the federal government has more scope for reverse discrimination than the states, but I would not insult the *Journal* by supposing that its grandiose rhetoric rests on such a pinpoint of logic.)

Is it massive quotas that offend the *Journal*'s principles, as opposed to individual acts of reverse discrimination? It makes no difference—either in principle or to the victim—if he is alone or part of a group. Nor does it matter if the racial preference was only a "factor" or a hard-and-fast rule: If race or sex is a "factor" it will sometimes be the determining factor. It clearly was with Lucas: A white man with his exact qualifications (apart from race) would never in a million years have been offered the job.

When the *Journal* says it doesn't mind if employers "go out of their way to find . . . minority job candidates," it seems to be seeking refuge in the old "recruitment and training" dodge. This holds that special searches and remedial help for minorities are permissible as long as the hiring decision itself is race-neutral. (Lucas, for example, appeared to know almost nothing about civil rights law, but promised to study hard and catch up.) But for any job (even assistant attorney general for civil rights) there are also potentially qualified whites who could benefit equally from "recruitment and training." Special efforts of this sort for blacks are reverse discrimination against them.

So if it was permissible for President Bush to take William Lucas's race into account, what is left of the alleged color-blind principle? Answer: very little. The *Journal* (which I dwell on because it states a widespread view so clearly—and also because it's so much fun to poke at) actually concedes the two best arguments for reverse discrimination. First is that "in many cases . . . the black experience in itself adds a unique qualification." That certainly is true in the case of an assistant attorney general for civil rights. Second is rough justice, helping victims of past overt discrimination to "make up for lost time."

(A third argument was outlined in this space a couple of months ago by Hendrik Hertzberg: that we need to force-feed a black middle class for one generation so that its children can avail themselves of "equal opportunity" in the traditional American fashion. To me it's a bit hard to justify the costs to individuals of reverse discrimination on the basis of this kind of speculative social engineering.)

The problems with affirmative action are less in principle than in practice. It stirs understandable resentments. It stigmatizes people who would have made it without any special help. If it leads to the hiring of unqualified people (which it sometimes does), it carries an economic cost. As presently administered, it is often a bureaucratic and litigation nightmare. Government contract set-asides and other forms of preferential treatment for minority businesses are simply stupid—affirmative action for the affluent—and an open invitation to corruption.

It would be good to get the affirmative action debate off the theological plane and onto some of these practical questions. But I suppose that will have to wait until *The Wall Street Journal* sorts out its theology.

Attitude Problem

(*The New Republic*, OCTOBER 9, 1989)

Because in wartime the various outlets of popular culture behaved almost entirely as if they were the creatures of their governments, it is hardly surprising to find that they spoke with one voice. Together with skepticism, irony, and doubt, an early casualty was a wide variety of views about current events.

—PAUL FUSSELL, *WARTIME: UNDERSTANDING AND BEHAVIOR IN THE SECOND WORLD WAR*

If we're going to win this war, it's going to take a long time. It's going to take a persistence in attitude. And this kind of garbage isn't very helpful. . . . For . . . this magazine, The New Republic, *to publish that if all you have in life is bad choices, crack may not be the most unpleasant of them, is irresponsible to an incredible degree.*

—WILLIAM BENNETT, TESTIFYING BEFORE CONGRESS, SEPTEMBER 14

Thus spake the drug czar, reacting to an article by Jefferson Morley in last week's *TNR*, describing his (very limited) experience with crack. The article in question did not urge anyone to use crack, did not say crack should be legalized, did not say drugs are not a serious national problem. In fact, it specifically said the opposite of all this, though perhaps without the usual catechistic reverence.

The purpose of the article was simply to describe what a crack high is like, for readers who may have experienced marijuana or powdered cocaine but know nothing about the drug of the moment. In the fuss this short piece has generated, no one has accused it of being inaccurate. The indictment is: "unhelpful." In the current state of drug-war frenzy, truth is no defense. As drug freak Ken Kesey famously put it (in Tom Wolfe's *The Electric Kool-Aid Acid Test*): "You're either on the bus or off the bus."

Although its purpose was mainly descriptive, the article made two points, one directly and one by implication. The direct point is that a crack high is pleasant, while it lasts. To any calm, rational person, this obviously is not a denial of the crack problem. It is an explanation for the crack problem. If using crack were an unpleasant experience from beginning to end, no one would use crack. Some critics have said this point is banal, but surely the fuss disproves that. It's hard on a journalist struggling to say something true and fresh about crack, after the millions of words that have appeared, to be told simultaneously that his point is (a) too dangerous to acknowledge, and (b) too obvious to need repeating.

The drug czar takes special umbrage at the sentence "If all you have in life is bad choices, crack may not be the most unpleasant of them." But the subject is short-term pleasure, not wisdom. And the article hardly ignores the ample downside of crack use (". . . stupefying . . . conducive to paranoia . . . cause of anti-social behavior . . . untold bodily damage . . ."). If it is now impermissible to note that the appeal of a chemical escape from life depends on the quality of the life you're escaping—and that this may help explain why crack has swept through the underclass—the drug war has become totally unhinged from reality.

The point Morley's article makes by implication is that it is possible to use crack once or twice without ruining your life. He is still functioning as a free-lance writer and an editor at *The Nation* (if you call that living), no more or less normal than he was before. Some crack experimenters will not be so lucky. Some will get sucked into the abyss, especially those facing the bleak alternatives we apparently are not allowed to mention. In that sense, perhaps, advertising the fact that one crack use may not be fatal "isn't very helpful."

But the journalist's job is not to be helpful. The journalist's job is to be truthful. If the authorities think that exaggerating—that is, lying—about the addictive nature of crack might be considered more helpful than telling the truth, one good answer is: That's too bad. Most journalists, though, adhere to the philosophy that the truth generally is helpful. That's why we do it. In this case, kids tempted by crack don't need *The New Republic* to tell them that crack use isn't invariably fatal. Pretending otherwise surely weakens the credibility and persuasiveness of the antidrug message more than telling the truth.

Yet on one of the weekend political chat-'n'-grunt shows, a conservative journalist and a liberal one agreed that Morley's article was not only "garbage" but "disgraceful journalism." This is what it must have been like to say in 1943 that the Japanese were human beings. Not to say that they weren't evil or that the war shouldn't be won—not to contradict the orthodoxy, simply to depart from it. Maybe that kind of agitprop mentality is necessary, or at least inevitable, in a real war. (Fussell, in his new book, is tart on the subject.) But the "war" on drugs shouldn't require the sacrifice of simple honesty in the name of promulgating the correct attitude.

The emphasis on "attitude" in this phase of the drug war is a political expedient. The Bush administration wants to make a big, big deal over drugs without spending much extra money—on enforcement, prisons, interdiction, rehabilitation, or anything else. So the administration takes the line that miracles can be achieved cost-free (or at least off-budget) through changes in attitude.

Social attitudes surely are important. But that war has been won. Could anyone have labored under the impression, the day before Bush announced his drug plan, that American society did not strongly disapprove of drug use? In schools, on television, in the movies, in the press, the message has been clear for years. Whatever good that message can do is being done. Fanning the flames of hysteria at this point is demagogic mischief. It is unhelpful.

Unlike most others, I think Bush will "win" the drug war. Attitudes have changed. Cocaine use is dropping; it will continue to drop. Middle-class trends will percolate downward, as they usually do. This problem won't disappear but will become less urgent; others will become more urgent. Bennett's main goal is a mere 10 percent reduction in cocaine use over two years. Come the next election season, Bush will pull a George Aiken: declare victory and come home. The Democrats, demanding more spending, will look like fools.

But all this will have very little to do with the present Kulturkampf. It's all too easy to whip up a pleasing froth of wartime national spirit if you're not actually calling on the nation's mainstream to sacrifice anything. Bush has become addicted to this kind of cheap political fix, first with the flag, now with drugs. Unfortunately, it takes ever-stronger doses to get the same high.

The game of moral one-upsmanship can always be won by taking the extreme position: Nothing is more important than this pressing crisis. Those who say wait a minute, this is complicated, other values are at stake, are criminally callous. A few years ago it was the antinuclear movement playing the game with great success: What could be more urgent than ending the risk of nuclear war? Standing in front of that moral bulldozer was a fearsome experience. Now it's drugs. The starting players come from the opposite sides of the political spectrum, but the newsmagazines and television networks pile on as usual. Fortunately for all of them, memories are short.

Monetary Democracy

(*The New Republic*, OCTOBER 30, 1989)

The Federal Reserve Board is indefensible in theory and indispensable in practice. Twelve unelected people have their collective finger on the second most important button in America: the one that controls the money supply, the biggest controllable factor in the equation of our economy. Seven of the twelve, the Federal Reserve governors, are appointed by the president to virtually uncurtailable fourteen-year terms. The other five, regional Federal Reserve bank presidents, are appointed by people appointed by the first seven. Their decisions are made in secret and kept secret for six weeks. Their budget is also secret. They probably affect your life more than the Supreme Court. How many of them can you even name?

At least the Supreme Court is in the Constitution. The Fed is merely a conceit of Congress, and wasn't fully vested with its current authority until 1935. Its mystical trappings are all quite recent. And the Court's seemingly undemocratic power has a clear basis in democratic theory: It protects individuals and minorities against the tyranny of the majority. The best that can be said of the Fed along those lines is that it protects the majority against itself—a dubious democratic safeguard.

Why should such an important body be "independent" of democracy? Other major democracies don't let unelected officials make such important national policy. In an informational pamphlet about itself, the Fed answers the question by denying the premise that the Federal Reserve is independent. "It is more accurate to characterize the System as 'independent within government,' " the Fed explains blandly. The pamphlet goes on to emphasize how often members have lunch with folks from the executive and legislative branches.

Gosh, surely we can do just a bit better than that. A better argument is that the Fed isn't really undemocratic. It's just democracy on a long fuse. The president does appoint the Fed's governors, and Congress can always change the rules if it wants to. The institutions of our representative democracy are all on fuses of various lengths, from the House elected every other year to the life-tenured Supreme Court interpreting a Constitution that itself is protected from short-term democratic storms but not long-term democratic tides. The Fed is in there somewhere between the Food and Drug Administration and the Circuit Court of Appeals.

Persuaded? I'm not, really. On the other hand, in the current state of American politics, no sane person would want it any other way. It was ten years ago this month that the Federal Reserve proved its worth, acting while the democratic branches of government were paralyzed to control inflation, then running at 14 percent. On October 6, 1979, Fed Chairman Paul Volcker announced that the Fed would "target" the money supply rather than interest rates. Like almost all pronouncements about monetary policy—from politicians as well as Fed chairmen—this was a question of political courage masked as a technical issue. Volcker was willing to put the country through high interest rates and a recession in order to conquer inflation.

It worked, at great cost. President Carter (who appointed Volcker) endorsed the Fed medicine and President Reagan—who had to reign over its most agonizing period—generally refrained from complaint. But it was surely a great relief to both of them that they didn't have to administer the injections themselves. And it's unlikely either would have had the guts to do so. What made the inflation cure possible was elected officials' ability to blame the Fed for the pain while taking credit for the cure themselves.

In the past decade, the American political system has become much more self-indulgent and shortsighted than it was in 1979. Reagan and Bush have taught the country to believe that no short-term sacrifice, however small, is necessary for any long-term benefit, however large. It is laughable to suppose that the president and Congress, who are now busy cooking up yet another tax cut in the face of a $140 billion deficit, could be trusted with the power to create a short-term rush of prosperity anytime they wanted, at the cost of future inflation and decay.

The Republican party has had it every which way on the question of Fed independence. The party's 1980 platform, at a time when inflation was public enemy number one, sternly declared: "The independence of the Federal Reserve Board must be preserved." By 1984 the inflation threat was past—thanks to the Fed's independence—but the party was still taking heat for the 1981–82 recession. "The Federal Reserve Board's destabilizing actions must stop," declared the 1984 platform, which also called for more "coordination between fiscal and monetary policy"—code for accommodating Reagan's huge deficits by printing more money.

In 1988 the Republican platform merely said blandly: "To keep markets on an even keel, we urge objective Federal Reserve policies to achieve long-run price stability." If this means anything at all, it is a veiled reference to something like a gold standard. But you can be sure that the next time such an objective guide to monetary policy produced a bit of a squeeze, politicians of both parties would be complaining again about "destabilizing actions."

The cleverness of the present Fed arrangement is that it allows politicians to complain about monetary discipline without being able to stop it. That is a great advantage, not just for the good of the country but for the politicians themselves. That is also the Fed's greatest defect, from a democratic point of view: not so much that unelected officials make the key decisions, but that elected officials don't have to take responsibility for the consequences. Still, who'd want to give these guys that kind of responsibility?

GEORGE ON MY MIND

(*The New Republic*, NOVEMBER 6, 1989)*

Some agency in Tokyo announced recently, to much gnashing of teeth on this side of the Pacific, that Japan is now richer than the United States. Thanks largely to the explosion in Japanese land prices (which roughly doubled from 1985 to 1988), the total value of that country's assets is now higher than our own.

Adherents of the American economic philosopher Henry George (1839–97) will recognize the fallacy immediately. Rising land prices don't make a nation any richer. How is a society enriched by the fact that the same land now sells for twice as much? This simply represents a transfer of wealth to landowners from those who need to rent or wish to own land: overwhelmingly, other Japanese. Indeed, although average hourly earnings in Tokyo are now the highest in the world, the average New Yorker's earnings go twice as far in buying power. The cost of real estate is a big reason.

Henry George was born seventy-five years before *The New Republic* in Philadelphia. He dropped out of school at age thirteen, went to sea shortly thereafter, and wound up working as a printer in San Francisco. In 1879, at age forty, he self-published his brilliant, obtuse, eloquent, grandiloquent masterwork, *Progress and Poverty*. After a slow start it became a best-seller and George himself became "the third most famous man in the United States" after Mark Twain and Thomas Edison, according to his granddaughter Agnes George de Mille (yes, *the* Agnes de Mille, the choreographer). He ran a legendary independent race for mayor of New York in 1886, losing to the Democrat but walloping the Republican, Theodore Roosevelt. By the time Roosevelt's great admirer Herbert Croly founded *The New Republic* in 1914, however, George and his theories were almost completely forgotten. Since then the lamp has been kept lit, only dimly, by a small group of earnest cranks who tend to repel potential enthusiasts with their extreme zeal.

This article appeared in the seventy-fifth-anniversary issue of The New Republic. TNR's *founding editor, Herbert Croly, was the author of an influential book entitled* The Promise of American Life.

George himself was a crank, but a wise one. His book addressed the question of how grinding poverty could exist in the midst of the great wealth and industrial progress of the late nineteenth century. A summary cannot do it justice. Nevertheless: George began from the premise that there are three factors of production: labor, capital, and natural resources (primarily land). All the world's wealth is created from these elements, and all the proceeds are divided among the worker, the capitalist, and the landlord. But whereas the return to labor is a reward for effort and the return to capital is a reward for saving, the return to land is a reward for nothing more than monopoly possession of a limited resource. (As real estate investors have noted throughout the ages, "They're not making any more of it.")

The ever-rising value of land, George reasoned, is not the result of the owner's efforts but rather a result of the growth of society itself—a larger population with increased wealth. If you own land, "you need do nothing more. You may sit down and smoke your pipe; you may lie around like the lazzaroni of Naples or the leperos of Mexico; you may go up in a balloon, or down a hole in the ground; and without doing one stroke of work, without adding one iota to the wealth of the community . . . you will be rich."

The landowner's profit, George maintained, is merely a tax on the truly productive factors of production, labor, and capital. And George's solution was to tax away the entire rental value of land, using the proceeds to abolish all other taxes. "Taxation which diminishes the earnings of the laborer or the returns of the capitalist," George argued in good supply-side fashion, "tends to render the one less industrious and intelligent, the other less disposed to save and invest." But a tax on land cannot reduce productivity since land alone is not productive and in any event cannot be withdrawn. George believed his proposal would, in one swoop, "raise wages, increase the earnings of capital, extirpate pauperism, abolish poverty, give remunerative employment to whoever wishes it, afford free scope to human powers, lessen crime, elevate morals and taste and intelligence, purify government, and carry civilization to yet nobler heights."

Obviously there are problems with this magic cure-all. George exaggerates the importance of land as the root of all economic evil, and he certainly was wrong that economic progress would inevitably bring increasing squalor and impoverishment if his ideas were not adopted.

On the other hand, his instinct that the hidden "landowners' tax" on the productive elements of society would grow with time and prosperity is probably correct. According to Federal Reserve figures, during the postwar boom era the share of America's national wealth represented by the value of land has grown from a fifth ($155 billion out of $786 billion) in 1946 to a quarter ($3.53 trillion out of $14.6 trillion) in 1988. There is the same amount of land in America as there was in 1946, but landowners' claims on all the wealth that has been produced since then—buildings, cars, Cuisinarts, Chicken McNuggets—have grown disproportionately.

Real estate has always led the "Forbes 400" list of the richest Americans as the primary source of large fortunes. In the 1989 list, just published, it slips behind manufacturing for the first time with 77 (compared with 80) out of 400. Forbes blames the recent price dip. But few on the list don't owe at least a part of their wealth to the long previous run-up in real estate or to ownership of mineral resources such as oil and gas. Outside of the United States, seven of the ten biggest fortunes are based primarily on real estate. America's richest man, John Kluge, increased his fortune by $2 billion (to $5.2 billion) last year by the simple expedient of owning cellular telephone franchises given away free by the U.S. government. Henry George was viciously witty about fortunes built on government-granted monopolies, "which are commonly confounded with the earnings of capital."

The most vehement objection to Georgism, through the years, has been that it's too late. Few current owners of land and other natural resources (or even government-granted monopolies) obtained them for free. To essentially expropriate their property (through 100 percent taxation of the profits) would be unfair. George is unsympathetic. He notes that even innocent landowners can lose their property in a legal dispute "if Quirk, Gammon and Snap can mouse out a technical flaw in your parchments or hunt up some forgotten heir. Why should it be any different in the case of *The People* v. *The Landowners*?" A clever point, but it doesn't really answer the question.

Nevertheless, George's ideas offer a useful lens through which to look at the world. What I like best about Henry George is the way he combines radical egalitarianism with an equally radical belief in free-market capitalism. Indeed, he saw his theories as a bulwark against socialism, protectionism, and William Jennings Bryan's style of populist demagoguery. But he noted the difference between capitalism in theory and the actual economy he saw around him. He distinguished between the accumulation of wealth and the creation of wealth. And he recognized that wealth accumulated in nonproductive ways was essentially taken from others' share: not merely unfair but actually bad for economic growth.

Although George's 100 percent land tax is impracticable, there are practical implications from his theories. George would sneer at the policy of giving away broadcast licenses for free. (Partly because of this policy, media is now the third-largest category of the Forbes 400.) He would understand the logic of an excess-profits tax on domestic oil and gas at the time of the OPEC energy hijack. He would see the futility of various current liberal schemes to "help" first-time home buyers through government subsidies, all of which will simply get capitalized into higher home prices. He would go ballistic over the idea of reopening the capital gains tax break for real estate.

Above all, perhaps, George would observe how the developed world has been suffering in recent years from real estate sickness. At times when the reward for happening to own a middle-class house has been greater than the reward for middle-class labor, this disease has twisted values, sucked away productivity, and redistributed wealth at random. And if, as many believe, the process is now going into reverse, the dislocations will be just as severe.

But *Progress and Poverty* is unavoidably a product of its time and place. That, more than its universal application, is what makes it a good read. Henry George was a self-educated American original, full of optimism and schemes for national improvement. Flush with Darwin and Herbert Spencer, he was a great one for proclaiming scientific "laws" of this, that, or the other aspect of the human condition—including, ultimately, the "law of human progress," with which I won't detain you. (Oh, well: It's "association in equality.")

Like Herbert Croly, Henry George felt that the closing off of the western frontier meant that American life would have to change. The Jeffersonian ideal of equality through widespread small land ownership would become impossible. But while Croly thought this logic dictated a centralized economy, with a large government role, George thought his more radical expedient could allow us to have more freedom and more equality, too. It was a more American prescription, even if it didn't carry the day.

Electioneering Etiquette

(*The New Republic*, NOVEMBER 13, 1989)

"It was a stark and jarring sixty seconds. By far Richard Nixon's toughest commercial of the campaign." This was the 1968 presidential campaign, the one that gave Roger Ailes his start, as immortalized in Joe McGinnis's book *The Selling of the President.* The ad was a montage of riots and war scenes interspersed with a laughing photo of Hubert Humphrey. It was pulled after complaints that it seemed to suggest Humphrey was laughing at American soldiers.

But Ailes had the last laugh. Not only did Nixon win, but with Ailes's help the art of the political commercial has sunk to a level that makes this early effort look like a PBS documentary. (Including the leisurely pace—sixty seconds!) McGinnis's book is an artifact of a lost age of innocence. Nixon is shown actually composing his own commercial messages on the spot. Ailes's brainchild is a series of hour-long (!) unrehearsed Q and A sessions with voters. The allegedly shocking deception is that the questioners are chosen with demographic calculation rather than at random. (Ailes: "You know what I'd like? . . . A good, mean, Wallaceite cabdriver. Wouldn't that be great? Some guy to sit there and say, 'Awright, mac, what about these niggers?' ")

Twenty years of Gresham's law—the bad politics driving out the good—brought us to last year's George Bush campaign. That is now the model and standard for political campaigns at every level. Of this year's three big races—for governor of New Jersey and Virginia and mayor of New York—the one in which the Democrat is surest of victory is New Jersey, where Jim Florio bushed first with a ludicrous commercial about how the Republican, Jim Courter, keeps toxic waste in his backyard. (Several drums of unused heating oil were left on some property Courter co-owned with his brother.)

However, all the tut-tutting about "negative campaigning" is a bit imprecise. There is nothing wrong with pointing out the failings of the opposition. After all, voting no is a more powerful expression of the democratic spirit than voting yes. Furthermore, the insistence that only "the issues" matter—that we should be talking about the future of our schools, not about my five past drunken-driving convictions—is a tiresome conceit. Personal history illumines character, and character is a valid "issue." New York Democrat David Dinkins's failure to file his income tax for four years and Virginia Democrat Doug Wilder's official reprimand for bungling a legal case are both relevant, even though they happened many years ago.

Nor is there anything wrong with dwelling on past views an opponent has abandoned. All three Democrats are having a good time with extreme antiabortion positions their Republican rivals held as recently as a few months ago, but now disown. Virginia Republican Marshall Coleman accuses Wilder of "spreading fear" for suggesting that Coleman might act on his alleged belief that even victims of rape and incest should be ineligible for abortion. Courter says he would not "impose my personal views" on the women of New Jersey. Pshaw. In Coleman's case at least, and that of New York Republican Rudolph Giuliani, the man's more moderate current position is undoubtedly closer to his genuine beliefs. But there is nothing wrong with nailing them to the cross of past demagoguery. And "flip-flops" are a valid issue in themselves, raising the question of whether a candidate genuinely believes in anything at all.

So what is wrong with today's negative campaigning? The basic standard, it seems to me, should be honesty. If a campaign thrust is honest, the voters can weigh its merits. But honesty must be broadly defined. Literal accuracy is the least of it. How you make something an issue is as important as whether you make it an issue.

First, much of the stuff being put forward as campaign issues, though literally true, is basically deceptive. Courter is running an ad saying, "Ten times Florio has taken campaign money from a corrupt union linked to organized crime." That's true, except that the contributions (all of $5,900) were made either before the union was under investigation or after it had been taken over by the feds. And Republican incumbent Governor Thomas Kean took contributions from the same union. If voters knew these facts, it would not merely weaken but totally destroy the power of the accusation.

Second, some campaign accusations, though accurate, are trivial, like Courter's drums of heating oil or building code violations in a house Wilder once owned in Richmond. They are the reductio ad absurdum of the fad for "negative research," a partisan version of investigative journalism in which paid gumshoes go after everything down to an opponent's elementary school report cards looking for usable dirt. The dishonesty here lies in implying these things matter, when you know perfectly well they don't.

Third, even accurate assertions become dishonest through a kind of campaign shorthand. The classic example is Bush's use of Michael Dukakis's court-approved decision to veto as unconstitutional a bill requiring teachers to recite the Pledge of Allegiance against their will. This became "Dukakis's veto of the Pledge of Allegiance." Republicans happily promoted this deceptive elision, but inevitably it was taken up by the press, too, out of totally nonmalicious need for compression.

Even in the relatively expansive precincts of a column, it is hard to tell the whole story of Florio's appearance as a character witness on behalf of an employee involved in a fatal car accident, but "interfering in the judicial process" on behalf of an accused killer—which is how Courter's ad puts it (although the man was acquitted)—is pretty unfair. Wilder's ethical lapse as a lawyer eleven years ago may be relevant, but the way Coleman's commercial zooms in on some boilerplate language in the official reprimand ("PROTECT THE PUBLIC") implies that Wilder is some kind of marauding Ted Bundy of the legal profession. Forced to discuss this so-called issue, the press usually just refers to an "ethical lapse"—as I just did—because who's got room to explain that it involved missing a filing deadline?

Fourth, there is—or ought to be—a statute of limitations on flip-flops. Coleman's latest ad is a staged mini-melodrama based on Wilder's support—in 1972—for a bill that would allow cross-examination of rape victims about their sexual history. That bill went nowhere and Wilder later—1976—supported a bill doing exactly the opposite. The ad omits all that. Some things in a candidate's record are simply not relevant. Wilder is not attempting a cynical "repositioning" on the question of rape, as other candidates are doing on abortion, and to imply based on this ancient matter that his current beliefs are untrustworthy amounts to a lie.

Finally, there is the question of proportionality. The lie is in the emphasis given to matters that may not be trivial but are hardly worth making the centerpiece of a campaign. This fundamental deception is a feature of all three major campaigns this year. Once again Bush is to blame, with his flags-'n'-furloughs festival last year. It will probably take a war to get American politics back up to the high level of Richard Nixon and Roger Ailes in 1968.

ESSENTIAL READING

(*The New Republic*, DECEMBER 18, 1989)

S omebody once held a contest: If you were the author of a book, and could have any words of praise to feature in an ad for it, what would they be? Most entries were on the order of, "Destroys the philosophical basis of all previous human thought—Hannah Arendt" or "I laughed till I cried—Mohandas K. Gandhi" or "If you read only one book this year, that's one more than I've read . . . I mean, make it this one—Ronald Reagan." But the winner was eloquent in its simplicity: "six-figure paperback sale."

This efficiently makes the key point about book blurbs: fine words butter no parsnips. Has anyone ever actually bought a book because John Kenneth Galbraith—to name one of America's most prolific blurbists—said it was important, or scintillating, or a laff-riot, or an incredible turn-on, or whatever? Yet publishers continue to solicit blurbs from the author's friends and to scavenge reviews for phrases to quote out of context. It's a treasured industry ritual (of which book publishing has many) rather than a rational business practice.

Because excessive praise for books has become so routine, I've started a collection (contributions welcome) of comments, either solicited or in reviews, that for one reason or another are double-edged. Sometimes it's the name attached that makes the intended puff self-defeating. A recent issue of the *Washington Monthly,* for example, contained an ad for a book titled *How to Win in Washington.* Emblazoned across the top was the inspirational message: "Essential reading—Stuart E. Eisenstat." Eisenstat, younger readers may need to be told, was one of President Jimmy Carter's top strategists. It would be like a book titled *How to Win in Afghanistan* with a blurb from Leonid Brezhnev.

More often the ambiguity is a matter of careless—or perhaps subconsciously subversive—wording. Former CIA Director William Colby has the following to say in an ad for *Guardians of the Arsenal: The Politics of Nuclear Strategy* by Janne Nolan (recently published by—ahem—New Republic Books): "Einstein's comment about the nuclear age remains true: a whole new way of thinking is needed. Janne Nolan shows how far we still have to go."

If they're not careful, the publishers of *Advise and Dissent*, the memoirs of former Senator James G. Abourezk, may be tempted to use for promotional purposes the opening lines of Philip Geyelin's recent favorable review in the *Washington Post Book World:* "You have never read—and are unlikely ever to read—political memoirs the likes of these." How true.

Sometimes the subversion seems less subconscious than consciously self-defensive. A recent *New York Times Book Review* carried a large, blurb-chocked ad for *On Becoming a Leader* by someone named Warren Bennis. Peter Drucker offered the artfully qualified encomium: "This is Warren Bennis's most important book." In fact, on close reading, several of the blurbs in this ad seemed strangely off-key. *USA Today* said of the book: "Its ideas are wise enough to stand re-examination." Management guru Rosabeth Moss Kanter opined: "Sure to launch an exciting journey of self-exploration for future leaders." Is that good?

But the weariest and most implausible bit of puffery is the one Eisenstat offered: "essential reading." For the hell of it, I searched for the phrase "essential reading" in Nexis, the electronic database of newspaper and magazine articles. There were seventy-three references so far in 1989. Strangely, the *Financial Times*, the *Christian Science Monitor*, and the *Wall Street Journal* have all found the occasion this year to publish articles asserting that they themselves are "essential reading." But most of the references are to books. *Life Insurance: A Consumer's Handbook* is "absolutely essential reading," says *Forbes*. *Football in Its Place: An Environmental Psychology of Football Grounds* is "as they say, essential reading," says the *Guardian* of London, with justified defensiveness.

Arnold Beichman of the Hoover Institution announces in the *Washington Times* that a book called *The Liberal Conspiracy* is essential reading. That's easy for him to say, of course, lounging under a palm out there in Palo Alto with a glass of chardonnay, *The Liberal Conspiracy*, and a fellowship to pay the rent. Those of us with jobs may demur about this, as well as about *White Bandits of the West: The Silent Brotherhood Inside America's Racist Underground*. Charles Johnson declares in the *Los Angeles Times* that this book is "essential reading for all Americans." In fact, he says, "it is a work we cannot ignore if, as a nation, we hope to survive this century." I guess at least that gives me eleven years to get around to it.

Reviewers usually let most readers off the hook by specifying a subgroup of humanity to whom the tome is essential. *Hemingway in Paris* is essential reading only for "Hemingway fanatics." On the other hand, *Armand Hammer: The Untold Story* is essential "for anyone *who was ever* fascinated by Armand Hammer" (emphasis added). Current lack of interest is no excuse. A book that is "essential reading for visitors to southern Venezuela" leaves visitors to northern Venezuela free to enjoy their trip. But few will escape a history of the American suburb; according to a *New York Times* reviewer, it is essential reading for "residents of Philadelphia, Chicago, Westchester County, Forest Hills, Queens, Shaker Heights, Ohio, and former borderlands everywhere."

I feel safe in skipping *Field Artillery and Firepower* by J.B.A. Bailey, which is essential reading only "for planners of army requirements, tactical operations, and joint operations." Ditto *The Arkrights: Spinners of Fortune* by R. S. Fulton, which is essential "for all serious students of early industrialism." But what about *Hector Berlioz* by David Cairns? It is "essential reading not only for the ardent Berliozian"—fair enough—"but for anyone with an interest in the history of romanticism." What courageous philistine dares to admit that he or she has no interest whatsoever in the history of romanticism? True, if I have such an interest, I have never done anything to feed it. But where better to start than with the "essential reading"?

I certainly can skip *Starting and Running a Bookshop*, which is "essential reading for anyone contemplating going into bookselling." Also that article in the *American Scholar* that, according to the *Washington Post*, is "essential reading for all those who love literature and suspect not much of it is being produced these days." I suspect all too much of it is being produced these days. In fact, as I logged out of my Nexis search for "essential reading," the computer popped me a message: "Additional items were added to this file while your research was in progress." Yikes! That's unfair. Hope there's no surprise quiz.

Democracy Theater

(*The New Republic*, JANUARY 1, 1990)

I say, old boy, PBS suddenly has a rival for the Anglophile market. C-SPAN, the cable network that transmits the House and Senate, is showing excerpts from the British House of Commons, which allowed in the television cameras last month. *Masterpiece Theatre* buffs may be slightly disappointed: Only one man, the Speaker, wears a wig, and the queen appears only once a year. What's more, there is no fruity music and no reassuring Alistair Cooke figure to explain what's going on.

Still, there are pleasures. The names, the accents, the suits, are magnificent. There is someone called Sir Fergus Montgomery complaining of injustice to war widows, with reference to a letter in yesterday's *Times*. A Scottish lady is discoursing earnestly about what sounds like "genital affairs." Wait, make that "general affairs." The Tory benches are a forest of foppish pinstripes. The U.S. House, by contrast, generally goes in for silly diminutive nicknames ("Newt," "Vin," "Buz") and baggy suits of solid blue. I watched a few hours of C-SPAN coverage of each House recently, for purposes of scientific comparison. Comparison number one: In lieu of stripes, the American members tend to festoon themselves with little pins and badges representing various political causes and patriotic themes.

Disappointingly, there is not a lot of Wildean witticism in Parliament. Prime Minister Margaret Thatcher's style, aped by a chorus of young Tory sycophants, is one of heavy-handed sarcasm. "Perhaps we had better wait and see so we can pontificate in the light of the facts," she sneers in response to a complaint about the impending water industry privatization. More entertaining are the old-fashioned class-war thrusts from the venerable members of the Labour party. It's less Oscar Wilde than Clifford Odets. "The home secretary has never lived in a cardboard box." (Crowd: "You tell 'em, Frank.") "The minister can shake his head. . . . Don't shake your head at me. . . . He's got a garage with a couple of cars in it. I've got people back in my constituency who have to walk because they can't even afford a flippin' bus." To a setup question to Thatcher from one of the Young Sycophants (something like: "Would the prime minister agree that the past ten years have been the most glorious chapter of British history since mankind was expelled from Eden?"), a Labourite yells, "Get off your knees!"

It is a tradition of this column to celebrate the superiority of the parliamentary system of government. This was a constant theme of Richard Strout, who wrote in this space from 1942 until 1983. The major advantage, compared with our system, is the merger of the executive and legislative functions. A national leader who wins an election by promising to do something can actually do it, and has no excuse for not doing it. This is excellent discipline for politicians and voters alike. It makes politics a more serious business. Logically, it should also make parliamentary debates less urgent, since the outcome is more likely to be predetermined by party-line voting. But the C-SPAN Parliament show demonstrates the opposite. Parliament debates focus much more on issues that really matter and on legislation that might really be enacted. They are also more like real debates, rather than sequential speeches. The tradition of "yielding" to another member in mid-speech, which in Parliament means giving an opponent the chance to take a shot at you, has evolved in the U.S. House into little more than a method of divvying up the allotted time among members of the same party.

Even among political opponents, there is far more debilitating politesse in the American House than in the British one. Vast amounts of time are wasted praising bipartisanship, thanking the member from the other party for his cooperation, and so forth. The only actual disagreement I heard in hours of a recent House session was a polite tiff between two Florida representatives about which one had more "seniors" in his district.

A second advantage of the parliamentary system is even more on display on C-SPAN: the distinction between the head of government and the head of state. Margaret Thatcher, world renowned for her haughtiness, undergoes a twice-a-week ritual of humiliation-by-questioning that would be an unthinkable act of *lèse-majesté* if inflicted on our jes' folks president. "Will the prime minister now make a public apology for this gross incompetence?" Has she not been rendered "a pygmy on the world stage" by something or other? Will she not "be swept from office and dumped in the garbage" very soon? All accompanied by cheers from one side and jeers from the other. Thatcher gives as good as she gets, but the whole process has a democratically healthy leveling effect. Indeed, after watching Parliament for a while, C-SPAN's House of Representatives show suddenly seems like *Hamlet* without the Prince of Denmark. The lead character in the drama—President Bush—is constantly referred to but never appears.

Question Time—the twice-a-week session where the prime minister and her Cabinet are interrogated by other members—replaces two institutions of American democracy: congressional committee testimony by Cabinet department heads, and presidential press conferences. It is superior to both. American Cabinet members justifiably complain of the vast amount of time they spend preparing for and appearing at redundant committee hearings. Usually in these sessions the Cabinet member and the interrogating legislator are both just mouthpieces for aides, who can often be seen on C-SPAN striking the classic Washington pose of leaning forward from behind and whispering in the boss's ear. In Parliament, the questions and answers are to the point, and there are no aides in sight.

As for the presidential press conference, Question Time offers the perfect answer to the perennial question, "Who elected Sam Donaldson?" Free of the need to appear objective or fair, opposition MPs ask tougher questions than White House correspondents would dare. Better framed, too. "Why are there more young people now begging on the streets of London and our other big cities?" Mrs. Thatcher was asked the other day. Could even Sam Donaldson have put it that straight, without a little speechlet to blunt its force?

C-SPAN, established a decade ago by the enterprising Brian Lamb, has turned into a wonderful adventure in true-life political theater. Funded by the cable industry and run on a shoestring, it fills the airtime between congressional sessions with what might be called "found democracy." You never know what you're going to stumble across on its two channels: House committee hearings, think-tank seminars, State Department briefings, a charity "roast" in honor of a big-shot journalist, a showing of campaign commercials by the Democratic Senatorial Campaign Committee, the weekly staff meeting of *The New Republic*. And now the Mother of Parliaments.

And there's more fun ahead. Lamb was just in Jerusalem trying to get permission to broadcast the Israeli Knesset. Mel Brooks, look to your laurels!

T HE M ANET I LLUSION

(*The New Republic*, JANUARY 22, 1990)

When the price of something goes up, the supply of it increases. That is the great consolation offered by economists throughout the ages. A higher price for apples will induce more people to grow apples. But no such consolation is available in the case of paintings by dead artists. The skyrocketing prices of established art masterpieces will not produce more such masterpieces. One or two may come out of hiding, and perhaps few forgeries will add to the world's enjoyment of great art until they are exposed and denounced. But the main economic effect of the art masterpiece price explosion is to transfer wealth to present owners of art masterpieces.

Economists call the mistaken feeling of increased wealth caused by general inflation "the money illusion." The inflation in art prices is slightly different: Call it "the Manet illusion." When an Impressionist painting thought to be worth $15 million is suddenly worth $30 million, the world is not $15 million richer. However, the owner's claim on the world's existing wealth has doubled.

For this reason, it's hard to understand all the hair-pulling about the terrible effect on the public of the art masterpiece price explosion. After all, most art masterpieces are owned by institutions that are owned, in turn, by the public—or at least dedicated to serving the public interest. "From the point of view of American museums, the art-market boom is an unmitigated disaster," wrote *Time*'s art critic Robert Hughes late last year in a woeful cover story. But why? Museums are the OPEC of art. They have a virtual monopoly on old masters and own a large proportion of the Impressionists, Postimpressionists, and so on. Economically, they are by far the biggest beneficiaries of higher art prices. So why have so many art mavens entered their blue period?

The reason of course is that museums only buy art, as a rule. They don't sell it. That is their great mistake. If museums could only overcome their antiselling fetish, they could exploit the enormous power the art boom has given them. They might use this power for at least three different purposes.

First, to break the back of the art market, if they want to. The market is already shaky. There was talk of Picasso's *Au Lapin Agile* (*Time*'s cover picture) breaking the world record of $53.9 million set two years ago by van Gogh's *Irises* and hitting as much as $75 million; it went for $40.7. Manet's *Rue Mosnier, Paris, Decorated with Flags* was supposed to bring in $30 million to $40 million; it went for $26.4 million.

Revelations about fancy financing arrangements and other manipulative practices by the auction houses make it all look increasingly like a classic speculative bubble. William Grampp, a University of Chicago professor, notes in his recent book about the economics of art, *Pricing the Priceless* (Basic Books), that historically, art has never been a particularly good investment.

If the high priests of the art world really think that exorbitant prices are turning art into a commodity, corroding aesthetic sensibilities, spreading philistinism like a plague, and so on, nothing could be easier than bursting the bubble. The fact that the vast majority of great paintings are permanently off the market is what keeps prices so high. Even the possibility of a small fraction of these coming up for sale would cause prices to plummet. One museum alone, such as the Metropolitan or the National Gallery, could probably create a crash simply by threatening to dump a van Gogh or two.

Billionaire publisher S. I. Newhouse is widely suspected of paying $17.7 million for a Jasper Johns last year in order to raise the value of the Johnses he already owned. Many might think that is a shrewder way to manipulate the market than by driving prices down. But if museums are really determined to reduce the market value of their own collections, they could pull a reverse Newhouse and sell a masterpiece or two. They might even be able to buy them back again for less once the panic takes hold.

Second, rather than destroy their own newfound wealth, museums might wish to exploit it more efficiently. At any level of art prices, museums can afford almost any painting they want, provided they are willing to sell others. That is what the Museum of Modern Art did in November to acquire an important van Gogh, though it was needlessly defensive about the transaction. High prices don't prevent museums from improving their collections—merely from expanding them indefinitely. And a visitor can't help noticing that MOMA, like other major museums, is already, er, full.

Although museums complain that the price explosion has made their acquisition budgets almost worthless, it has had the opposite effect on hundreds of paintings they keep in storage. Since it is a cardinal belief of the commercialization deplorers that the philistines are especially partial to inferior works by big-name painters, the museums should have a golden opportunity for a sort of aesthetic arbitrage.

Third, if museum trustees really believe that great paintings are insanely overvalued financially—but undervalued aesthetically—they may want to consider selling off their inventory and not replacing it. If you wouldn't pay $50 million for a van Gogh, why should you keep a van Gogh you could get $50 million for? Use the money for the homeless, or art education, or some other worthy cause.

Harvard political scientist Edward Banfield proposed in a book several years ago that museums free themselves from the cult of the original and replace their paintings with high-quality reproductions. His argument was that a reproduction incorporates all or almost all of a painting's aesthetic value, yet costs a small fraction of the original because it lacks the investment value. If it is investment values (in both senses: the financial value of paintings and the spiritual values of the financial world) that are such a threat to museums today, Banfield's solution seems even more tempting. The *Time* cover story reported that the canvas on tour in Australia representing itself as the world's most expensive painting, van Gogh's *Irises,* may actually be a copy! This reinforces Banfield's contention that the difference between real and fake is not even in the eye of the beholder.

It ill behooves Americans to fret that we are losing great European painting to the Japanese. How did we get them? As Grampp wittily points out, works of art have been moving west "for millennia": from the Middle East to Greece and Rome in ancient times; then from Italy to northern Europe; in the nineteenth century, from Europe to the American East Coast; more recently, across America to Texas and California; and now to Japan. Someday, Grampp predicts, they'll all end up back where they started. All the more reason for museums to think of their collections as assets to be used shrewdly, not as sacrosanct national treasures.

QUALITY TIME

(*The New Republic*, FEBRUARY 12, 1990)

It may seem presumptuous, but I have decided to apply for the 1990 Malcolm Baldrige National Quality Award. This government-sponsored honor was created by an act of Congress in 1987, in memory of the secretary of commerce who died that year in a rodeo accident. It is given in three categories: manufacturing, services, and small business. Not being sure which category the production of an opinion column falls into, I may apply in all three. Please, don't try to dissuade me. As George Bush himself puts it, in Mao-like cadences, on the cover of the application brochure: "The improvement of quality in products and the improvement of quality in services—these are national priorities as never before."

Quite right. It had been in the back of my mind that I ought to take steps to improve the quality of this column, now that Japanese and Korean pundits are breathing down my neck and threatening my market share. But well, frankly, what with the end of history and everything, I just couldn't be bothered.* However, when a fellow is offered the chance to win "a three-part solid crystal stele standing 14 inches tall" with "an 18 karat gold plated medal . . . embedded in its central form," the medal itself inscribed with " 'Malcolm Baldrige National Quality Award' and 'The Quest for Excellence' on one side and the Presidential seal on the other side," it really gets him off his heinie and puts him to work upping his "quality excellence criteria," as the brochure adroitly puts it.

Of course, merely applying for a "Malcolm" will take up most of my time for the rest of 1990, leaving little opportunity for actual column production. The instructions alone run thirty-nine pages. First you submit an "Eligibility Determination Form." Then you submit an "Application Package" (fifteen copies) composed of an "Eligibility Determination Form with official eligibility confirmation," an "Application Form," a "Site Listing and Descriptors Form," and an "Application Report," which (you will

---

An influential article entitled "The End of History" had recently been published and was the talk of the op-ed pages. Its thesis has not worn well.

be pleased to hear) "is limited to a maximum of 75 single-sided pages"—
not counting "Supplemental Sections" of fifty pages each, and also not
counting "two-page overviews, dividers, covers, tab separators, title pages,
and tables of contents."

The "Application Report" must be typed "using a fixed pitch font of
12 or fewer characters per inch or a proportional spacing font of point size
10 or larger. Any type may be used." (Gosh, thanks.) The report must
address itself to seven "Examination Categories." "Each of the seven Examination Categories has two or more Examination Items. Items are designated by two-digit numbers from 1.1 to 7.8." And, just to make your
joy complete, "each Examination Item includes a set of Areas to Address
(Areas) designated by lower case letters and enclosed in a rectangle." Enclosed in a rectangle! That'll show those Japanese a thing or two. As the
current commerce secretary, Robert Mosbacher, truly notes, the Baldrige
Award "has demonstrated that government and industry, working together, can foster excellence."

So here we are, for example, working together for excellence at Category Four, "Human Resource Utilization," Item 4.1, "Human Resource
Management," Area (a): "how the company integrates its human resource
plans with the quality requirements of business plans." I am ashamed to
say that in my writing business I have given this matter no thought whatsoever. And there are 132 more quality considerations just like it that must
be addressed if one is to win a "Malcolm."

Although I hate to lend succor to rivals, let me strongly urge all "Malcolm" applicants to read the instructions carefully. They are full of helpful
hints. "Items in Categories 1, 2, 3 and 5 should not be interpreted to
require the types of data which are requested in Categories 4, 6, and 7."
In my haste to make the April 25 deadline, I almost missed this sage
advice.

After April 25, I will have three or four months to tidy up my office
in preparation for the Site Visit Review, "conducted by at least five members of the Board of Examiners." And don't suppose that this Board is
just some undifferentiated mass of quality expertise. Oh, no. It has members "of three types: Examiners, Senior Examiners, and Judges." Rest assured that "all members of the Board take part in an examination
preparation course. . . . "

Then in "October or November" comes the great moment when I
receive my award. Last year the awards were presented by President Bush

himself. Past winners have included companies like General Motors and IBM. I can't help thinking they'll be looking for something a bit more postindustrial this time around. I'm feeling lucky. But even if I lose, I'll get a consolation prize, absolutely free (apart from the $2,500 application fee, $1,000 for small businesses): a "Feedback Report" summarizing my strengths, my "areas for improvement"—tactful phrasing there—and my "overall quality management profile." Then all I have to do is get my mommy to sign it and return it to Secretary Mosbacher for a little gold star.

TRY A LITTLE HARDER

(*Time*, FEBRUARY 19, 1990)

In 1947 the U.S. gross national product was $235 billion. That's about $1.4 trillion in today's money. Over the next four years, America spent $13.6 billion—almost $80 billion in today's money—reviving capitalism and securing democracy in Western Europe under the Marshall Plan.

If anyone had told the Americans of 1947 that in 1990 their nation would be more than four times as rich, they would not have been surprised. America, after all, was the greatest country in the history of the world. It could do anything. If anyone had told them, though, that the America of 1990 would be unwilling to spend more than $300 million ($51 million in 1947 dollars) to complete the job begun in 1947 by claiming Eastern Europe for capitalism and democracy—that they would have had trouble believing. Yet $300 million plus dribs and drabs is what President Bush is offering next year in foreign aid to Poland and Hungary. The other East bloc nations get nothing but dribs and drabs. Think of it per person. That $13.6 billion was $94 for each of the 144 million Americans in 1947, or $553 in today's money. An equivalent sacrifice by today's affluent standards would be more than $1,200 per person. By contrast, even if we continue that $300 million a year for four years, it works out to $4.80 for each of today's 250 million Americans.

There is no special shame in not being the world's greatest nation. The Swiss and the Swedes lead happy lives. Perhaps, having remained steadfast for four decades of cold war, we have done enough. Prosperous isolation has genuine appeal. But it is embarrassing to hear a president proclaim, as Bush did in his State of the Union speech, that "America stands at the center of a widening circle of freedom," with so little to back it up. Surely the transformation of communism to capitalism, totalitarianism to democracy is the great adventure of the next generation. Do we want to be part of it in a serious way or not?

Bush spoke grandly of "the revolution of '89," the explosion of freedom, then pathetically listed Panama as item number one. This only drew attention to our sideline role in the truly historic developments of 1989, in Eastern Europe. Perhaps there is little more we should or could have done in 1989. But 1990 and beyond will be different.

In all the disputes over Eastern Europe's future, everyone agrees about two things. First, that the quick, magical part is over and the hard, slow, painful part has just begun. And second, that while free markets will make these nations more prosperous in the end, the wrenching and novel process of converting command economies into free markets will make things even worse for at least a while. Poland's courageous total-immersion reform plan is expected to reduce workers' wages by 20 percent from their already desperate levels. Poland begins this experiment owing $40 billion to the West from the disastrous 1970s. Yugoslavia, Hungary, and East Germany owe about $20 billion apiece.

"It is time to offer our hand to the emerging democracies of Eastern Europe," said Bush. But an empty hand is not enough. It is absurd to say, as some do, that money is not what Eastern Europe needs. Yes, capitalist expertise and rapid integration into the Western economic system are equally important. But this is no excuse for refusing simple cash. Nor is the fact that so much Western money was squandered in the 1970s. That was a different world.

It is worse than absurd to say we cannot afford to be generous because of our own debts and social problems. As Bush proclaimed in the State of the Union, we are the most productive nation in the world, at least for the moment. The very collapse of communism will save us billions. If we choose to consume our riches (and more) rather than invest and share them, that is a statement about our spiritual condition, not our economic one. Which brings us back to the question of greatness.

America's role in World War II reflected national greatness of a traditional kind: economic and military strength and courage. The Marshall Plan reflected national greatness of an especially American kind: generosity and farsighted promotion of our own values. To be sure, generosity was not all of it. We feared that Stalin would be the "receiver in bankruptcy" of an impoverished Europe, as *Time* wrote the week the plan was announced. That fear may be gone. But it is not the end of history. Because of what could still go wrong in Eastern Europe, and to set an example for the rest of the world, the successful conversion of these nations to capitalism and democracy is vital to America.

In 1947 we even bankrolled the recovery of our defeated enemy, Germany. In 1990 we debate whether perestroika in the Soviet Union will collapse into economic chaos and archaic nationalism, without any suggestion that we ought to do something about it. Meanwhile, Senator Robert Dole wins acclaim by suggesting that what little aid we give to Eastern Europe ought to come out of our mite of aid to the rest of the world.

Have we now lost that special American kind of greatness? Do we now think that spraying bullets in a place like Panama makes you a superpower? Bush has been criticized for spending much of last week inspecting the troops, yesterday's pastime, when he should have been concocting a "new vision." But lack of vision doesn't threaten America's greatness. What does is a simple unwillingness to make the effort.

Second Thoughts

(The New Republic, FEBRUARY 26, 1990)

Around the world, national theologies are crumbling: communism, apartheid, and, here in America, the worship of guns—to foreigners, the single craziest thing about us. Do you sense an outbreak of sanity about gun control? I do. There was retired Chief Justice Warren Burger preaching sacrilege on the cover of *Parade* magazine a couple of weeks ago. A Time/CNN poll reports that 87 percent of gun owners themselves favor a seven-day waiting period for handgun purchases; three quarters favor registration of semiautomatic weapons and handguns; and half favor registration of rifles and shotguns.

Unfortunately, there is the Second Amendment to the Constitution: "A well regulated militia, being necessary to the security of a free State, the right of the people to keep and bear Arms, shall not be infringed." As Sanford Levinson, a professor at Texas Law School, points out in the

December *Yale Law Journal* (the article is called "The Embarrassing Second Amendment"), no prominent legal scholar has ever tackled this provision. The leading constitutional reference book dismisses it in a footnote.

Most right thinkers take comfort in that funny stuff about the militia. Since the amendment's stated purpose is arming state militias, they reason, it creates no individual right to own a gun—especially today when the only state militias are the National Guard. That reasoning is good enough for the ACLU. But would civil libertarians be so stinting in interpreting an amendment they felt more fond of? Say, the First?

The purpose of the First Amendment's free-speech guarantee was pretty clearly to protect political discourse. But liberals reject the notion that free speech is therefore limited to political topics, even broadly defined. True, that purpose is not inscribed in the amendment itself. But why leap to the conclusion that a broadly worded constitutional freedom ("the right of the people to keep and bear arms") is narrowly limited by its stated purpose, unless you're trying to explain it away?

That word "infringed" is also pesky. First Amendment freedoms, by contrast, may not be "abridged." Wouldn't you say (if you didn't know the subject matter) that a freedom guaranteed against mere "infringement" deserves at least as robust a reading as one protected only against actual "abridgement"? *TNR*'s Mickey Kaus says that if liberals interpreted the Second Amendment the way they interpret the rest of the Bill of Rights, there would be law professors arguing that gun ownership is mandatory.

Of course the hypocrisy is not just on one side. Second Amendment enthusiasts tend to be the sort who, in other contexts, are horrified at the thought of unelected judges overruling the will of the majority. They are happy to see other folks' dubious enthusiasms suppressed for the alleged good of society. Guns don't kill people—only pornography, drugs, etc., etc., kill people. But this doesn't free liberals to be hypocritical ourselves.

The most thorough parsing of the Second Amendment is a 1983 article in the *Michigan Law Review* by Don Kates, a gun enthusiast. Kates expends most energy demonstrating that at the time of the Bill of Rights, the word "militia" did not mean a separate, organized military force. All able-bodied men were considered to be part of the "militia" and were expected to defend the state if necessary. I'm not sure this is as clinching an argument as Kates seems to think. The fact that once upon a time everyone was a member of the militia doesn't prove that everyone still has a right to a gun even after the composition of the militia has changed.

But Kates has other bullets in his belt. The phrase "right of the people" appears four other times in the Bill of Rights (including the First Amendment). In all these other cases, everyone agrees that it creates a right for individual citizens, and not just some collective right of states as a whole. Then there is the phrase, "keep and bear." The right merely to "bear" arms might just mean serving in the militia. But what does "keep" mean? Finally, Kates marshals impressive historical evidence that the Second Amendment, like other Bill of Rights protections, was intended to incorporate English common law rights of the time, which pretty clearly included the right to keep a gun in your home for reasons having nothing to do with the militia.

So there we are. If there is a good reply to Kates's fusillade, the controllers haven't made it. In a videotape distributed by Handgun Control, Inc. (of which I'm a member) for use in high schools, Harvard Law professor Alan Dershowitz blusters that "asking about what the Framers would have done about handguns is absurd. No one can know." He compares it to another modern development, wiretapping. It's an unfortunate example. The Supreme Court has ruled—and even Robert Bork agrees—that, reasoning by analogy, the Framers would have wanted the Fourth Amendment's protection against "unreasonable searches and seizures" to apply to wiretapping.

Of course the existence of an individual right to own guns doesn't mean that it is absolute. What are the limits? In the Supreme Court's one twentieth-century treatment of the Second Amendment, in 1939, it held somewhat ambiguously that sawed-off shotguns aren't necessarily protected by the Constitution without proof that they are the kind of weapon a militia might have used. Working from that decision and the common law, Kates says the amendment's protection should be limited to weapons "in common use among law-abiding people," useful for law enforcement or personal defense, and lineally descended from weapons known to the Framers. (No nuclear bombs.) He adds that they must be light enough for an ordinary person to carry ("bear"), and even that they can't be especially "dangerous or unusual." He says—NRA take note—that the amendment places no limit on mandatory registration or laws against concealed weapons in public (since state militias were required to produce their guns for inspection).

This list seems quite reasonable and moderate, though where it all comes from is not all that clear. In suggesting, for example, that it would be okay to ban automatic rifles but not semiautomatics, he is slicing the constitutional salami pretty thin. But in what I suspect was the main purpose of his exercise—establishing that a flat ban on handguns would be hard to justify under the Constitution—Kates builds a distressingly good case.

The downside of having a Bill of Rights is that the protection of individual rights usually entails social costs. This is as true of the Second Amendment as it is of the First, Fourth, Fifth, and Sixth. The downside of having those rights inscribed in a Constitution, protected from the whims of majority rule, is that they can't be redefined as life changes. It would be remarkable indeed if none of the provisions in the Bill of Rights became less sensible and more burdensome with time. Talking and writing are as central to American politics as they ever were; shooting just isn't. Gun nuts are unconvincing (at least to me) in their attempts to argue that the individual right to bear arms is still as vital to freedom as it was in 1792. But the right is still there.

WHO WON NICARAGUA?

(*The New Republic*, MARCH 19, 1990)

Two years ago, after Congress finally cut off all U.S. support for the contra war in Nicaragua, President Reagan declared: "Those who led the fight against our package of assistance to the democratic resistance cannot escape responsibility for what followed." What followed—cease-fire, free election, victory for the opposition, voluntary surrender of political power by the Sandinistas—turned out to be pleasanter than anyone would have dared to predict. And, wouldn't you know, suddenly it turns out that contra opponents were not responsible after all. It was the contras themselves who achieved this splendid result, we are now told. Only yesterday they were (said their supporters) a spent force, thanks to the perfidy of Congress. Now they have undergone a stunning retrospective recovery.

"Let it be on your head" was a major theme of contra supporters during the years of bitter ideological struggle here in Washington. "Which side are you on?" challenged White House communications director Patrick Buchanan in a notorious 1986 *Washington Post* op-ed piece. "Whether

Central America becomes the next appendage of Soviet Empire is a question to which the Democratic Party in Congress now holds the answer." Failure to fund the contras "would lead, as night follows day, to loss of Central America." And, "if Central America goes the way of Nicaragua, they will be in San Diego."

The New Republic: "If in Nicaragua transition to democracy were possible without war, we too would oppose any fighting. But that option does not exist. Does anyone believe that the Sandinistas will ever . . . permit a free allocation of power by election?" War is brutal, but: "The liquidation of the democratic side of the Nicaraguan civil war will bring infinitely more tragedy to Nicaragua, to Central America, and ultimately to the rest of the hemisphere." The pro-contra argument was that without continuous active military resistance—war, in other words—the Sandinistas were certain to consolidate their power. Anyone who thought otherwise—who held out hope for regional negotiations, for moral suasion, for internal discontent, for the natural economic catastrophe of a Marxist economy—was either hopelessly naive or a secret Communist sympathizer.

Now, Congress did briefly approve military aid to the contras in 1986, and "humanitarian" aid at other times. And the Reagan administration sneaked in some illegal military assistance before that. The contra war managed to kill more than thirty thousand Nicaraguans over the years. In proportion to Nicaragua's tiny population, that's the equivalent of almost three million Americans. Those who wish to give the contras credit for the triumph of democracy in Nicaragua are reduced to arguing that our on-again, off-again support for the rebels—the zigs and zags for which they had nothing but contempt at the time—was, in retrospect, exactly the right approach. By a remarkable coincidence, thirty-thousand deaths was precisely the right number: More would have been otiose, but fewer would have been insufficient.

Actually, there could be a grain of truth in this. What may have helped, if anything, is a sort of bad-cop, good-cop strategy, with the White House threatening war and Congress offering negotiations. But how many more Nicaraguans would have died—died unnecessarily, as it turns out—if contra supporters had had their way all along? And where would Nicaragua be today? Probably in the midst of a bloody civil war, with the Sandinistas still in charge. At best, there would be a militarily installed junta more to U.S. liking, with no electoral legitimacy and the ousted Sandinistas fighting their own renewed guerrilla war from the hills. Surely it is more wholesome to speculate whether today's happier result might have been achieved with only twenty-thousand war deaths, or ten-thousand, or even none at all.

To be honest, I didn't predict this outcome, either. In fact, I even wrote an article a couple of years ago titled "Who Lost Nicaragua?" Succumbing to the romantic realpolitik of Washington in the 1980s, when hard noses were de rigueur, I accepted the premise that cutting off the contras would probably mean permanent Sandinista rule and argued that contra aid was a bad idea anyway. That was unduly pessimistic. But at least I was prepared to accept responsibility for the probable consequences of my position, unlike most contra supporters, who never acknowledged the cost in blood and destruction they were willing to impose. Ronald Reagan apparently spent his entire administration believing that the contras were not the sorts of people who blew up power stations, because "this would hurt the people of Nicaragua."

Impoverishing the people of Nicaragua was precisely the point of the contra war and the parallel policy of economic boycott and veto of international development loans. American thinking has been at its most Orwellian on this point, blaming the Sandinistas for wrecking the Nicaraguan economy while devoting our best efforts to doing precisely that ourselves. The Sandinistas might well have been able to wreck the economy on their own, but we didn't give them the chance. I opposed economic sanctions against Nicaragua on the Reaganite grounds that they hurt the people they were intended to help. But it must be conceded that the economic disaster was probably the victorious opposition's best election issue. Nevertheless, it was Orwellian once again for the United States, having done this, to be posturing as the exhorter and arbiter of fair elections in Nicaragua.

Of course the most important factor in explaining the unexpected collapse of communism in Nicaragua is the unexpected collapse of communism in the Soviet Union. To what extent American policies of the past decade (as opposed to the broader bipartisan American policies of the past two generations) are responsible for this pleasant surprise is a larger question.

One way to think about these things, though, is to ask what the Reagan-did-it crowd would be saying today if the opposite had happened. What if the Soviet Union were as unreconstructed and malevolent as ever? Would they be saying, "Well, I guess Reagan's policies were a mistake"? Or would that also, in their view, have proved the wisdom of the arms buildup, Star Wars, and so on? If Daniel Ortega by now had declared himself emperor and launched a full-scale invasion of El Salvador, would contra supporters be taking credit for that outcome? Or would "responsibility" be back on the backs of contra opponents? The question answers itself.

IRANAMOK FINALE

(The New Republic, APRIL 9, 1990)

L ike most Americans, I haven't been following the John Poindexter trial with rapt attention. Like somewhat fewer, I feel a bit guilty about this. When Representative David Obey was upbraided last year for his tiresome curiosity about the Iran-contra affair, he said, "I didn't swear to uphold the Constitution until I got bored." Most of us never swore to uphold the Constitution at all. Still, it makes something of a mockery of our former outrage about the scandal that we can't even be bothered to follow the denouement. Were the skeptics right all along that the whole thing was blown out of proportion?

One small matter, though, has penetrated the thick skin of my indifference, and perhaps yours, too. Don't I vaguely remember that the scandal fizzled three years ago when former National Security Adviser John Poindexter declared to the Iran-contra congressional committee: "The buck stops here, with me"? When Poindexter refused to finger President Reagan, the Media Central Committee decreed that, as a national obsession, the case was closed. And yet Poindexter is now defending himself—defending himself on charges of lying to Congress, no less—by claiming that he was acting on orders from President Reagan. Gosh, isn't that a little, er, inconsistent?

Answer: It's not quite as inconsistent as it seems. When Poindexter said, "The buck stops here," he was talking specifically about the diversion of profits from the Iran arms sale to the Nicaraguan contras. Poindexter's trial is about the subsequent cover-up, and that is what he is trying to blame on President Reagan. However, in mounting his defense he actually does now allege that Reagan knew about the diversion—exactly what he denied in his immunized 1987 testimony. Yet in the court of public opinion, the case remains closed. Rulings of the Media Central Committee are unappealable.

Confusion and boredom turn out to be far more effective than a traditional cover-up. There was outrage the summer of 1987 when it was suggested that Reagan should simply pardon Poindexter and Oliver North. Yet what has happened, to general indifference, is a sort of round-robin of pardoning. Poindexter and North pardon Reagan by taking the blame upon themselves, then go for a pardon in turn by shifting the blame back onto Reagan. Responsibility is like a hot potato that gets passed around, but is always magically in the hands of whoever isn't the focus of attention at the moment.

North was acquitted on nine of twelve counts, including the most important, by persuading the jury that he had been made the fall guy by higher-ups. Now at the trial of Poindexter, North's next higher-up, North has suffered repeated bouts of those tragic failures of memory that strike everyone in this case from Reagan on down. When the fog of North's memory did clear, the figure who usually stood revealed was Robert McFarlane, Poindexter's predecessor, who conveniently has already copped a plea.

Most irritating of all, the cumulative effect of the round-robin guilt-shifting is to leave the impression that they've all been vindicated and there was nothing to be outraged about in the first place. Every time one of them gets off by blaming one of the others, *The Wall Street Journal* runs an editorial saying, "See? It's all nonsense." Who can keep track of what so-and-so said three years ago, compared with what he's saying today, and have time for golf?

The round-robin has been especially useful to President Bush. He has been able to claim that, as vice president, he knew nothing about these appalling goings-on, while at the same time embracing North for whatever political advantage can be derived from that.

Poindexter's own guilt on the principal charges against him is so obvious it's hardly worth discussing. The obfuscation necessary to mount a half-plausible defense is one of the things that makes the case so confusing. One main accusation is that Poindexter lied to members of Congress when he told them, in November 1986, that he knew nothing about one of the major shipments of missiles to Iran at the time it occurred a year earlier. At the Iran-contra hearings in 1987, he testified the exact opposite—that he was intimately involved in the deal—but this was under a grant of immunity, so it can't be used against him. Poindexter now doesn't claim he wasn't involved in the 1985 shipments, but he claims he suffered a "memory lapse" when asked about it a year later. Oddly, this "memory lapse" produced the same erroneous details as a false chronology prepared by a group at the NSC, for which North has already been convicted.

The same day as the "memory lapse," Poindexter tore up a document, signed by Reagan, justifying the November 1985 HAWK missile sale as part of a deal for release of the hostages. Poindexter concedes this. His defense is that he tore it up so as not to mislead Congress! It wasn't an arms-for-hostages deal after all, you see. Poindexter "wanted Congress to get accurate information and by golly he delivered accurate information to Congress," says his lawyer. Unfortunately, North, the impresario of the deal, wrote at the time (in a memo that accidentally didn't get destroyed), "120 HAWKS = 1) 5 Amcits; 2) Guarantee no more." Amcits is North-speak for American citizens. "Guarantee no more" meant no more hostages would be taken. The Iranians ratted on both parts of the deal.

The other major accusation is that Poindexter lied when he wrote to three congressional committees in July 1986 that the NSC was obeying "the spirit and the letter" of the Boland Amendment, which banned support for the contras. Poindexter's defense is that the Boland Amendment didn't apply to the NSC; therefore the NSC was obeying its "spirit and letter" by ignoring it. There is an argument—unconvincing, but at least serious—that the Boland Amendment was so badly worded that it did leave the NSC off the hook, though its obvious purpose was to cut off the contras completely. There is even an argument—also unconvincing but serious—that the Boland Amendment was unconstitutional. There is no serious argument that Poindexter was not trying to deceive Congress when he wrote that letter. He wanted legislators to think that the contras had been cut off, not that he'd found a scintillating new legal theory. They would have rewritten the law in five minutes if they'd known this was how the administration interpreted it.

Only a "sparse crowd," says *The Washington Post,* attended the first public airing of Reagan's taped testimony in the Poindexter trial. He duly played his part in the round-robin by declaring that the entire Iran-contra affair "was a covert action that was taken at my behest." That was no damaging confession since, he insisted, the arms sale was not a swap for hostages; it involved Iranian "moderates" unconnected to Khomeini; no one lied to Congress; Eugene Hasenfus, the operative whose capture by the Nicaraguans began the unraveling of the secret contra war, was just a private citizen; and so on—all matters long ago proved false.

The consensus of those who paid any attention to Reagan's amazing recital was: "Poor fellow, he's finally losing it." But Reagan's convenient senility is contagious—it has infected all the principal Iran-contra players at various points. In fact, it has now struck the entire nation. Is "Khashoggi" a person or a type of missile? What was all that about the cake? Who was Elliott Abrams again?

And thus they've gotten away with it. Right before our eyes.

Regrets Only

(*The New Republic*, APRIL 30, 1990)

Although I have no special desire to be governor of Texas, and would actively prefer *not* to become head of the Office of Thrift Supervision (the poor soul charged with cleaning up the savings and loan mess), the traumas of aspirants to these posts in recent days compel me to make the following statement. It has been cleared with political consultants of both parties.

Like many members of my generation—Senator Al Gore and Representative Newt Gingrich, to name but two—I too have experimented with marijuana in the distant past.

It was in a party situation during my freshman year in college. Someone handed me a marijuana cigarette and I took a puff. Maybe two. I deeply regret this youthful indiscretion. I found the drug had no effect on me whatsoever, and I determined not to experiment with illicit substances any further. Instead, I got throwing-up drunk in a manner more suited to one with aspirations toward a leadership role in this great country of ours.

However, a few days later I experimented with marijuana once again. On that occasion I enjoyed it a good deal more. This youthful indiscretion I also deeply regret. During the next several years, overcome by the spirit of scientific inquiry, I experimented with marijuana perhaps two hundred or more times. I am not sure of the exact number, but I do know that I deeply, deeply regret all of these youthful indiscretions.

As a law school student in the mid-1970s, I continued to conduct occasional experiments with marijuana—heedless of the baleful influence this apparently was having on impressionable members of the faculty such as Professor (later Judge) Douglas Ginsburg. Years afterward, in 1987, Ginsburg lost his chance to become a Supreme Court justice after it was revealed that he had smoked pot while teaching at that very law school. Although my law school experiments were few in number, I deeply regret each one of them.

Unlike the string of prominent Americans who have come forward lately to confess their dope experiences, I cannot pinpoint with the same remarkable clarity the last time I experimented with marijuana. Specifically, I cannot guarantee that it was in the "distant" past. All I can say for sure is that it was in the past, somewhat distant, that it was an indiscretion, somewhat less youthful, and that I deeply regret it.

These days my drug of choice is decaf. I drink it to forget. Knocks me right out. But if, perchance, I find myself experimenting with marijuana on some future occasion—which I won't until the law, or at least the zeitgeist, has changed; but if that should ever happen—it will be an elderly indiscretion, which I regret all the same. Deeply.

The 1960s are said to have been a period of cultural revolution, with marijuana playing a big part. Surely, though, the lesson we are learning as more and more prominent people come forward with tales of their "experiments" with marijuana is how little effect it all really had on the culture. The fact that nerds like Douglas Ginsburg (yes, or the author of this column), slick goody-goodies like Al Gore, and fast operators like Newt Gingrich all smoked dope shows both how widespread the phenomenon was and how little it mattered.

How little it mattered is a rebuke to marijuana's fans as well as its foes. Pot didn't stop Ginsburg from becoming a right-wing legal scholar or Gingrich from becoming House Republican whip, which is hardly what Flower Power was supposed to lead to. On the other hand, it didn't leave Timothy Ryan unwilling or unable to tackle the S&L catastrophe. (Most people would have to be stoned to even consider taking on that assignment.) The Great Pot Experiment of the 1960s and 1970s produced millions of conventional, productive, upstanding citizens, plus a few journalists.

After Ginsburg fell, a lawyer friend of mine expressed dismay that "the only members of our generation who will get to run the country will be sanctimonious liars." I reassured him that this is true of every generation. But it appears now that Ginsburg was an aberration, a victim of temporary cultural confusion: On the marijuana question, out-and-out lying may not be necessary. Both President Bush and drug czar William Bennett have agreed that past pot-smoking should not disqualify someone from future high office. The revelation simply needs to contain the right ingredients: experiment . . . distant past . . . party situation . . . like many members of generation . . . youthful indiscretion . . . deeply regret. . . .

Where is the line between youthful indiscretion and adult depravity? Is it about age twenty-one? If so, the evolving standard about marijuana use is in odd contrast to the standard of recent years about alcohol consumption. Under the influence of Mothers Against Drunk Driving, the federal government has pressured the states into raising the drinking age from eighteen to twenty-one. In America, it seems, it's morally and politically acceptable to be stoned as a minor or drunk as an adult, but not the other way around.

Of course that's not really true. You can't be excused for "experimenting" with marijuana as a college kid today—only twenty years ago. Czar Bennett would like to take away the scholarships of students caught using marijuana. Massachusetts Attorney General James Shannon, age thirty-seven, recently made the boilerplate confession about past "experimentation," but now favors mandatory prison time for even casual users caught twice. He says that his attitude has now changed. Well, as the Church Lady says on *Saturday Night Live* . . . How *convenient*.

What has really changed since twenty years ago except for the fact that those who were breaking the law then are making the laws now? Marijuana was just as illegal back then as it is today. And there have been no dramatic discoveries about any harmful effects of using it casually. All that has changed is the zeitgeist. Yet young lives will be ruined while older lives proceed unmolested along their placid course.

All these ex-Communist-style confessions-cum-recantations about past drug use leave a bad taste in my mouth. What I'm waiting for is some politician to announce that he used to indulge in marijuana every now and then and that—whatever he thinks about more serious drug problems—he *doesn't* especially regret it. Maybe even that what he really regrets is all the experiments he *didn't* conduct in his youth, perhaps because he was too busy plotting his scramble up the establishment heights. To have used marijuana in the 1960s and 1970s, when everyone was supposed to use marijuana, and to deplore marijuana in the 1980s and 1990s, when everyone is supposed to deplore it, is just a bit too unsurprising.

Sour Milken

(*The New Republic*, MAY 21, 1990)

But . . . *it came to be said of him that he had been more sinned against than sinning; and that, but for the jealousy of the old stagers in the mercantile world, he would have done very wonderful things.*

Those words dispatch the great crooked financier Augustus Melmotte in Trollope's 1874 novel *The Way We Live Now*. The same is being said about the greatest real-life crooked financier of our own day, Michael Milken: that he was a brilliant innovator done in by the envy of lesser mortals and older money. The most hysterical (in both senses) reaction to Milken's guilty plea came from Evans and Novak: "His surrender suggests that in its judicial handling of individuals, the United States is running counter to the worldwide trend toward freedom."

Yet one of Milken's most ardent defenders in the past, newspaper magnate Ralph Ingersoll II, has turned oddly silent. When Milken was indicted last year, Ingersoll praised him as a hero on *Nightline* and said the prosecution was "as revolting as . . . the McCarthy hearings." Ingersoll and others signed a newspaper headlined MIKE MILKEN, WE BELIEVE IN YOU: "Mike cares about people. . . . Mike has always performed according to the highest standards of professionalism, honesty, integrity and ethical conduct."

"Mike" helped Ingersoll to raise $500 million in junk bonds (or, if you prefer, "high-yield, fixed-return securities"), which he used to buy up newspaper companies, often at startlingly high prices. Now the revenues from the newspapers don't begin to cover the interest payments, and Ingersoll is sleazily offering to buy back his debts for as little as twenty-eight cents on the dollar. William Farley, another former loudmouth about the virtues of risk, debt, and Michael Milken, has defaulted on $1.5 billion of bonds he used to overpay for companies.

The case against the case against Michael Milken has three parts. One, his crimes were "technical," not serious. Two, they were a minor sideshow, unrelated to his real work, which was the creation of the junk bond market. Three, Milken's junk bonds served America by enabling small, risky companies to raise capital and create jobs; and by financing the takeover movement that forced big corporations to become more efficient.

The word "technical" can mean two different things here (as noted by Professor Ronald Gilson of Stanford Law School). Most of the crimes Milken pled guilty to are arguably "technical" in the sense that they were violations of rules designed to assure an orderly and fair financial marketplace. These rules, by their nature, are somewhat arbitrary—like the 55-mile-per-hour speed limit—and the behavior they outlaw might not otherwise seem obviously immoral. But the laws Milken has admitted breaking are not "technical" in the sense that they were broken unintentionally, by stepping slightly over a fuzzy line. He knew he was breaking important laws. And in a couple of cases—helping an associate to arrange a phony tax loss, and "point shaving" (essentially, ripping off customers by tiny fractions that add up to big money)—the inherent rights and wrongs are not even ambiguous.

So why did he do it, when he was making hundreds of millions of dollars legally? The answer, I think, is that the manipulative shenanigans were not just a sideshow. The exchange of favors—buy this troubled bond for me, and I'll buy a bond or do something else for you—was part of his modus operandi. It's just that many of the favors were illegal. Those who wish to blame the government's removal of Milken for the collapse of the junk bond market are not completely wrong. It required a master juggler to keep all those balls in the air.

Thus to question three: How wonderful were junk bonds? Only about half went to finance those little entrepreneurial companies that were deemed too risky to float a traditional bond. And even much of this money was spent, as Ingersoll spent most of his, buying established operations rather than creating new ones.

Although the bondholders were paid high interest to compensate them for the extra risk, it's clear in retrospect (and not very long retrospect: reality has struck within a year) that the risk was often wildly underestimated. Sometimes, as in the case of the savings and loans that bought 7 percent of junk bonds, buyers were numb to the risk because they were essentially protected from it by federal deposit insurance. Sometimes Milken's own juggling kept buyers buying despite the risk. Mostly, though, it was just the willing suspension of disbelief.

Whatever the reason, it was too easy. Many of those spunky little companies that couldn't get financing in the bad old days shouldn't have gotten financing after all. Today the average junk bond trades at about 75 percent of its face value, reflecting an assumption that it has a one-in-four chance of going bust. No one figured on that.

About half of all junk bonds financed takeovers of larger companies or restructurings to ward off takeovers. By replacing equity with debt (borrowing money to buy shares), they turned companies that weren't inherently risky into companies that were. Companies like Southland (7-Eleven stores), J. P. Stevens, and maybe even Milken's Drexel Burnham Lambert itself wouldn't have gotten into trouble if they didn't have huge interest payments to pay (instead of optional dividends).

Did the takeover movement make corporate America more efficient? This was always a bolder claim than many of its proponents realized. If the huge premiums that takeover artists offered for company shares reflected genuine improvements they could make in corporate management, this is a devastating indictment of American capitalism. Widespread public share ownership, a professional management class, the stock market—pillars of our economic system—topple under the weight of this argument, if true.

It is true, to some extent. But as takeover frenzy spread, speculative fever and too-easy access to financing became better explanations of the prices being offered. Milken's contribution was to greatly increase the proportion of unproductive paper shuffling in the takeover boom. It's an old story. "There was not one of them," Trollope writes of Melmotte's business colleagues "who had not . . . been given to understand that his fortune was to be made, not by the construction of the railway but by the floating of the railway shares."

WHERE ARE THEY NOW?

(*The New Republic*, JUNE 11, 1990)

"Democrats buy, Republicans rent" used to be the maxim of the Washington real estate market—meaning that Republicans served their terms in Washington and then went back to the real America, whereas Democrats, with their commitment to Big Government, put down roots in the capital. Everyone knows that hasn't been true for decades, but conservatives still make a big noise about their alleged distaste for Washington: its isolation, its elitism, its reliance on the public sector and estrangement from the productive economy.

No politician played on this kind of anti-Washington imagery more successfully than Ronald Reagan (although Jimmy Carter tried). In Reagan's own mind, his administration was probably some Jeffersonian dreamworld of hardy yeomen who had reluctantly set down their plows for a brief term of government service before returning to the land that had nurtured their fine American values.

In fact, the Reaganites are already just another layer of sediment in the geology of Washington. At law firms, lobbying outfits, think tanks, and expense-account restaurants, the Reagan people have sprinkled down and settled in on top of the Carterites, Nixonites, New Frontier, and Great Society types, and so on back to a few remaining New Dealers.

Do you doubt it? Let's put the proposition to a test. In May 1985— the high noon of Reaganism, after the triumphal reelection, before Iran-contra—*National Journal* published its quadrennial special issue purporting to identify the top "decision makers" of the Reagan administration. From this source, a crack *New Republic* research team (Dan Gross) compiled a roster of 102 top officials: all those listed from the White House, the National Security Council, the Office of Management and Budget, etc., plus the 13 Cabinet officers and heads of 34 executive, independent, and regulatory agencies.

How many of them were in Washington before morning arrived in America with Reagan in 1980? How many are still here now? Four of the 102 have died, leaving 98 in our semiscientific sample. Of these, by my count, 40 were in Washington before the Reagan administration and are still here; 9 were in Washington beforehand but are now gone; 23 came from elsewhere and stuck around; and 26 came from elsewhere and left.

Instant analysis: Exactly half (49) of Reagan's top appointees at the zenith of his reign came from the permanent Washington establishment, while half were hardy yeomen tilling the soil at places like Merrill Lynch in New York (staff chief Donald Regan . . . still here). Of the Washingtonians, I spotted only one—communications Director Patrick Buchanan—who is a genuine native. The rest were capital arrivistes at some point in their careers. Of the ones who came from outside Washington, slightly more left after the party (26) than stuck around (23). But in all, 63 of our Reaganites are still in Washington, while only 35 have made new lives or resumed old ones outside the Beltway. That's almost two-to-one.

Sixteen of those who are still in Washington are working for the Bush administration, including the president himself. So they are still in public service. That's a mitigating factor for those who see the Washington Problem as one of a leech culture on the rest of the country, but not for those who see the Washington Problem as one of a permanent governing class.

On the other hand, many of those who have left Washington physically haven't really left it spiritually. Five are ambassadors. At least one is back in his home state running for Congress in order to get back here. Those who left did not necessarily go back where they came from. Several—such as David Stockman, a representative from western Michigan before becoming budget director—have moved on to New York. Some might see that kind of movement as a natural progression of elitism, rather than a reassuring populist ebb and flow.

Few of the Reagan 98, whether in Washington or elsewhere, have returned to anything Thomas Jefferson would recognize as the private sector. They are regulatory lawyers or fellows somewhere or in "government affairs" at large corporations. An astonishing number now identify themselves as "consultant," a term that covers a variety of sins. Secretary of Agriculture John Block actually *was* a farmer in Illinois when he was appointed in 1981. Now he is president of the National American Wholesale Grocers' Association in Falls Church, Virginia (that's inside the Beltway).

Bud McFarlane is still here as a "consultant." Years ago, shortly after *Washington Post* reporter Janet Cooke was exposed as a fraud and lost her Pulitzer Prize, I heard a fellow journalist express her impassioned affront at having run into Cooke at the local Safeway. A clot of colleagues agreed that the miscreant's very presence in town was an outrage. Apparently the notion was that anyone so deeply disgraced should be physically banished as well. This struck me at the time as a parochial attitude that you wouldn't find in, say, New York.

But isn't it time for everyone to give up this tiresome conceit that there's something immoral about living and working in Washington? The editors of *The Wall Street Journal* were at it again the other day, using a marketing study showing that Washingtonians prefer tennis and gourmet cooking to hunting and "tinker[ing] with the Chevy" as an occasion to sneer about "an elite culture, a sort of American royal court divorced from the common tastes." Maybe I'm going out on a limb here, but how much bowling, Bible reading, and tabaccy chawing do you suppose goes on among editorial writers of *The Wall Street Journal*?

The draw of provincials to the capital city, and their self-reinvention as metropolitan sophisticates, is a constant in all nations. Unlike, say, Britain and France, the United States has different capitals for government and business, with cultural leadership split between the business capital and a third city, L.A. That impoverishes life in Washington, but it's probably good for the country.

In terms of cultural isolation, New York is far worse off than Washington. The texture of life in Washington—how you get to work, how you do your laundry, what you do on weekends—is more or less like the texture of middle-class life in the rest of the country. In New York, these day-to-day details are completely different.

Unlike New York and Los Angeles, Washington at least worries about what the rest of the country is thinking, and tortures itself about being out of touch. And Washington—like New York and Los Angeles, but unlike other places in America—is nourished by a constant stream of new arrivals from everywhere else in the country. If most of them don't go back, is that so awful?

THE CORN IS GREEN

(*The New Republic*, JUNE 18, 1990)

On Sunday morning, when they ought to be in church, many Americans are worshiping at the shrine of Public Affairs, watching the TV interview shows. A strange subgenre of advertising has evolved to service these shows, in which corporations tout their patriotism rather than their products. We learn how General Electric brought freedom to Eastern Europe, how Merrill Lynch is enriching the nation, and so on.

But Sunday morning is dominated by a mysterious company that is virtually unknown for anything *except* its public affairs commercials: Archer Daniels Midland ("supermarket to the world"). ADM's only other claim to fame is its chairman, Dwayne Andreas, who is notorious for his large campaign contributions to both parties (Bush *and* Dukakis in the last presidential election), and for running a resort in Florida where Bob and Elizabeth Dole, Tip O'Neill, and Robert Strauss own units.

On a typical recent Sunday, May 27, ADM had five different ads running in various combinations on all three network shows: ABC's *This Week with David Brinkley*, NBC's *Meet the Press*, and CBS's *Face the Nation*. (Brinkley is another resident of Andreas's Florida resort.) The ADM ads are like *Twin Peaks:* Lavishly produced and full of plot, they convey an ominous feeling that something is going on, without any clear sense of what that might be. I can't begin to explain *Twin Peaks*, but the comically deceptive ADM commercials are not all that hard to decode. Prizes are hereby awarded in the following categories:

Most offensive. This one begins with a clip of JFK proclaiming, "Ask not what your country can do for you," and goes on to declare—in one of those warm, gravelly voices corporations choose to impersonate themselves—"At the Archer Daniels Midland Company, history has taught us that doing what's good for our country can also be good for business." ADM's main line of business is refining corn into high-fructose corn sweetener and ethanol, a gasoline additive. Both products depend on massive government subsidies and trade protection. There is probably no company in America where the question "what your country can do for you" is asked more often or answered more successfully.

Most dishonest. A man is climbing an ever-steeper staircase. Each step represents the number of minutes the average citizen of a particular country has to work to afford a pound of sugar—ranging from the United States (little bump) at 1.47 to China (sheer cliff face) at 74. The point is supposed to be that America is blessed with cheap sugar. The purpose is to quell any doubts about the government's insane sugar price support program.

What's wonderful is that ADM *doesn't make sugar!* Its interest in sugar price supports is solely as maker of a rival product, corn sweetener for food and soft drinks, which would have no market if sugar could be sold here at the world price. Artificially high sugar prices, maintained by quotas on foreign sugar, cost consumers more than $3 billion a year. The quotas are devastating to emerging democracies such as the Philippines, far outweighing what we give in foreign aid.

Obviously, the fact that the average Chinese must work fifty times longer for a pound of sugar than the average American has almost nothing to do with the price of sugar and everything to do with relative national wealth. The average Chinese must work longer for *everything* because the average Chinese is paid so little. In fact, America's GDP per capita is *fifty-eight* times that of China, making sugar look like a relative bargain for the Chinese.

(Another ADM ad on the sugar theme, slightly less deceptive, merely notes that American sugar is—slightly—cheaper in absolute terms than sugar in other advanced countries such as France and Germany. That just demonstrates that we're not the only fools in the world. It certainly does *not* demonstrate that, as the ad puts it, sugar is "a sweet deal for everyone." It's a sweet deal for the average American sugarcane farmer, who makes a quarter of a million dollars from the sugar program, and for ADM, which makes millions. It's a big rip-off for the rest of us.)

Most cloying. A woman pulls up at the gas pump and, in a voice-over while filling up, expresses her joy over ethanol. "Now that pure grain ethanol has replaced lead in gas, the air's a lot cleaner for everyone, especially kids." Actually, of course, the air is exactly the same amount cleaner for kids as for adults. That's one of the things about air. And a recent study—controverted, to be sure—says that ethanol cuts carbon monoxide but *increases* nitrogen oxides and hydrocarbons, for a net increase in smog.

Gasoline using ethanol gets an exemption of six cents a gallon from the federal gas tax. Since ethanol is only one tenth of the combined product, this amounts to a whopping sixty-cents-a-gallon subsidy for ethanol itself, which otherwise would be uncompetitive. Including state tax breaks, the total government subsidy for ethanol since 1980 has been $4.6 billion. The government gave lavish tax credits and loan guarantees for construction of ethanol plants, and even has given free surplus corn to ethanol producers. ADM has three quarters of the ethanol market. Thanks to ethanol, says the ad, "we don't need as much foreign oil." In fact, it takes more energy to produce the corn and turn it into ethanol than the ethanol itself replaces.

Most mysterious. A recent addition to the ADM canon is similar in setting—a woman pumping gas into her car—but darker in tone. Remember all that stuff you heard during the last commercial break about how the air is getting cleaner—"especially for kids"? Well, forget it. "Every day there's a grim reminder hanging in the air over our cities, and . . . we all have to be concerned." Gasoline has gotten cleaner? No, "Gasoline has gotten dirtier. The chief culprit is benzene, a known deadly carcinogen." Poisonous gasoline vapors are threatening—yes—the children (shown tucked in sweet unknowing innocence in the backseat).

What to do? ADM recommends a procedure for pumping gas just short of the precautions you might take for changing the rods in a nuclear power plant. "Keep all of your car windows rolled up, so that the fumes can't get inside. Stand upwind or away from the nozzle. And if you get gas on your hands, be sure to wash it off. This message is brought to you in the interest of a cleaner, safer environment by the Archer Daniels Midland Company."

How thoughtful. But why this sudden concern about benzene? I looked up a *Washington Post* article referred to in the commercial and, unsurprisingly, it turned out that benzene and ethanol are competing additives for meeting clean air standards. All the horrorshow about standing upwind is just part of a campaign to get benzene banned or ethanol made mandatory. Maybe they're even right about benzene, but it's typical of the ADM method—and certainly gives you no confidence in their position—that they would approach the issue so obliquely.

You can almost count on any bit of ADM civic braggadocio to turn out to be dubious. So I was more pleased than shocked to learn that ADM's much-self-touted cornstarch additive for plastics—the one that supposedly causes them to decompose quicker in landfill—is widely considered pointless by environmentalists. It turns pieces of plastic into plastic powder. Maybe the high-fiber, low-fat, cholesterol-free vegetarian patty promoted in yet another ad is actually the boon to humankind ADM claims. But, knowing ADM, you have to wonder what's the catch.

Is Bush Nice?

(*Time*, JULY 16, 1990)*

George Bush seems like a hard man not to like. But some of us are up to the challenge. It's not a question of disagreeing with his policies, or despairing of his "vision," or worrying about his "timidity"—the usual charges. A few people retain what the president himself has called "this fantastically, diabolically anti-me" attitude. They dislike him personally.

When Bush is still remarkably high in the polls, this demands an explanation. The president's popularity is partly owing to the stream of good news on the economic and international fronts. But since he has barely even tried to put his personal stamp on these happy developments, credit must also go in large part to Bush's personality. He strikes people as a nice guy. Compared with Jimmy Carter (and, goodness knows, Michael Dukakis), he seems loose and human. Compared even with the saintly Ronald Reagan, he seems genuine, off the pedestal, really there. You can take him anywhere.

But is he nice? There are scattered reports that he can actually be testy and thin-skinned in private. But let's ignore these and stipulate that George Bush is a pleasant person and, more than that, genuinely decent in his personal dealings. There is a difference between that kind of niceness and decency on the public stage. Bush has perfected the art of substituting the one for the other.

In the current condition of our politics, of course, it's hard to make judgments from afar even about personality, let alone about character. Everything is so contrived. If that charming business a while back about

*Published at the peak of Bush's popularity, this piece was originally titled (by the editors at Time) "Is Bush Nice? A Contrarian View."

hating broccoli wasn't the result of extensive focus-group testing, it might as well have been. Bush is smart enough to know it would play well. And we do know that he exaggerates things, like his love of country music. (The Bushes actually also listen to classical in the White House.) Ironically, Bush wins points for genuineness, even with cynics like me, for the hints of self-awareness he's always dropping about the stage show he's putting on.

Yet, for one thing, Bush's facile ability and his willingness to switch off his niceness when convenient make you wonder how genuine it is. No one would have accused him of excessive niceness during the 1988 campaign, when he was more concerned with appearing tough. A really nice person doesn't stop being nice when it's inconvenient. More recently, about the budget deficit, there was this classic Bushism: "People understand that Congress bears a greater responsibility for this. But I'm not trying to assign blame." He's nice enough not to want to be associated with a nasty remark but not nice enough not to make it. Lacking the courage of one's nastiness does not make one nice.

Then there is what might be called Bush's lack of moral imagination and empathy. After the massacre in Tiananmen Square, he said, "This is not the time for an emotional response." In this case and others, like Lithuania, there have been realpolitik reasons—perhaps sufficient reasons—for not cutting off the offending regime. But Bush's repeated cool response to distant suffering and struggles gives the impression that at some level he just doesn't get it. He may give his coat to a beggar on the street—noblesse oblige—but his sleep is not disturbed by things he can't see.

In fact, Bush's personal friendliness seems to cut against this kind of moral empathy. He seems more concerned with not hurting the feelings of people he's met, like Deng Xiaoping, than about the fate of people he hasn't.

Something similar is at work on the domestic side. You don't have to be a big-spending, social-welfare liberal to qualify as a nice guy. But a certain level of indifference disqualifies you. Take one small example: measles. This disease, which was virtually wiped out in the United States in the early 1980s, is killing children again, in part because the government vaccination program has run out of money. In the richest nation in the world, children are dying from measles because society won't fork out enough for shots! We're talking a few million dollars.

Perhaps Bush didn't know about this until it was reported in *The New York Times*. It's a big bureaucracy. But, at that point, why didn't he pick up a phone and find out what the hell was going on? What else is the point of being nice and being President at the same time? That's what LBJ would have done—not a nice person, affabilitywise, but someone who connected his private heart and his public role in more than just talk.

What is least nice about George Bush as a public man is precisely his hypocrisy about the connection between alleged belief and action. Campaigning for President, he said, "We . . . need to assure that women do not have to worry about getting their jobs back after having a child or caring for a child during a serious illness. This is what I mean when I talk about a gentler nation . . . It's not right, and we've got to do something about it." Now he's vetoed the Parental and Medical Leave Bill, passed by both houses of Congress, on the grounds that the government should stay out of such matters. That's not what he was trying to imply two years ago. Was he lying then? Or just mouthing the words? Or does he see no connection between what he says and what he does?

Intellectual integrity—not saying one thing while meaning or doing another—is central to decency in public life. So is intellectual courage: saying what you honestly think (if there is anything you honestly think), even if it's unpopular. Bush lacks both these qualities.

In sum, Bush is basically a decent man whose decency, unfortunately, is about an eighth of an inch thick; a man whose personal decency masks, rather than enhances, his public role; a good person, if there's no reason not to be, but a sucker for a Faustian bargain. He can be had cheap—political convenience will certainly suffice. And that's not nice at all.

BART FOR PRESIDENT

(*The New Republic*, JULY 23, 1990)

 hy don't I learn? The answers to life's problems aren't at the bottom of a bottle. They're on TV!

—HOMER SIMPSON

A thirty-second spot on ABC's *Roseanne* will cost advertisers $375,000 next year. *Roseanne* is the number one show of the past television season. It's a comedy of lower-middle-class resentment, of a particularly modern kind. The heroine is a woman who struggles to balance the obligations of holding a job and raising a family in a world of sexism, oppressive bosses, dead-end jobs, pinched finances, and other social forces generally unhelpful to people in her position. It's often funny. And whenever I watch, I can't help thinking; If this is the most popular television show in the country, why can't the Democratic party win a national election? What has Hollywood figured out that the Democrats haven't?

I think something similar while watching *The Simpsons*, the fantastic cartoon family show on the Fox network, which has become a national obsession since its debut last January. In a typical recent week, *Roseanne* and *The Simpsons* were ranked first and second among women ages eighteen to forty-nine. Among men in that demographically desirable group, *The Simpsons* was number one. *Roseanne*, feminist tilt and all, was in sixth place with the boys, just ahead of two NBA playoff games.

Drug czar William Bennett, looking for another publicity hit, recently took on Bart, the bratty ten-year-old Simpson son. Spying a Bart poster at a drug rehabilitation center, Bennett scolded, "You guys aren't watching *The Simpsons*, are you? That's not going to help you." Apparently Bennett was taking his cue from a few humorless educators who have objected to a popular Bart Simpson T-shirt declaring, UNDERACHIEVER AND PROUD OF IT. The czar beat a hasty retreat when the entire country responded as one with another Bartism: "Don't have a cow, man." He claimed he'd never actually seen the show and had nothing against it.

However, Bennett's dismay, whether feigned or sincere, was justified. *The Simpsons* is no threat to drug rehabilitation. But, like *Roseanne*, it is a direct challenge to Republican claims to be the party that is addressing middle-American values and concerns. The Simpson family seems a bit better off than the Conners of *Roseanne*—the cartoon Marge Simpson doesn't work, an option not available to her all-too-fleshly sister, Roseanne Conner—but the Simpsons, too, suffer from economic and spiritual alienation, not to mention an environment ravaged by nuclear and toxic wastes.

Ever since Ginger Rogers's mother complained to the House Un-American Activities Committee that a movie featuring her daughter had contained the line "Share and share alike—that's democracy," right-wingers have worried that Hollywood lefties are infecting innocent audience minds with progressive notions. A recent newsletter from something called the Media Research Center reviews another successful sitcom, *Designing Women* (CBS). In one particular episode, the reviewer notes with distress, the characters "become union advocates after witnessing terrible working conditions at a curtain factory. . . . Conveniently ignored: mandatory union dues and membership, other approaches to solving labor problems, and American unions' long-standing track record of helping liberal Democrats and liberal causes." A disgraceful artistic lapse, to be sure.

But advertisers aren't paying $375,000 for thirty seconds to finance the spread of left-wing agitprop. They're paying because people are watching. The producers and writers of *Roseanne* and *The Simpsons*—though possibly Democrats and certainly not devoid of artistic ambition—are creatures of commerce as well. If their shows have a liberal slant, which they do, it's obviously a slant they think—correctly—will sell.

It's puzzling, therefore, that liberal politics can't sell. Even more puzzling: Hollywood's growing influence on the Democratic party is widely believed to hurt the party in its efforts to reclaim the middle-American "silent majority" that has been going Republican since Nixon. In their overt politics, Hollywood liberals are more interested in El Salvador and tropical rain forests than in the meat-and-potatoes concerns of traditional Democratic constituencies. Yet in its commercial life, Hollywood is brilliant at appealing to these very constituencies on liberalish themes.

Roseanne and *The Simpsons* both celebrate "family values," but with a left-wing twist: the family as a haven from the cruelties of the economic marketplace, and as threatened by those same economic forces. Roseanne loses her job when she won't work overtime on the weekend. She is reduced to selling magazines by telephone. (To one prospect: "Well, I'm not interested either, but it's my job.") Up for a position as secretary to some deskbound big shot (alienated personnel director, a black woman: "the man doesn't even need a secretary, he doesn't do anything"), she's disqualified because she doesn't know how to use a computer. Homer Simpson, meanwhile, loses his job at the nuclear plant but despairs of qualifying for one at the toxic waste dump: "I'm not a supervising technician, I'm a technical supervisor!"

Roseanne and Homer are obviously heirs of Ralph Kramden and Archie Bunker. But the American Everyman has changed, and not just because one of them is a woman. For one thing, compared with their TV ancestors, the Simpsons and the Conners are well off. They live in nice houses, unlike Ralph and Alice Kramden's stark walk-up flat. Homer Simpson wears a tie to work. Dan Conner is some kind of independent construction contractor. In short, they are not your traditional "working class." They are the new middle class, making a good living during good times at postindustrial sorts of jobs, but obsessed with what the social critic Barbara Ehrenreich calls "fear of falling." It is this sense of the precariousness of middle-class life—fed by two decades of stagnant median family income—that the Democratic party has spectacularly failed to tap.

Then there's Bart. He's not a bad kid, merely an independent spirit. That makes him genuinely dangerous. We cheer when he cheats on an IQ test, because the teacher has explained: This won't affect your grade in class; it will merely determine your fate for the rest of your life. "How important is it to be popular?" he asks his father. "I'm glad you asked, son," says the hapless Homer. "Being popular is the most important thing in the world." Of course the point of the episode is to teach the opposite lesson. And by pursuing his own independent course, true to his ideals, Bart now is even more popular than Mr. Popularity-Above-All, George Bush. Which is a lot more than any flesh-and-blood Democrat can claim.

FEAR OF CHANGE

(The New Republic, JULY 30, 1990)

Is the United States still a great nation, capable of facing unafraid the challenges of the future? Or are we paralyzed by fear of change and capable only of wallowing in nostalgia for past greatness? Declinists might take as two small bits of evidence for their side of this argument the penny and the dollar bill. American coinage and currency have become ridiculous. A dollar is barely worth what a quarter was twenty years ago. At an average worker's wage, the time it takes to pick up a penny on the sidewalk is more than a penny is worth. Yet the U.S. Mint will manufacture almost thirteen billion of these items in 1990. You have to whip out your wallet to buy a ride on most public transit systems, and the machine designed to take your paper money, if it exists, is probably broken. We have forgotten the pleasure of walking around with the weight of real, valuable "walking around" money jingling in our pockets.

Other nations have come to grips with past inflation and redignified their money. In Britain and France, the highest-value coin is worth about $1.70. In Germany and Japan, it's about $3. The smallest British bill is now a £5 note, worth about $8. Japan's smallest note, 1,000 yen, is worth about $6.60. Canada eliminated the dollar bill last year.

A great nation makes national policy decisions based on the interests of society as a whole. A nation past its days of greatness is a cacophony of self-protective interest groups. There is legislation before Congress to replace the dollar bill with a coin and eliminate the penny. Leading the charge for currency reform is the Coin Coalition, dominated by vending machine interests. Leading the opposition is Americans for Common Cents, a front for the zinc lobby. Today's pennies are 97 percent zinc. Ironically, copper interests favor currency reform. They hope that a dollar coin will contain copper, as pennies no longer do. Opponents, by contrast, claim the support of the Industry Council for Tangible Assets (whatever that is), the Professional Numismatics Guild, and the Bowie Coin Club.

As is standard in this sort of legislative battle, both sides assert a touching concern for disadvantaged groups. The Coin Coalition notes that a dollar coin "would be a boon to the visually impaired." Americans for Common Cents counters that eliminating the penny would harm "those with incomes under $10,000, non-whites, and Hispanics, and those adults with less than twelve years of education." Offered in support of this proposition is a study by an economics professor at Penn State University. Using an elaborate computer simulation, he concludes that even if the law requires rounding cash transactions up or down to the nearest nickel, the rounding will be up an average of 70 percent of the time. Further research demonstrates that the aforesaid disfavored groups are more likely to do business in cash. QED.

On the other hand, the Coin Coalition offers evidence (in the form of a "Dear Abby" column) that the proliferation of near-worthless pennies is a threat to the health of household pets, who swallow them and develop "vomiting, sudden anemia, and in some cases serious illness and even death" from ingestion of zinc.

The pros flaunt a recent General Accounting Office study that concluded, with comic exactitude, that replacing the dollar bill with a coin would save the federal government $318 million a year. They play down the same study's conclusion that eliminating the penny would lose the government $2 million a year, since pennies still cost less than a cent to produce. Instead, they trumpet a 1987 study by the National Association of Convenience Stores, which figured that eliminating the penny would save two seconds per transaction for its members. Times 10 billion transactions a year, that's 5.5 million hours, or "$22 million in lost productivity."

The economist from Penn State ridicules the idea that clerks "will suddenly be free to stock shelves or clean stores" without the penny to deal with. He notes the cost of training them in the intricacies of rounding up and down. And he asserts that the inflationary effect of the "rounding up" could eventually increase cost-of-living adjustments by as much as $1.5 billion a year. That wins the prize for the largest number either side has been able to throw around so far.

Then there is the vexing and subtle issue of cash register drawers. Most have five coin compartments. The GAO notes that this should allow for a dollar coin without the need to eliminate pennies. True, some stores now use the fifth compartment for rolled coins. But this, the agency notes puritanically, "is not advisable due to the weight this imposes on open cash register drawers." Could the rolled coins go into the space now reserved for dollar bills? Only if such bills are eliminated, and if the Coin Coalition is thwarted in its design to reintroduce the two-dollar bill. And what about checks and Food Stamps? To the judicious mind, neither side has morality totally on its side in the cash register aspect of the controversy. There is much to be said for both points of view.

No one would ever design a coinage and currency system like the one inflation has bequeathed us. For all the studies one way and another, there can't be any serious question that eliminating the penny and moving to a dollar coin would be efficient. The question is whether we are too backward-looking to take the step forward.

The government is traumatized by the failure of the Susan B. Anthony dollar coin in 1979. But that was badly bungled. Among other problems, the Anthony dollar looked like a quarter. The GAO believes the key failure was not forcing people to use the coin. The next time, "Congress and the administration must jointly reach, and agree to sustain, an agreement to eliminate the dollar note in the face of negative public reaction." But what would be the point of such antidemocratic fortitude? Why not give people another chance to come to their senses voluntarily? After all, the dollar has lost almost half its value since that last experiment. As a paper currency, it's a joke. As a handsome, weighty coin, it could be great once more.

Here We Go Again

(*The New Republic*, AUGUST 13, 1990)

P resident Bush says he has no idea where David Souter stands on abortion, affirmative action, and the other hot constitutional issues. Seeking a formula that will reassure liberals without alarming conservatives, and vice versa, he said there was no "litmus test," but that his Supreme Court nominee would "interpret the Constitution and not legislate." And thus the Summer Supreme Court Hypocrisy Festival is under way once more. All the players know their parts, but the audience may need help understanding the script. Herewith a handy guide to some of the major buzzwords.

Advice and consent. A "strict construction" (see page 137) of these words would seem to entitle the Senate to a major say in choosing Supreme Court justices. The "original intent" (see page 136) of the Constitution's authors apparently was to compromise between different proposals giving exclusive authority to the Senate and to the president. Yet conservatives generally interpret this phrase to mean that the Senate must approve anyone the president nominates unless he actually can't tie his shoes on the third attempt.

A Supreme Court justice is not a member of the president's team, like a Cabinet officer, and the Senate owes the president's choice no special deference. This is not a recipe for paralysis, as some have charged. It is a recipe for compromise. Clearly, Strict Constructionist Bush made no serious attempt to seek the Senate's "advice" before choosing Souter. That should make its "consent" harder to come by.

Balance. What liberals now claim they want among the nine justices. History does not record any liberal calls for "balance" when the Court was tilted to the left and liberal presidents were doing the appointing.

Conservative. This can mean two things. It can mean a principled belief that unelected judges shouldn't thwart democracy by sticking their own political values into the Constitution. Or it can mean, "Here is a golden opportunity to stick conservative political values into the Constitution. Liberals did it for years—why shouldn't we?" (See "judicial restraint," below.) Liberals like to argue that "conservative" also should mean a reluctance to overturn established precedents. But conservatives are not stupid enough to fall for that.

Election returns. Commentators seem unable to resist Mr. Dooley's hackneyed line, "Th' Supreme Coort follows th'iliction returns"—even though the entire controversy over the Court centers on the fact that it does *not* follow the election returns. Conservatives resent this. However, when liberals choose to mount a campaign against a nominee, conservatives complain about the "politicization" of the judiciary. They've got it backward. The Supreme Court is supposed to be above politics—protecting our constitutional rights against the whims of the majority. Choosing justices, by contrast, is where politics is supposed to come into it.

Fifth Amendment. A perfect example, say conservatives, of a provision the liberals have run wild with, allowing criminals to get off on technicalities. Deplorable, unless the criminal happens to be Oliver North. The North prosecution just got trashed on an exquisite Fifth Amendment technicality by a conservative-tilted federal appeals court panel.

Ideology. Very bad for a judge to have, everyone agrees. (But see "philosophy," page 136.) In announcing Souter, Bush reaffirmed the traditional pretense that he sought "excellence" and that he would never dream of finding out whether a potential justice agreed with him on issues he has long claimed to be vitally important. In fact, judicial selections have become much more ideological. The chance of a Republican president choosing another Brennan, as Eisenhower did, is nil. Fair enough. But this gives the Senate the right to pass judgment on the same basis.

Judicial activism and *judicial restraint.* Conservatives believe that activism is bad and restraint is good. Except that the 1988 Republican platform calls for judges who hold that "the Fourteenth Amendment's protections apply to unborn children," which means judges who ban abortion no matter what the legislature votes. Oh yes, and conservatives think the special-prosecutor law is unconstitutional, and so is affirmative action, and maybe New York City rent control, and so on and so forth.

Litmus tests. Sometimes called "single-issue litmus tests." Bad, very bad. Especially the other side's. While prochoice senators were warning President Bush not to apply a prolife "litmus test" to his nominee, prochoice groups were sending out mass mailings promising to oppose anyone who would vote to reverse *Roe* v. *Wade*.

Philosophy. A good thing to have, as long as it doesn't make you an "ideologue" (see page 135) or suggest that you have "prejudged" anything (see below). There is the germ of a legitimate distinction here, between having a theory of the role of the judiciary (philosophy) and merely being determined to impose your political will (ideology). But usually a "philosophy" is what I have and an "ideology" is what you have.

Original intent. What conservatives say they want judges to follow. Makes it sound simple, which it isn't. What was the original intent of the Framers about how to interpret their original intent?

Prejudge. A very, very bad thing to do, it seems. Preferable: an "open mind." In the Bork episode, Republicans savaged Democrats for having "prejudged" his suitability before the hearings (as if the Republicans hadn't). Then Democrats savaged Bork for having "prejudged" constitutional issues that might come before him on the Court.

The Supreme Court is not a trial court, in which factual evidence must be presented afresh. The whole point of having a judicial "philosophy"—good, remember?—is that it leads you to understandings on specific issues. Abortion, for example, has been the predominant constitutional issue for almost two decades. Anyone who hasn't thought it through and reached a conclusion by now shouldn't be eligible to graduate law school, let alone sit on the Supreme Court. Which leads directly to . . .

Questions on specific issues. Should a Supreme Court nominee have to answer them? Of course. Except for Bush's understandable desire to have it both ways, why should this be a guessing game? That would indeed— as Robert Bork has charged—put a premium on candidates with no record of having thought about the issues they will have to deal with. Nominees shouldn't be expected to answer an endless string of hypothetical questions. But on the great constitutional questions—does the Bill of Rights apply to the states?—and on the big 5-4 issues of recent years—abortion, reverse discrimination, flag burning—there's no reason the Senate shouldn't expect an answer and an explanation of how it was derived.

Prochoice. "We must stop any nominee who is not prochoice," says abortion-rights leader Kate Michelman. But you can be prochoice and still think that abortion is not in the Constitution. Indeed, that is what I think. The reaction to last year's *Webster* decision has demonstrated that not only can the political process protect abortion rights, but this can be a great revival issue for liberals (just as *Roe* made abortion a great revival issue for conservatives).

Reverse discrimination. A no-no, needless to say. Conservatives are all for judicial activism when it means judges knocking down affirmative action plans. And yet Bush almost bragged of his intention to take ethnic criteria into account in appointing future Supreme Court justices. Ronald Reagan promised in the 1980 campaign to name the first woman to the Court, and did so. Go figure.

Strict constructionism. The third component of the great conservative judicial trinity, along with "judicial restraint" and "original intent." These values are not always compatible. For example, the First Amendment says: "Congress shall make no law . . . abridging the freedom of speech." A strict construction of those words would lead to a broad, "activist" approach. Yet few self-proclaimed strict constructionists are First Amendment absolutists. Where does Judge Souter stand? The only way to find out is to ask.

You Must Be Very Busy

(*Time*, AUGUST 20, 1990)

It wasn't enough, was it? Millions of Americans are coming to the end of their annual summer vacations. You've enjoyed a couple of weeks off from work—maybe three if you're very lucky. You're right to want more. The American chintziness about vacations is absurd.

In Washington, at least, the easiest way to flatter someone is to say, "You must be very busy." (And the most disconcerting answer is, "No, not really.") It is today's ritualistic form of obeisance. It means, "You must be very important." We've come a long way in the century since Thorstein Veblen wrote about "conspicuous" or even "honorific leisure" as a way of displaying social status. "Gosh, you must have nothing at all to do all day" would not be considered a compliment.

The equation of busyness with importance may help to explain Americans' queasiness about vacations. *The Washington Post* reports that two days before Iraq invaded Kuwait, when troops were already massed on the border, someone tried to reach the head of Kuwait's civil defense, only to be told he was on vacation for the next three weeks. Go ahead and laugh. But is that any more absurd than Dan Rather, who was on vacation in France, spending the day of the invasion desperately scouring the Middle East for a place to broadcast from and ultimately settling for London—rather than permitting a war to occur while he was off duty?

Last year I worked for a spell at *The Economist* in London. The attitude there was a revelation. They take pride in their work, and can be as self-important about it as any group of American journalists. But they also take five weeks of vacation every year, plus nearly a week at Easter and nearly two weeks at Christmas when the office is shut, plus the usual holidays. And it would take more than a mere war somewhere to get an *Economist* editor to cancel his or her summer "hol."

American vacations compare poorly with those of most other advanced countries. According to the Bureau of Labor Statistics, the average American full-time worker puts in a 40-hour week, gets 11 official holidays and 12 days—slightly more than two weeks—of paid vacation. That's typically after five years on the job. Among major industrial countries, only the United States doles out vacation time primarily as a reward for seniority rather than as a basic job benefit.

The British on average work 39 hours a week, get 8 paid holidays and enjoy 25 days—5 weeks—of paid vacation a year. The French by law work a standard week of 39 hours, have 8 holidays and get 25.5 days of annual vacation. The Germans—the Germans!—work a 38-hour week, get 10 holidays and have 30 days—6 weeks—of paid vacation.

Yes, yes, you say. But what about Japan? As they reluctantly phase out Saturday work, the Japanese are down to an average of 42 hours a week. They are entitled to an average of 16 days of paid vacation, but characteristically use only 9 of them, though the government is urging them to use more. However, the Japanese get another 20 days off a year that are labeled holidays, only 11 of which are national celebrations. The others are, in effect, vacation days bunched at high summer and year's end. In short, although many Japanese still work on Saturday, the typical Japanese worker gets more actual vacation time than the typical American. While the Japanese move toward more days off, the United States is moving toward fewer. The BLS finds, unsurprisingly, that vacation policies tend to be more generous in unionized companies and in manufacturing, both of which are declining.

As they become more affluent, individuals and societies face the same choice. They can enjoy the increased value of their labor in the form of more goods and services, or they can enjoy it in the form of less work. It is humbling, for an American, to note that the war-wrecked societies of Europe and Japan have made their remarkable comeback while devoting an ever greater share of their productivity to "buying" themselves time off. The standard-of-living statistics, which still usually show the United States ahead, do not include the value of an extra two or three weeks of leisure every year.

Of course the notion of a trade-off between productivity and leisure assumes that if people work 50 weeks a year, their output is greater than if they work 46 or 47. For the prototypical assembly-line job, that might be true. But fewer and fewer jobs are like that. For most "brainworker" jobs, there isn't such a clear relation between time put in and what comes out. (Any writer can tell you that.) At some point, the relationship reverses itself. That old businessman's saw, "I can do a year's work in 11 months but not in 12," contains a lot of truth. But who admits, these days, to taking a month off?

At the upper reaches of the American economy, where official vacation time is more generous anyway, there is a lot of "work" that would look like vacations to most people: entertaining clients at golf tournaments, board of directors' meetings at luxury hotels, conventions in Hawaii, conferences of the Trilateral Commission, and so on. Dispensing with a couple of weeks' worth of these frivolities—in favor of real time off—would do the American economy no harm.

On the other hand, time off is not always a function of affluence. Sometimes it takes the unwanted form of unemployment. If we are heading into a recession, it would be more sensible as well as more compassionate for employees to share the reduced available work and increased available leisure, rather than imposing more leisure than anyone wants on an unfortunate few.

One of the most admirable things about Ronald Reagan as president was his freedom from time snobbery. There was a man who didn't worry that his importance was measured by the number of hours or days he spent at his desk. George Bush seems to have inherited the same healthy attitude. (Although he does suffer from a related preppy affectation of taking leisure activities such as games and sports terribly seriously.) Let the nation learn from its leaders.

Law and Order

(*The New Republic*, OCTOBER 1, 1990)

A*merica and the world must support the rule of law. And we will.*
—PRESIDENT BUSH TO A JOINT SESSION OF CONGRESS, SEPTEMBER 11

Kuwait, embarrassingly, was not a democracy or a "free" country, as the term is commonly understood, before August 2, and still won't be one when and if the Emir is restored. Saudi Arabia suffers the same unfortunate defect. So to justify American actions in the Persian Gulf, President Bush cannot call upon the usual rhetoric about democracy and freedom. Instead the reigning concept is "order." Saddam Hussein, he says, has assaulted the "very essence of international order and civilized ideals."

The notion of "order" as a supreme value in the affairs of nations is not universally accepted. In fact, it is at the heart of international law, an area of thought the U.S. government has not had much time for during the past decade. "Order," and the related concept of "sovereignty," assert that the status quo has its own legitimate claims, simply because it is the status quo, and disturbing it risks "chaos"—war, misery, death—as Bush now says.

The Reagan Doctrine was a specific rejection of international law as the illogical elevation of sovereignty over more important values such as democracy and freedom. Why should the forces for good sign a charter of self-abnegation? Legal rules are fine for fishing treaties, but not for more important matters. In Grenada, in Nicaragua, as recently as nine months ago in Panama, the Reagan and Bush administrations gave scant attention to the claims of sovereignty, or of various treaties we have signed promising to eschew force against fellow signatories.

International law can be ambiguous. And even under international law, sovereignty doesn't trump everything. State Department lawyers usually have been able to cobble together some legal rationalization for various American adventures over the decade. But the efforts became more and more halfhearted. By the end, the contradiction could no longer be contained in any gray area. Our assertion of America's right to promote American values by violent means was incompatible with even the least ambitious claims of international law to protect sovereignty and limit the use of force.

Conservative thinkers circled in for the kill. As Daniel Patrick Moynihan writes, with endearing overstatement, in his new book, *On the Law of Nations:* "In the annals of forgetfulness there is nothing quite to compare with the fading from the American mind of the idea of the law of nations."

Yet suddenly, in the Gulf crisis, Bush cannot cite international law often enough. "The occupation of Kuwait is illegal under international law." Iraq is "an outrageous violator of international law." "And so my message to Iraq is . . . 'Adhere to international law.' " The economic sanctions: "International law . . . must be enforced." The hostages: "contrary to international law." Negotiate with Hussein? He "has been so resistant to complying with international law" that there is no point.

International law—it's not just for sissies, anymore. Why the unacknowledged change of heart? International law serves two vital purposes for the United States in this crisis. First, with democracy unavailable, it is a high-minded value we can legitimately claim to be protecting, thereby avoiding undue emphasis on oil and other unromantic and narrowly strategic concerns. Oh sure, a police state like Iraq is worse than a feudal kingdom like Kuwait. But you cannot ask Americans to die for that kind of comparative awfulocracy. Something nobler is required.

Second, the principles and procedures of international law have been essential to gaining the support of the rest of the world. And everyone agrees that gaining the world's support is Bush's greatest triumph.

Robert Bork has written: "The major difficulty with international law is that it converts what are essentially problems of international morality . . . into arguments about law that are largely drained of morality." In fact, this is actually an advantage of all law, not just international law. Even without an automatic enforcement mechanism (international law's obvious defect), it is easier to get people to agree to apply a preexisting set of rules than to agree ad hoc on the moral merits of a particular policy. And even if we disagree on the morality of a specific case, we still share a vested interest in the rule of law generally, which inclines us to follow the rules even when a particular application doesn't suit us.

Furthermore, as Moynihan presciently points out in his book: "Allied and nonaligned nations . . . can far more readily support (or at least accept) American policies if our conduct is seen to be based on law that binds us as well as them." *The New York Times* reports, as if revealing something, that the Bush administration's early resort to the United Nations was a pragmatic decision, "rather than flowing from a set of lofty principles."

That's the point. International law is valuable—useful—even to super-power America.

To take one small example within the large one, there are already disputes about what constitutes "humanitarian" food supplies under the UN embargo of Iraq. To what extent you bend the embargo to alleviate the suffering of innocents is a tough moral question on which reasonable people can surely differ. It is extremely useful for the United States to be able to say, You may not decide this for yourself. Under the law, exceptions are up to the Security Council. That is far easier than stopping each ship for a moral argument.

Is international law more than just a rhetorical convenience? Having sneered at it for a decade, then having found it necessary, will the United States abandon it once again when it ceases to be convenient? This is not merely a hoity-toity question of not wishing one's country to appear hypocritical. Obviously, even the rhetorical usefulness of international law depends on others believing that this time we really mean it.

Really meaning it means giving up our own freedom of action on occasion, and allowing our own case-by-case moral assessments to be constrained by rules that will sometimes strike us as wrong. It means respecting the sovereignty of governments we rightly don't like. It means allowing the judgment of other nations to stay our hand sometimes, even when we think that judgment is mistaken. Law that need not be obeyed if you disagree with it is not law. If we want meaningful international law to be available when we find it useful, we must respect it even when we don't.

Docutrauma

(*The New Republic*, OCTOBER 22, 1990)

It was hard to watch the Civil War series on PBS without thinking, Please, let's not have a war in the Persian Gulf. When I read in *The Washington Post* that local stores had been running out of blank videotape, I figured that Ken Burns's justly hyped documentary had given Saddam Hussein a good three extra months to come to his senses. I hope I'm right.

But there was a second reaction as well. The series would not have been as gripping if it merely portrayed the war as a hell of slaughter. There was also a sense of sharing in an epic drama, a sense that the actual participants on both sides had as well. For most of those who survived—and most did survive—the Civil War was the most important event in their lives. In fact, it was one of the main things that gave their lives meaning. The TV series emphasizes this. Almost its very first lines are a quotation from Oliver Wendell Holmes, Jr.: "We have shared in the incommunicable experience of war. We have felt . . . the passion of life to its top. . . . In our youths, our hearts were touched by fire."

This second reaction—almost of envy for those who lived through the Civil War—also has implications for the current foreign policy debate. Do we, as a nation, need great purposes in the world? Opposition to war in the Persian Gulf has been monopolized by a newly resurgent right-wing isolationism of the pre–World War II variety. Even before August 2, the innate American skepticism of "foreign entanglements" (George Washington) was being exploited by those who oppose not merely bloodshed but any "extranational ideal" such as promoting democracy or ending hunger that "treats our Republic as a means to some larger end" (Patrick Buchanan).

The death of communism gives these conservatives a chance to complete the vision they are pleased to call "nationalism" but which is in fact a vision of a passive nation, both domestically and internationally. It is the job of society, through the government, to protect America from incoming missiles, to keep the streets safe and free of potholes, and to enforce norms of sexual behavior and expression. That's about it. They see nothing spiritually ennobling about larger national goals.

The desire to lay down the weary burdens of the cold war, and resentment over the refusal of wealthy allies to pull their own weight, are both legitimate. It is typical of the Democrats to have fumbled the issue of "burden sharing," which has been there for the taking for years. But the conservative isolationists retreat too far.

Americans want to live in history. They want their lives to have meaning beyond having lived, prospered amid family and friends, and died at a ripe age. To be sure, throughout history most people have gotten more history than they wanted: wars and other plagues that denied them the comforts of normal life. Part of America's blessing, emphasized by leaders since Washington, has been a geographical exemption from most of this kind of history. The Civil War is the great exception. But a hunger for history helps to explain our fascination with the Civil War.

Francis Fukuyama has been rightly mocked for declaring last year that history was over. But he was shrewd and correct to observe that without history, life would be boring. And he was honest to note within himself "a powerful nostalgia" for reasons to live "that called forth daring, courage, imagination, and idealism." The PBS Civil War series sent conflicting messages: War is hell, but struggling for a great cause (even the wrong cause) is grand.

One tremendously appealing thing about Israel, to Americans who visit there, is that here is a country full of people very much like us— modern, middle-class, educated—who are nevertheless living in history. They don't have to waste time pondering the purpose of life. They are inventing a nation. And they are dramatically at risk every day, no matter how normal the day seems otherwise. We American visitors are hypocrites, of course: We could trade places, but don't. Still.

While today's Republicans seem to have no interest in anything between bellicosity on the one hand and national passivity on the other, the challenge and opportunity for Democrats is to find alternatives that satisfy both the craving for peace and the craving for crusade. Yes, William James and Jimmy Carter: the moral equivalent of war. This is what Democrats are sometimes pleased to call a "basic human need." There are extreme libertarians who want to privatize the potholes, who oppose any national endeavor, foreign or domestic, as an infringement on individual freedom, and who are deeply suspicious of all talk of national purpose as potentially fascistic. But even these libertarian zealots would find their lives quite empty if the great campaign they are dedicating themselves to were suddenly won.

Ronald Reagan did not mind treating our Republic as a means to some larger end. He understood that Americans like to have a sense of national purpose. Thus his endless references to America as "the last, best hope of mankind" and "a shining city on a hill." But Reagan refused to call upon Americans as individuals to do anything more than sit there and shine. George Bush, by inaugurating our biggest "foreign entanglement" since Vietnam from his golf cart at Kennebunkport, found the perfect expression of our hypocritical desire to be in history and eat it too. Unfortunately, the adventure he started probably can't be completed without interrupting the golf game.

There are missions for America in the world that don't require bloodshed. There are ways to feed the hunger for national purpose that neither recklessly ask for too much sacrifice nor fatuously ask for none at all.

Democrats used to be good at this sort of thing. The Marshall Plan and the Peace Corps are two stellar examples.

The hunger for larger purpose is a refined appetite, arguably even a decadent one. The people of Eastern Europe are thrilled to anticipate a time when they can turn their backs on politics and enjoy the boredom and comfort of bourgeois life. But at the ends of their lives, they will still look back on the struggles leading up to and following the year 1989, as Oliver Wendell Holmes looked back on the Civil War, as the great adventure of their lives. Will today's Americans have anything like that to look back on? Maybe the Persian Gulf. But let's hope we can find something better—more noble and less costly—than that.*

Uncle Sam Doesn't Want You: The Ballad of the Woodstock Brigade

(*The New Republic*, NOVEMBER 26, 1990)

So I'm sitting in my office minding my own business a few weeks back, reading a report from the Congressional Budget Office, as is my wont of a brisk fall afternoon, when Will Davenport calls, very agitated, from Knoxville, Tennessee. Mr. Davenport, who is a stranger, says he is about to turn forty.

I say I know the feeling.

Well, he says, he was watching the Civil War documentary on PBS and was overcome by the desire to serve his country. And you're calling me, I interrupt triumphantly, because you were inspired by my recent column about the Civil War and the need for national purpose.

No, actually, he is unaware of that column. He is calling me because he wants to enlist in the Army and fight in the Persian Gulf. But he has been told by his local Army recruiter that he is too old. Various politicians' offices have given him the polite brush-off. He is looking for some strings to pull, and he thinks that I might have an in with his senator, Al Gore. A perfectly reasonable assumption for any regular reader of *The New Re-*

---

*In the event, the Persian Gulf war turned out to be both less costly and less monumental than seemed likely in October 1990. It faded from the national consciousness with amazing speed.

public, but not, alas, correct.* Nevertheless, we chat.

Mr. Davenport is a bouillabaisse of yuppie emotions, all of them honorable, many all too familiar. Facing forty naturally induces morose contemplation. Another factor, Mr. Davenport admits, is "the adolescent and probably very foolish idea that a real man becomes a soldier for a while." With no special exertion, he avoided service during Vietnam. He doesn't really regret this, because he thinks that war was wrong. But he does feel he missed something important. And he shares the widespread concern that in Vietnam and again in the Gulf, the fighting and dying is done by poor boys (and now girls) while those of what he calls "a better background" escape. During the 1980s he worked in California as an electrical engineer on the Stealth bomber. He was struck that even most of the people building America's weapons had no firsthand knowledge of war.

In the Vietnam debate, which will never end, the fact that the elite escaped most of the bloodshed has been invoked by both hawks and doves: the hawks to sneer that real American boys made the sacrifice while the fancy pants protested; the doves to say that the war would never have gone on so long if the Establishment's children were dying. Mr. Davenport's views are closer to the latter. But he is uncomfortable with the Vietnam era's rejection of all things military, and he is intrigued by the idea of a citizen army, such as both sides of the Civil War, which even elected their own officers.

Not part of Mr. Davenport's thinking is any great enthusiasm for President Bush's purposes in the Gulf enterprise. Indeed, when I talk to him more recently, to see how his quest is progressing, he concedes that he has become "cooler on thumping Saddam Hussein." But he still feels that a "Woodstock Brigade" (his nice term) in the Persian Gulf, which he could join, would be good for him and good for the country. He says a lot of the soldiers he sees on TV look about his age.

Most of us may not share Mr. Davenport's eccentric determination. But his general feelings touch a chord. And what aging yupster will not feel aggrieved to discover that he is considered too old for military service? After all, what have we been jogging for all these years? But a call to a local Army recruiting office confirms the insult. The lady on the phone says pleasantly but firmly that she is not interested in my business unless I am under age

---

Al Gore is close friends with several editors of The New Republic, *including the editor in chief. The magazine has endorsed him twice for president (as of this writing, in early 1995). But I am merely a distant admirer. See page 14.*

thirty-five. "And if it's just a couple days before your thirty-fifth birthday, we couldn't get you in," she adds with unnecessary cruelty. If I want to be an officer, it's even worse: the age limit for enlistment is twenty-nine.

The recruiter says she hears from one or two overage would-be enlistees a week. A senatorial aide who specializes in military casework says he gets ten to fifteen inquiries of this sort a month. The Woodstock Brigade awaits the call.

But Mr. Davenport has chosen the worst possible moment to have his crisis of conscience. The biggest personnel challenge to the military right now is getting rid of people. Under the recent budget agreement, the uniformed services will be reduced by 425,000 over the next five years, out of a current total of slightly more than 2 million. The problem will be finding ways to keep people who have chosen a military career and have been trained at great expense.

This particular dilemma illustrates the larger irony facing all proposals, such as reviving the draft, intended to address concerns about the isolation of the military from society in general and decision-making elites in particular. The services don't need more people. Anyone who enters the military against his will or out of a guilty conscience will take the place of someone who is there for more practical reasons. That person may not be grateful to be shut out so that some yuppie can enjoy an egalitarian moral frisson.

Colonel Lamar Crosby, a personnel manager in the office of the secretary of defense, denies that the current all-volunteer force is unrepresentative. He says it draws in rough proportion from all socioeconomic groups. But why is it, then, that practically no one in the White House, Congress, the Washington press corps, and so on has a family member serving in the Gulf? According to Colonel Crosby, the explanation is that the absolute numbers are so small, compared with earlier military festivities like World War II. It's not skewed demographics.

Well, since I've got you on the phone, could a thirty-nine-year-old guy be of service in Saudi Arabia? Colonel Crosby is doubtful. Contrary to Mr. Davenport's impression, very few infantrymen in Project Desert Shield are even over thirty, let alone approaching forty. (Like many folks our age, Mr. Davenport is losing his ability to judge the age of younger people.) "It's been shown time and again that war is a young man's game," the colonel says. Yes, it was different in the Civil War. But by World War I and World War II we had learned our lesson. The colonel goes on to a brisk discussion of things like "going days without sleep or rest . . . in a combat environment" that leaves me feeling Will Davenport's years.

Anyway, the colonel adds, things are moving pretty fast in the Middle East and it would take sixteen weeks of training before Will could get there. Then he'd be even older, I disloyally volunteer. "He'd be a lot older," says the colonel.

Point made. But couldn't there be a place for Will Davenport? Not at a desk. And not in some exercise of noble humility like emptying bedpans at an old people's home. (He could have done that as a CO during Vietnam.) But something that allows him to buckle his swash as well as serve his nation. Applications for the Woodstock Brigade might not be overwhelming. Even Will, during our last conversation, says, "Gosh, what if I got my wish? Well"—pause—"I guess I would still go."

W<small>AR</small> P<small>OWERS</small> W<small>AR</small>

(*The New Republic*, DECEMBER 31, 1990)

I s it clear beyond dispute that President Bush cannot launch a war against Iraq without the prior consent of Congress? Last week this column said so, but that, tragically, does not make it so. The administration, while promising "consultation," maintains that it has all the legal authority it needs to make good on its threats of war if necessary. Conservative legal scholars are beavering away on theories to explain why the words "Congress shall have power . . . to declare war" don't mean what they say.

We have reached the reductio ad absurdum of the conservative campaign of recent years to give the president dictatorial powers in making foreign policy. The last decade has seen a rich variety of foreign adventures: among them Grenada, Panama, the funding of the Nicaraguan contras, the Libya bombing, the sale of arms to the Ayatollah, the reflagging of the Kuwaiti tankers. (Remember that one? The idea was to help Kuwait's ally Iraq in the war against Iran. "It's a funny old world," as Margaret Thatcher said the other day.) Each episode came with a theory—often produced after the fact—about how Congress would be exceeding its constitutional mandate if it chose to interfere. "Micromanage" was the general accusation.

But "micromanagement" is not the issue now. If the president can send half a million troops halfway around the world and make a deliberate, leisurely, unilateral decision to start a massive land war, then the constitutional provision about Congress declaring war has become meaningless.

Let us pause only briefly to relish the irony of those who usually campaign under the banners of "strict construction" and "original intent" fleeing on this occasion from the plain meaning of words. First they snip away at the "declare war" clause until there is nothing left. Then, with a gusto that would make any liberal activist proud, they build fantasy castles on the clause making the president "commander in chief" of the armed forces. A commander is an operational leader. The commander of a battalion cannot decide alone to commit his soldiers to war. The words "commander in chief," given their commonsense meaning, don't confer that authority either—especially when the authority is explicitly conferred on others.

The busy beavers have three counterarguments. One is that the authors of the Constitution considered and explicitly rejected language giving Congress the power to "make war," rather than merely "declare war." The standard reply is that this change was intended to leave the president, in James Madison's words, "the power to repel sudden attacks." The original-intent game is usually a war of quotes. But the other side has no return fire for this one. It is about as clear as anything can be in constitutional interpretation that the Framers did not intend to give the president carte blanche to start a war.

And so the second counterargument: Forget the Framers. In real life, over two centuries, the president has taken on the war power. A favorite statistic is that the United States has sent forces abroad some two hundred times, while there have been only five declarations of war. What's one more time?

One simple answer to this is that 196 wrongs don't make a right. But this 200-wars statistic is one of those supposed facts that take on a life of their own in ideological struggles. In their book on the war power, *To Chain the Dog of War*, Francis Wormuth and Edwin Firmage have an amusing chapter on what they call "Lists of Wars." The lists melt away when you start eliminating minor episodes with little or no actual fighting; rogue actions by distant officers authorized by neither the president nor Congress; actions Congress did approve, though not by a formal declaration, and so on. Although presidents have waged war unconstitutionally on occasion, the authors conclude, no president has ever attempted to justify his action by a bald assertion of unilateral authority. At least not yet.

No question the trend since World War II has been toward even broader assertions of presidential war-making power. And Congress has not always resisted. But a trend is not a mandate. Reversing the postwar trend away from strict construction of the Constitution is just what conservatives aspire to in areas like individual rights and criminal procedure. Why should war powers be exempt?

A third counterargument against taking the "declare war" clause seriously is that Congress can stop a war anytime it wants through its control over government spending. But the Constitution gives Congress the spending power and the power to declare war. The one doesn't make the other meaningless. Furthermore, when Congress passed the Boland Amendment—using its "power of the purse" in an effort to stop American support for the Nicaraguan contras—these same conservative theorists declared that this was an unconstitutional abuse of the spending power to interfere with the president's foreign policy authority. And when the Reagan administration raised money for the contras abroad, this was declared to be beyond Congress's power to prevent. Operation Desert Shield is also being financed, supposedly, by foreign contributions. If Congress tried to cut off spending for a war against Iraq, our theorist friends would surely argue that Congress cannot foreclose the spending of other people's money.

Forty-five Democratic members of Congress have asked the federal district court in Washington to stop President Bush from going to war against Iraq without congressional consent. It would certainly be a first if Judge Harold Greene granted the injunction. But if he declines, that doesn't mean the constitutional question is answered. There are good practical reasons why courts should not try to settle disputes between the other two branches. But the president cannot ignore the Constitution just because no court will force him to obey it.*

---

*In the end President Bush did get a resolution of approval from Congress, but only after half a million troops were already in place, making rejection difficult. And he continued to insist on his right and intention to launch the fighting whether Congress approved or not. This is one of several issues on which the parties have now amusingly reversed positions, with Republicans asserting Congress's right to pass judgment on all military actions—including many far short of the scope of the Persian Gulf war—and Democrats indignantly defending the president's inherent foreign-policy authority.

Dollars for Scholars

(The New Republic, JANUARY 7, 1991)

The Reuben Baker Scholarship at Harvard College is for "a resident of Latrobe, Pennsylvania, or, there being no such resident, a resident of the western part of Pennsylvania." The Borden Scholarship is for people "bearing the surname of Borden or Anderson." The Arthur Anderson Brooks Scholarship is for "deserving Protestant Christian young men . . . preferably of New England stock." The Helen E. Millington Memorial Scholarship is for "students whose fathers are deceased and whose mothers have not remarried." The Henry Harrison Sprague Scholarship is for those "in whole or in large part of New England Colonial descent." The Augustus Woodbury Scholarship is for those who "prepared for college at Phillips Exeter Academy." The list goes on for 250 pages.

The point is not that it still sometimes helps to be white. (Harvard, in practice, guarantees financial aid to all comers.) The point is that fate spews out all sorts of arbitrary advantages and disadvantages. Yet some people in government seem obsessed with one tiny category: the occasional advantage that comes from being black. Many who opposed the Civil Rights Act of 1964 *in* 1964, including Ronald Reagan and George Bush, now posture as guardians at the portals of its "true meaning." Who among these "reverse discrimination" obsessives believes that when all the advantages and disadvantages in the game of life are weighed and balanced, the advantage—even in 1991—goes to people of color?

Three years ago Reagan vetoed the so-called Grove City bill, named for the Supreme Court decision it was designed to countermand. The bill authorized federal civil rights enforcement in all departments of universities where any department accepts federal funds. Congress overrode Reagan's veto, and the Bush administration now wants to use this very law to restrict minority-targeted scholarships. Conservatives who condemned the Grove City bill at the time as an unwarranted government intrusion into the private sphere seem to have forgotten their objection now that the enemy is reverse discrimination rather than discrimination of the classic kind.

Bush is obviously sorry he ever wandered into this thicket. He says the original decision to ban minority scholarships "was made without the knowledge of the White House." But he cannot blame a rogue assistant secretary of education for his sorrows. The conservatives are right: Michael Williams's ruling was the logical extension of everything Bush professes to believe about civil rights, in particular the principle that it must be "color-blind" or "racially neutral." Republican operatives have been plotting to ride resentment against reverse discrimination to reelection in 1992. And minority-only scholarships are surely reverse discrimination.

By contrast, there is no coherent principle or logic in the policy the administration has settled on after a few mad days of backtracking. That policy holds that universities receiving federal funds (virtually all universities) may not finance minority scholarships themselves, but may administer minority-targeted scholarships that are financed by others.

Well, it's a distinction (as my old law professor used to say). It might even thread the needle of the civil rights laws to some judge's satisfaction. But it hardly solves the moral puzzle of reverse discrimination. Bush now says that privately funded minority scholarships are not merely tolerable but actually a good thing: "I've long been committed to them." Yet how can scholarships based on race be morally repugnant when financed by universities but praiseworthy when financed by individuals?

Furthermore, the policy is not racially neutral, unless the administration is prepared to allow—if not encourage—whites-only scholarships at universities, provided they are financed by outsiders. I can't believe it is.

Even before the official backtrack, the policy was full of contradictions and violations of the alleged principle at stake. There is an exception for minority scholarships funded by the federal government itself. So, according to the Bush principles, it is the proper role of the federal government to (1) pay for minority scholarships itself; (2) ban minority scholarships paid for by universities; and (3) encourage minority scholarships paid for by private individuals. Go figure. As a final fillip, the revised version declares that the administration takes no position on minority scholarships funded by state and local governments. Probably a good thing.

Similarly, there is an exception for universities acting under a "court order to desegregate." Courts have used minority scholarships as a remedy in civil rights cases. And that's okay, apparently. Thus, according to the Bush interpretation, the same civil rights laws that sometimes *require* you to create minority scholarships at other times *forbid* you to do the exact same thing. The principle is getting a little muddy.

More generally, the administration suggests that minority scholarships may be okay even without a court order to make up for past discrimination, or simply to promote diversity in the student body. This is called reinventing the wheel. Universities don't create minority scholarships just for the heck of it, or because they hate white people. They do it to promote diversity and make up for past discrimination. If those are good enough reasons to overcome the supposed anathema on reverse discrimination, then the principle is reduced to an empty debating point.

Finally, according to the administration, there is nothing wrong with using race as "a factor" in awarding scholarships, as long as it is not the "overriding" factor. This bit of sophistry derives from Justice Lewis Powell's opinion in the 1978 *Bakke* case. Yet anything that is a factor in a decision will sometimes be the determining factor. Otherwise, it is not a factor at all.

And taking race into account as a "factor" is still reverse discrimination. What is the moral difference between, say, reserving 10 percent of all scholarships for blacks and awarding enough extra points for blackness as a "factor" under some formula system that blacks win 10 percent of all scholarships anyway? Darned if I can see. And once again, this exception is not "color-blind." The administration surely does not approve of using white skin as a "factor" in awarding scholarships. I hope.

So what's the moral? The moral, to me, is that in applying the principles of civil rights, there is no truly "color-blind" standard that any reasonable person, including George Bush, would actually be willing to enforce. It is possible to stir up white resentment against reverse discrimination. It is possible to recognize that reverse discrimination is dangerous medicine that should be used sparingly. It is not possible to get all self-righteous about "color blindness" as an absolute principle, and really mean it. The choice is either to abandon the laws protecting blacks and other minorities, or to recognize that they can't always be applied equally in both directions.

DEAD IRAQIS

(*The New Republic*, MARCH 18, 1991)

Maybe I missed something, but the first news report I read discussing the question of Iraqi casualties in Operation Desert Storm appeared in *The Washington Post* on February 18, the thirty-fourth day of the war. The figures it cited, unconfirmed, were 20,000 dead and 60,000 wounded up to that point. It added that "wounded soldiers were dying for lack of treatment amid conditions that recalled the American Civil War." The story was on page 7.

As of this writing, the Persian Gulf war still lacks its Mathew Brady to record the acres of bodies incinerated in their bunkers or buried alive in the sand. But eighty thousand losses by mid-February hardly seems unrealistic. After all, there has been no effort to minimize Iraqi military, as opposed to civilian, casualties. Quite the opposite. By the time the Iraqi Army is forced out of Kuwait, said General Thomas Kelly on February 23, "there won't be many of them left."

Obviously a wartime enemy cannot be allowed to hold his own soldiers as hostages. War means killing soldiers, and concern for our own troops dictates that it be done efficiently. America has clearly decided the benefit was worth the cost. But the way we have shielded ourselves from the cost being imposed on Iraqi soldiers—human beings, after all, mostly draftees, with families—is unpleasant.

Like everything else about this war, the spread of callousness on the home front happened at lightning speed. This is partly due to what a *Post* editorial called "the Nintendo effect": those tapes of exploding buildings that made bombing seem like a video game. It is partly because of the remarkably few American casualties. The other week I found myself saying, "When the war starts . . . ," meaning the ground war, at a time when American bombs were undoubtedly killing thousands of Arabs a day. There's a lot we still don't know—partly of necessity and partly because our leaders have kept it from us. But there is also a blinding moral self-righteousness that keeps us from seeing what's going on before our eyes.

A neat little example of this process concerns a device known as a "fuel-air explosive" (FAE). The FAE works, in essence, by filling a wide area with combustible gas, then lighting a match. A search through Nexis, the computerized news media database, reveals that the FAE entered public discussion as something the Iraqis might have. It was described as a terror weapon: an "exotic explosive" with "a devastating blast similar to a small nuclear explosion over an area several miles wide." "Unlike Iraq's arsenal of chemical and biological weapons," reported the *Los Angeles Times* on October 5, "there is no ready defense against" the FAE—which, by the way, "the United States does not have in its arsenal."

The FAE soon acquired the moniker "the poor man's nuclear weapon." The Reagan and Bush administrations stood accused of encouraging the transfer of technology for it, back when Iraq was our pal. A *Los Angeles Times* article on January 15, about potential casualties, said the allies were prepared for "massive burns" from "powerful Iraqi fuel-air explosives." *The New York Times* reported on January 24: "Hussein might be planning to use an even more horrific weapon, never before employed in combat, known as the fuel air bomb, which spreads a circle of fire."

A *Boston Globe* article on February 6 cited a U.S. War College study suggesting that Iraq might have used fuel-air weapons, and not chemical weapons, during the Iran-Iraq war— the implication being that there was little to choose between them. This article also said: "Some independent analysts believe that both the U.S. and Iraqi arsenals include" FAEs—the first hint that the good guys might have this weapon—although "it is not clear whether Iraq or any other nation has succeeded in perfecting them."

Clarity was not long in coming. The *Los Angeles Times* reported on February 7 that "the United States stockpiled exotic fuel-air weapons" in Saudi Arabia for use against Iraq. And what's the big deal? Although some "experts call them 'the poor man's nuclear weapon . . . ,' others say the bombs pack about as much punch as conventional explosives." The poor-mouthing continued in *The Wall Street Journal* on February 8, which reported that FAEs "are derided by U.S. military technologists, despite outside talk they could be 'superbomb' response to any Iraqi chemical attack."

The notion that FAEs are so horrible that they would be used only in response to a chemical attack lasted less than a week. *The Washington Post* on February 16: "U.S. warplanes have begun dropping . . . fuel-air explosives on Iraqi positions to 'experiment' with their effectiveness in clearing mine fields or blasting away berms and clusters of trucks and armored vehicles." *The New York Times* ran a diagram the same day titled "How Fuel-Air Explosives Work," implying that their only function and effect is to clear minefields. The explosion creates pressure that sets off the mines, "clearing an area large enough for a helicopter to land," the *Times* helpfully explained.

On February 17, the *Post,* having repeated that FAEs are "employed against mines and light equipment such as trucks," added en passant: "Their fireballs also suck away oxygen, which specialists pointed out could lead to asphyxiation of Iraqi troops hiding in bunkers." A *Los Angeles Times* editorial the same day, discussing possible use of nuclear weapons, noted that they may "be no more inhumane than, say, fuel-air explosives, which kill by sucking every particle of oxygen from the air."

But in general, the papers continued to play down the fact that FAEs, former terror weapon, actually kill people. The *Los Angeles Times* on February 17 (same day as its frank editorial) reported that FAEs "clear mine fields, pack down sand to ease movement of allied armored columns, and further terrorize and demoralize the lightly armed Iraqi infantry troops. . . . " A *USA Today* chart on February 19 explained that FAEs create a "pressure wave that detonates mines, destroys buildings, aircraft."

On February 23, the day the ground war started, *The Washington Post* reported about this weapon that at first we didn't have, then would never use except against a chemical attack, then were using to clear mine fields and pack down sand: "All of the front-line Iraqi troops have been subjected to extensive bombardment, including many detonations of 10,000-pound BLU-82 bombs, containing fuel-air explosives." But by then, who cared?

FROM CLARK CLIFFORD TO RON BROWN

(The New Republic, APRIL 22, 1991)

In his forthcoming memoir, *Counsel to the President,* Clark Clifford recalls consulting New Deal Brahmin David Lilienthal about the propriety of setting up as a Washington lawyer after leaving the Truman White House. Clifford quotes Lilienthal's journal: "I said of course he shouldn't go [back] to St. Louis, that the fact that others had been greedy and not too principled in how they practiced law didn't mean that he needed to, nor would he."

Clifford opened shop early in 1950. A phone call brought him his second client: "Mr. Clifford, this is Howard Hughes. . . . I have followed your career with interest and we all thank you for the contribution you have made to the nation. I understand you have gone into private law practice. . . . " But before signing Hughes up, Clifford says, he delivered "a well-rehearsed little speech" that he gave to every client: " 'Before we proceed, there is one point I must make clear. I do not consider that this firm will have any influence of any kind here in Washington. . . . If you want influence, you should consider going elsewhere.' Hughes said he understood my point completely."

Hughes understood, all right. "By the late spring of 1950," Clifford writes happily, "it seemed clear that the firm . . . would prosper." And indeed it did. Clifford and Warnke became one of the prominent Washington law firms of the postwar era. Clifford writes that he is "proud of my profession." But he adds stuffily that this is "law as I knew it . . . not necessarily the kind of work done by so many young lawyers in large firms today." Clifford settled into his role as "Washington's ultimate insider" (his publisher's description) and "the Democratic Party's pre-eminent wise man" (ditto).

Clifford's memoirs do not include the most famous anecdote, possibly apocryphal, about his law practice. That's the one about the client who is having trouble with a regulatory agency and asks Clifford what to do. Clifford advises, "Do nothing," and sends a bill for $5,000. The client calls Clifford and says, "At least tell me why I should do nothing." Clifford says, "Because I said so," and sends a bill for $10,000.

In the twilight of his career, at age eighty-four, Clifford is now in trouble over his connection to a crooked foreign bank called BCCI. A group of investors associated with BCCI hired Clifford ten years ago to help them buy a bank here in Washington. BCCI had been refused permission to buy two other American banks, but Clifford assured regulators that BCCI would have no connection to this purchase. The sale was approved, Clifford became chairman of First American, as the bank was renamed, and his firm made millions in fees.

Lo and behold, it turns out that BCCI has actually been the secret owner of First American all along! In a hastily added footnote to his memoir, Clifford plays Captain Renault, straight out of *Casablanca*. He is shocked, shocked: "When I was first informed that United States law might have been violated, I was both appalled and embarrassed. . . . It was possible that I had been used, I realized with a combination of outrage and deep concern. . . . "

Two misconceptions color Washington's reaction to Clifford's distress. One is that this was an aberration in his distinguished legal career. The other is that Clifford's "smell detector" should have warned him off. What BCCI was buying from Clark Clifford is exactly what many of his clients have bought over the years: Washington respectability. Selling respectability is like living off the family silver: You have to dole it out sparingly, because once it's gone it can't be replaced. But you could say that Clifford's timing was perfect. He hoarded most of his respectability until the end, then cashed it in before it was too late.

When you're selling respectability, an oversensitive smell detector is no asset. Far more useful is the kind of monumental lack of curiosity that may yet save Clifford from total disgrace. Perhaps Clifford really didn't know that his clients were fronting for BCCI. But he did know that they were being "advised" by BCCI, and that BCCI was corrupt. Of course if they didn't have a little problem of some sort, they wouldn't have needed to hire Clark Clifford, would they?

Two decades ago Clifford rented his respectability to another bank, the National Bank of Washington, then owned by the notoriously corrupt United Mineworkers Union headed by Tony Boyle. Boyle hadn't yet been convicted of murder when Clifford graced NBW's board, but it surprised few when he was. The *Washington Monthly* had tried to shame Clifford into quitting, without success. Another lustrous achievement Clifford omits from his memoirs is his legendary work for DuPont in 1962, saving the company hundreds of millions (big money back then) with a specially legislated tax break.

Influence peddling is rarely as crude as making a phone call (though Clifford did make that phone call for BCCI, effectively stifling a congressional investigation of BCCI's drug money laundering by ringing up Senator Claiborne Pell). Sometimes it is a matter of what lobbyists like to call "access": opening the right door so that the client can make his own case. Sometimes it actually is what Clifford insists in his memoirs, merely "advice on how best to present your position to the appropriate departments and agencies." Sometimes it is more ephemeral yet: mere propinquity—the right to say, "Clark Clifford represents me." Whatever the specific service being rendered, however, clients are paying to tip the balance of democratic government in their favor. And a lot of the time (though not always), they're getting their money's worth.

To help it out of its current mess, First American has hired Patton,

Boggs and Blow, the law firm of the present chairman of the Democratic party, Ron Brown. Patton, Boggs is just the sort of large modern law firm that Clark Clifford sticks up his nose at. But much of its business is essentially the same as Clifford's: trading on influence. In the franker modern style, Brown and his partners no doubt spare their clients that sanctimonious little speech. And there may be less emphasis on respectability and more on raw connections. But the principle, or lack thereof, is the same.

Brown's been in the news lately, too. He's a board member and stockholder of a Louisiana company called Chemfix Technologies, which contracts with cities to turn sewage into landfill. *Newsday* reports that New York City awarded Chemfix a $210 million contract about the same time the Democrats chose New York as the site of their next convention, and despite complaints from other cities that Chemfix's operations "stunk to high heaven."

Since a federal ban on ocean dumping of sewage in 1988, the sewage conversion business has become highly politicized. Rival firms have hired Tip O'Neill's son and Al D'Amato's brother. There is absolutely no evidence that Ron Brown ever called up Mayor Dinkins and said, "If you want the convention, give me the sludge contract." But that's not how it works. There's only one reason a Louisiana sewage company would want a Washington lawyer high in Democratic politics on its board, and it's not his knowledge of sewage.

Brown is a lobbyist for several Japanese electronics firms, as well as for AUTOPAC, the trade group for imported-car dealers. He has represented the Sultan of Oman. Jack Anderson reported in 1988 that for most of the 1980s Brown had a $150,000-a-year contract to represent the Haitian government of Jean-Claude "Baby Doc" Duvalier. Brown told Anderson he had "apprehensions" about this, but thought he could "do more good than harm." Among other services, Brown helped the dictator's brother-in-law deal with an arrest for drug trafficking. Brown's contract with Haiti ended shortly after Baby Doc fled the country one step ahead of the lynch mob.

In 1986, NBC agreed with a group called the National Black Media Coalition to sell one of its radio stations to a minority-controlled firm. In 1989 it sold Washington station WKYS to a company of which Brown owns 10 percent. NBC got a special tax break designed to make it easier for minorities to afford to buy broadcast stations. NBC also lent the buyers part of the purchase price. Brown has consistently refused to say how much of his own money he had to put up for a share of a broadcast property that is worth many millions.

Brown got this deal because he is black, but not just because he is black. He got it because he is one of Washington's most prominent and politically influential blacks. Having Ron Brown in your minority group when you're trying to obtain a broadcast license is like having Clark Clifford on your board when you're trying to get approval from bank regulators.

Someday Ron Brown may be regarded as "the Democratic party's preeminent wise man."* Is that progress? It's sad that Washington's Democratic graybeards have tended to be men who built fortunes peddling their influence: Clark Clifford . . . Robert Strauss . . . Ron Brown. . . .

Of course many prominent Republicans have done the same. Indeed, it was Republicans who pioneered most of the grossest excesses of influence peddling during the innovative 1980s, stripping away the delicate veneers painstakingly maintained over decades by the Clark Clifford types. But you expect Republicans to be whores for business, and to be cynical about the processes of government. For a Republican politico to be available for hire may be equally corrupt, but it is less hypocritical.

Anyway, for the Republicans now—as for the Democrats during Clark Clifford's prime—it doesn't matter so much. But it's different if you're a party in desperate need of redefining yourself in your own mind and the public's. In that situation, it's a substantial disadvantage when your so-called leaders and wise men can be bought by anyone who walks in the door with enough money.

COVER-UP

(*The New Republic*, APRIL 29, 1991)

onald Reagan will never be bald as long as he lives. But he may very well get gray in Washington.
                    —A REAGAN SPOKESMAN QUOTED IN *THE NEW YORK TIMES*,
                                                        DECEMBER 18, 1980

But he never did. Or did he? There is no entry on "hair" in the index to Lou Cannon's fat new book on the Reagan presidency, *President Rea-*

---

*I guess not.

gan: The Role of a Lifetime. Reagan's own recent autobiography, *An American Life,* suffers the same unfortunate lacuna. Nor is there any index reference to hair in *For the Record,* the otherwise vindictive memoir of Reagan's chief of staff Donald T. Regan—though Regan does have three citations under "Reagan, Ronald, hearing problem of"—or in the grand-daddy of Reaganite kiss-and-tells, David Stockman's *The Triumph of Politics.*

So we must rely on Kitty Kelley. Not only does the index of her *Nancy Reagan: The Unauthorized Biography* contain a generous three citations under "Reagan, Ronald Wilson, hair color of" (plus a fourth under "hairstyle of"). But under "Reagan, Nancy Davis, hairdressers of," the citations go on for three lines. The key reference is on page 292. After explaining how Clairol paid Nancy Reagan's hairdresser $20,000 a year to fly from Beverly Hills to Washington every three weeks and do her hair for free, Kelley notes: "Whenever he visited the White House to color the First Lady's hair, Julius also dyed the President's gray roots, which he had been doing secretly since 1968."

This revelation might strike most people as less interesting than Kelley's allegation that Nancy was canoodling with Jerry Lewis on the desk in the Oval Office. (Have I got that right?)* But many will find it a good deal more plausible. Most people probably assume by now that of course a man of Reagan's age can't have a full head of naturally brown hair. And yet the Reagans and their spokespeople continue to deny that he dyes it.

A small matter, perhaps. But you can read the saga of Ronald Reagan's hair as a metaphor for the 1980s, a time when deceit by public officials reached new levels of respectability. Reagan set a standard of brazen duplicity of which George Bush and future presidents are the beneficiaries. I spent the last couple of years of the 1970s in a frenzy of rage against Jimmy Carter for transparent propaganda falsehoods of the sort that are our daily diet in the age of Bush. Now it is just "spin control."

Reagan is legendary for his ability to insist with seeming sincerity that black is white (or, in this case, that white is black). Although the hair question may not be as vital to historians as, say, his role in Iran-contra, it is worth cherishing for its starkness. The usual muddling devices are not available. He cannot claim he didn't know whether they were dyeing

---

The actual suggestion was Frank Sinatra in the upstairs White House living quarters.

his hair, as he claimed not to know about the trading of arms for hostages. He cannot claim that he can't remember, since it has to be done regularly. He cannot blame Congress for dying his hair against his will, as with the deficit. He can't say it's a matter of national security. And it's not one of those complicated questions the nation soon learned to give Ronald Reagan a pass on, like how Strategic Defense would work.

The press's approach to the hair question went through phases, similar to the phases in the press's general approach to Reagan's truthfulness. Phase one, during his campaign for president, was a fairly energetic skepticism. Reagan was forced repeatedly to deny that he colored his hair. The first interviews with sycophantic barbers appeared, parodying the posture of the loyal presidential aide with their praise of his wavy texture and insistence that the hair was natural down to the roots.

Reagan claimed that during his governorship, Sacramento reporters had stolen some of his clippings from the barbershop floor for closer inspection, and found no artifice. This became a treasured part of the Ronald Reagan Anecdote Collection, repeated by Nancy as recently as 1989, embroidered with the assertion that the hair had been sent out for laboratory tests. This version surfaced just last year in a "Dear Abby" column. Dear Abby moved the time frame to the Reagan presidency and enhanced it by having the reporter work "for one of those gossipy newspapers (sold primarily in supermarkets)."

Phase two came in the early White House years, as reporters grew used to the Reagan style and wearied of trying to catch and expose every falsehood. Most reporters undoubtedly assumed that he dyed his hair, but despaired of ever proving it or making anyone care. The issue slipped from sight.

It was at this point that a second theme started to emerge: Reagan is starting to turn gray. In May 1982, *The New York Times* reported that Senate Majority Leader Howard Baker "confided to some of his aides that for the first time he had noticed some gray in Mr. Reagan's hair." The next month the *Times* itself reported that Reagan's "new, puffier style seemed to do more to show off his traces of gray." (Presidential barber Milton Pitts characteristically stonewalled: "There is no new hairstyle.") In November 1982 the London *Guardian* observed that "the miracle hair, sleek brown and shiny when he took office, is notably grayer now." And *The Washington Post* confirmed the next month: "His once jet-black hair is now streaked with gray."

Phase three was during and after the triumphal 1984 reelection campaign. Even the cynical Washington press corps came to believe in the Reagan magic. Maybe a man who can carry forty-nine states really can approach his eighties with a full head of naturally brown hair. Only Geraldine Ferraro had the guts to note "the fact that Ronald Reagan dyes his hair." Meanwhile, the London *Financial Times* observed, in January 1985: "His still luxuriant brown hair may be beginning to show traces of gray." (Milton Pitts: "His hair color has not changed any time in the last four years.")

In phase four, the failures and disappointments of Reagan's second term reignited a few doubts, but the myth basically survived. A conservative activist, enraged at the president's halfhearted support for Supreme Court nominee Robert Bork, said, "Maybe Reagan does dye his hair."

Meanwhile, the hair monitors continued to detect the beginning of the end. The *Financial Times* observed in August 1987: "The loss of public trust is at last turning Ronald Reagan's hair gray." In September 1988, *The Washington Post* detected "a few gray [hairs] poking through." And a December 1988 *Post* valedictory noted: "There are streaks of gray in the mane of black hair, so envied by his rivals."

Then came phase five. Shortly after he left office, Reagan's head was shaved for brain surgery, and briefly, as it grew back, his hair was completely gray. How to explain it? In October 1989, on his famous $2 million speechmaking visit to Japan, *The New York Times* reported that his crew cut "appears considerably more gray than his characteristically long brown locks." But "a spokesman for Reagan vehemently denied that any artificial color had ever been applied." In December 1989, at a speech in California, "Mostly the audience stared at Reagan, whose gray hair was the main subject of conversation."

But soon Reagan's hair was once again just beginning to turn gray. A *Washington Post* review of his televised testimony in the John Poindexter trial: "His still wavy hair has swirls of gray." The *Post*, February 1991: "Except for the streaks of gray in his black hair, Reagan seems to have aged little since he left the White House."

Maybe he doesn't dye his hair. A decade of repeated shock discoveries that his hair is at last starting to turn gray suggests a scarier possibility than this rather mundane lie: His hair's been gray all along! But Ronald Reagan's had us so hypnotized that we can't even see it. How did Kitty Kelley miss this one?

INADMISSIBLE

(*The New Republic*, MAY 6, 1991)

The U.S. prison population has tripled in the past two decades, to more than a million. This country has more of its population behind bars than any other nation with reliable statistics. South Africa is second, the Soviet Union is third. Now that South Africa has a moratorium on executions, we're also the only advanced Western nation with a death penalty. It is absurd to say the answer to rising crime is locking up even more people for even longer periods, or chopping off more heads. But few politicians can resist.

Jeremy Bentham, who first elaborated the theory of prison as a deterrent to crime, might look at America's choked prisons and say we've got it all wrong. As James Q. Wilson and Richard Herrnstein, no softies, put it in their book, *Crime and Human Nature:* "It may be easier to reduce crime by making penalties swifter or more certain, rather than more severe." America's absurdly long prison terms often come at the end of a lengthy and random process that nullifies their power as a deterrent to crime.

One element of President Bush's crime bill that can't be laughed off immediately, therefore, is his proposal to limit the exclusionary rule. This is the rule that evidence obtained in violation of a person's constitutional rights cannot be used against him in court, even if it proves him guilty. Or, as Benjamin Cardozo famously derided the exclusionary rule, it is the doctrine that "the criminal is to go free because the constable has blundered."

The exclusionary rule usually involves evidence obtained in violation of the Fourth Amendment right against unreasonable searches and seizures. Unlike a coerced confession, illegally seized evidence is just as probative as evidence seized properly. In the war of statistics about how often the guilty go free because good evidence against them can't be used, liberals are a bit disingenuous. It is rare that the exclusionary rule is rarely invoked at a trial. But trials themselves are rare. Far more often, potentially excludable evidence will lead prosecutors to drop the case or negotiate a plea bargain for a shorter term.

Indeed, the best case against all the elaborate procedural safeguards created by the Warren Supreme Court is that they have created a level of protection for defendants that we can't afford to offer, and don't really offer. Practically all criminal defendants are actually tried in a much more rough-and-ready process—plea bargaining—in which there are no safeguards for the innocent or those whose constitutional rights have been violated, but where potential procedural claims are translated into shorter sentences. Meanwhile, legislatures increase the official sentences for crimes to counteract the plea bargaining effect.

So dump the exclusionary rule? Not so fast. There is a logical flaw in the argument that excluding wrongfully obtained evidence lets the guilty go free. That is, the guilty would also go free if the evidence hadn't been wrongly obtained in the first place. Conservatives complain about the burden of the exclusionary rule on cops and prosecutors. But the rule is a burden only to the extent that it actually works in deterring unconstitutional behavior. The complaint, in short, is not with the exclusionary rule. It is with the Fourth Amendment itself. Eliminating the exclusionary rule would only lead to more guilty people being punished if it also led to more illegal searches, seizures, and confessions: an effect the rule's critics take great pains to deny.

In fact, the Fourth Amendment—as interpreted by the Supreme Court—could use some pruning back. Most guilty-going-free horror stories you read in attacks on the exclusionary rule involve a piece of evidence ruled inadmissible on some overly exquisite chain of logic involving some cop's failure to curtsy in the right direction. But cops also violate real Fourth Amendment rights that most people treasure and everyone—criminals included—is entitled to. And they would do it a lot more often if it weren't for the exclusionary rule (as they did before the rule was imposed in 1961).

Most calls for reforming or eliminating the exclusionary rule, including President Bush's, come with deeply disingenuous alternative proposals for protecting Fourth and Fifth amendment rights. These generally involve internal police department disciplinary procedures and/or an enhanced right for victims to sue. You will not be surprised to hear that the record of police departments punishing their own for rights violations is laughable, as is the record of juries sympathizing with criminals who sue cops.

And isn't it odd for conservative antilegalistas to be proposing a whole new layer of bureaucratic and legal procedure? Addressing this concern, a recent Justice Department report notes—without apparent irony—that claims will be minimal since those whose rights were violated will not qualify for free legal counsel as they do in criminal trials. How very reassuring.

But the main problem with alternatives to the exclusionary rule is that if they worked, they would be just as burdensome to law enforcement as the exclusionary rule itself. The assumption has to be, therefore, that proponents assume they would not work. That certainly sounds like Attorney General Richard Thornburgh's assumption when he complains: "If police feel that someone's perched on their shoulder watching every action they're going to take, you're not going to get the kind of aggressive law enforcement that you need."

PLEASE DON'T QUOTE ME

(*Time*, MAY 13, 1991)

An article devoid of [quotes], one that consists entirely of the author's own observations and conclusions, will generally leave readers dissatisfied and unpersuaded, as well as bored.
—FEDERAL APPEALS JUDGE ALEX KOZINSKI (DISSENTING),
MASSON V. NEW YORKER MAGAZINE, INC.

During the last election a television journalist called up to say he wanted to interview me. Puzzled—this man knows far more than I do about politics—but flattered, I said sure. He showed up at my office, set up his lights and camera, and asked, "Mike, would you say that . . ." Then he proceeded to enunciate some theory about the course of the campaign.

Me (eager to please): Good point. You're absolutely right about that. I never thought of it before.

Him (testy): No. Would you *say* it.

Ah. He didn't want my wisdom. He wanted a sound bite. Or, in the outmoded argot of print, a quote. Under the conventions of American journalism, his insight was worthless to him until he could get someone else to utter it, thus conferring on his nugget some spurious authority and relieving himself of any taint of opinion or bias. I could just as easily quote him to the same purpose. Someday I will.

In a way, American journalism has brought *Masson* v. *New Yorker*

Magazine, Inc., on itself by worshiping at the shrine of the quote. The case is now before the Supreme Court. Most journalists would probably agree with Judge Kozinski of the lower court that an article without quotes just doesn't hack it.

Jeffrey Masson, a psychiatrist, was the subject of a *New Yorker* profile by Janet Malcolm. Masson claims that Malcolm libeled him by putting in his mouth words he never said, such as describing himself as an "intellectual gigolo." Malcolm denies making up quotes but also claims a constitutional right to do so.

Despite all the fuss, the issue doesn't seem very complicated. "X said Y" is a factual assertion. If X didn't say Y, it is a false assertion. But falsehood is just one part of a libel case. You have to prove the falsehood was defamatory. You have to prove you've been harmed. These constraints will take care of most of the nightmare scenarios journalists worry about, such as being sued for "cleaning up" quotes. Above all, if X is a public figure, you have to prove the misquote was committed with "reckless disregard for the truth." (The lawyers call this "actual malice"—the "actual" being a lawyer's way of indicating that it doesn't actually mean malice at all.)

The Supreme Court has given limited constitutional protection to falsehoods in order to give the truth some breathing room—to protect honest mistakes. In a tort-crazed nation, this is a great luxury. In other countries journalists live in fear of lawsuits. In America all professionals *except* journalists live in fear of lawsuits. Journalists are rightly alarmed that the mere accusation of fake quotes could land a journalist in a costly lawsuit, and the Supreme Court should protect us against that. But if quotes are made up, this alone surely displays reckless disregard for the truth. The claim of Malcolm and her defenders that the Constitution should protect even purposely made-up quotes, as long as the author thinks they reflect the subject's views, is an embarrassment.

How *The New Yorker*'s reputation can survive this assertion of privilege is a puzzle. Nowhere in journalism is the quote more sanctified. A typical *New Yorker* profile is nothing but a string of lengthy quotations from the subject and his or her associates, with a connecting tissue of irrelevant scene-setting detail. Malcolm has admitted to fabricating some of this detail, such as moving the site of a conversation from her flat in New York City to a restaurant in California. The myth is that by relying so heavily on seemingly verbatim quotations, the journalist is functioning as a crystal-clear piece of glass through which the reader can see the subject whole and true. But if the quotes are the result of art and not tape recording, the whole genre needs rethinking.

Newsmagazines also rely heavily on quotes, though their style emphasizes compression and bustle, in contrast to *The New Yorker*'s leisurely pace. Each point the writer wishes to make comes with a quote to add color and authority. The color and the authority often take up more precious space than the point itself: "Iraq may not become a quagmire. 'We'll feed the Kurds and then amscray,' says retired Lieutenant Colonel William Finnegan, now a senior fellow at the Center for War, Pestilence, Famine and Death in Washington."

Newspapers treasure quotes from "ordinary" people, for authenticity rather than authority. A poll, conducted at great expense with the best psephological technique, is thought to gain extra credibility if one out of 250 million citizens can be found to restate its findings in prose. "Seventy percent of Americans list inflation as one of their top five concerns. 'These prices are just getting out of sight,' says Judy Draper, 38, a data processor and mother of three in Molina, Mo."

At the opposite extreme, a foreign correspondent I used to edit would weave elaborate tales of international intrigue, ending each delirious paragraph with the vestigial incantation, ". . . according to sources." Even he felt that by merely *declaring* he had "sources"—never mind who or where—he was allaying suspicions that he might be making it all up.

Maybe what American journalism needs is not just better quotes but fewer quotes. The Masson case is a reminder that the accuracy and wisdom of a piece of journalism inevitably depends on "the author's own observations and conclusions," as Judge Kozinski puts it. It is often more efficient, not to say more honest, to express these directly. Quotes can become a crutch. Or rather, "Quotes can become a crutch," says one observer of the journalistic scene.

P.C. B.S.

(*The New Republic*, MAY 20, 1991)

I t's been years, I suspect, since the term "politically correct" has been used without irony. And I beg leave to doubt that anyone ever has accused anyone else of being "politically incorrect" with a straight face. The present ubiquity of these terms is a brilliant propaganda victory by *critics* of the alleged regime of left-wing intolerance at America's universities. *The Wall Street Journal* claims that "we are far worse off now as regards the threat to intellectual freedom, the pressures to conform ideologically, than during the McCarthy era."

Flaw number one in this theory is that it's evident, even from afar, that conservative activism is thriving on campus. In my day, twenty years ago, you could spend four years at a major university without running into anyone who admitted to being so much as a liberal Republican. Now there are conservative newspapers, student groups, faculty caucuses, all busily claiming suppression.

No doubt the zeitgeist at universities is still to the left of the zeitgeist in American society as a whole. And no doubt there are idiots, some with tenure, saying idiotic things. But that's not the accusation. The accusation is that dissent is being stifled in order to enforce an "orthodoxy."

In 1951, William F. Buckley, Jr., published his first book, *God and Man at Yale,* making a similar complaint that universities were indoctrinating their students with left-wing propaganda. But Buckley at least was honest. His book—subtitled *The Superstitions of "Academic Freedom"*—was an attack on the notion of the university as a neutral forum where ideas do battle. Buckley's sermon was that Yale should impose an orthodoxy on its students—a conservative orthodoxy of capitalism and Christianity. In short, political correctness, conservative-style.

By contrast, Dinesh D'Souza, the would-be Buckley of 1991, calls his book *Illiberal Education* (Free Press), and styles himself the defender of tolerance, openness, academic freedom, and so on. Unlike Buckley's, D'Souza's book is not a sustained argument but rather an any-weapon-to-hand collection of slightly suspect anecdotes. Example: To support his peculiar assertion that racism is less prevalent at universities in the South than in the North, he reports that white fraternities at the University of Mississippi raised money to help "repair" a black fraternity whose "house was vandalized," as he puts it. In fact, the black fraternity house was completely destroyed by arson, an episode that apparently has no bearing on the question of race relations.

After wading through much of the anecdotage of PC hysteria, my own conclusion is that very little of it supports the charge that anyone's right of free expression is being stifled, let alone that there is a reign of terror on campus. The stories break down roughly into two categories.

One category consists of Buckley-like objections to a lack of orthodoxy. Stanford may have been right or wrong to drop its "Western culture" requirement, but surely it is those who want the requirement restored who deserve the accusation (if it is an accusation) of demanding "correctness." Stanford students may still take all the courses they want about dead white males. The question is whether they should be forced to.

Many anti-PC diatribes are just lists of things the writer finds objectionable and would like—in the spirit of toleration and free inquiry—to expunge from the college curricula. "Academic Marxists deny the autonomy of culture," intones George Will in *Newsweek*. Of course anyone sensible denies the autonomy of culture. Will's example of a transparent Marxist absurdity—"Shakespeare's *Tempest* reflects the imperialist rape of the Third World"—will not strike everyone as a worthless way to look at the play. And the notion that all political interpretation of Shakespeare is invalid—because it offends against "the autonomy of culture"—is surely more philistine than any theory academic Marxists have cooked up. Nevertheless, I would not have a fit if George Will was hired to teach English full-time at Duke. In fact, I would encourage it.

A second category of "PC" complaints involves people who are "accused" of or "ran into trouble" for making some remark that offends someone's "ethnic, racial, religious [or] political sensitivity." The quoted phrases come from Representative Henry Hyde, Republican of Illinois, who has taken this up as a cause. Although PC hysterics—correctly—mock excessive concern about "sensitivity" as a threat to robust debate, many of their own complaints amount to offended sensitivity at someone else's over-robust exercise of free expression.

Phrases like "accused" and "ran into trouble" often turn out to mean that someone was yelled at, or picketed, or vilified in the student newspaper. How is that censorship? How is it censorship if the students and faculty choose not to have a conservative commencement speaker? Or if some lunatic puts out a memo condemning the phrase "a nip in the air"? The complainers like to observe that minority students are being taught to revel in their status as victims, to wallow in "sensitivity," and to demand exemption from criticism. But much of the "PC" criticism itself reflects the romance of victimization and false martyrdom.

Then there are the so-called speech codes: official university rules designed to protect sensitivity and promote civility. Hyde, backed by the ACLU, is pushing a bill to curtail these codes by applying First Amendment free-speech standards to private universities (as they already apply to public ones). There are some genuine horrors here, such as the already legendary rule against "inappropriately directed laughter," and the one attempting to outlaw "conspicuous exclusions of others from conversations." But there is also a lot of exaggeration.

The statistic that 70 percent of American universities have speech codes of some sort, based on a survey, has now taken on a life of its own. It is grossly misleading. Most of the rules in these codes don't infringe First Amendment values in any way. In fact, they are intended to promote First Amendment values. The prototypical "speech code" rule would be one forbidding the shouting down of another speaker.

Many of these codes, as it happens, have their roots in the early 1970s, when they were a conservative response to left-wing student activism. In those ancient days, it was academic conservatives who argued that the life of the mind required a higher standard of civility and respect for the views of others than could be tolerated in society at large, and insisted that students who could not agree to such a standard did not belong in the academic community. Now Brown throws out a drunk for yelling racist and homophobic slogans in the middle of the night, and conservatives scream totalitarianism. Next they'll be occupying the dean's office.

O<small>NLY</small> C<small>ORRECT</small>

(The New Republic, JUNE 17, 1991*)*

T*he New York Times* recently ran the following item in its popular "Corrections" column:

An article in The Living Section on April 24 about yerba mate, a Par-
aguayan beverage, referred imprecisely to a group of herbs used medicinally
in Paraguay. Some of them, including palo santo and naranjo, have Span-
ish names.

Now, that is magnificent. It has everything one looks for in a correction: lyricism, romance, pathos, mystery. In two brief sentences, on a page
otherwise devoted to the routine betrayals of diplomats and politicians,
one is plunged into a world of exotic beverages and medicinal herbs.

Like all great corrections, this one hints at—but does not totally reveal—two dramas: the making of the original error and the making of the
correction itself. Thus the mind indulges in delightful speculation. What
desperation of consumer novelty-seeking reduced the *Times*'s Living Section to writing about Paraguayan refreshments? Down what byway had
we wandered to be misinformed that certain Paraguayan medicinal herbs
don't have Spanish names? What oversensitive Hispanophile took such
umbrage at this implication that he or she demanded a correction, and
why was he or she not told to go away and drink a yerba mate? And then,
as a final delight, there is the note of grudging contrition ("referred imprecisely"), especially prized by corrections connoisseurs.

As self-flagellation has come into fashion in American journalism,
corrections have blossomed. Most major papers now run a box full of them
every day, along with variants such as "clarifications" and "editor's notes."
I read corrections avidly. Not solely in the spirit of schadenfreude—we all
make mistakes—but as a sort of poetry. Corrections are the haiku of journalism: short, rich in imagery, hedged about by rigid stylistic rules.

The main rule, imposed most rigidly by the *Times* (but not invariably
even there), is that the correction should avoid repeating the original error.
The purpose is high-minded, but the effect is often exotic or comic as the
author tries to characterize the nature of the mistake without letting on
what exactly it was. An example from my collection: "A report in the Style
Makers column on May 20 about Judith Neidermaier, a display designer
in Chicago, misstated her role in creating mannequins shaped like wooden
clothespins for the Fendi boutique in New York. . . . " One could dig up
the May 20 *Times* to learn what Ms. Neidermaier's role in the creation of
mannequins shaped like wooden clothespins was wrongly alleged to be.
But how could the actual allegation compare to the options the imagination provides?

Although most *Times* readers, like me, may have skipped that article "about shoes and handbags for evening," who could fail to be charmed by the correction (which, like most poetry, is best read aloud)?

The affected paragraph should have read:

Bergdorf's has Carey Adina's satin trapezoid in fuchsia, chartreuse, purple, or bright blue with a jeweled clasp and a stiff handle ($425); Paloma Picasso's asymmetric heart-shaped bag in rose or black with a golden globe on the handle ($565), and a Bergdorf-label pyramid in gold satin with a handle of gilded rope ($280).

Of all corrections, the least interesting to connoisseurs are the ones addressing mere typographical errors, such as the classic missing "not." But even connoisseurs are not above enjoying the slapstick effect of certain editing mistakes, such as the *Times* attributing the comment that it was "fashionable to be racist" during the Reagan administration to Lee Atwater instead of Spike Lee. Last November the *Times* had to correct an article about former drug czar William Bennett and Representative Charles Rangel: "It was Mr. Bennett who called Mr. Rangel a 'gasbag,' not the other way around."

A while back, *The Washington Post* ran a correction admitting it had misquoted the same Bill Bennett "in saying his 'brother and his mother are the two best counselors I've got.' The quotation should have cited his brother and his wife." This was funny enough. It would have been funnier in *Times* style, though, which would have apologized for having "mischaracterized the relationship between William J. Bennett and one of his two best counselors. She is his wife."

Math seems to be a special problem for the *Times*. In January the paper apologized for having "misstated the value of 52 factorial, or $52 \times 51 \times 50$, etc." in an article about card shuffling. Then in May it apologized for having "misstated the product of $100 \times 99 \times 98$ and so on" in an article about "finding the shortest path around a group of cities." The latter correction was a true groveler, listing four other errors in the same article and ending with an apology for not having run the correction sooner.

Excessive groveling is enjoyable; inadequate groveling is more so. With the jovial headline OOPS! a local hardware chain recently took space in the *Post* to correct an earlier ad:

> *This week's Hechinger circular incorrectly states on page 15, "Free stainless steel sink with any kitchen cabinet purchase." The correct copy should read, "Free kitchen installation videotape with purchase of 8 or more cabinets."*

"Oops," my eye. Despite the effort to laugh off the error as a mere typo, something more sinister is clearly going on.

Although the paper cannot possibly own up, it's perfectly evident what's going on in this delicious golden oldie (1984) from the *Post*. "An article yesterday incorrectly identified the race of attorney Rufus King III, who was selected by President Reagan for a D.C. Superior Court judgeship." Stop right there. Can you guess? Yes, "King is white." What I especially love about this one is the suspicion that the Reagan people may have made the same mistake.

But from the poetical point of view, the best corrections are those that totally fail in their clarifying purpose, leaving the reader more contentedly bewildered than ever. Consider this, from the June *Vanity Fair:*

> CORRECTION: *In "Publish and Perish" by Bob Colacello in the April issue, Primrose Dunlop was referred to as Primrose Potter. Primrose Dunlop's mother is Lady Potter, whose first name is also Primrose.*

Wonderful. Gilbert and Sullivan could set it to music.

Keiretsuphobia

(The New Republic, JULY 1, 1991)

You don't hear much about MITI anymore. For a while, Tokyo's Ministry of International Trade and Industry was more widely feared in America than the Kremlin (and this was when the Kremlin was still the Kremlin). MITI was said to be the central government authority directing Japan's diabolical plot to take over the world one industry at a time. Well, MITI is still there, doing whatever evil it did before. But it has been replaced in the anti-Japanese demonology by an even more diabolical organism: the keiretsu.

Keiretsu (same word, singular or plural) are networks or families of corporations. There are "horizontal" keiretsu, spanning several industries and generally organized around a bank, and "vertical" keiretsu, composed of a major industrial corporation and its suppliers in a particular industry. Toyota, for example, heads an auto industry keiretsu. Through interlocking directorates, share-holdings, and simple buying power, Toyota dominates its family of parts manufacturers.

As I was struggling to explain the alarm over keiretsu to a *New Republic* editorial meeting last week, "It's a gigantic conspiracy to . . . to . . . to . . ."

"To build cars?" suggested the editor helpfully.

Exactly.

Keiretsu are said to have roots in the ancient relationship between feudal landlords—*daimyo*—and their samurai, and also in the huge industrial combines—*zaibatsu*—that built the Japanese war machine of the first half of this century, which MacArthur naively thought he had dismantled. And companies like Toyota are now said to be importing this un-American concept, with its associated blizzard of foreign words, into the United States, when they open plants here and form relationships with American suppliers.

In the *Harvard Business Review* last winter, the founder of a Japanese supplier described the nightmare of life inside a keiretsu: "I went to the president of this big company, not to demand my freedom but to profess my sincere desire to support his company's growth. . . . 'Your words are like an expression of affection from an ugly woman,' he answered. . . . My loyalty was taken for granted." Well!

T. Boone Pickens, the legendary Texas self-publicist, has done the most to spread keiretsu alarm. Two years ago he acquired a 26 percent interest in a Toyota headlight supplier. The company, Koito, would not put him on its board or provide him information that, he said, would expose the evils of the keiretsu system. Recently he announced he was giving up in despair and disposing of his stock.

In fact, as Koito had alleged all along, it came out a few months ago that Pickens never really owned the stock. The Japanese financial sharpster who had "sold" it to him had also loaned him the money and guaranteed him against loss. It was all part of a scheme to create so much noise that Toyota would buy the shares back at a premium ("greenmail," it's called). But the sharpster suffered other reversals and needed his shares back. That, not despair over keiretsu, is what led Boone to abandon his quest.

As with other allegedly nefarious Japanese practices—trade protectionism, MITI itself—the critics of keiretsu don't make clear whether they think this is an outrage that ought to be eliminated or a brilliant stroke that ought to be copied. "Keiretsu is a great part of Japan's economic success," writes Pickens. "It reinforces Japan's stable business environment, providing corporate managers with the time and capital to plan for the long term." If so, why fear the arrival of keiretsu in America? Because "keiretsu fits the classic definition of . . . business monopolies. Suppliers become captives. Worker freedom is restricted. And consumers pay more."

Consumers pay more? Wait a minute. A main accusation against keiretsu is that they enable a Toyota to squeeze its suppliers and unfairly undercut American rivals. That means consumers pay less. Meanwhile, the Federal Trade Commission is investigating whether Japanese companies with American plants discriminate against American suppliers in favor of their keiretsu-mates back home. But if being a "captive supplier" is so awful, why complain about being left out?

And then there's a consulting firm study of keiretsu in America, financed by Pickens, which raises yet another contradictory worry: that "Japanese automobile manufacturers could induce low-cost Japanese auto parts suppliers in their respective keiretsu systems to refuse to sell to U.S. automobile manufacturers." In other words, the system will discriminate in favor of American parts manufacturers by denying GM and Ford access to Japanese parts.

Clearly, explanations for keiretsuphobia lie more in the realm of psychology than in the realm of economics. Growing up in Detroit, I several times took the public tour of Ford's great River Rouge plant. The guide would explain how, for maximum efficiency, virtually everything that went into a car was manufactured from scratch on-site. Later that kind of thinking went out of fashion. It came to be thought that "contracting out" different bits of the manufacturing process and buying supplies "off the shelf" was more efficient. Who knows? But American companies still do it both ways, and Japanese vertical keiretsu are just a middle way between these two extremes. General Motors still makes far more of its own parts than Toyota buys from "captive" suppliers.

Robert Z. Lawrence of the Brookings Institution has done what is regarded as the most important study of keiretsu in Japan. Are they an efficient method of production, or just a cozy arrangement that blocks opportunity for American suppliers? Lawrence found that keiretsu tend to reduce imports but have no significant effect on exports. From this he reasoned, logically, that keiretsu are an unjustified impediment to trade: If they actually made products more efficiently, they would increase exports as well as reducing imports. So American trade negotiators are right to try to break them open.

That's fine. But a corollary of this logic is that keiretsu are doing Japan no good either. Far from a nefarious plot, they are a foolish archaism. Yet keiretsuphobes don't take that point of view. Indeed, the *Harvard Business Review,* which seems to be developing a specialty in anti-Japanese alarmism, published another article last year on keiretsu, this one urging American and European computer manufacturers to join in a giant keiretsu-style combine with all their suppliers to take on the Japanese. At the same time, T. Boone Pickens wants to "use the antitrust laws to prevent Japan from exporting its keiretsu cartels to the U.S."

Are Japan's keiretsu to be envied or to be deplored? Copied or banned? The answer, I think, is none of the above.

THE PERCEPTION OF IMPROPRIETY

(The New Republic, JULY 8, 1991)

Sometime in the next couple of months, Washington will have its traditional summer scandal. It will descend suddenly and be brief but intense, like a summer thunderstorm. But it will drench the parched political landscape and give welcome relief to desperate journalists and politicos during the hot dry season. Then it will go away.

This happens almost every year. The first one I lived through involved Bert Lance, President Carter's budget director. It had something to do with a bank, I dimly recall, and his wife had a funny name. But it all seemed quite thrilling at the time.

At some point in this future episode, someone will declare that the problem is not any misbehavior itself but rather the "appearance" of impropriety or the "perception" of a conflict of interest. (Or "the possibility of even the appearance of any conflict of interest," as Representative Stephen L. Neal of North Carolina put it on his 1991 financial disclosure form, explaining that he was investing only in mutual funds and North Carolina bonds, plus Quaker Oats stock because oats reduce cholesterol.) And thus, with general agreement that the problem is one of appearances or perceptions, the scandal will drift off into a misty afterlife realm where Tongsun Park is eternally dancing with Donna Rice while the Wedtech Orchestra plays hits from the Watergate tapes.

What's nice about the appearances/perceptions fudge is its versatility. It can be useful to any part in an unfolding scandal: the alleged wrongdoer and his or her allies, the accuser, the official tribunal, the press.

For the unfortunate person who awakes one muggy August morning to find his picture in *The Washington Post* and three camera crews camped out on his doorstep, "appearances" are a way of turning a mortal sin into a venial one, of conceding error without confessing guilt. In announcing that John Sununu would henceforth have to clear his air travel plans with the White House counsel, President Bush said, "I want this administration to continue to be above the perception of impropriety." Was the perception of Sununu's impropriety a correct perception? Bush was never forced to say.

Senator Mark Hatfield has had a series of ethical stumbles. In 1984, discussing a controversial payment to his wife by a foreign businessman, he said the problem was "insensitivity to the appearance of impropriety." In May of this year, discussing favors Hatfield received from the crooked president of the University of South Carolina, an unnamed friend told the *Post:* "He's really had to do some soul-searching about the importance of perception in the public's trust."

And this one's wonderful. The general counsel of the University of Nevada at Las Vegas said recently the school's regents were "extremely concerned about . . . even the appearance of a relationship" between UNLV's basketball team and a convicted game fixer. The "appearance" of a relationship was a published photograph of three UNLV players and Richard "The Fixer" Perry sitting in a hot tub together.

But "appearances" can also be a way of accusing someone of wrongdoing without saying what, if anything, is really wrong. It is a shortcut to moral outrage, for those who are in a hurry to get there. And there is a self-fulfilling quality to such accusations, since the accusations themselves help to create the perception they complain about.

Democrats on the House Judiciary Committee demanded that Richard Thornburgh resign as attorney general when he announced his intention to run for the Senate. Why? According to the *Post,* they say "he has created the appearance of a conflict of interest by deciding to stay on." Now, either there is a conflict of interest or there isn't. It's possible there's a genuine conflict, but it's intellectually lazy and unfair to Thornburgh to fry him for the mere appearance of one.

The most egregious use of the appearances dodge recently was in the Senate Ethics Committee's treatment of the Keating Five. The committee cited Alan Cranston for actually breaking the rules, John Glenn and John McCain for "poor judgment," and Dennis Deconcini and Don Riegle for "conduct that gave the appearance of being improper." It hardly requires the elaborate and costly proceedings of the Senate Ethics Committee to determine that there has been an appearance of impropriety. Of course there's the appearance of impropriety. The appearance of impropriety is precisely why the Ethics Committee was convened. What we want to know is: *Was there impropriety?* If they cannot tell us that, we are not interested in their views on how things appear.

It's especially puzzling when journalists resort to the appearances cop-out. There was a small ethical flurry in May over Robert Clarke, a senior federal bank regulator, who was borrowing money from banks to play the market in stocks and junk bonds. The usual: *The New York Times* reported that "critics on Capitol Hill said he was insensitive to the appearance of impropriety"; Clarke apologized for having "inadvertently contributed to a public perception of conflict of interest." Then along came the *Times* editorial page to accuse Clarke of "a shocking appearance of impropriety. At best, he's been morally obtuse."

So the press has done its duty and reality has been brought into line with perceptions: Mr. Clarke has put his investments into a blind trust. Surely, though, it is the function of *The New York Times* to bring perceptions into line with reality, not the other way around. Were Mr. Clarke's investments ethically wrong, or not? Perhaps the news pages cannot settle this question, but the writers on the editorial page ought to be able to settle it at least to their own satisfaction.

Emphasis on the appearance of an ethical conflict can lead to the appearance of an ethical solution. In Illinois a few months ago, the leading state labor and business PACs agreed to boycott fund-raisers by state legislators during the months of April, May, and June. "We've been concerned about the appearance of impropriety," one lobbyist explained to the *Chicago Tribune*, which reported that the goal was "to curb appearances of vote buying by lobbyists and a shakedown by lawmakers." Of course what the lobbyists manage to avoid with their ostentatious three months of self-restraint is not *even* the appearance of impropriety—it's *only* the appearance of impropriety. The impropriety itself remains. The PACs are still there, still contributing to politicians, and if they are not managing to buy a few votes they are a fraud on their members. But at least the perceptions are taken care of.

LIFE TERMS

(*The New Republic*, JULY 15, 1991)

The great advantage of the right-to-life side in the abortion debate is its moral clarity. Louisiana's new antiabortion law, enacted June 18 over Governor Buddy Roemer's veto, declares: "Life begins at conception and . . . is a continuum until the time of death." It defines the term "unborn child" as "offspring of human beings from the moment of conception. . . . "

If the fetus is a fully human being with the same moral claims as any other from the moment of conception, it is only reasonable that doctors who kill fetuses by performing abortions should be punished with up to ten years in prison and a $100,000 fine. What's harder to understand, given this presumption, is why this statute—the toughest in the nation, a direct challenge to *Roe* v. *Wade*—should explicitly exempt from any punishment the woman who procures an abortion. Yet it does.

The same anomaly arose during one of the 1988 presidential debates. Michael Dukakis accused George Bush of wanting to brand women who seek abortions as criminals. Bush burbled that while he opposes abortion, "I haven't sorted out the penalties." The next morning campaign manager James Baker declared, "Frankly, he [Bush] thinks that a woman in a situation like that would be more properly considered an additional victim."

That sounds compassionate, but it is nonsense. If every fetus is a fully human being, a woman who procures an abortion is exactly like someone who hires a gunman to murder her child. Hardly a victim. Yet when a prochoice Louisiana legislator introduced an amendment to the abortion bill imposing penalties on the patient as well as the doctor, the prolife majority saw this—quite accurately—as sabotage and it got only two votes.

In January, Utah enacted an antiabortion law almost as restrictive as Louisiana's. After the bill passed, the ACLU discovered that this law, combined with an earlier law defining murder to include the killing of a fetus except in a legal abortion, could lead to the death penalty (by firing squad!) for both doctor and patient. The bill's author protested, "It was an innocent oversight. We specifically amended the bill to try to avoid penalties on the woman." Nevertheless, to make absolutely sure the patient would not be punished, and even the doctor would not be tried for murder, the abortion law and the murder statute were both amended once again.

According to the National Abortion Rights Action League, before *Roe* v. *Wade* (1973), sixteen states actually did have laws on the books punishing women who had abortions, and others made the woman patient potentially liable under statutes about aiding and abetting crimes, etc. If states are allowed to ban abortion once again, it will require Utah-style contortions to make sure that the normal logic of criminal law—that someone who desires, seeks, arranges, and pays for a crime is guilty of the crime—is derailed in this particular situation.

There will be problems, too, with self-administered abortifacients like RU 486. Is the woman who doses herself a victimizing doctor or a victimized patient? There is already a dispute over whether the new Louisiana law covers forms of birth control, like the IUD, that may technically work postconception. A National Right to Life Committee spokesman insists airily that all that stuff about "life beginning at conception" is just "in the preamble," and therefore apparently doesn't count. The "actual operative language of the bill" requires "specific intent" to terminate a known pregnancy, and therefore mere use of an IUD wouldn't count. That may be correct as statutory interpretation, but as moral logic it doesn't work. If the fetus is a human being from the moment of conception, using a device that would destroy such a fetus is, at best, like setting a house on fire with the intention of killing anyone inside but without knowing for sure who is there. Hardly blameless.

The point, though, is not that women are likely to be punished as criminals for seeking an abortion or using birth control. The point is that even abortion's strongest opponents turn logical somersaults to avoid punishing women abortion customers. What this reveals is that they don't really think abortion is the equivalent of murder. That is, they don't really believe that every fetus from the moment of conception has the same moral claims as a postbirth human being. Or at least they are unwilling to defend the implications of that belief. Exceptions permitting abortions for victims of rape and incest, which most right-to-lifers support, raise the same logical problem.

If abortion opponents would abandon their false claim to moral clarity, we could have a useful debate about what reasons for abortion are better than others and when in its development the fetus acquires claims that can override the various reasons a woman might have for wishing to terminate her pregnancy. But abandoning abortion-is-baby-killing would mean giving up the best weapon in the propaganda battle. And admitting that the moral issue is inherently muddled might dangerously incline an honest person to the prochoicers' conclusion: that, in most circumstances at least, the decision should be left to the woman who has to live with the consequences.

That's why people cling to absolutist rhetoric who can't possibly believe it. The official Republican party position, as expressed in its 1988 platform, is that "the Fourteenth Amendment's protections apply to unborn children."* The Fourteenth Amendment guarantees to every person "the equal protection of the laws." If the fetus is to be considered a person under the Fourteenth Amendment, then states that punish murder (all states, of course) would have to treat abortion—the purposeful killing of a fetus—exactly like murder. If a state regards people who arrange for a murder to be guilty of murder themselves (as all states do), that state would have to prosecute as murderers women who procure abortions. If a state has the death penalty (as the Republican platform strongly recommends), that penalty would have to apply equally to murderers of fetuses.

In a way, though, such ridiculous absolutism is just a response to the absolutism of the other side of the abortion debate. Prochoicers have insisted since 1973 that the extreme abortion-rights view is inscribed somewhere in the Constitution. The debate for eighteen years has not been over who decides about abortion—the state or the individual? It has been over who decides who decides—the legislature or the courts?

If one message of the prochoice movement is that abortion is not a question that lends itself to simple moral absolutes, doesn't it follow that the question is not one for courts to settle absolutely one way or the other? Isn't it better treated as a matter for the democratic process to struggle with and reach a decision that the majority can feel comfortable with?

*The 1992 platform, too

Judges, Democracy, and Natural Law

(*Time,* AUGUST 12, 1991)*

Though people on both sides deplore them, these annual summer brawls over Supreme Court nominees can be valuable exercises in civic education. The Robert Borkathon of 1987 forced millions of Americans to think about the role of a constitution in a democracy: the proper way to interpret two-hundred-year-old phrases, the conflict between majority rule and individual freedom, and so on.

This summer President Bush's nomination of Clarence Thomas has unexpectedly plunged the nation even deeper into the pool of first principles. America finds itself debating natural law. An enthusiasm for something called "natural law" is one of the repeated themes in Thomas's slim collection of writings and speeches. What he means by natural law and what uses he would put it to as a life-tenured Supreme Court justice are not clear. This justifiably alarms some people, who are worried that "natural law" could become an excuse for a conservative judge to impose his political agenda—just as conservatives have accused liberal judges of using "privacy" to do.

In fact, though, the two questions can be separated. Is there something called natural law? And is it a legitimate basis for judges to overrule the wishes of the majority as expressed in laws of a less exalted sort?

At this point in American history, the answer to the first question is beyond challenge. Yes, as far as the United States is concerned, natural law exists. The "Laws of Nature" are right there in the first sentence of the Declaration of Independence. The second and most famous sentence provides a perfect definition of natural law: human beings are "endowed by their Creator with certain inalienable Rights," including "Life, Liberty and the pursuit of Happiness."

Where do these rights come from? Some may have trouble with the concept of a divine creator. Others may find it overly metaphysical to insist

---

*My prediction that the Clarence Thomas confirmation hearings would center on a discussion of natural-law theory turned out to be laughably wide of the mark.

that every human being has these rights in a world where most people are patently unfree to exercise them. But few can doubt that life, liberty, and the pursuit of happiness are what a civilized society ought to strive to provide its members. As the Declaration says, that is the reason "Governments are instituted." It is "self-evident." That's good enough for me.

But just because rights exist, this does not mean it is the role of judges to enforce them. The institution of judicial review—the power of unelected judges to overrule the democratic branches of government—is a funny business. Judges do not have that power in other major democracies, and it is not explicitly authorized in the U.S. Constitution. It emerges, rather, from the structure of our government. As Justice John Marshall first reasoned in *Marbury* v. *Madison* (1803): Faced with a conflict between a law and a constitutional provision, judges must honor the Constitution. All government officials should do the same. The Supreme Court's interpretation of the Constitution is definitive only because procedurally it comes last.

The Constitution lists certain rights, and others (such as the right to vote) are implied in the structure of government it sets up. But nothing in the constitutional structure of the government gives the Supreme Court authority to overrule the other branches on the basis of unwritten natural law. Judicial review, a bold claim at first, is now so well established that we've come to feel that a right doesn't exist unless a judge can enforce it. But enforcing a right means interpreting it, and exclusive power to interpret a concept as vague as natural law should not be given to the unelected branch of government. The job of protecting our nonconstitutional rights belongs to those who most directly "deriv[e] their just powers from the consent of the governed," as the Declaration has it: elected officials.

The Declaration speaks of "Life, Liberty and the pursuit of Happiness." The Constitution refers more prosaically to "life, liberty, or property." It's an illuminating difference. Furthermore, the Constitution does not guarantee these values in absolute terms. It protects them only from deprivation by the government itself, and even in that regard it promises only procedural fairness and equal treatment. The authors were surely wise to narrow the focus. What would be left of democracy if judges could roam the landscape striking down anything that—in their opinion—interfered with somebody's pursuit of happiness?

All this is not to say that natural-law concepts have no role to play in constitutional interpretation. Many people, for example, find it hard to understand why freedom of speech must be extended to Nazis and others who do not believe in free speech themselves and would deny it to others if they could. The answer is that the Bill of Rights is based on the theory of natural law, not on the alternative theory of a social contract. You are entitled to these rights simply because you are a human being, not because you have agreed, literally or metaphorically, to honor them.

Majestic phrases like "due process of law" require parsing. Even the strictest constructionists would accept that the natural-law thinking of the eighteenth century is useful in divining the Framers' "original intent."

Some enthusiasts see the Ninth Amendment—which provides that the list of rights in the Constitution "shall not be construed to deny or disparage others retained by the people"—as a direct incorporation of natural law. The fact that these enthusiasts include would-be judicial activists of both the Left and the Right ought to dim the enthusiasm of both groups. The point is that the people do have rights not derived from the Constitution—natural rights, if you will—but judges have no special authority to enforce those rights.

Clarence Thomas may well be claiming no special authority for judges when he invokes natural law and natural rights. In that case, there is no problem. If he has more ambitious notions, there is a serious problem. And the fact that liberal justices may have had overreaching notions of their own in the past is mere irony.

Class, Not Race?

(*The New Republic*, AUGUST 19, 1991)

The nomination of Clarence Thomas for the Supreme Court has usefully confused the debate over affirmative action. Not only was Thomas's race the determining factor in his selection for the Court (despite President Bush's farcical attempts to deny it) but at every stage in his career he had enjoyed favorable treatment because of his race and background rather than his "qualifications" in some clinical sense.

It does not strike me as terminally hypocritical for Thomas to have taken advantage of reverse discrimination—for example, an explicit 10 percent minority quota that got him into Yale Law School—while claiming to be morally opposed. Unless you are Gandhi, you live in society as you find it while you work to reform it. I oppose the home mortgage interest deduction, and have written often urging that it be curtailed, but I still take it every year.

What complicates the affirmative action debate, though, is the evident reasonableness of giving someone like Clarence Thomas a leg up in the game of life. Even the purest of meritocratic purists can see that Thomas's history of overcoming poverty and racism is itself meritorious. And few would argue that, in getting as far as Yale Law School, Thomas found the advantages of a deprived background to outweigh the disadvantages.

The moral of the Thomas saga therefore, some have suggested, is that affirmative action should be revised, not discarded. The basis should be social class rather than race. At meritocratic crisis points, a Clarence Thomas should get extra credit for having been born in poverty, but not because of the color of his skin per se.

This is not a new idea. In *Illiberal Education,* his recent attack on the American university, Dinesh D'Souza complains for pages about affirmative action, only to conclude that "universities should retain their policies of preferential treatment but alter their criteria . . . from race to socioeconomic disadvantage." Twelve years ago, before he was a judge, Antonin Scalia interrupted a screed against affirmative action to remark: "I do not, on the other hand, oppose—indeed I strongly favor—what might be called . . . 'affirmative action programs' of many types of help for the poor and disadvantaged even if most of those benefited would be members of minority races."

The idea is very tempting. Some even maintain that this was the original concept of affirmative action, before it got perverted and bureaucratized. Certainly it is hard to explain why a prep-school-educated child of two black professionals should get admissions preference to Harvard over, say, the kid of an unemployed white coal miner from a run-down public school in Appalachia.

Situations like that are somewhat rarer in real life than in the imaginations of affirmative action opponents. Trading race for social class sounds like a very good deal for affirmative action supporters, especially if this would actually end the toxic debate over racial preference. But would it? Only if opponents are prepared to abandon many of the principles they ostensibly have been fighting for.

First, affirmative action by social class is still a departure from what D'Souza is pleased to call "a neutral standard of academic excellence." If "qualifications" are measured by ability to do the job or to succeed at school, any form of affirmative action is a departure from the principle that scarce spaces should go to the best-qualified candidate.

A few months ago there was a triumphant fuss when a student working in the admissions office at Georgetown University's law school revealed that blacks on average had lower admissions test scores. "Gotcha!" was the general attitude among critics. But under a system of preferential treatment by "socioeconomic disadvantage," blacks admitted to Georgetown would still have lower average scores than whites. If that is intolerable, so is affirmative action of any sort.

Second, affirmative action by social class is still a form of zero-sum social engineering, and for every winner there will still be an equal and opposite loser. Will the white man in that famous Jesse Helms commercial—crumbling his rejection letter in disgust—be comforted because he lost his job to someone else adjudged to be socioeconomically preferable rather than racially preferable? More to the point, would Jesse Helms be prepared to explain to this man—or, for that matter, to Justice Scalia's immigrant father, who (wrote the son) "never profited from the sweat of any black man's brow"—that his lost job is merely making up for past injustice?

Third, affirmative action by social class would not address the highbrows' favorite complaint: that affirmative action stigmatizes the beneficiaries in their own minds and in the minds of others. This is a recurrent theme in D'Souza's book and the dominant theme in the writings of Shelby Steele. It is a trump card for critics of any social policy that the policy in question "hurts the very people it is trying to help."

Any debilitating self-doubt that exists because of affirmative action is not going to be mitigated by being told that you got into Harvard because of your "socioeconomic disadvantage" rather than your race. To be sure, the beneficiaries of "new, improved" affirmative action wouldn't wear the stamp of it on their faces in quite the same way. But they themselves would know, their friends and advisers would know, and all but a very few blacks would be assumed anyway to be affirmative action beneficiaries.

Affirmative action by social class might bring its own innovative horrors. Definitions, to start. Does Clarence Thomas the sharecropper's kid get more or fewer preference points than the unemployed miner's son from Appalachia? Is a large suburban public high school a bigger or smaller minus than a second-rank prep school? In Communist societies, such as

Mao's China, they have produced hierarchies of reverse social discrimination that match the social distinctions of the most rigidly stratified traditional society. Do we want to start playing that sort of game here?

Reverse social snobbery is already a minor irritant in the public debate that should not be encouraged. Nor should a whole new category of imagined victimization. A few days ago in *The Washington Post*, the conservative literary critic Carol Iannone suggested that the reason the Senate rejected her nomination for the advisory board of the National Endowment for the Humanities was that she is working-class. That is ludicrous. Even the children of Supreme Court Justice Clarence Thomas will surely feel the sting of prejudice more than Carol Iannone ever will.

But this doesn't mean the children of a Supreme Court justice need or deserve preferential treatment (though, of course, in real life they will get it, whatever their parent's race). Affirmative action by social disadvantage does have a certain logic that traditional affirmative action lacks, not to mention a seductive freedom from the poison of racial consciousness. To embrace it honestly, though, critics of reverse discrimination would have to give up about three quarters of their case—and about 99 percent of the political power of their argument. That I doubt they are prepared to do.

DON'T BE PUSHY

(*The New Republic*, OCTOBER 14, 1991)

The cringing ethnic is a pathetic specimen in American culture. It might be Uncle Tom meekly defending his master for selling him down the river. ("It goes agin me to hear one word agin Mas'r. . . . He couldn't be spected to think so much of poor Tom. Mas'rs is used to havin' all these yer things done for 'em, and nat'lly they don't think so much on't. They can't be spected to, no way.") Or it might be Walter Lippmann oleaginously agreeing with Harvard's WASP president, A. Lawrence Lowell, that the university ought to have fewer Jews ("bad for the immigrant Jews as well as for Harvard if there were too great a concentration"). One blessing of the creation of Israel is that it relieved pressure on Jews elsewhere to cringe, assimilate, "normalize" themselves. Being Jewish became normal.

Nevertheless, Alan Dershowitz's best-selling book, *Chutzpah,* makes me, as an American Jew, cringe. Dershowitz says: "American Jews need more chutzpah." They "are not pushy or assertive enough" to protect their own interests or Israel's. They still act like "second-class citizens," overly worried about how they appear to gentiles. He discerns a subtle new form of anti-Jewishness, replacing the cruder anti-Semitism of the past, which he clumsily calls "Judeopathy." It consists of a "double standard" under which Jews and Israel are held up to "super-scrutiny" and criticized for behavior tolerated uncritically in others. In particular, the role of Jews in helping Israel through the American political process is simply an exercise in first-class citizenship. "That is the American way." Chutzpah is patriotic!

But are there not limits to chutzpah, both as a political strategy and as a lifestyle?

To start, claiming that the fruits of Jewish political chutzpah are merely Jews' fair share in the American system moves you onto dangerous logical ground. Because of their organized determination, general civic involvement, social prominence, and—yes—financial success, Jews enjoy political influence out of proportion to their share in the population. That does not mean disproportionate in any right-and-wrong sense. Nor does it say anything about the substantive merits of any particular Jewish cause. But the suggestion that American politics is or should be a scramble among interest groups to split the American pie does not lead to the conclusion that Jews are entitled to a bigger piece.

Furthermore, one problem with American politics is that too much of it is indeed an interest group scramble. The days when "pluralism" seemed an unalloyed blessing are long gone. The demands of Americans as members of narrow interest groups often undermine their interests as citizens of society as a whole. The deficit is a concrete expression of this problem. Urging Jews to flex their chutzpah without restraint, then granting them absolution on grounds that this is "the American way," is advice less patriotic and more cynical than it seems at first.

But, even measured cynically, is it good advice? Moderating your chutzpah for fear of appearing "pushy" may be psychologically demeaning, but it may also be politically sensible. AIPAC, the American pro-Israel lobby, will be happy to explain to Professor Dershowitz that what the gentiles think does matter. Appearances do count, after all, and the appearance of an all-powerful Jewish lobby that will stop at nothing to get its way is self-defeating. In a way, American Jewish political influence is like the Israeli nuclear capability: It must be denied, but not too convincingly. Unabashed chutzpah is not the best tool for this delicate task.

On a personal level, what is wrong with not wanting to seem pushy? The standard chutzpah jokes—the man who kills his parents then pleads for mercy because he is an orphan, etc.—are funny precisely because the behavior they describe is appalling. Ethnic traits are a sensitive subject, and rightly so. I don't even object to the unwritten rule that you—especially if you are an outsider—can ascribe good traits to an ethnic group (music, humor, intelligence) but not bad ones. Logically, though, the possibility of good ethnic traits suggests the possibility of bad ones, too.

But leave that aside. Unattractive behavior is unattractive, whether or not it is an ethnic stereotype and whether or not that stereotype has any validity. Irishmen, like anyone else, shouldn't drink too much. It would be a foolish response to the stereotype of Irishmen to say, "I'll show them," and go get plastered. Pushiness isn't nice behavior, and I intend to try to avoid it. I hope that doesn't make me an Uncle Tom, or an Uncle Walter.

As for the double standard Dershowitz complains of, it certainly exists and is not new. That double standard is a large part of the basis for American financial support of Israel: $77 billion in aid (1991 dollars) in the past quarter century. In a world of nations clamoring for American support—many of them poorer than Israel or more directly vital to America's national interest—Israel's moral superiority to other nations has been its Unique Selling Proposition. That is a practical asset the Shamir government seems intent on squandering.

Theologically, Jews are supposed to believe that they are held under "super-scrutiny" not just by gentiles but by God himself. We are the "chosen people"—remember?—and are expected to behave better than others. History certainly confirms this special burden on Jews, as well as their pretty impressive record of rising to meet the challenge. Here in America, where the burden is after all pretty light, even those Jews who don't necessarily buy into the God part generally take pride in the history, happily accept the challenge, and wouldn't trade either for a mess of chutzpah. We don't want to be that normal.

Iᴛ'ꜱ Yᴏᴜʀ Fᴀᴜʟᴛ

(*The New Republic*, OCTOBER 28, 1991)

Everyone can agree that congressional check-kiting and related scandals, though small matters in themselves, are symbolic of a larger problem in American democracy. We just might disagree about what that larger problem is. The problem as generally presented is that members of Congress dwell in an inside-the-Beltway cocoon of special privileges, isolated from the concerns of the real world. The fact that they can't keep their own accounts in order is taken as a metaphor for the mess they've made of the government budget.

It's a metaphor, all right. My favorite aspect of the story is the hundreds of thousands of dollars in unpaid bills at the House restaurant and catering service. It turns out that most of this money is actually owed by constituent groups that get a member's authorization to use House catering facilities and then stiff him or her for the bill. The member, being a politician, is naturally hesitant to press for payment.

So the dining bills are indeed just like the federal budget. The citizenry makes demands for benefits, refuses to pay for them, runs up a huge tab called the national debt, then blames the politicians for being irresponsible, spendthrift, etc., etc., etc. This is not to say that the politicians are blameless. But they are far from entirely to blame.

The check-kiting story is generating a whole new wave of anti-Washington posturing identified as "populism." I'm not sure what "populism" means, but if this is it, it is smugger and more complacent than any common form of inside-the-Beltway elitism. It has been taken up by columnists and commentators who make many times what a member of Congress does, and are far more steeped in the culture of Washington than a congressman who goes home every weekend. Editorial writers at *The Wall Street Journal* join the chorus from their aerie at the World Financial Center in downtown New York.

The last outbreak of this virus was a year ago, when the government almost shut down as Congress and President Bush struggled to produce the controversial budget agreement. Bush himself preposterously piled it on: "Oh, how nice it is to be out where the real people are, outside of

Washington," he said while campaigning in Nebraska. A Tampa, Florida, retiree named Jack Gargen bought himself some publicity with newspaper ads declaring: "I'm appalled . . . I'm bitter . . . I'm outraged . . . I'm angry . . . I'm incensed . . . I'm livid . . . I'm even more livid . . ." at various congressional malefactions. He announced an organization called THRO, for "Throw the Hypocritical Rascals Out."

Unfortunately, the blight of hypocrisy is not restricted to within the Washington Beltway. Even Mr. Gargen was afflicted. Although he was "appalled" by the national debt and "outraged" at the thought of higher taxes to reduce it, he offered no alternatives besides the usual red herrings: "sheer government waste," Food Stamps for people wearing designer jeans, and so on. He opposed "federal giveaway programs," but stood like Horatio at the Bridge against any imposition on "our retired senior citizens"— who are, of course, the overwhelming beneficiaries of federal giveaways. In his hypocrisy, Mr. Gargen was exactly what he professed to be: the voice of the American Everyman.

You could lock any two ideologues of the Left and Right in a room and together they could come up with a set of taxes and spending programs that was both fairer and better for the economy than the budget we have now. Provided, that is, that they didn't need to submit their handiwork to the voters for approval.

Every now and then *Time* magazine runs a special feature bewailing the supposed dearth of leadership. Maybe it's time for one bewailing the lack of followership. Americans don't want leadership. They want alchemy. True, they have been told by politicians that alchemy is possible, that the gap between the government they want and the amount they're willing to pay for it can be closed by magic. But in their hearts, they must know that's not the case. Or at least anyone carrying on about a lack of "leadership" in Washington must already know this. And it's absurd to accuse leaders of failing to persuade you of something you already know.

It's even more absurd to vote time and again for leaders you believe have failed, and then to demand their mass removal. Goodness knows our elected leaders, most of them, would win no prize at a medium-sized state fair. But who elected them? The current fad for term limits on Congress and other elected offices is the silliest expression of America's failure of democratic followership. As has been noted, its message is: Stop me before I vote again.

Of course most American citizens don't vote most of the time. There are commentators who excuse this, too, as demonstrating a healthy contempt for politicians or, more grandly, a healthy democratic contentment. People should not be scolded for ignoring their franchise, the argument goes. In a properly functioning society, politics is rightly of marginal concern to good citizens. They are far wiser to attend to their families instead, or bake cookies, chase butterflies, write poetry.

For a seemingly populist argument, this is amazingly patronizing. After all, those making it spend much of their own waking hours thinking about politics and public policy. They do not do so because they think that such matters are of marginal importance. They are not showing humility by taking over this grim duty of caring about politics, as a saint might by washing the feet of the poor and sick. They think about politics precisely because they do believe it's an important subject, and they believe their views on the subject are especially important. It's just other people's views that don't matter, apparently.

Criticizing the citizenry for the sins of the politicians sounds undemocratic. It is reminiscent of Brecht's famous caustic crack that when people lose confidence in the government, the government should "dissolve the people and elect a new one." Politicians prefer to tell the people they're wonderful. Even Jimmy Carter, in his legendarily downbeat "malaise" speech, burbled about "my belief in the decency and the strength and the wisdom of the American people." George Bush says "real people" have it all over those icky politicians.

Respect for democracy does not require this type of pandering. It does not assume that the people are inherently wise and any error of the political system is a failure of the officials they choose to elect. Genuine respect for democracy does not let the voters off the hook by putting all the blame on leaders—like blaming parents for their misbehaving children. Real respect for democracy takes it for granted that government is by the people when it performs badly, just as when it performs well.

Jimmy Carter's campaign slogan was "A government as good as its people." That's just about what we've got.

W HO B EAT C OMMUNISM?

(*Time,* NOVEMBER 4, 1991)

I n 1977, President Jimmy Carter gave a speech renouncing America's "inordinate fear of communism." This line came to haunt Carter and established his reputation for global naïveté. It is often contrasted with President Ronald Reagan's "evil empire" speech of 1983, although the two phrases are not logically contradictory. Carter didn't say inordinate moral revulsion against communism or inordinate military opposition to the Soviets. He said "fear," meaning an inordinate belief in the power of communism as a political and economic system.

And hasn't history borne him out? Even after six years of remarkable change, the fragility of communism after the August coup attempt surprised nearly everyone. Meanwhile in Washington, the hearings on Robert Gates for CIA director have exposed the mechanisms that produced inordinate fear.

Senator Daniel Patrick Moynihan has developed a magnificent obsession with the CIA's odd role in the cold war as a cheerleader for the success of the Soviet experiment. "Every President since Dwight Eisenhower has been told that the Soviet Union [had] growth rates vastly in excess of ours," he says. The CIA regularly predicted that the Soviets were catching up. In the late 1970s, it claimed, absurdly in retrospect, that the Soviet economy was two-thirds the size of America's. While exaggerating the importance of Communist regimes in such places as Angola and Nicaragua, the agency also completely missed the ethnic and nationalist time bombs inside the Soviet Union itself.

The Gates hearings revealed the CIA in the 1980s as an institution determined to portray Soviet communism as an ever-growing threat, no matter what the evidence. The agency produced an intentionally one-sided report on possible Soviet involvement in the assassination attempt on the pope and presented it as a balanced view—in support of Director William Casey's conviction that the Soviets were behind all international terror. It offered retrospective justification for selling weapons to the Ayatollah on grounds that the Soviets were making inroads in Iran—something that even Gates now admits was incorrect.

The argument between liberals and conservatives about what caused communism's fall, and who got it right or wrong, will go on for a long time. On the main cause—the utter hopelessness of communism as an economic system—both sides got it right in their hearts but somehow wrong in their heads. They knew communism couldn't work but forgot it. Of the two sides of the argument, though, it seems to me that conservatives were wronger here. They are the ones who kept emphasizing that military strength could grow indefinitely, no matter how decrepit the economy.

On the second most important cause—the spirit of freedom in individual people, which survived seventy years of totalitarian rule—both sides were caught by surprise. The Communists had more than three generations in which to mold a New Soviet Man. Few outsiders suspected they had failed so completely. Given half an opportunity, it turned out, people knew immediately what they wanted and demanded it. The freedom-enhancing advent of electronic gizmos like televisions and computers—so different from the role Orwell envisioned for them in *1984*—helped but can't fully explain it. Perhaps conservatives deserve an edge on this item for their greater doubts about social engineering in general.

The third cause of the Soviet downfall was the decades-long American, and Western, policy of containment. Both sides of the argument can take equal bows for this one.

The real bone of contention, of course, is the role played by Reagan's military escalation of the 1980s. It's hard to argue that this was worthless or counterproductive and impossible to know how the world would look today if America had followed a different course. But a few skeptical points might be kept in mind.

First, Reagan certainly never advertised his strategy as one of capitalizing on growing Soviet weakness by engaging the USSR in an arms race in which it couldn't hope to compete for long. Quite the opposite: Per those CIA estimates, the arms buildup of the 1980s was presented as a question of desperately trying to keep up with the Joneskis. So, at the very least, Reagan misled the American people into a highly aggressive policy by presenting it as defensive.

Few will object to having been misled if the policy worked. But did it? All you can say for sure is that if things had turned out differently—if communism was still standing tall, the Soviet Army and its proxies was still marauding around the world, and the CIA was still churning out rosy estimates of Soviet growth—that also would have been held to vindicate the Reagan policy.*

On the question of what degree of hostility is best designed to hasten the collapse of a Communist regime, it is at least worth pondering the example of Castro's Cuba. That is the Communist country to which American opposition has been most consistently implacable. For four decades, no trade, no détente, no summits, no nothing. Now it is the last totally unreformed Communist country left, though probably not for long. Is that just a coincidence?

And in considering whether, just maybe, a Soviet system whose economy is currently shrinking at the rate of 10 percent a year might have collapsed even without the help of an extra push from America, remember that the push was enormously costly to our side as well. Although defense spending is down from its peak and heading lower, the United States will be paying off the bills run up in the early 1980s for decades to come. If those weapons made the difference, it was money well spent. But maybe we were merely victims of our own "inordinate fear."

David Duke and American Decline

(*Time*, NOVEMBER 25, 1991)

Our mental image of a major nation in decline is Britain. And, in retrospect, the British handled their decline pretty gracefully. In just a couple of generations, Great Britain sank from economic and political superpower to second-rank member of a second-rank regional bloc. Yet the transformation happened without much domestic rancor, despite Britain's supposedly bitter class divisions. At worst, the general attitude was a certain sullen resignation. At best, there was a jolly, fatalistic insouciance. The Brits almost seemed to enjoy their ride down.

America will not be so lucky. In David Duke, we have seen the face of American decline. Of course you can argue about whether the United States has entered a long-term decline similar to Britain's. And even if it has, you can argue whether politicians of one party or the other have the right formula for reversing course. But if decline is America's des-

---

A well-known principle of logic holds that a proposition that can't be falsified has no meaning.

tiny, American society is not likely to take it as mildly as the British did.

America is so much more diverse and so much more contentious. Americans may be about to discover just how much of our ability to get along with one another has depended on that spiritual sense of American manifest destiny—and, more practically, on a steady rise in the average person's prosperity. For almost two decades now this rise, which Americans take as their birthright, has stalled or at least slowed dramatically. David Duke is a political expression of that reality.

The former Nazi and Ku Klux Klan Grand Wizard ran for governor of Louisiana in a campaign based on an open appeal to white people who feel they are being cheated of their American birthright by blacks, immigrants, liberals, New Yorkers, and similar bogeys.

The message is enticing because people are frightened about their standard of living. Yet whatever you may think about affirmative action, immigration, and other "hot button" issues, economic stagnation is far more responsible than these controversial social policies for the sense of shrinking opportunity off which the David Dukes feed. When the pie isn't growing, people become more obsessed with their slice.

America is not homogeneous. We have no ethnic or religious bonds to unite us. We are proud of having built a working nation out of so many disparate parts, and proud of the tolerance that has made that possible. But was ever-increasing prosperity the crucial glue? It's easy to welcome newcomers to the party when the banquet table is overflowing. It's easy to settle disagreements by splitting the difference if there's plenty to go around. In bad times hospitality shrivels and disagreements fester.

Firm class divisions may actually have helped Britain weather its decline. They made for social stability. By contrast, America's social stability came from opportunity. Our "classlessness," as many observers have noted throughout the years, has always rested on the possibility of self-improvement. With unlimited opportunity, no one ever needed to feel stuck in his or her place.

The first time people worried that this special American dispensation might be ending was a century ago, with the end of western expansion. The West was America's social safety valve. American philosopher Henry George went even further. In his famous book *Progress and Poverty* (1879), he wrote that the empty West was responsible for America's egalitarian and optimistic spirit. "The child of the people, as he grows to manhood in Europe, finds all the best seats at the banquet of life marked 'taken.' "

Freedom from such limitations, George believed, could explain "all that we are proud of in the American character." But this gift was imperiled, he predicted, now that "our advance has reached the Pacific."

Henry George was wrong. Geography ran out but prosperity didn't. America remained the land of opportunity. But he was right that America's sense of itself as a nation is wrapped up in the promise of ever-rising prosperity in a way that is not true of other nations. The closing off of the West didn't shut the social safety valve, but a long period of stagnation might. Geographical claustrophobia didn't pervert the American character, but economic claustrophobia could do so.

The current wave of "declinism" got its start with Paul Kennedy's 1988 best-seller, *The Rise and Fall of the Great Powers*. That book posed a conundrum: A nation's military strength rests on its economic strength, but economic strength tends to wither when a nation devotes too many resources to the military. "Imperial overstretch," Kennedy called it.

The world has changed since 1987, and the danger of the United States bankrupting itself through military overextension seems a lot slimmer. Furthermore, the thought of losing our status as a military "great power" with defense commitments all over the world does not traumatize most Americans, I suspect. What does traumatize Americans is the thought of economic stagnation as a permanent condition.

But there's another conundrum: The politics of decline produce exactly the wrong formula for reversing the economics of decline. The result: As decline becomes more evident, it also becomes harder to correct. We need politicians who can persuade the voters to make short-term sacrifice for long-term gain, and small personal sacrifices for the good of society as a whole. Yet the more people suffer from economic claustrophobia, the less amenable they are to such an appeal. Instead, they listen to David Duke, who tells them that Others are stealing their lifestyle.

TERM LIMITS FOR COLUMNISTS

(Unpublished, NOVEMBER 1991)

I have changed my mind.

I used to think I could happily read George Will's column twice a week for the rest of my life, or his. But Will's widely noted recent column announcing his conversion on the subject of term limits for politicians (it began with the historic declaration, "I have changed my mind") has persuaded me to think again. On reflection, I now believe that I was mistaken.

I come to this new belief with a becoming reluctance, but I hold it with a certainty if anything even greater than that with which I held the opposite belief only moments ago. The conclusion is unavoidable: If we are to compete successfully with the Japanese and a united Europe, America simply cannot go on reading the same columnists year after year. There must be strict term limits—by constitutional amendment if necessary—on pundits.

Nonrenewable twelve-year terms for commentators would assure a constant infusion of fresh blood for the nation's op-ed pages, public affairs TV shows, and journals of opinion. For practitioners, opinionizing would come to be thought of as a mere interval in the real work of life—be it lobbying, running for office, or chiropractic—rather than a career in itself. Stale professionals, whose desperation for a column idea often leaves them beholden to Beltway interest groups, would be replaced by "amateurs" in the original Latin sense of those who love what they're doing. Pretentious etymological references and other obvious padding would disappear.

Far more than elected politicians, after all, the Washington punditocracy comprises an insular class, permanent and prosperous, remote from the concerns of working Americans. If an obscure congressman is likely to suffer from swollen self-importance after twelve years, a member of the McLaughlin Group is unlikely to avoid the curse. If it is democratically healthy for politicians to be expelled from this Eden of governance every now and then, how much healthier must it be for members of the Fourth Estate.

And how comforting it will be for those bands of disconsolate excongresspersons, trekking south along I-95 on their way out of town, to be joined by the occasional Rowland Evans or William Safire, who can read to them from his collected columns by the campfire at night. George Will can take comfort that, in whatever congressional district the future may hold for him, there he will find a forcibly retired member of Congress already—thanks to Will's own exertions—settled in and available for the occasional fix of legislative gossip for old times' sake.

"Whatever happened to old H.R. 278?"

"Vetoed again, I hear."

"You don't say. Well, I never . . ."

Supporters of my proposal must face squarely the fact that it will untimely rip from the nation's bosom many fine commentators. I have nothing against any particular pundit, least of all George Will. Well, least of all myself and second least of all George Will. The question, as Will describes it, is whether "more talent is excluded from public service by clogging the system with immovable incumbents—and by the atrophy of the talents of incumbents once interested in things other than job security—than would be lost by term limits." How well put! It will be sad to see that fellow go.

But is it not hypocritical for someone who has spent his own adult life entirely in Washington, climbing the pundit pole, to suggest that a professional pundit class is bad for the country? Don't ask me. Ask Dan Quayle, the Bush administration's point man in the fight for congressional term limits. He has spent almost his entire adult life in electoral politics, arriving in Washington as a congressman in his early thirties and showing no signs of eagerness to leave. Yet he has no qualms in arguing vehemently that the existence of a permanent political class in Washington is the source of all our ills. Congressman Newt Gingrich and other term limits enthusiasts share a similar history of being, for better or worse, professional politicians who crave politics as a lifetime's career. No doubt they have thought of some explanation for this seeming contradiction, though I can't. But whatever it is, I second it.

There is a larger contradiction among supporters of congressional term limits. Most supporters see it as a populist measure, addressing the problem that elected officials grow "out of touch" with the voters. George Will sees it as precisely the opposite: a way to liberate politicians from the narrow, petty demands of their constituents and free them to consider the larger national interest. Both theories cannot be right. But either one applies equally well to columnists. George Will, of course, does not hesitate even now to take the Larger and Longer View. He does not whore after cheap popularity by endorsing faddish causes—or at least, when he does so, he does it for counterintuitive reasons. Not every columnist, though, can afford Will's austere self-discipline. We must please readers, as politicians must please voters. Term limits would free us from such constraints, and allow us to concentrate on what is good and right and just.

Of course, columnists, unlike politicians, must meet the test of the marketplace. But politicians, unlike columnists, must meet the test of the voting booth. Readers, like voters, can always say "no." But that is considered insufficient discipline. For their own good, people must be stopped from reading George Will, even if they want to.

The B List

(*The New Republic*, DECEMBER 9, 1991)

Well, I didn't make the list. Did you? According to a special report on CNN, the government has a secret list of people who will succeed to the presidency in case of nuclear war. The official list prescribed by law and the Constitution—call it the A list—begins with the vice president and descends through the speaker of the House, the president pro tem of the Senate, and fourteen Cabinet officers, ending with the secretary of veterans affairs in seventeenth place.

But there is apparently another list, a B list, that begins with number eighteen and runs who knows how far. According to CNN, it has at times included such people as former United Nations Ambassador Jeane Kirkpatrick, former White House Chief of Staff Howard Baker, and former CIA Director Richard Helms. All of them refused to comment to CNN, but they are undoubtedly feeling rather smug. In Washington, being secretly in line for the presidency is sure to become the newest status symbol.

According to CNN, the plan to install what it calls "the Doomsday Government" was created by the Reagan administration in 1982 and entrusted to a secret agency with the wonderfully deadpan name National Program Office. Oliver North was intimately involved, wouldn't you know. "National Program Office" does not sound like the kind of thing

Ronald Reagan ought to approve of, though that could be deliberate, to put people off the scent. More satisfactory sci-fi vibes are given off by the actual name of the B list itself—the Presidential Successor Support System, or PS-cubed for short. So far, says CNN, PS-cubed has cost the taxpayers $8 billion.

The CNN report was most alarmed about the constitutional implications of a secret line of succession, unknown and unapproved by the body politic. But how worrisome is that? After all, the connection between democracy and the official, nonsecret line of succession is pretty attenuated. Or did you consider Manuel Lujan's qualifications to be president when you voted for your senator, who voted to confirm him as secretary of . . . well, as secretary of whatever he is?

More interesting are the questions of how Ollie North and Company came up with their list of potential presidents, and who is on it. Making lists of names is a favorite occupation of the power-mad. Sometimes these are lists you want to be on, such as those determining who gets invited to a party or who wins a National Medal of Freedom or who gets selected as the ABC Person of the Week. Sometimes they are lists you'd just as soon not be on, for example, who cleans up the kitchen or who has to testify before the House Un-American Activities Committee or who gets executed by Stalin. But the list-maker can take pleasure in either type. Whether for good or evil, the opportunity to exert power by inclusion and exclusion is the same.

I suppose being on the list of who gets to become president of the United States after a nuclear holocaust lies somewhere in between the two categories in terms of desirability. It's like a party you wish to have it known you were invited to but are not particularly eager to attend. Or maybe it's like not being invited to the party itself but being told you can come around the next day and eat the leftovers.

Reagan's commitment to keeping the federal government going under any circumstance is touching. You would have thought that, for a true conservative, one of the bright spots of a nuclear holocaust would be the cessation of the government. Sort of the ultimate in term limits. Is a list of seventeen successors to the president not long enough? That is exactly the sort of bureaucratic mentality Reagan claimed to oppose.

In its report CNN interviewed a source identified only as "Bob." Bob was said to be "knowledgeable." And according to Bob, "In some cases, it may be necessary to even go outside of the active current government to bring in that expertise in a period of crisis." Good old Bob has stumbled onto the perennial dream of good-government types: that, in a crisis, the nation will reach out to Father Theodore Hesburgh (or is it Lee Iacocca? Felix Rohatyn? Magic Johnson?) to take command. What a pity it will take a nuclear catastrophe to bring America to its senses.

CNN does not report how long the B list is. But clearly there is no logical stopping point. If 17 successors to the President are insufficient, so are 34 or 68 or 136. To do this thing right, the National Program Office would have to rank the entire population from one to 250 million in terms of each person's qualifications to be president. It's not easy. Sure, it starts out a snap. But after you've slotted Bill Moyers in number 1 and Willie Horton in number 250,000,000 (and no furlough even then), you still have to face that vast middle ground. Does my Aunt Evelyn come before or after your Uncle Benny? Does Madonna outrank Arthur Schlesinger, Jr.? And don't forget yourself, Ollie. You squeeze right in there between Pee-wee Herman and Orrin Hatch.

In *The New York Times,* Duke law professor William van Alstyne points out another problem with the B list. Since it's secret, how will you prove that your number has come up? It would be like winning the lottery but losing the ticket. As the *Times* states the dilemma: "Who . . . would believe an obscure figure claiming to be president under a top-secret plan no one had ever heard of." For myself, I wouldn't even believe Jeane Kirkpatrick or Howard Baker.

Obviously, the solution is to make the list public. And, just to be sure, we should tattoo every American citizen with his or her presidential succession number (PSN). That way, survivors stumbling through the wreckage of American civilization would merely have to compare numbers to know who should take orders from whom.

As nuclear war becomes a more distant possibility, though, the real significance of the B list is here and now. For prestige, there's been nothing like it since Nixon's enemies list. In fact, this is the enemies list in reverse. It can be only a matter of time before lobbyists are offering to get your name on the presidential succession list and PR firms are offering to promote your presence on it, whether truthfully or not.

Come to think of it, I may have been hasty in admitting that I am not on the list. Keep in mind that that may have been disinformation.

Naturally, anyone who is on such a list would be required to pretend otherwise, whereas anyone left off would be sorely tempted to bluff. Be nice to me and I'll make you ambassador to Afghanistan. After a nuclear war, that could be one of the more desirable postings.

Dɪᴅ Hᴇ Sᴀʏ Iᴛ?

(*The Washington Post*, DECEMBER 12, 1991)

Now that Justice Clarence Thomas is safely installed on the Supreme Court, his supporters are proceeding, in good Stalinist fashion, to rewrite the past. This being America, they cannot erase history. What they can do is to obfuscate and confuse until the truth gets lost.

The issue is what Thomas said at his confirmation hearing about his views on *Roe* v. *Wade*. As summarized by this column, Thomas testified "that he had never discussed *Roe* v. *Wade* and had no opinion about it." Many other journalists used a similar formulation. The point is of interest because the assertion—made under oath—is so implausible. *Roe* is the most controversial Supreme Court ruling of a generation, especially in Thomas's conservative circles. It came down while he was actually in law school.

It is now being asserted that Thomas never said any such thing. Anyone who has ever suggested that Thomas denied discussing *Roe* is guilty of a brazen falsehood—"a whopper," according to the ever-vigilant *Wall Street Journal* editorial page. One prominent legal affairs writer—Stuart Taylor, Jr., of *Legal Times*—has already succumbed to a fever of scrupulousness and printed a retraction.

Before this goes any further, here is the key passage:

> *Sen. Leahy:* Have you ever had discussion of *Roe* v. *Wade* other than in this room? In the 17 or 18 years it's been there?
>
> *Judge Thomas:* Only, I guess, senator, in the fact that, in the most general sense, that other individuals express concerns one way or the other, and you listen and you try to be thoughtful. If you're asking me whether or not I've ever debated the contents of it, the answer to that is no, senator.

> *Sen. Leahy:* Have you ever . . . stated whether you felt that it was properly decided or not?
>
> *Judge Thomas:* Senator, in trying to recall and reflect on that, I don't recollect commenting one way or the other.

Thomas also testified that he "cannot remember personally engaging" in discussions of *Roe* during law school and that he had no "personal opinion" at the time of the hearings about *Roe*'s correctness. About the only permutation Leahy negligently failed to explore is whether Thomas had once had an opinion about *Roe* that he had never expressed and subsequently misplaced.

So. Is it unfair to summarize this mess of verbiage as an assertion by Thomas that he had "never discussed" *Roe*? As we try to parse these purposely evasive phrases, what form of "discussion" do they leave room for? No "discussion" at all during law school, or at least no discussion that Thomas can remember. After law school, it is true, Thomas's statements would allow for a somewhat strained form of discussion in which "other individuals" expressed "concerns" about *Roe* while Clarence Thomas perhaps stood mute, his head tilted at a "thoughtful" angle, but not "commenting one way or another."

Then, too, there is the fascinating question of the distinction, if any, between "discussing" *Roe* and "debating" *Roe*. Thomas outright denied having ever done the latter. I suppose it might have been possible, in the halls of the Reagan administration where Clarence Thomas spent the 1980s, to have many vigorous "discussions" about *Roe* that didn't amount to "debates" because no one disagreed:

Reaganite 1: Terrible decision.

Reaganite 2: Terrible, terrible decision.

Reaganite 1: Really awful, don't you think?

Reaganite 2: Absolutely. Bad, bad, bad.

Et cetera. It might even have been possible, in such a context, for Thomas to overcome the seemingly difficult challenge of being "thoughtful" without "commenting one way or another." An energetic nodding of the head no doubt would have been quite well received.

At worst, by using the term "discuss" rather than (say) the term "comment" to summarize what Clarence Thomas claimed never to have done in connection with *Roe* v. *Wade,* the press has overlooked the possibility that Thomas was trying to say that he had participated in discussions without expressing a view himself on the ruling's merits. A sort of Ted Koppel role, perhaps. For eighteen years. Mea culpa.

And yet, conceding all this, how far have we retreated from the wilder regions of implausibility? Thomas said explicitly that he has (or had as of September) no opinion about *Roe*—which is at least as hard to believe as the notion that he had never expressed whatever opinion he might have. Thomas's fellow justices have expressed firm opinions about *Roe* in past rulings and dissents. But Thomas persuaded the senators that having no opinion is a virtue or even a necessity for a Supreme Court nominee. In truth it's hardly even a possibility.

Take It Away

(*The New Republic,* JANUARY 6, 1992)

The Taking Clause of the Fifth Amendment ("nor shall private property be taken for public use, without just compensation") is not one of your more fashionable constitutional freedoms. But it has a cult following among conservatives, who see it as the vehicle for a revival of so-called economic rights. "Economic rights" in this context does not mean anything so bleeding-heart as a right to food or shelter or a job. It means the right to conduct your business unmolested by the government.

The Supreme Court has taken a couple of Taking cases this term. By June, then, we should have an answer to the question that has been hanging over the Court for years. Once conservatives have a secure majority, will they be content to make good on their own rhetoric about "judicial restraint"? Or will they use the Court's power to impose their political agenda on the elected branches of government?*

The legal issue is: When does government action short of actually seizing your property amount to the same thing, and therefore require compensation? In one of this year's cases, a man paid $975,000 for two beachfront lots in South Carolina. Before he could put up houses, the state rezoned the lots to forbid building. The lots are now worthless. The man argues, with some justice, that he is no better off than if the state had

---

*The Court fudged, and the question is still open.

simply taken the land away—in which case the Constitution would have required that he be paid.

The fact that the two lots' market value was totally destroyed makes this an especially sympathetic case. But logically, the owner is no worse off than if, say, he'd owned four lots and a zoning change had reduced their value by half. If the government takes one of your ten acres of land, no one has any trouble seeing that as a "taking," even though you have nine acres left. How is it any different if the government does something that reduces the value of all ten acres by one tenth?

As University of Chicago law professor Richard Epstein argues in his 1985 book, *Takings,* any government action that reduces the value of someone's private property can be defined as the total deprivation of something. Law students are taught that property ownership is, in fact, a "bundle of rights." If a person is told he can't build a building over a certain height, he has been denied his "air rights" just as completely as if the air rights were all he owned.

Or look at it this way (reasons Epstein). How is imposing a regulation that reduces the value of your property any different from taking that property away from you and then giving it back to you subject to the regulation? And yet the property at its new reduced value is clearly not "just compensation" for taking the property at its old full value.

Epstein is the godfather of the Taking Revival. Senator Joe Biden waved a copy of *Takings* with alarm in the Clarence Thomas hearings. But Epstein's thinking is actually more of a problem for Taking Clause enthusiasts than for skeptics. Epstein sees most of what the government now does as a violation of the Taking Clause: progressive taxation, all Social Security and welfare programs, virtually all regulations, in short any action by the government that burdens some citizens more than others. Most Taking cultists don't go so far. But Epstein's logic is rigorous. By contrast, his halfhearted followers have no logical explanation for why and where they stop short.

It used to be conservatives who argued that constitutional provisions should be interpreted modestly and in line with the original understanding of the Framers. One such modest interpretation of the Taking Clause would be that it applies only to actual, physical seizures of property by eminent domain. That is what the Framers had in mind by "taking." Anything else is metaphor. And once you enter the land of metaphor, you are on a very slippery slope toward Epsteinism.

Attempts to define the limits of the Taking Clause have generated a vast scholarly literature, which can't be summarized here (mainly because I haven't read most of it). Past Supreme Court cases are a muddle. Much is made of the distinction between regulations aimed at preventing a public nuisance, like pollution, and those aimed at conferring a public benefit. But what is the difference? In the South Carolina case, the purpose of the zoning was to prevent beach erosion. Is that a nuisance or a benefit? And why should the landowner be paid all or nothing at all based on such a shadowy distinction?

The Supreme Court has held that a "permanent physical invasion" is a taking, no matter how small. Thus when New York City required apartment building owners to allow cable TV wiring—a trivial imposition that, if anything, enhanced the buildings' value—that was a "taking." But when the city forbade the owner of Grand Central Station to build an office tower above it—which reduced the property's value by hundreds of millions—the owner was out of luck.

If the Court starts defining many government regulations as "takings" requiring compensation, those regulations will become unaffordable and will have to be abandoned. That, of course, is the conservative agenda. But good liberals must take the Bill of Rights seriously, including the parts that are inconvenient. The Taking Clause, like the Second Amendment, is one of these.

In one sense, property rights are more at risk from the tyranny of the majority than the liberty rights civil libertarians usually concern themselves with. The distribution of property, unlike the distribution of liberty, is a zero-sum game. More freedom of speech for me need not mean less for you. But if 51 percent of the citizenry decides to vote itself more property, that property can only come from the other 49 percent. That is the abuse the Taking Clause is intended to prevent.

Nevertheless, my liberal heart does not bleed much for the "victims" of democratically enacted government regulations. Taking Clause enthusiasts overlook its one-sidedness. What about the many situations where government actions *increase* the value of someone's private property? Zoning is a classic example. The South Carolina saga is often reversed: A zoning change will add millions to the value of some property. Yet there is no constitutional mechanism for society to recoup that value. (Epstein would say that this too is an unconstitutional "taking"— from everybody else except the landowner. But, as noted, few of Epstein's followers actually follow him over the cliff of logical consistency.)

It is a characteristic flaw of the American mind-set to be overly concerned with discrete injustices and not concerned enough with the injustice of life in general. Thus we have an overblown medical malpractice law and no national health insurance. In the (worthy) cause of reducing litigiousness, conservatives want to make it harder for people harmed by private fault to sue for compensation. Yet they don't worry about the swamp of litigiousness that would open up if people could sue whenever they were affected in any material way by a government regulation for the common good. Is the man whose land value is reduced through zoning more to be pitied than the man who has no land to begin with?

Can We Stand Pat?

(The New Republic, JANUARY 27, 1992)

Patrick Buchanan will never be president of the United States for many excellent reasons and one bad one. The good reasons are obvious. The bad reason is that he has spent most of his adult life as a purveyor of political opinions, in newspapers and on television. Goodness knows I don't pine for a world where television commentators are routinely elevated to genuine power. But a political system that punishes strongly held and vividly expressed opinions—whatever their merits—has defects of its own.

Even now, "negative research" munchkins in the Bush campaign are undoubtedly plowing through thousands of Buchanan newspaper columns and television transcripts, in search of material. It's hard not to feel a bit sorry for Pat as you contemplate the embarrassment of riches available to them.

There is, to pluck just one example, his 1977 column in praise of Adolf Hitler as "an individual of great courage with an intuitive sense of the mushiness, the character flaws, the weakness masquerading as morality that was in the hearts of the statesmen who stood in his path." The column goes on to compare current-day statesmen to those flawed statesmen of the 1930s.

Is that column an indefensible defense of the indefensible, disqualifying its author from national office? Read in its entirety, including parts not quoted here, no. Read in the context of Buchanan's other writings on related matters, it becomes troubling once more. That's the usual pattern with Buchanan's more incendiary stuff: explainable taken alone, hard to explain taken together. But in a political campaign, the column will get neither reading. It will be boiled down to: Buchanan praised Hitler. Imagine what Roger Ailes could do with that, if necessary.

Of course the take-no-prisoners style of political campaigning is one Buchanan himself has promoted and participated in since Hitler, I mean since Nixon. So perhaps it serves him right. But does it serve us right? To be sure, as a man of opinions Pat Buchanan is an extreme case. But even as saintly and moderate a commentator as, say, David Broder has left far too many hostages to fortune to contemplate political office.

The psychology of the commentator and that of the politician are completely different. A commentator must have opinions on everything and spew them like an open fire hydrant. Pat Buchanan the journalist needs dozens of opinions a week to fulfill his professional obligations. Furthermore, as a matter of character a good political commentator looks for things to say that will disconcert people, confound settled views, even give offense.

By contrast, what is a great line for a commentator is, for a politician, a "gaffe." A gaffe, as this column never tires of pointing out, is when a politician tells the truth. Not necessarily the objective truth, but the truth about what he or she really thinks. The serious presidential candidate must hoard his or her opinions, if indeed he or she has any. Each one must be shaped with care, the rough edges must be polished away, before it is produced. The fewer old opinions lying around out there, the easier it is to mold new ones to current exigencies.

Buchanan's problem is not merely his paper trail of old opinions but his commentator's reflexive tendency to say unnecessarily interesting things. Like a smoker, he knows he should quit but he apparently can't. Interviewed recently by the London *Sunday Telegraph*, for example, he explained his distaste for recent cultural developments with this anecdote about a visit by his wife to downtown Washington: "The other day Shelley went down Connecticut Avenue and these guys were sitting on the corner playing bongo drums. I mean, this is the town I grew up in." If it's possible to be charmed and offended at the same time, that's my reaction to this remark. Charmed by the double naïveté—about modern culture, about modern politics. Offended by the implication that people playing bongo drums (and we know who they are) don't belong in Washington.

And what about this, from the same *Sunday Telegraph* interview? "The U.S. should stand up for values, shared values. Why are we more shocked when a dozen people are killed in Vilnius than a massacre in Burundi? Because they are white people. That's who we are. That's where America comes from." The only faintly charming thing about this is Buchanan's touching belief that "we" actually do care much about those people killed in Vilnius. Pat thinks America not only shares his neoisolationism, but also shares his own Baltic and Balkan exceptions to it.

Nevertheless, give Buchanan this: Unlike his rival for the Republican nomination, George Bush, he's got principles. True, they're mostly the wrong principles. But Bush versus Buchanan is a tempting illustration of the maxim that in some ways the wrong principles are better than no principles at all.

They're better, first, aesthetically. It is pleasing to see a candidate on the hustings promoting long-held beliefs with sincere passion. Of course, there are limits to this pleasure. Our friend Hitler was no fun for decent people to watch on the stump. But you don't have to agree with Buchanan to admire his straightforwardness (so far) when reporters ask him questions, or to cringe at the shrieky campaign style of George Bush when he tries to make up in pitch and volume what he lacks in conviction.

Second, the wrong principles at least create a focus for honest political debate. On issues ranging from civil rights to free trade, Bush has pursued a strategy of making clarity impossible. It's not just the politicians who like to avoid clarity; the voters do too. Buchanan will not promise to be the "environmental president." If he were the Republican nominee, America would not merely have the opportunity but would have no choice except to decide how much environmental protection it wants.

Third, there are some issues on which we might actually be better off seeing the wrong principles enacted than to continue in principle-free drift. Federal spending is one of these. For eleven years, two Republican presidents have been claiming to oppose the growth in federal spending without actually proposing the necessary cuts. Two trillion dollars of added national debt is the result. We can argue endlessly about whether spending should be reduced or taxes should be increased. But either solution would be better for the country than another decade of no solution.

Unlike other candidates who can prattle disingenuously about flexible

freezes and bureaucracy and waste, fraud and abuse, Buchanan is on record, repeatedly, endorsing most of the genuine ways federal spending
could be cut. Bring home all the troops. Eliminate foreign aid. End all
farm subsidies. Cut Social Security, Medicare, Medicaid, college loans,
and so on. Now that he's a politician, he'll be strongly tempted to fudge,
on this and other matters. Don't do it, Pat. We've got plenty of other
reasons to vote against you already.

Eт Tu, Bugsy?

(*The New Republic*, FEBRUARY 3, 1992)

Oliver Stone is in the doghouse over his movie *JFK*. He stands
accused of trashing history in his presentation of the Kennedy
assassination; of glorifying a disreputable if not lunatic character
in the person of New Orleans prosecutor Jim Garrison; and of polluting
the minds of a generation too young to remember the real events. They
may draw the lesson that America is controlled by a vast conspiracy in the
government and media, of which Lee Harvey Oswald was just a minor
player and possibly an innocent dupe.

But the problem goes far beyond Oliver Stone. He is just a minor
player, and possibly an innocent dupe, of a conspiracy to twist the truth
that includes virtually all of Hollywood if not most artists throughout
history. The media, I'm sorry to report, are involved in this conspiracy as
well. How else to explain their obsessive critical focus on Oliver Stone and
JFK, while more dangerous malefactors escape unscathed?

Is it just a coincidence that Oliver Stone is vilified for glamorizing Jim
Garrison, while Warren Beatty gets nothing but praise for glamorizing
the far more odious figure of mobster Bugsy Siegel? In a mild way, *Bugsy*
even uses some of the same verisimilitude-inducing techniques as *JFK*,
such as mixing in real footage (a final shot of present-day Las Vegas, which
Siegel ostensibly founded in 1946), and telling you what happened to the
characters after the movie's story ended.

To be sure, the hero of *Bugsy* kills a couple of people. But who can
hold that against such an irresistible charmer and visionary? "He's classically heroic, in a way," explains Beatty's co-star Annette Bening, accurately
capturing the movie's viewpoint. "He has a fatal flaw—he has hubris. And

fate is unkind." Says Meyer Lansky in the movie itself: "He isn't even interested in money. He's interested in the idea." Sex and ideas: a veritable Gary Hart.

Bugsy, writes *The New York Times* approvingly, is "the archetypal American dreamer." In the movie, standing in the middle of a barren desert, Beatty/Bugsy imagines Las Vegas. "It came to me like a vision, like a religious epiphany," the character says. In fact, according to *Little Man*, Robert Lacey's recent biography of Meyer Lansky, Siegel didn't even come close to inventing Las Vegas. By the end of World War II, there were already two large luxury casino-hotels on the Las Vegas "Strip." A local newspaper reported in 1946 that every rich person who came to town said, "I'm going to build a hotel." Even the Flamingo Hotel itself wasn't Bugsy's idea. He invested in it after construction had started, and later forced out the real founder in the usual unsavory manner.

Bugsy makes much of Siegel's alleged desire to assassinate Mussolini, although even in the movie he never acts on it. This is supposed to give a gloss of patriotism to the hero's murderous instincts. In fact, according to *We Only Kill Each Other*, a 1967 biography of Siegel by Dean Jennings, Bugsy actually did business with Mussolini. The dictator sent him $40,000 as an advance on delivery of a new kind of explosive in which Siegel—visionary as ever—had invested. Only after the failure of a test explosion—for which Siegel went to Italy, socialized with Mussolini (plus Goebbels and Göring), and notably failed to assassinate him—did relations deteriorate. Now that story would have made a great movie.

Clearly, then, Warren Beatty and *The New York Times* are involved in a conspiracy, along with the rest of the entertainment-informational complex, to destroy the American Dream for generations too young to remember where they were the day Bugsy Siegel was shot. By glamorizing bloody criminals, they are poisoning children's minds against real American heroes like Lee Iacocca and Robert Stempel.*

But Bugsy is not this conspiracy's darkest achievement of late. That encomium belongs to Walt Disney Studios' vicious misrepresentation of *Beauty and the Beast*. This subversively entertaining work of propaganda distorts several key episodes, makes up new characters out of whole cloth, and undermines the psychological structure of the tale.

Psychiatrist Bruno Bettelheim discusses "Beauty and the Beast" at

Chairmen of Chrysler and General Motors

length in his classic book on fairy tales, *The Uses of Enchantment*. If I've got this right, the tale is really about the healthy transformation of a child's Oedipal attachment to a parent into romantic love for a more suitable object. When Beauty's love turns the Beast into a handsome prince, "this foreshadows by centuries the Freudian view that sex must be experienced by the child as disgusting as long as his sexual longings are attached to his parent," but when directed at someone else, "sexual longings no longer seem beastly."

So much for Beauty. As for the Beast, his side of the story is about "an evolution from a self-centered, immature (phallic-aggressive-destructive) sexuality to one that finds its fulfillment in a human relation of deep devotion." In short, "the marriage of Beauty and the Beast is the humanization and socialization of the id by the superego."

The Disney people mangle all these subconscious themes in ways that inevitably will cause grave psychological trauma to young viewers. If the transferal of affection from father to lover is disrupted, the long-term effect on our gross national product could be severe.

In the movie, Beauty rejects the equation between handsomeness and virtue from the very beginning, in the person of an invented lothario named Gaston, thus short-circuiting the tale's crucial moral development. In the original story, Beauty asks her father for a rose, symbolizing her Oedipal attachment to him. When he breaks one off its stem to give to her, says Bettelheim, it symbolizes her loss of virginity. In the movie, it is the Beast who possesses a rose, wilting in a glass case for lack of love. Goodness only knows what tender ids will make of that.

In the Beast's house, Beauty can have anything she wants—"a narcissistic fantasy typically engaged in by children." But "the fairy story tells that such a life, far from being satisfying, soon becomes empty and boring." In the Disney version, though, aesthetic considerations (a brilliant production number called "Be Our Guest") prevent any hint of boredom with material things. Are we thereby guaranteeing future generations of greedheads?

Space limitations prevent full delineation of Hollywood's plot against our nation's future. Clearly *The Addams Family*, with its celebration of dysfunctional parents and children, is part of the conspiracy. I'm not saying that *JFK* was intended to distract us from the real danger. I'm just raising the possibility.

BUCHANAN AGAIN

(The New Republic, FEBRUARY 24, 1992)

Reluctantly, this column returns to the subject of Patrick Buchanan. The editor in chief of this journal writes that I have failed to denounce Buchanan as an anti-Semite because I am "structurally enmeshed" with him. (In my few waking hours not toiling away for *The New Republic,* I moonlight on the CNN program *Crossfire,* where Buchanan was my cohost until he launched his presidential bid.) *Washington Post* columnist Richard Cohen charges that whatever views I may have on Buchanan and anti-Semitism are discredited because of a "conflict of interest." Ditto the views of others who have appeared regularly on TV with Buchanan, including *TNR*'s Fred Barnes and Morton Kondracke.

It's not clear what Cohen thinks we should do about this alleged conflict of interest. As the editor in chief indeed complains, I have not forced my views about Buchanan and anti-Semitism on anyone. Until now, I have not even volunteered them. But when fellow journalists call up to ask my opinion, I have answered as best I can. My *Crossfire* connection with Buchanan is the only reason anyone cares about my opinion in the first place. Should I refuse to discuss it? Or would my "conflict of interest" disappear if I happened to agree with Cohen?

I confess, if that's the word, that I have allowed my opinion of Buchanan to be influenced by the experience of working closely with him— being "structurally enmeshed," as the editor in chief would have it. Is that a "conflict of interest" or common sense? I was surprised to discover that, despite Buchanan's snarly reputation, he was genuinely friendly and gracious. As a Jew, I never felt any hostility from Buchanan on that score, never heard him make a disparaging remark about Jews, never noticed any difference in the way he treats Jews and non-Jews. Of course all this is not proof that he isn't, at heart, an anti-Semite. But it surely is relevant evidence, not a "conflict of interest."

To be sure, closeness can be distorting as well as clarifying. Although I am not a close pal of Patrick Buchanan, it is too late for him or me (or Richard Cohen or Marty Peretz) to claim immunity from the inside-the-

Beltway coziness that can corrupt judgment. All I can say is that I have not been engaged in a whitewash of Buchanan. When he appeared recently as a guest on *Crossfire*, I worked him over harder on the anti-Semitism issue, among others, than any other TV interviewer has done so far. Transcripts available. In a recent column, I offered up a couple of arguably racist Buchananisms that the American media had missed. (They have since been widely repeated.) Unlike, perhaps, some other Washington journalists who have worked closely with Buchanan, I do not think the anti-Semitism charge is outrageous or patently false. Buchanan has said many things that legitimately raise the question. But to raise it is not to answer it.

None of Buchanan's individual remarks is, in my view, the "smoking sound bite." Consider, for example, his drumbeat of support for those accused of Nazi war crimes. (And leave aside irksome recent evidence that Buchanan may be vindicated on his favorite case, John Demjanjuk.) If Richard Cohen or I took up falsely accused Nazis as a hobbyhorse, no reasonable person (I hope) would accuse us of anti-Semitism. It would be seen, quite rightly, as good journalistic iconoclasm and/or admirable defense of civil liberties in extremis.

Buchanan can't get off so easy. His other published comments on Nazis, Israel, the Jewish lobby—and his general indifference to civil liberties—put this eccentric passion for accused Nazis in an eerie light. But they don't make it prima facie anti-Semitic.

Anti-Semitism is not a disease you can give a blood test for and get a definitive yes or no. Three factors make me hesitate to apply the label to Buchanan. First, he does have warm personal relations with many Jews. Despite the old saw about "some of my best friends," that surely counts for something. Second, I believe Buchanan sincerely thinks the accusations are unfair; in his heart, he doesn't think he is an anti-Semite. Of course it's possible to be an anti-Semite without knowing it—but surely it's harder. Third, Buchanan's controversial remarks about the Israel lobby, Nazis, and so on do not, I think, hide coarser views. Buchanan is—or at least he was until he started running for president—a frank man. He says—or used to say—what he thinks. Make what you wish of his past public statements, but I believe they are not a case of the mask slipping.

In all this Buchanan is different from, say, David Duke. Duke surely does not work and socialize comfortably with Jews. He surely does not deny in his own heart that he is a Jew hater. And Duke's record and personality give you every reason to assume that what he says is the palest dilution of what he really thinks.

My real answer to the question "Is Buchanan an anti-Semite?" is: Give me a definition and I'll tell you. If your definition is someone who viscerally hates Jews as individuals and as a race, the answer is no. If you have a more sophisticated and nuanced definition, my answer might be different. But the trouble with more sophisticated definitions is that they tar someone like Buchanan with the same brush as David Duke and Adolf Hitler and other anti-Semites by any definition. And the proper response to a Pat Buchanan is surely not the same as the proper response to a David Duke.

William F. Buckley, whom Marty Peretz quotes with approval as having concluded that Buchanan's past statements "amounted to anti-Semitism," said the other day that he would vote for Buchanan if he were a New Hampshire resident. Presumably that is not the right response to a genuine anti-Semite.

I hesitate to apply the label "anti-Semite" for one more reason. Some of those most eager to brand Buchanan are also among those who deplore (as part of the deplorable "political correctness" epidemic) the facile overuse of terms like "racist" and "sexist." And they're right: Words like that work as censors of debate and ultimately lose their power when used promiscuously. The magazine you hold in your hands has been the loudest voice in the land condemning such labels as the enemies of openness and complexity in the public debate. The same is true, in spades, of a term like anti-Semite. There are times, of course, when all these labels are appropriate. But in today's political culture, there is no particular courage in being the first to use them, and no special shame in hanging back.

COLONEL OF TRUTH

(The New Republic, MARCH 9, 1992)

**H**ow can I ever repay you for your kindness, Mr. Reed?" said Luke, overjoyed.
"I have taken a fancy to you, Luke," said his companion. "I hope to do more for you soon."

—STRUGGLING UPWARD, OR LUKE LARKIN'S LUCK,
BY HORATIO ALGER, JR. (1886)

First, I want to thank you, not just for saving me from the draft, but for being so kind and decent to me last summer. . . .
Please say hello to Col. Jones for me.

—LETTER TO COL. EUGENE HOLMES OF THE ARKANSAS ROTC,
BY BILL CLINTON (1969)

Until last week, the most vivid depiction of a Rhodes scholar in literature was in Max Beerbohm's 1911 novel of Oxford, *Zuleika Dobson*. Beerbohm's joke was that Americans are unconsciously verbose:

> *"Like most of my countrymen, I am a man of few words. We are habituated out there to act rather than talk. Judged from the viewpoint of your beautiful old civilization, I am aware my curtness must seem crude. But, gentlemen, believe me, right here—"*
> *"Dinner is served, your Grace."*
> *Thus interrupted, Mr. Oover, with the resourcefulness of a practiced orator, brought his thanks to a quick but not abrupt conclusion.*

But we now have a far richer exposition of the Rhodes scholar mentality in Bill Clinton's famous letter—written exactly half a lifetime ago—explaining why he would not after all be joining the University of Arkansas Reserve Officers Training Corps. Connoisseurs recognized it immediately as a masterpiece of the genre. The release of Clinton's twenty-three-year-old letter confirms that he is a classic Rhodes scholar type. That's not, or at least not entirely, an insult: It's a classic American type, too.

What is most poignant about the letter is that Clinton didn't need to write it. He had already reneged on his previous summer's commitment to join ROTC. And he was already safe from the draft, due to a high number in the lottery two days before. But he had cultivated a relationship with this Colonel Holmes, had "promised to let you hear from me at least once a month." He clearly couldn't bear the thought that Colonel Holmes might turn against him for this betrayal. And very likely he couldn't bear the thought in his own mind that his friendship with the older man had been a mere cynical calculation. So he writes of his "depth of feeling," his "anguish," his sleepless nights. He hopes to impress the colonel—and himself—with the shining sincerity of his confession that "I had no interest in the ROTC program in itself."

The letter ends with the fatal words, "Please say hello to Col. Jones for me." Another colonel! Young Clinton had had a busy summer. But this colonel was not impressed. In an ironic twist Horatio Alger would not have appreciated, Colonel Jones saved the letter and nursed his resentment for twenty-three years, then released both.

When people talk about a "Horatio Alger success story," they usually have in mind someone who lifts himself up by his own bootstraps. But that is not what Horatio Alger's stories were like at all. The typical Horatio Alger hero succeeds by impressing a successful older man or men with his sterling qualities. " 'A thoroughly good boy, and a smart boy, too!' said Armstrong to himself. 'I must see if I can't give him a chance to rise. He seems absolutely reliable.' " These days we call this sort of thing "mentoring."

The way you get a Rhodes scholarship is to solicit eight recommendations, compose a personal essay, and then submit to a series of intense interviews by a selection committee. The committee is composed of local dignitaries, mostly former Rhodes scholars, in your state and region. The whole procedure is an institutionalized Horatio Alger story, an orgy of mentoring.

The qualities this process tends to reward are well displayed in the Clinton letter. Above all, there is the difficult combination of slick ambition and earnest, almost naive, idealism. Unction and real charm do battle almost sentence by sentence. No one reading Clinton's letter can doubt that this intelligent young man is sincerely opposed to the Vietnam War. Equally, no one can doubt that he buffaloed the ROTC colonels and is trying to buffalo them again. His anguish over making the right moral choices in his life is believable and touching. Less touching is the suspicion that what's best for Bill Clinton will usually turn out to be the right thing to do.

A related quality is self-dramatization—also partly appealing in a heartfelt youthful way, but not completely attractive. At one level, there is the reflexive bragging of the practiced résumé stuffer: "One of the national organizers of the Vietnam Moratorium is a close friend of mine. . . . For a law seminar at Georgetown, I wrote a paper . . ." At another level, there is the melodrama of anguish and self-doubt, the "eating compulsively and reading until exhaustion brought sleep." (However, "the particulars of my personal life are not nearly as important to me as the principles involved.") At yet another level is the bland conviction that destiny calls: "For years I have worked to prepare myself for a political life characterized by both practical political ability and concern for rapid social progress. It is a life I still feel compelled to try to lead."

It's no surprise that so many Rhodes scholars go into politics. Idealism and ambition observe a strange but comfortable truce in the heads of the best politicians as well. Politicians tend to have the same ravenous need for approval, and the same skill at evoking it.

Some observers of the Rhodes phenomenon (and there are those who study it obsessively, including some of the lab specimens themselves) believe that Rhodes scholars actually make bad politicians because they expect to be handed rewards rather than begging for them. Rhodes scholars thrive, goes the theory, at being appointed to prestigious posts, not at winning mass elections. They're good at sucking up, not so good at sucking down. That's why a Rhodes scholar will never be president. Goes the theory.

We shall see. It's true that someone like Bill Bradley seems to think he should be selected for the presidency by a panel of distinguished fellows, and beyond that he won't trouble to exert himself. But Clinton is, from all reports, a natural-born politician who truly enjoys it in its most retail aspects.

Let's not be too hard on Bill Clinton. He's a good boy, and a smart boy, too. We must see if we can't give him a chance to rise. He seems relatively reliable.

ARTS AND CRAFTS

(The New Republic, MARCH 16, 1992)

There's nothing important George Bush knew about John Frohn-mayer the day he fired him, February 20, that he didn't already know the day he hired Frohnmayer two and a half years ago. And indeed, the unceremonious dumping of the chairman of the Arts Endowment tells us nothing we didn't already know about George Bush. But it's a timely reminder.

In 1989, when Frohnmayer was appointed, Bush was just beginning his presidency. He had won the 1988 election with a remarkable exercise of hateful demagoguery, but now he was eager to show that the real George Bush was classier than that. He was in his "kinder, gentler" phase. He wanted to differentiate himself from Ronald Reagan. He wanted to win back the respect of establishment elites, if not of actual liberals.

Politics, to George Bush, is performance art. Not unlike the notorious Karen Finley,* he had smeared himself with symbolic excrement. Now the performance was over and he wanted a shower.

So he picked John Frohnmayer, a high-minded Oregon lawyer and certified artsy-fartsy, to head the controversial National Endowment for the Arts. And Frohnmayer did exactly what Bush wanted. He threaded the needle between right-wing arts bashers and the arts establishment, attempting to minimize offense to either group. He canceled a grant to an AIDS art exhibit when the Right started barking, then restored the grant when the artsies barked louder. His tenure was not always an exercise in principle, but it was a moderate Republican's earnest approximation. It was, in short, George Bush's presidency on its best behavior.

Total courage would not be expected of—or even recommended to— a man in Frohnmayer's position. Frohnmayer generally doled out his cour-age in wisely calibrated amounts. But any dose of political courage is apparently intolerable to George Bush in election season. With Pat Bu-chanan on the stump denouncing the Arts Endowment as "the uphol-

*A performance artist best known for covering her body in chocolate

stered playpen of the arts-and-crafts auxiliary of the Eastern liberal establishment," Frohnmayer had to go.

The rise and fall of John Frohnmayer is thus a small metaphor for George Bush as a person and as a president. He knows what's right and he'll do it—if there's no reason not to. He sincerely wants to be virtuous. He just doesn't want it very badly. If it's a choice between virtue and something else he wants, like reelection, virtue is the first to go.

Bush doesn't even have the courage of his lack of convictions. Look at the snaky way he let Frohnmayer go: pretending Frohnmeyer had quit, praising his integrity and decency, but adding that "some of the art funded by the NEA does not have my enthusiastic approval." What an artfully qualified remark. Give that man a grant. But does Bush share Buchanan's disapproval of Frohnmayer's NEA or does he not? Don't ask.

In a country that's going down the rathole in several dozen ways, this question of arts subsidies plays an absurdly overblown role in the public debate. For the Reverend Donald Wildmons and Senator Jesse Helmses, it's a valuable "hot button" issue to use in direct-mail fund-raising. For them, and for a presidential candidate like Buchanan, it's junk-food populism: a high-calorie, low-nutrition substitute for serious politics. To hear Helms and Buchanan, you would think that a large part of the federal deficit could be eliminated if we would only stop paying people to take pictures of themselves with a bullwhip up their rectums.*

Even some longtime supporters of government arts subsidies are starting to wonder if these battles are worth it. Other rich countries manage to subsidize the arts far more generously than we do without much fuss. But maybe our political culture just isn't up to it. In real life, as distinct from the theater of politics, the NEA is just one way the government subsidizes art. Even without direct subsidies there would still be the indirect subsidy of tax-deductible private contributions. And there is the huge unacknowledged subsidy of performing artists called unemployment compensation.

From a liberal point of view, the case for government arts subsidies is not without flaws. The typical customer of the subsidized arts—museums, opera, public television, etc.—is clearly more affluent than the typical taxpayer. Heroic efforts of arts advocates to prove otherwise are unconvincing. Movies, baseball games, and rock concerts get no government subsidy.

*A reference to Jesse Helms's favorite Robert Mapplethorpe photograph

Why should the customers of these entertainments help to finance the entertainments of those who are, on average, better heeled than themselves?

And the preening self-righteousness of the arts crowd can get on your nerves, as they insist on this subsidy as a kind of right. There is something irksome about people wanting to be a counterculture on the majority's nickel.

On the other hand, the unavoidable fact is that much if not most of the art we treasure from past centuries—paintings, cathedrals, most classical music, even some of Shakespeare's plays—was created under government (or official church) sponsorship. If our democratic society is going to produce similar gifts for future generations—not to mention our own—we probably need some institutional substitute for the commissioning function of kings and cardinals. The NEA is it.

Furthermore, there is no way to subsidize the creation of new art (as opposed to merely helping the New York Philharmonic to perform Beethoven's Ninth Symphony again) without subsidizing art that gives offense to someone. Senator Jesse Helms and the Reverend Donald Wildmon are always going to find something to make a fuss about.

The latest fuss is typical, in that the actual connection between the offensive material and the NEA is indirect. The fuss concerns a single passage in a single poem in a single publication of a group that received a whopping $5,000 NEA grant for general purposes. To expect the NEA to inspect and warrant the purity of every product of a grantee is absurd. To expect politicians to show a bit of backbone when these fusses are raised is not absurd, but if the politicians aren't up to that, we might as well forget the whole exercise.

Supporters of arts subsidies often make the mistake of defending any item a Helms or a Wildmon attacks. That is foolish. Not only is it inevitable that an arts agency will subsidize works that are offensive to a minority, it is inevitable that the agency will sometimes find itself subsidizing works that are rightly offensive to the majority of people—on moral grounds or on political grounds or simply as bad art. Arts funding is not a science. If the majority itself isn't prepared to shrug off a few genuine mistakes every year, then it isn't ready to be in the arts subsidy business.

Oh, Grow Up

(*The New Republic*, APRIL 6, 1992)

One of the most entertaining things about the news is its arbitrariness. When is some story a huge outrage worthy of screaming headlines on page 1, and when does it deserve burial on page 23? Just lately *The Washington Post*, like every other news medium, has been giving the screaming page 1 treatment to the story of rubber checks at the so-called House Bank. But just two years ago the same newspaper thought the same story was worth page 23.

On February 7, 1990, the General Accounting Office, Congress's investigative arm, released a report on the House Bank. The *Post* reported it the next day. That article, by Walter Pincus, contained all the major elements of today's scandal: the existence of a special "bank" where House members' pay was deposited; the fact that members could overdraw their accounts without penalty; the fact that many members were abusing this privilege.

A search through Nexis, the computerized media database, indicates that only one other newspaper, the *Los Angeles Times*, picked up this story—running it two months late, April 8, on page 11. Last week the *Times* editorialized indignantly about "politicians being out of touch with commonsense principles." The *Miami Herald*, which surely has access to *The Washington Post* wire service, and which huffed last week about "justified public outrage" at congressional check kiting, ignored the story completely two years ago. So did all the radio talk show hosts who are now up in arms, some of whom must have seen it even on page 11 or 23.

Even before 1990 the House Bank was no secret. *Roll Call*, the Capitol Hill newspaper, reported in 1988 that some freshman senators, envying the "efficiency" (!) of the House side, wanted a bank of their own where "members who overdraw their accounts are not penalized." According to last week's House ethics committee report on the bank scandal, the GAO complained in 1954 that "some members frequently overdraw their accounts, sometimes in excess of their monthly salary and expenses . . . and one-third of all active members" were in arrears during one typical period. The GAO has issued regular reports to Congress on the workings of the

House Bank, and these reports have been public since 1977. These reports show that more bad checks were written in the 1960s and 1970s than in recent years.

Of course the Republican politicians now waxing self-righteous about the bank's casual practices did not need GAO reports to know all about them long ago. Minority Whip Newt Gingrich shamelessly compares himself to Vaclav Havel for having the courage to challenge the House leadership on this, although he himself has admitted to twenty or more bad checks. These admissions by Republican miscreants are based on their own records, not on information supplied by investigators. So no one hid their own bad checks from them, as they try to imply.

The fact that the abuse was widely known for years may indeed reflect poorly on the Democratic leadership. But what does that same fact say about the sincerity of Gingrich's present outrage? It's a funny kind of "scandal" that has been public knowledge for years if not decades.

This "bank" was really just a pot of money consisting mainly of House members' salary payments. The money sat there, interest-free, until a member withdrew it. There was an open, if not official, policy that members could draw up to a month's salary in advance; but the money came from the pot, not from the taxpayers. The members overall have been in surplus continuously since 1947. In fact, the biggest beneficiary of this curious arrangement was the U.S. Treasury. It got the float on House members' salaries that otherwise would have been deposited in real, interest-paying banks a lot sooner.

This is not meant to absolve Congress completely. The bank's operation was an embarrassing, amateurish mess. Speaker Tom Foley badly bungled the cleanup operation. There were some real abusers of the overdraw privilege. And some may even be criminals—if, for example, they used their free loans to pay for election campaigns (as Gingrich characteristically has been implying without evidence). Furthermore, it is hard not to take some pleasure in seeing your typical representative—who lives for reelection and who figures he's thought of everything—being hit with this unexpected pie in the face.

But if a tidal wave of public revulsion sweeps a third of Congress out of office over this, as some are predicting, you've got to wonder about the seriousness of the American electorate. It's not that most members of Congress deserve the virtually automatic reelection prospects they traditionally enjoy. Quite the opposite. It's that there are so many good reasons to vote against the typical incumbent politician (including those in the executive branch).

What serious citizen tolerates a $400 billion deficit but draws the line at a $400 rubber check? If 125 members of Congress were voted out over their failure to enact a capital gains tax cut, or over too much foreign aid, that would be a mistaken but responsible exercise in democracy. If a similar massacre occurs over the House Bank, that will be a joke.

Or is the House Bank "symbolic"—a "metaphor" for something larger, such as out-of-control government spending? That is the justification of those who are busy fanning the flames of public outrage. That is always the justification invoked by the promoters of our increasingly symbolic politics. Whether the trivial, irrelevant, or wholly concocted issue is the Pledge of Allegiance or prison furloughs or rubber checks or whatever comes next, there is always a fancy metaphorical explanation available on demand. Meanwhile, the hard, genuine issues of politics are evaded.

Even now, rich Washington-based political consultants of both parties are plotting how they will use the check-kiting scandal as an anti-Washington theme in next fall's campaigns. The manipulators of this issue are more a part of the insular Beltway culture than their victims, and the issue itself is more of an inside-the-Beltway phenomenon than the vice it purports to attack. Of all the inhabitants of the inside-the-Beltway culture, members of Congress as a group are probably the least affluent, the least coddled, and the least isolated from life outside the magic circle.

It's hard to go against the tide on an issue like this one without getting branded an elitist and being told that you "just don't get it"—in the reigning political cliché of the season. Check bouncing, you get told, is something ordinary people can relate to. This, it seems to me, is the more elitist position: that ordinary folks need to be spoon-fed mock issues because they can't handle the real ones. The truly democratic position is to say to your fellow citizens: Get serious. Grow up.

Message: I Don't Care

(*The New Republic*, APRIL 27, 1992)

By the end of Ronald Reagan's first term as president, supporters and opponents alike had begun to use the term "Reaganism" to refer to his governing ideology. As we approach a similar point in George Bush's presidency, no one uses the word "Bushism" to mean any coherent set of political beliefs, or even a recognizable presidential style. Instead, a "Bushism" has come to mean the incumbent's funny way of talking.

Everyone can identify the components of a typical Bushism. The staccato sentences with no pronouns. The long, meandering nonsentences that reverse course or get lost completely halfway through. The fractured syntax. The weird mixed metaphors and non sequiturs. But no one has yet explained convincingly why he talks this way or what it means. My colleagues at *The New Republic* have put together a collection of some classic Bushisms, to be published in May by Workman Press. Reading these classics all at once does not solve the mystery, but it does shed some light.

The last president so widely mocked for his way of talking was Eisenhower. The most famous Eisenhowerism was not even uttered by Eisenhower himself. It is an Eisenhowerized version of the Gettysburg Address, composed by Oliver Jenson: "I haven't checked these figures, but eighty-seven years ago, I think it was, a number of individuals organized a governmental setup here in this country, I believe it covered certain eastern areas, with this idea they were following up, based on a sort of national independence arrangement," and so on.

Bush's rambly, semicoherent style has been compared with Ike's. But actually, even this parody is reasonably coherent compared with some of Bush's riffs. And Eisenhower's verbiage lacked Bush's essential frantic quality ("frantic" being, oddly, one of Bush's favorite criticisms of others). Eisenhower's admirers believe he could turn the fog machine on or off at will, and used it purposely to divert and confuse. No one has ever tried to make that case about Bush, so far.

The positive spin on Bushism is different. It's that his inarticulateness illustrates his sincerity and lack of artifice. It shows he's a regular guy, a

small-"d" democrat, uncomfortable with fancy-pants rhetoric. Bush himself advanced this theory in what was, as it happens, the most eloquent
performance he's ever given: his acceptance speech at the 1988 Republican
convention. Naturally he didn't write it himself (any more than Lincoln,
these days, would dream of writing the Gettysburg Address). The author
was Peggy Noonan, Official Purveyor of Soaring Lyricism to Republican
Presidents.

In one of that speech's most absurd flights of Noonanism, Bush read
from his teleprompter: "Now I may be—may not be the most eloquent,
but I learned that early on the eloquence won't draw oil from the ground.
And I may sometimes be a little awkward, but there's nothing self-
conscious in my love of country. And I'm a quiet man, but I hear the quiet
people others don't."

In fact, no one has ever accused Bush of being a "quiet man." In fact,
he's a babbler. And in fact, some of his silliest and most patently insincere
babbling comes when he is trying to be demotic. ("When I need a little
free advice about Saddam Hussein, I turn to country music." Or, "Look,
I want to give the high-five symbol to high-tech.") The best case for
Bushspeak as an expression of the democratic impulse is slightly different.
It was made by Jacob Weisberg of TNR, who compared Bush to "a big,
clumsy golden retriever, drooling and knocking over furniture in his eagerness" to please everyone.

The canniest description of Bush's strange discursiveness belongs to
Timothy Noah of The Wall Street Journal, who compares it to call-waiting:
Bush is always putting one half-finished thought on hold to take up the
next one. Closely related to this is the intensely self-conscious tendency
described by Meg Greenfield in Newsweek: "Bush is always telling you
how to look at what he is doing, or what the impression is he is trying to
create." ("We have—I have—want to be positioned in that I could not
possibly support David Duke, because of the racism and because of the
bigotry and all of this.") What these tics share is a clear view of the mind
at work. Bush's mental processes lie close to the surface.

This is honesty of a sort. Bush is famous for his attitude that politics
is a thing apart from one's true self—a distateful business one stoops to
when one has to. When he denies a remark he has just made ("People
understand that Congress bears a greater responsibility for this—but I'm
not trying to assign blame") or reads his stage directions aloud ("Message:
I care"), he is telegraphing, perhaps involuntarily, that he doesn't really

mean what he says, that it's all just politics. It's sort of a verbal wink. The implication is that as long as we're all in on the joke, it doesn't matter. ("I've told you I don't live and die by the polls. Thus I will refrain from pointing out that we're not doing too bad in those polls.")

But maybe it does matter. What Bush seems to have no interest in is not just politics in the narrowest sense but political ideas of any kind. He is constantly revealing this in unconsciously dismissive references to "freedom and democracy and things of that nature" or "values that—that have made this country the greatest, freedom, democracy, choices to do things—you know." When he says, "I think in politics there are certain moral values. I'm one who—we believe strongly in pluralism . . . , but when you get into some questions there are some moral overtones. Murder, that kind of thing . . . ," he is pretty transparently faking it. The transparency is to his credit, in a way, but the faking it is not.

Bush's problem is not a lack of intelligence—or (as some have suggested) an excess of the prescription tranquilizer Halcion. At bottom, his problem is a simple lack of anything to say. That's why he babbles. That's why he contradicts himself. That's why he tells you how you should perceive what he's saying, instead of just saying it. That's why he tells transparent whoppers.

A man anchored in true beliefs of some sort not only would be more articulate in expressing those beliefs, he would make a better liar, too. He wouldn't wreck a story about how faith sustained him while he waited to be rescued from the Pacific during World War II by adding, preposterously, that he was also sustained by thoughts of "the separation of church and state." Ronald Reagan, a man of a few clear, rock-hard beliefs, was a brilliant liar.

If there were a real Bushism, in other words, there might not be all those Bushisms. Is that clear at all?

The Case for Ross

(*The New Republic*, MAY 18, 1992)

As a person and as a political phenomenon, H. Ross Perot is deplorable in many ways. Let us list some of them.

First, from a partisan perspective, it is hard to believe that his candidacy won't hurt Bill Clinton more than George Bush in the end. Clinton can only win by turning the election into a referendum on the incumbent, and Perot will be there to split the "no" vote.*

Second, Perot's popularity illustrates either the decadence of the political system or the political immaturity of the electorate (take your pick). Whichever, it is pathetic that so many voters are so eager to reach outside the system for a name to vote for. Perot is the ultimate antipolitics candidate in a year when antipolitics is the most fatuous politics of all.

Then there is the related tiresome convention that anyone truly qualified to be president shouldn't want the job. Perot's "I'll run if you beg me" approach is working for him the way it never worked for Mario Cuomo because he is completely outside the political system. It's an update on the myth of Cincinnatus, the farmer who reluctantly lays down his plow to solve the mess in government, then returns to the private sector with the thanks of a grateful nation.

Perot's candidacy is also the latest expression of the 1980s myth of the businessman as popular hero and savior. Lee Iacocca and Peter Ueberroth enjoyed earlier fantasy flights on the notion that what this country needs is a good CEO.

Indeed, if the Perot phenomenon has any recognizable political flavor, it's fascism. He was a tough but loving paterfamilias in his company, and he'll do the same for his country. He will sweep aside the dithering politicians to carry out the true will of the people. He will make the trains run on time. What Alberto Fujimori is doing for Peru, Ross Perot will do for the United States. If he hears the call.

Perot's personality seems perfectly suited to this role. He has the successful businessman's nearly demented self-confidence—I can do brain

*Well, this was wrong.

surgery because I'm rich—and the short man's strutting egomania. He has the revealing habit of incessantly quoting himself. As I was saying just the other day, that is a sure sign of an ego out of control. And yet he believes deeply in his own humility—prides himself on it, in fact.

Especially for a nonpolitician, Perot is a brilliant sound-bite artist. He favors silver bullet solutions and strikes a can-do posture—as if running the country were a matter of boldness and organization, like rescuing hostages from Iran.

Finally, it is not a happy development that Perot is prepared to spend $100 million of his own money on his campaign. There are too many other people who wouldn't miss $100 million if it would get them on the cover of *Newsweek*. In *The Theory of the Leisure Class*, Thorstein Veblen movingly discussed the challenge to rich people of giving meaning to fortunes too large to be appreciated in normal material terms. But traditional solutions such as mansions, yachts, and racehorses at least have the advantage of not perverting the democratic system. It's true that PAC money is also corrupting. But why must we choose one or the other?

All that said, though, I have a soft spot for Ross Perot. I've had it since I found myself trapped in a room where he was giving a speech on education reform in Texas. Perot headed a governor's commission on the subject. To my surprise, he delivered an eloquent plea for government spending and for redistribution on the basis of shared communal values. It wasn't fair, he said, and it wasn't good for Texas, that poor school districts had less money for education than rich ones. He made social spending sound like good business sense. He persuaded the state both to raise taxes and to shift expenditures from rich to poor. Quite a feat, in 1985.

Perot is accused of having no coherent set of political values, of choosing his issues on the cafeteria line. He himself brags predictably that he is more interested in practical solutions than in ideology. "I hate labels. I'm an independent." And so on. And yet Perot's cafeteria choices don't seem so incoherent to me. Or at least, they disconcertingly resemble my own.

Above all, Perot is the only presidential candidate who is emphasizing the most important issue. That is the deficit, broadly defined to mean our general failure to invest in the future as well as the federal budget gap itself. Perot is not completely honest about how he would close the gap. He babbles about "waste and abuse" like a pro. But he is more forthright than his rivals in calling for curbs on entitlement payments to the affluent and for an end to the military subsidy of Europe and Japan. And he is reasonably straight about saying that if the citizenry finds serious spending cuts indigestible, higher taxes are the only alternative.

Perot is prochoice on abortion, live-and-let-live on gay rights and other questions of lifestyle freedom, pro-gun control. On foreign policy he opposed the Gulf war but supports aid to the former Soviet Union. He thinks that growing income inequality is socially unhealthy and favors a heavier tax burden on the rich like himself. He is obviously "probusiness," but whether this means a belief in free markets or some corporate-statist vision of government subsidies and protectionism is not clear.

This set of views may be less ideologically coherent than those of Karl Marx or Milton Friedman. But they do not suffer much in that respect compared with George Bush or Bill Clinton. I detect no gaping inconsistencies.

Nor does it seem fair to charge Perot with vagueness. It's true he has not prepared eighteen-point position papers on various topics like Clinton and, selectively, Bush. And he is clearly benefiting in the opinion polls from a fairy-godmother syndrome: the hope, masquerading as a belief, that someone will come along with a magic wand and wave away all our problems. But Perot himself has been slightly better than Clinton and miles ahead of Bush in conveying the essential message of no gain without pain.

I wouldn't vote for Ross Perot over Bill Clinton. But I'd vote for him in two seconds over George Bush. And if I lived in a state where Perot could win but Clinton couldn't, I'd vote strategically. Others will vote for Perot in the spirit of "Let's take a flier. What have we got to lose?" That's a sentiment deserving of sympathy, if not total respect.

In Defense of Good Intentions

(*Time*, JUNE 1, 1992)

> *or many years we tried many different programs. All of them—let's*
> *understand this—had noble intentions.*
> —PRESIDENT BUSH IN LOS ANGELES, MAY 9

These days, one of the worst things you can be accused of is good intentions. George Bush imputes good intentions to the antipoverty efforts of the 1960s and 1970s as a preface to saying they've backfired. Bush's Republican rival, Patrick Buchanan, then trumps him by preemptively tarring any new antipoverty efforts with the same brush. "In the wake of Los Angeles," Buchanan declares, "everyone has a 'solution' to the 'problem.' And these solutions come from earnest and well-intentioned men and women." Officer, stop that man! He's armed with good intentions and presumed dangerous.

A check through Nexis, the computerized news-media database, confirms that virtually every time someone is described as having "good" or "noble" or "best of" intentions, that person is about to be accused of doing something wrong. It may just be improperly removing a hook from a fish ("Good intentions notwithstanding, the result of such handling can be a severely injured fish . . ."). But most often since the Los Angeles riot, the subject has been the cities and the underclass.

Good intentions do sometimes go awry, in helping the poor as in any other human endeavor. Go see the current movie of E. M. Forster's *Howards End*—or read the novel—for an exploration of that theme. But the reflexive crediting of "good intentions" has become a standard throat-clearing exercise by those who wish to attack government antipoverty programs. This serves their rhetorical purposes in two ways.

First, while good intentions might seem like an admirable thing to have, the phrase also conjures up an image of woolly-minded naïveté. Those dear old liberals, sitting in their ivory-tower rocking chairs, knitting vast social-welfare blankets from skeins of good intentions and taxpayer money: What do they know about the real world? The implication is that good intentions are not merely insufficient but even detrimental to the hard business of facing up to the hard truths about poverty and race. Good intentions are for sissies.

At the same time, crediting others with good intentions is a subtle way of claiming them for yourself. After all, it is hardly necessary to vouch for the good intentions of Lyndon Johnson, who wanted to spend billions fighting poverty. The one who needs credit for good intentions is Bush, who says such efforts are unnecessary or even destructive and—by a remarkable coincidence—the true solutions to the problems of the ghetto are those that ask virtually nothing of the white middle class. Naturally, Bush would like to stipulate good intentions all around.

It is shocking to read President Johnson's words from the 1960s. He spoke bluntly about "white guilt" and "equality [of] result." These phrases violate the taboos of 1992's conservative political correctness. And of course anything as grandiose as a "war on poverty" is unthinkable today. Why is that? People say we have lost the economic optimism and national self-confidence of the 1960s. But the 1980s were also a period of national economic optimism; yet that is when the War on Poverty was officially declared unwinnable. And even the sad-sack 1990s are objectively richer than the 1960s. The difference must be a matter of good intentions.

To be sure, there is some hard-earned pessimism about government programs at work. But much of the pessimism is mere posturing. Bush and others have said repeatedly in recent weeks that the government has spent "$3 trillion over 25 years" fighting poverty, with the implication that this money has been lavished on the underclass. According to the White House's own figures, most of this mystical $3 trillion went for such non-underclass and politically sacrosanct programs as Medicare (more than a trillion) and veterans' benefits ($287 billion). The good intentions of anyone who talks about $3 trillion spent fighting poverty are suspect from the start.

Like Jimmy Carter after the Soviet invasion of Afghanistan, Bush would like it known that after Los Angeles the scales fell from his eyes. "The time really has come to try a new way . . . making our commitment to end poverty and despair greater than ever before." However, the distinguishing feature of the conservative antipoverty agenda that Bush has now embraced is not its newness—or even its rightness or wrongness—but its cheapness. At the state level, in the name of welfare "reform," benefits are simply being slashed. The cost of "enterprise zones" is hidden in the form of tax cuts (with the usual claim that these cuts will pay for themselves).

Some favorite conservative nostrums would actually cost plenty, such as privatizing public housing; or changing current welfare rules that penalize people for taking a job, saving money, or keeping their families intact. But conservatives usually pretend the cost doesn't exist. It isn't recalcitrant liberals standing in the way of such reforms. It is a national reluctance to spend the money, nurtured by conservatives themselves.

Fine words butter no parsnips, as the Brits like to say. The test of good intentions is a willingness to put yourself out for them. Yet the political message Bush and company are sending is: You have already put yourselves out too much. After Los Angeles, it's a comforting message. What a relief to be told that good intentions are futile.

Last Resort

(The New Republic, JUNE 1, 1992)

"It is the Congress that appropriates every dime," said President Bush, attacking "the spending habits of the Congress" at a Bush-Quayle fund-raiser the other day. "It is the Congress that tells the Executive how to spend every dime."

To puncture this tiresome conceit is one reason I'm for Senator Paul Simon's balanced budget constitutional amendment. Each year, it declares, "the President shall transmit to the Congress a proposed budget . . . in which total outlays do not exceed total receipts." Neither Ronald Reagan nor George Bush has ever come close. In fact, the total amounts Congress has appropriated over the years aren't too different from the amounts these two presidents have requested, whatever disagreements there may have been about where the money goes (defense versus domestic, etc.). Simon's proposed amendment would call this hoary Republican bluff.

The amendment also would require Congress to enact a deficit-free budget, unless a three-fifths majority in both houses voted not to. Congress, terrified of the sour public mood, is apparently near-certain to pass some kind of balanced budget amendment next month and send it on to the states for ratification.* But voting for a balanced budget amendment

*Didn't happen—at least in 1992

is not just a desperate short-term political expedient. For Democrats, it is good long-term politics as well.

The voters are hypocrites about federal spending: hating it in general, cherishing it in the particular. The deficit—a government now spending four dollars for every three dollars it brings in—is the concrete expression of this voter hypocrisy. Politicians of both parties cater to this hypocrisy. But by and large it is Republicans who since 1980 have made it the central feature of American politics and Republicans who have benefited politically from it. Republicans have gained the political advantage of being perceived as the party more opposed to government spending, without paying the political cost of opposing specific expenditures.

A balanced budget amendment, if it worked, might lead to lower spending or higher taxes or some combination. But at least it would lead to an honest debate. That would not just be hygienic. It would be helpful to the party that's been losing the dishonest debate of the past decade.

Of course mere partisan advantage is not a good enough reason to amend the Constitution (though tell that to the term limits boys). There are those who think that the goal of a balanced budget is neither necessary nor wise. And there are those who support the goal but doubt the means.

The argument against the desirability of a balanced budget has many byways, but the main point is the traditional Keynesian one that the stimulus of a deficit should be available during recessions: The proper goal is balance over the course of an economic cycle. Simon's three-fifths escape clause is intended to allow for deficits during bad times (without even requiring an offsetting surplus in good times). If exercised promiscuously, this escape clause could make the amendment worthless. But the medicine is there if needed.

What's driven some liberals to support a balanced budget amendment, however, is the realization that deficit spending has become a medicine we Americans can't be trusted with. We use it when we're sick, then when we're healthy we just increase the dosage. When, inevitably, we get sick again, even gargantuan doses don't have their usual therapeutic effect. Even to use this drug properly in the future, we first will have to clear it out of our system for a while.

The deficit also makes new forms of government activism nearly impossible. If liberal politics are to be anything more than a holding action ("reactionary liberalism," in Kevin Phillips's devastating phrase), the nation's deficit addiction must first be cured.

The Washington Post says that a balanced budget amendment would be "trivializing the Constitution" and creating a "permanent monument to a temporary failure of political will." This is a serious objection. As a general rule the Constitution ought to dictate the procedures of democracy and the protection of individual rights, not specific policy outcomes. As Justice Holmes famously put it: "A constitution is not intended to embody a particular economic theory. . . . It is made for people of fundamentally differing views." Then, too, you don't want to encourage all those constitutional cowboys out there with other ideas for fiddling with the sacred text. ("We can amend that dang Constitution if we have to," said Ross Perot recently, with insufficient reverence.)

But have you read the Constitution lately? Many of its clauses address concerns that now seem trivial. See the Third Amendment, about quartering soldiers. We should only be so lucky that fiscal responsibility seems a passé issue in future years. And the balanced budget amendment, despite its name, is arguably procedural, not substantive. It doesn't mandate a balanced budget, but simply amends the legislative process to counteract the current bias against one.

Then there's the question of enforcement. The conservative enthusiasm for this amendment is ironic, since—far more than the typical constitutional provision—it is an invitation to judicial freelancing of exactly the sort they claim to abhor. What happens if president and Congress don't meet the requirements? Do judges have these officials arrested? Do they institute across-the-board budget cuts of their own? Or do they duck the issue by calling it a "political question" and refusing to act?

The answer, I hope, is the last. The amendment would probably be judicially unenforceable. But that doesn't make it worthless. The Constitution depends, to some extent, on the willing suspension of disbelief. Judges have no real power to force the other branches to obey any constitutional provisions—even those mandating elections and so on. And yet the Constitution is generally obeyed.

Robert Reischauer, head of the Congressional Budget Office, calls the balanced budget amendment a "cruel hoax" on the public because—like Gramm-Rudman before it—it substitutes procedure for substance. It allows politicians to pretend they're addressing the deficit while actually putting off the painful slicing for later. (The amendment takes effect two years after ratification by the states, which also could take years.)

Reischauer is right that the amendment is a hoax on the public, which is not being told what a balanced budget would actually entail. But is it a cruel hoax? It would be if the three-fifths escape clause became a routine exercise. But if the amendment actually produced genuine fiscal discipline, even four or five years down the road, it would be a kind hoax, not a cruel one—sort of like enticing a beloved relative into a drug treatment program.

It is cowardly, to be sure, for today's politicians to support a balanced budget amendment instead of actually taking action toward a balanced budget. But that cowardice will catch up with them one way or another. They'll either have to face the music in four or five years or retire in order to avoid it. In fact, the balanced budget amendment could make that other constitutional cure-all—term limits—superfluous.

Happy Families

(*The New Republic*, JUNE 15, 1992)*

What Vice President Dan Quayle complacently mocks as "indulgence and self-gratification," the founders of this nation referred to as "the pursuit of happiness." They were for it. And they believed the government's job was to provide the conditions for that pursuit, not to dictate its terms.

Dan Quayle's own pursuit of happiness has been conventional and easy, though he seems to think he deserves a prize. For most others, the pursuit is a struggle. That sound you hear across the land is millions of hands slapping on foreheads as deserted wives, gays and lesbians, men and women (and children) trapped in miserable marriages, assorted misfits, and—yes—even some lonely middle-aged professional women who somehow never got married but want a baby anyway say, "Why didn't I think of that? I should just be a member of a happy two-parent family with a couple of normal, healthy kids. In fact, why not go all the way and inherit a newspaper fortune while I'm at it?"

The liberating social developments of the past few decades have surely had their downside, but to dismiss them all as a ghastly mistake is smug

---

*Quayle later claimed vindication for his famous "Murphy Brown" salvo when illegitimacy became a fashionable topic with politicians across the political spectrum. But the later discussion focused entirely (whether correctly or otherwise) on welfare as the alleged cause of the illegitimacy epidemic. Quayle's attempted alarums about television, etc.—the focus of his speech—went nowhere.

and cheap and stupid. The pill, easier divorce laws, gay rights, the increased toleration of single parenthood and other eccentric living arrangements—all these have undermined the traditional family. They also have offered paths to happiness for millions who would otherwise be trapped by the conventions that provide the plots of so many gloomy nineteenth-century novels. "Happy families are all alike, but each unhappy family is unhappy in its own way," wrote Tolstoy in *Anna Karenina*. Well, we've disinvented at least a few of those ways.

Is it self-indulgent and irresponsible for "Murphy Brown" to bring a child into the world without a father? (Even twenty years ago, "Mary Richards" couldn't have gotten away with it.) Yes, that child would be better off with two parents. But surely the child of an intelligent, loving, affluent, educated, mature single mother will have his pursuit of happiness greased at least as much as the average kid who is brought into this world. Unless you think kids shouldn't be brought into the world under less than perfect conditions—in which case there would be no kids—Murphy Brown has nothing to feel guilty about.

But Murphy Brown is a fictional character. Should her inventors feel guilty for a plotline that will influence poor, uneducated, immature women to have babies without fathers? Or, to put the guilt trip in its more general form, does "the turbulent legacy of the 1960s and 1970s" include a breakdown of traditional values that members of the middle class may have managed to survive but "the poor, with less to fall back on, did not"? (The words are from Quayle's speech; the point is a neocon bromide.)

It is hard to know which is more exaggerated: the notion that the problems of the ghetto can be explained "predominantly" (Quayle again) as "a poverty of values," or the notion that the poor values of the underclass trickled down from the counterculture. Let us concede a grain of truth to both points. But if you're looking for social forces that contribute to the breakdown of traditional values and the epidemic of self-indulgence, it's absurd to obsess about Woodstock.

Even conservative social critics have made the point that free-market capitalism, in its constant stimulation and satisfaction of appetites, is the most powerful force eroding traditional values and social arrangements. The very decision to give Murphy Brown a fatherless baby was more a product of capitalist forces—the quest for ratings—than of any leftover 1960s ideology.

As it happens, Bill Kristol, the vice presidential chief of staff, is the son of Irving Kristol, the prominent conservative social critic. Kristol the Younger bears approximately the same relationship to "Dan Quayle" that series creator Diane English bears to "Murphy Brown" (or, for that matter, that Candice Bergen's father, Edgar, bore to "Charlie McCarthy"). So "Quayle" must be familiar with the argument. And "Quayle" also lived through the Reaganite 1980s. In the search for cultural influences promoting self-indulgence and immediate gratification of appetites, that decade is a livelier suspect than the distant and bedraggled 1960s. Kids weren't shooting other kids over $150 gym shoes in 1969.

To paraphrase Göring, whenever I hear the word "values" I reach for my gym shoes—in case I want to run away. The problem isn't "family values" themselves. They're swell, in their way. The problem is the government trying to impose them. But I don't seriously worry that Quayle's speech is the beginning of any right-wing family values Kulturkampf. That would require more courage of its alleged convictions than this Republican administration has got. And the more cynical uses of a new "family values" campaign are so transparent.

First, "values" are a convenient excuse for the failure of two Republican presidents to do much of anything about the cities and the underclass. They are another free lunch—a seeming answer to some pressing national challenge that requires nothing of the mass of middle-class voters. If only poor people would pull up their socks and stop watching TV shows written by liberals, their problems would be solved.

Second, "values" are, since Spiro Agnew, a traditional weapon in the Republican presidential campaign arsenal. If the "values" debate were a real one, that would be fair enough. But it is not. The Republican technique is to create a straw man—a parody "liberal" who doesn't salute the flag, doesn't love the family, and so on. It worked in 1988, and if you can successfully portray Michael Dukakis as Abbie Hoffman, anything's possible.

When you've controlled the White House for twelve years and people are palpably unhappy with the country's condition, it's useful to have someone else to pin the blame on. Congress serves this function in our constitutional system. But there's also that old bogey, the "cultural elite" that's been secretly running the country while the president and vice president were off playing golf.

Thus "family values" are part of a campaign technique that predates even Spiro Agnew. It's the stigmatization of a Great Other: a group of people within the country but different from normal people and therefore responsible for everything that's going wrong. No wonder we're running a $400 billion deficit when unmarried middle-aged women think they can just go off and have babies by themselves.

ASK A SILLY QUESTION

(*The New Republic*, JULY 6, 1992)

On June 4, President Bush held a traditional, full-dress evening news conference at which he was questioned by the professional journalists of the White House press corps. One week later Ross Perot appeared on NBC's *Today* show, where viewers questioned him by telephone for two hours.

Here, condensed (and omitting follow-ups), are the first ten questions the professionals asked Bush: (1) Will you debate Ross Perot in the fall campaign? (2) Is it proper for a man like Perot to use his wealth to run for president, and is Perot an insider or an outsider? (3) Do the opinion polls reflect a rejection of your message? (4) Do you agree with Dan Quayle that Perot was wrong in opposing the Gulf war? (5) If you're reelected, will you submit a balanced budget in 1994?

(6) Why are you going to the Rio Earth Summit since you're being so heavily criticized there? (7) Even though the economy is improving, you are still unpopular. What are you going to do about it? (8) When are you going to do in Yugoslavia what you did in Kuwait? (9) Why won't you use the "bully pulpit" of the presidency to take on pressure groups that prevent a balanced budget? (10) What were your dealings with Ross Perot on the MIA issue?

Here, similarly condensed (and omitting a joke inquiry involving the sexual organ of a popular radio talk-show host), are the first ten questions the nonprofessionals asked Perot: (1) When are you planning to declare your candidacy officially? (2) Are you prochoice or prolife? (3) What would you do as president to put unemployed Americans back to work? (4) What are your views on farm policy, especially concerning dairy farms? (5) Would you raise taxes to balance the budget? (6) How do women figure in your plans? (7) Do you support the Brady (waiting period for handguns) bill? (8) Do you support national health care, and if not, what is your plan for health care reform? (9) An article in *Texas Monthly* portrays you as a ruthless businessman. Why should Americans trust someone like that? (10) Can you describe some positive qualities of your opponents?

Now, I do not subscribe to today's fashionable pseudo-populism, which holds that all wisdom lies with ordinary citizens, who are rightly outraged at all those out-of-touch, inside-the-Beltway cultural elitists who are wrecking the country, etc., etc., etc. On the other hand, based on this one sample, I would be hard-put to argue that on balance the insider professionals with press passes dangling from their necks asked better questions than the amateurs who got through to *Today*'s 800 number. How about you?

Journalists love to agonize about their calling. Every election cycle there's something new to agonize about. Spin control and sound bites are now old hat. This year's agony is whether the candidates, especially Ross Perot, are completely avoiding the crucial mediation of journalists by abandoning the traditional campaign mechanisms—speeches, press conferences, traveling circuses, appearances on *David Brinkley*—in favor of TV shows like *Donahue* and *Larry King* where they are questioned primarily by members of the public. Or *Arsenio Hall*, where they simply play the saxophone.

There are two concerns here. First, that untrained amateurs are no match for skilled professionals in exposing a candidate's flaws and weaknesses. And second, that semijournalists like Donahue and King, not to mention nonjournalists like Arsenio, unhealthily—or at least surrealistically—muddy the distinction between serious politics and trivial show biz. There is, no question, something eerie about the same show discussing men-who-would-be-president one day and women-who-ate-their-husbands the next. Whether this juxtaposition demeans democracy or merely reflects it is too heavy a question for today's sermonette. But the first concern, about amateur questioning, seems exaggerated. The amateurs could teach the pros a thing or two.

The most striking difference between the two sets of questions, of course, is that the pros are obsessed with process while the amateurs are obsessed with substance. It doesn't do to be too pious about this. We all want to know what Bush thinks about Ross Perot. But three out of the first five questions? And is the most pressing question, even about Ross Perot, whether Bush will commit right now to debate him come the fall? This is not looking for insight or even information. It's looking for a lead.

Ditto the invitations to criticize Perot for bankrolling his own campaign, or to agree with Quayle that Perot was wrong to oppose the Gulf war.

To be sure, presidential candidates should be subjected to questions more rigorous than, "Sir, what is your position on issue X?" And at this point it is hardly worth asking George Bush if he is "prochoice or prolife" (as much as one would dearly love to know). But the pros' questions seemed less in the commendable spirit of "gotcha!" than in the silly spirit of "nyah nyah." Did anyone expect Bush to say, "Yes, as a matter of fact you're right—the opinion polls do demonstrate that the voters have rejected my message"?

As I know from personal experience, the defense has all the advantages in this game. It is virtually impossible to corner an even semiexperienced pol who doesn't wish to be cornered. Nevertheless, if a man has just delivered a pep talk for a balanced budget amendment, why ask him if he'll propose a balanced budget two years from now? Surely the "gotcha" question is why he hasn't proposed a balanced budget for the past four years.

By contrast, the single cleverest question in either session was asked by "Gene in Los Angeles" on *Today*, who challenged Perot to list the "positive qualities" of his opponents. I can't think of a way to avoid an interesting answer. Perot actually handled it quite well, giving a gracious encomium to Clinton's achievements and revealing his contempt for George Bush by praising Barbara and the kids.

Even the straightforward "What about issue X?" questions gave Perot enough rope to hang himself a couple of times on the questions of farm policy and entitlement reform. This is better than the professional reporters' score with their body-English inquiries of the "Do you still beat your wife?" variety. And the single dumbest question was asked to Bush by one of the pros: What would you say to Ross Perot if you ran into him?

In the recent British election, all three candidates (including the incumbent prime minister) were appearing on radio call-in shows regularly until the day before the voting. There, too, the untrained amateurs occasionally were able to nail a politician where the trained professionals could not. That doesn't mean we pros aren't needed anymore. But all the resentful yelps about the amateurs sound less like upholding of standards and more like fear of competition.

Taxonomy

(The New Republic, AUGUST 31, 1992)

Massachusetts *Governor William Weld repeatedly referred to the 43 tax increases Clinton signed during 11 years as governor.*
                                                     —USA TODAY, JULY 7

Bill Clinton as governor of Arkansas raised taxes something like 128 different times.
                               —VICE PRESIDENT DAN QUAYLE, JULY 23, 1992

Well, take taxes. We're mad at George Bush because he raised taxes once. Bill Clinton has signed 121 tax increases. A hundred and twenty-one!
                              —REPRESENTATIVE NEWT GINGRICH, JULY 30

Like Joe McCarthy counting Communists in the State Department, Republicans had a hard time deciding exactly how many tax increases to accuse Bill Clinton of. They have settled on the number 128, and the Bush-Quayle campaign has issued a list. The list accompanies a press release featuring the infantile snideness deputy campaign manager Mary Matalin brings to all her literary efforts on behalf of the president of the United States. It accuses Clinton of being "the Pinocchio of this political season . . . an arsonist posing as a fire fighter . . . ," etc.

The exact number of tax increases in Arkansas while Clinton was governor is a meaningless question in any event, but the Republicans obviously think it's a telling point. As McCarthy understood, a number lends phony precision that gives weight to the general indictment—in this case, that Clinton is a "tax raiser." So the accuracy of the number is important, not for what it says about Clinton but for what it says about Bush. Bush has decided to campaign on the theme of "trust." Bear with me while we analyze the "128 tax increases," and see if you can trust anything Bush or his campaign says or does.

The Bush-Quayle list is hilariously shoddy. My favorite items are three (Nos. 31, 86, and 91) that aren't items at all. They are just places where the description of an alleged tax increase took more than one line. Similarly, No. 78 is a verbatim repetition of No. 74 (a twenty-five-cent tax increase per gallon on "light wine").

This list of 128 derives from a list of "120" alleged Clinton tax increases put out by his 1990 Republican rival for governor, Sheffield Nelson. The Bush-Quayle people were wise enough to leave off a few choice items such as a $250 fine added to the sentence for drug offenders, which Nelson chose to define as a tax increase. But the Bush-Quayle "tax increase" list does include (No. 92) a $1-per-conviction court-costs fee imposed on convicted criminals. One dollar, and the Bushies are complaining! These people are supposed to be tough on crime?

Item No. 46 is a 1987 law lengthening the season for dog racing. This is apparently a "tax increase" on the theory that a longer season increases state gambling tax revenues. No. 48 is a $500 license fee for abortion clinics. Does the GOP really object to this burden on commerce? Other supposed tax increases either never actually took effect (No. 71) or replaced another tax of equal size (No. 117). A fuel tax increase is counted as two because it applies to both gasoline and diesel. A general booze tax increase weighs in at five if you count categories like wine coolers separately—as they do.

Dick Alexander, an Arkansas law professor working for the Clinton campaign, figures a true count would be fifty-five or fifty-nine increases in various taxes and fees while Clinton was governor, depending on how you figure. He's so honest he includes ten that the Republicans somehow overlooked.

But in the real world, as opposed to Republican propaganda fantasies, taxes are adjusted up and down all the time. Alexander has produced a list of forty-eight Clinton tax *cuts* during his governorship. These include such George Bush favorites as a tax credit for businesses hiring employees in enterprise zones and a tax break for capital gains. They also include a general cut last year that reduced or eliminated income taxes on 374,000 low-income Arkansas citizens. Since, according to Alexander, seven of Clinton's fifty-five (or fifty-nine) tax increases have expired or been repealed, the actual number of tax "increases" and the number of tax "cuts" are about equal. If you care.

Arkansas is a very low tax state. It ranks forty-ninth in per capita state and local taxes and fiftieth in per capita expenditures. Of course Arkansas is also a very poor state. But even measuring taxes as a share of personal income, Arkansas ranks forty-seventh.

A "Factsheet [*sic*]: Clinton Fiscal Policy" put out by the Bush-Quayle Committee augments the "128 tax increases" canard with the assertion that "taxes are $397.1 million higher on an annual basis than when Clinton took office." This figure, of course, reflects inflation and real growth as well as any genuine tax increases. By the same moronic calculus, federal taxes are $476.4 billion higher than when Ronald Reagan and George Bush took office—almost double.

In fact, the absurdity of this whole count-the-taxes exercise is illustrated by applying it to George Bush's tenure as president. Just one tax increase? Forget it. The notorious 1990 tax increase was in fact at least 73 separate increases. And Bush signed tax bills in 1989 and 1991 as well, each one with multiple provisions. Who can forget his memorable decision in 1989 to "Limit nonrecognition treatment when securities are received in certain Section 351 transactions?" That one was a $1.4 billion tax increase over five years.

There have been dozens of federal excise tax increases during Bush's reign. For example, in 1990 he imposed a two-stage tax increase (to take place in 1991 and 1993) on both small and large cigars—two distinct categories in the statute. According to the Bush-Quayle rules, that counts as four separate tax increases.

Overall, by my count using his rules, Bush has raised taxes 133 times—more often in just four years than Clinton did in eleven. And that doesn't even include increased fees for government services such as campgrounds in national parks. Nor does it include criminal fines. The real total of Bush tax increases, as defined by the Bush rules, would be hundreds more.

Every day the Bush-Quayle machine puts out stuff like this malarkey about "128 tax increases," and every day Republican sound-bite artists fan out to spread the word—often word-for-word from the press release. The Clinton-Gore machine is certainly no less efficient, but I believe it is less dishonest. If anyone has an example of a similar raw deception propagated by the Democratic campaign, I would like to hear of it. Meanwhile, returning to the would-be Bush theme of "trust," I think I prefer Reagan's old mantra about negotiating arms control with the Soviets: "Trust, but verify."

128 Skiddoo

(*The New Republic*, SEPTEMBER 21, 1992)

Who do you trust in this election? The candidate who raised taxes one time . . . or the other candidate who raised taxes and fees 128 times . . . ?

—GEORGE BUSH, 1992

How can I help seeing what is in front of my eyes? Two and two are four.
Sometimes, Winston. Sometimes they are five. Sometimes they are three.
Sometimes they are all of them at once.

—GEORGE ORWELL, *1984*

All politicians lie. Bill Clinton, in my view, has at least shaded the truth about the draft and about Gennifer Flowers. But George Bush's acceptance speech line about the 128 tax increases is a lie of gemlike purity and distilled cynicism. It was false, he (or his speechwriters) knew it was false and knew it was widely known to be false, and he said it anyway.

In 1988, Michael Dukakis said the election was about competence, not ideology, then ran an incompetent campaign. In 1992, George Bush says the election is about "trust" and "character" (as opposed to, say, the economy), then neatly demonstrates his defects in exactly those departments. In doing so, he revealed not just his contempt for the truth, but his contempt for the American political process and his fellow citizens as well. We shall find out if that contempt is deserved.

The week before Bush's speech—when the 128-to-1 canard was already circulating among Republican sound-biters—I wrote a column establishing beyond all honest doubt that both numbers are wildly inaccurate. There's room for quibbles about the exact tally. But, however you measure it, Bush has presided over more separate tax increases in his four years as President than Clinton has in his twelve years as governor.

I do not flatter myself that the president of the United States reads my column. But I do know that the people who prepared Bush's speech had read it, because they cited the column in a supporting document released with the speech text. This document asserts—as if a sufficient refutation—that the piece was "written by liberal columnist Michael Kinsley, and his research assistant, a Clinton campaign volunteer." Research assistant? It's true that I contacted (and quoted) the Clinton campaign. I also got "research assistance" from the Bush campaign. In the journalism business, we call this "reporting."

No "research assistance" was necessary to see that the list of 128 alleged Clinton tax increases circulated by the Bush-Quayle people is a joke. A glance does it. To take the most egregious cases, three of the numbers on the list have no words attached to them at all. Another item is a verbatim repetition of a previous item. Even if these and other flaws escaped the notice of Bush-Quayle staffers as they eagerly retyped the list and faxed it around on Bush-Quayle campaign stationery, the problems were all laid out in my column and therefore known to those putting the false words in George Bush's mouth.

Maybe Bush didn't know when he spoke the words that they had been publicly established as untrue. But he knows now. What did he do when he found out? Did he perchance think, What would my idol, Harry Truman, have done?* Did he call someone on the carpet and say, "How dare you put lies in my mouth?" Apparently not, because the Bushies are still, incredibly, claiming that the statement was accurate. "We stand by the figure 128," said White House spokesman Marlin Fitzwater more than a week after Bush's speech.

The Bush campaign has circulated a four-page memo rebutting my previous column. It is headlined: CLINTON'S 128 TAXES AND FEES: UN-DENIABLE. It asserts that "every single substantive charge Michael Kinsley has leveled against the tax and fee list . . . is false or grossly misleading. The list is solid." But in fact the memo does not defend—how could it?—the three totally nonexistent items. Nor does it challenge my count—133—of Bush tax increases. It engages in scholastic quibbles about some—but not all—other items I questioned, and I could quibble back. It refuses to back down from the preposterous claim that an extension of dog-racing season was a "tax increase." It dismisses a counterlist of 40-odd Clinton tax cuts on the odd grounds that most of them "apply exclu-

---

*At this moment in the 1992 campaign, believe it or not, a major issue of dispute was whether Bill Clinton or George Bush was more like Harry Truman.

sively to businesses," as if that doesn't count and as if Bush objects to business tax cuts.

This memo can't be intended seriously to persuade anyone that the 128 figure is "solid." The Bush campaign's purpose is merely to create the impression that there is some honest controversy—which there isn't—about the truth of Bush's original sally. In this, the Bush people have taken cynical advantage of certain conventions of the press.

Journalists have actually done a good job of noting that the 128-taxes figure has been challenged, but they are hampered by a reluctance to say flat-out that the President is a liar. *The New York Times* did say the figure is "false, based on trickery." But more common are such descriptions as "exaggerated" (*Washington Post*), "highly misleading" (*Wall Street Journal*—which itself exposed the fraud early on), and "at best a distortion of Clinton's record" (*Boston Globe*).

Keep the phony dispute going and eventually the press throws up its hands and declares wearily that both sides have called the other one dishonest for long enough and it's time to move on. This has now happened. Meanwhile, voters who haven't followed the issue with my own neurotic obsession are left with the vague impression that Clinton has raised a lot of taxes and who cares exactly how many. Lately the papers have been quoting anonymous Bush aides saying exactly that, although Bush is the one who decided to make the demagogic point about the number 128.

This is not about taxes. It is about, as Bush says, character and trust. If Bush would knowingly tell an established falsehood in one of the most important and widely watched addresses of his life—and stick by it afterward—what wouldn't he say? Honesty rarely counts for enough with any politician, as I say, but with George Bush it apparently counts for nothing.

Am I belaboring a rather small point? I don't think so. Some lies are complicated, like Bush's assertion in the same speech that Congress forced the 1990 tax increase on him. Some essentially dishonest statements are technically truthful, like his assertion that the Democratic platform doesn't contain the letters G-O-D. (It doesn't, but it does contain the letters F-A-I-T-H, referred to as one of "the basic values that built this country and will always make it great," and a similar passage in praise of R-E-L-I-G-I-O-U-S I-N-S-T-I-T-U-T-I-O-N-S.)

The 128-tax-increases-to-1 lie may be a small lie as these things go, but it is crystal clear. As such, it is a test of character not just for Bush but for those around him. There are decent people in the Bush campaign and Republican leadership, and others who wish to be thought of as decent. Do they care if the president lies? If they remain silent—or defend the lie—we'll have our answer.*

Mamas, Don't Let Your Babies Grow Up to Be Pundits

(*The New Yorker*, OCTOBER 26, 1992)

You probably think it's easy being a pundit. Eric Alterman thinks it's heaven. As he demonstrates in his new book, *Sound and Fury: The Washington Punditocracy and the Collapse of American Politics*, pundits now rule the world, or at least the United States. Pundits command and official Washington obeys, and no one cares that the pundits are usually wrong.

From afar, it must look like a pretty soft life, making a living just spouting opinions. Sitting in front of the TV, watching the members of *The McLaughlin Group* as they rate on a scale of one to ten the likelihood of a thunderstorm in Milwaukee next week, you're tempted to think, Any idiot could do that. But it takes a special kind of idiot. Not to brag, but I know these people.

Favoring friends and family with beautifully wrought opinions about Ross Perot or the North American Free Trade Agreement in the comfort of your own home, you're like the competent amateur cook who thinks it would be neat to run a restaurant. But the professional pundit's life is hell. It's opine, opine, opine, day in and day out, until you never want to have another opinion again.

What used to be one of the day's great pleasures—perusing the newspapers over morning coffee—becomes a nightmare. At the crack of dawn, even as the professional restaurateur is out selecting fresh vegetables and fish so his customers can later enjoy a leisurely dinner, the professional pundit is feverishly assembling the day's haul of fresh opinions. Here's this

---

This idiotic controversy continued throughout the campaign, stoked by me among others. At one point a Clinton aide named Betsy Wright stupidly released a list of 127 Clinton tax increases, and the Bushies crowed. Depending on how you define a "tax increase," you can come up with almost any number you wish. But the essential point is that any given definition produces far more "tax increases" by Bush as president than by Clinton as governor—not the "1" Bush was claiming.

morning's *Times:* SENATE PASSES BILL TO CHARGE MAKERS FOR DRUG APPROVAL. *Shit.* What do I think of that? CIA CHIEF ORDERS INVES-TIGATION OF STATEMENTS IN IRAQ BANK CASE. That headline contains at least three words—"CIA," "investigation," and "bank"—that together carry the powerful subliminal message "Do not read this article. Life is too short." But for the pundit there is no escape.

NEW USE IS FOUND FOR ABORTION PILL . . . MAOIST CHIEF IN PERU IS SENTENCED TO LIFE (hmm, sounds like a good thing—but is there a catch?). . . . We're still on the *Times* front page and we haven't even got to the eighteen stories dissecting the presidential debates.

On something like the debates, it isn't sufficient to have one large opinion, however sound. You must supply opinions in infinite layers. Having an opinion on who won or will win is like being able to boil water. You have to have an opinion about whether the draft thing is backlashing against Bush, how Clinton should exploit Iraqgate, the potential effect of a decline in viewership between debates two and three, suits and ties: do they matter?, participating journalists: are they ethically compromised?, etc., etc.

And the eternal quest for novelty! The amateur home chef can re-create exquisite opinions by the masters—a view on the Maastricht treaty borrowed from George Will, a sermonette on voter alienation from a recipe by David Broder. But the professional pundit must concoct something different, something with a dash of originality. In a field as thoroughly picked over as the presidential debates, this requires flirting with absurdity: Can I get away with predicting that Stockdale will be the sure winner in the veepstakes? What if I say Perot's handling of foreign policy will be the key thing to watch for? Will that fly?

Punditry, you see, is not for the fainthearted. It doesn't matter whether what you say actually turns out to be correct. ("Never look back" is the watchword of our profession.) The fear is merely that a pearl of analysis will sound just too ridiculous at the time it is uttered. But the path between the sheer drop-offs of absurdity on the one side and banality on the other can be mighty narrow.

TV punditry adds a whole extra layer of terror, mainly of being ex-posed as an ignoramus. It's ten seconds to showtime and you suddenly realize you have no idea where Somalia is. You're on the air, opinions are flying like shrapnel, and you're about to demand that Nicholas Brady be fired as the secretary of the treasury when a small voice in your head whispers, "Are you *absolutely sure* he's not the secretary of commerce?" The words freeze in your throat. You gurgle. You decide to play it safe and demand that Richard Darman be fired as the head of the Office of Management and Budget. (*Wait!* Or is it the Council of Economic Advisers? Too late. . . .)

Is this man I'm talking to Senator Domenici or Senator Deconcini? And is he the one in the Keating Five or was it the other guy? (What was the Keating Five again?) Someone calling himself Senator Bob Smith of New Hampshire sits before you declaiming about big-spending Democrats. It's your turn to interrupt, but the only thing on your mind is: Can there really be a senator named Bob Smith? ("Senator, this is not a motel. What is your real name?")

Fast-moving world events generate intense pronunciation paranoia and a vicious competitive snobbery among the talking heads. Just think: Once upon a time it was a mark of sophistication to know that Gorbachev is pronounced Gorba-*chawv*. That didn't last long, but at least in those days the proper pronunciation of Gorbachev was about all you needed in order to have a third of the globe covered. The rise of Eduard Shevardnadze was an ominous portent. These days, you get no credit at all for knowing that Vaclav is pronounced *Vaht*-slahv, and successfully condemning "Slobodan Milosevic" for the rape of "Bosnia-Herzegovina" is barely a warm-up routine for opining on daily news out of the former Soviet bloc.

Yet to control the world would surely be worth some televised embarrassment. Alterman's eccentric but flattering argument is that pundits are more influential in the screaming TV age than they were in the stately days of Walter Lippmann. That's because, he says, the other institutions of democracy have decayed—politicians speak in tongues, the parties barely exist, unions and other voluntary organizations have retreated from the national stage—and the rest of the press is hamstrung by the conventions of "objectivity." Pundits reign supreme.

True, there is a downside. Because of pundit power, "our economy, our security, and most particularly our democracy are imperiled by the decrepit state of our national political discourse." But this is surely a small price to pay for the thrill of seeing strong governments wilt at the drop of your sound bite.

I must confess I hadn't noticed this power myself. But it's an interesting thesis. Give me a minute and I'll have an opinion about it.

Vindication

(*The New Republic*, NOVEMBER 23, 1992)*

No doubt it will all end in tears. But for the moment, I FEEL GREAT! It's like the lifting of a terrible headache, or like coming up for air after swimming underwater.

Yes, the euphoria is not entirely rational. I think I speak for all Clinton supporters in saying that we realize the election of our man as president will not magically solve all the nation's problems. Nor will it clear up our skin condition, improve our love life, pick up our dry cleaning, or stop that strange noise in the back of our car. Life goes on. Nevertheless, this victory is very, very sweet.

Partly it's just the sporting aspect. Democrats under age forty-five do not have much experience voting for the winner. Until last Tuesday, I'd done it only once—in 1976—and then with no special enthusiasm. In 1992, it was nice to feel that Lady Luck was on our side for a change. A friend who worked in the Carter White House says that watching Bush's repeated fumbles this year reminded her of those bleak months in 1980 when "everything we touched turned to shit."

Above all, this Democratic victory is sweet revenge on George Bush for the loathsome, dishonest, and empty campaign that won him the White House in 1988. His empty administration was a final comment on the emptiness of that campaign. What did Bush do about the alleged problem of prison furloughs in his four years as president? How often did he recite the Pledge of Allegiance to the Flag?

Bush is doomed to be remembered as a failed president. The only debate will be over whether his failure reflected the culmination of Reaganism or the betrayal of it. (The answer seems obvious to me.) And the only historical uncertainty is whether the Bush era will be seen as a dip between the prosperous Reagan and Clinton eras, or as the beginning of an extended national decline.

For years to come, the Democrats will be able to run against Bush the

---

This is a period piece. The period lasted about three months, from November 1992 through January 1993. I republish it without comment, except to note the opening sentence.

way the Republicans have run against Carter, and as Democrats ran against Hoover before that. Like the late 1970s, the early 1990s will be frozen in people's memories—inaccurately—as a terrible time, far worse than it really was. This injustice fills me with unwholesome glee. The best Bush can hope for is obscurity. A crossword puzzle president: "President after Reagan. Four letters. Begins with 'B.'" Polk? No. . . .

Meanwhile, after what seems like a century of stern sermonettes to Democrats about how we must "rethink," must purge ourselves of excesses and extremism, must listen to the people, must abase ourselves with public mea culpas, etc., etc., it is now the Republicans' turn for mandatory re-thinking and op-ed self-flagellation. They are in worse shape than the Democrats ever were; they don't even control the other elected branch of government (though they do, by now, have the courts). Supply-side eco-nomics and the whole range of social issues from abortion to school prayer are just two suitable subjects for orgies of conservative self-abuse. I intend to enjoy the show.

But schadenfreude (joy at others' misery) is not the only reason to feel euphoric. Defeat of the Republican presidential machine offers some hope that American politics can become more honest again. The dishonesty that has become institutionalized in our politics is of two sorts. In neither category are the Democrats blameless, but in both the Republicans have led the way.

The less important form of dishonesty is campaign sleaze. "Horton-ism" is the shorthand term for finding and exploiting an ugly symbolic issue, either literally false or false in the implications derived from it. The Bush campaign tried repeatedly to find its Willie Horton this year—Hil-lary, gays, Oxford, the trip to Moscow—but nothing stuck. Nor did the lies about Clinton's record as governor of Arkansas. In fact, many of these thrusts seem to have backfired. If political strategists, like generals, fight the last war, maybe there will be less poison gas next time.

The more important form of institutionalized political dishonesty is fiscal. Ronald Reagan made it impossible for any presidential candidate with a hope of winning to tell the truth about federal spending and taxes. The last major party nominee who tried was Walter Mondale. Clinton certainly did not tell the truth this time. But it surely was asking too much to expect Democrats to go on losing the White House by telling the truth about the federal budget while Republicans went on winning by lying about it.

Now, however, we're even. And Clinton, the winner, was marginally more forthright on the subject than Bush, the loser. So perhaps the great chain of lying can be broken. In particular, Clinton has shown that you can win an election without promising never to raise taxes in any way on anyone. So perhaps we have seen the end of a period of absurd policy gridlock (in which the average person's taxes have gone up anyway).

This election has restored my faith in my fellow citizens. Not just because they voted my way, but because they rejected ugly appeals to various forms of chauvinism and intolerance. Watching that GOP Festival of Hate in Houston, I felt sick. I thought, Here we go again. And I confess: I thought it would work. Why not? It worked the last time. To be sure, last time the economy wasn't so pressing. This year voters had more important things to be scared of than Republican-confected bogies. But intolerance usually flowers, rather than shrivels, in bad economic times. No, the voters deserve credit for not being fooled twice. I should have had more faith. I apologize.

This leads to the deepest reason I feel so euphoric at the election result: I feel connected with my country again. The single most repellent remark of this election year was Republican National Chairman Rich Bond's comment during the Houston convention, "We are America. Those other people are not." The words are hateful and un-American on their face. The fact that Bond himself is a New Yorker with political roots in Manhattan liberal Republicanism merely illustrates the depraved cynicism of this failed Republican culture war.

Nevertheless, a part of me feared it was true. For twelve years Democrats and liberals have suffered a rising crescendo of schoolyard taunts: You are outsiders, out of the mainstream, out of touch with ordinary Americans. Your political beliefs and cultural values are anathema in large swaths of your own country. Each election, however fraudulently won from our point of view, made the case harder to refute.

Well, apparently it ain't true. Those other people are the ones who are out of touch, who are outside the mainstream, whose values aren't widely shared.

And so my message to Republicans is: Wipe that damned smug grin off your faces at long last. And just hope that we're nicer to you in opposition than you've been to us all these years.

ELECTION FRAUD

(*Time*, NOVEMBER 23, 1992)

Democratic National Committee Chairman Ron Brown was beaming as he bounced into the CNN Washington bureau. And rightly so. It was midafternoon on Election Day, and exit polls showed that Bill Clinton was going to win big. But before going on-air, Brown sobered up. "I'd better not seem too happy," he said. "The polls are still open." Brown soon appeared on TV screens around the world expressing cautious optimism to an interviewer who knew as well as Brown did that the result was a foregone conclusion.

Bush deputy campaign director Mary Matalin was interviewed on CNN a few minutes after Brown. Her eyes said it was all over, but her mouth soldiered on. Reports of high voter turnout were very encouraging for hopes of a Bush upset, she insisted.

The drama that had you glued to your TV the evening of November 3 was a fraud perpetrated by a vast conspiracy. Virtually everyone you saw on-screen—reporters, analysts, candidates and their handlers—knew what everyone else was waiting to hear, yet pretended ignorance. Not just that Clinton would win, but by what margin in which states. And the Senate and governorship results, too. All, because of exit poll results, available at the punch of a computer button hours before they were reported to viewers.

The New York Times editorialized afterward that "the four networks deserve unstinting praise for threading a careful path between sensationalism and censorship." In fact, election-night broadcasts were an orgy of both vices, as all the networks generated false tension while suppressing the very information that would dissipate it.

And why? Because otherwise sane people believe—against all logic—that it somehow undermines democracy to project the result of an election before some people have voted. The networks are not to blame. Under pressure from Congress and sundry goody-goodies, they have agreed not to "characterize the outcome" in any state until the polls (the real polls) have closed in that state. This hasn't satisfied some westerners, who complain about announced results from the East before polls have closed in the West.

This year all four networks called the Clinton victory at 10:48 P.M. eastern time—7:48 P.M. in the West where polls closed at 8.00 P.M.— thereby denying westerners twelve precious minutes during which to vote in ignorance. Meanwhile, newspapers—including *The New York Times*— had hit the streets as early as 10:30 P.M. with CLINTON VICTORY head- lines.

Self-censorship inevitably blurs into outright deception as network anchors pretend the race hasn't been decided. "The only way Bush can win now is by carrying states X, Y, and Z," they say, knowing full well that Bush can't carry states X, Y, and Z and cannot win even if he does. Or they drop little hints of the true outcome—"The smell of change is in the air tonight, Peter"—as if these insights derive from years of experience and exquisitely sensitive journalistic nostrils rather than from cold, hard numbers on a computer screen in front of them.

The exit polls do provide a way of foreshadowing: "While we don't yet know who will carry Georgia, Dan, it's interesting to note that Clinton is running strongly there among people both under and over five foot six." Or they provide grist for tautological insights: "People who say that Bill Clinton reminds them of Jack the Ripper seem to be voting against Clin- ton in large numbers tonight, Tom."

What's the point? I have news for people voting late in the evening on the West Coast. It is virtually certain that the election result is settled by the time you vote. This is true whether or not that result is reported on TV. In fact, even those, like me, who voted early in the morning on the East Coast could do so with confidence that the election result would be determined despite our particular vote, if not before it.

But if reporting the result on TV leads people not to vote, however nutty their reason, isn't that a bad thing? Well, even studies purporting to show that early reporting reduces voter turnout don't claim that this affects the actual result—in the main race or in subsidiary contests. And that's only logical. Why should knowing the outcome discourage voters for the loser more than voters for the winner, or vice versa? High voter turnout is desirable for its own sake, I suppose. But surely, deceiving people into exercising their right to vote is high-mindedness gone badly astray.

Some argue that exit polls shouldn't be reported because they may be wrong. But aren't other citizens able to handle this possibility as well as the journalists and politicos? The main difference between exit polls and other polls is that exit polls are more likely to be accurate. Fear that they are right, not fear that they are wrong, is what upsets people.

The New York Times recommends "extending daylight time for two weeks in the West," keeping East Coast polls open until 9.00 P.M. and requiring western polls to shut at 7.00 P.M. The aim of this Rube Goldberg contrivance would be a uniform poll closing. Thus, to save westerners from the alleged danger of a devalued vote at, say, 7.30 P.M., they will be denied the right to vote that late at all. And even this won't solve the censorship problem, since the networks know the results long before the polls actually close.

I have a better idea. Why don't we forget about it? Voting is an act of democratic faith. You do it even though you know that elections are never determined by one vote. If you can't stand the thought that your vote doesn't "matter" in that sense, you'd better not vote at any hour in any time zone.

Bias and Baloney

(*The New Republic*, DECEMBER 14, 1992)

Aha! Gotcha! That undoubtedly is the reaction of conservatives across the land to evidence that American journalists tend to have liberal political views. The evidence comes in a survey of fourteen hundred journalists conducted over the summer and reported in *The American Journalist in the 1990s,* a study published by something called the Freedom Forum, a philanthropic spin-off of the Gannett media empire.

Few tears have been shed over the study's conclusion that the typical journalist earns less in real terms today than in the late 1960s. (Average age, 36; median 1992 income, $31,297.) Instead there has been gnashing of teeth over the news that 44.1 percent of journalists consider themselves Democrats and only 16.3 percent Republicans. The gap has grown since a similar survey in 1982 and is far larger than the gap in polls of the general population, some of which have shown the parties close to even. At a time when Republicans are toying with a variety of stab-in-the-back theories of why they lost the last election, most involving the press, such findings are red meat to right-wing conspiratorialists.

Why do journalists tend to be liberals? The extent of this tendency is exaggerated in paranoid conservative minds. And there is the countervailing reality that media owners and editorial pages tend to be conservative. Two decades after George Will was discovered sipping a cherry soda at a local drugstore, the Washington punditocracy—on the op-ed pages and TV yack shows—also has a definite conservative slant. Nevertheless, the general liberal inclination of journalists would be hard to deny.

Perhaps I am not the best person to try to solve the mystery of why. My own political views are more or less liberal. They were not genetically implanted, and I hold them under no form of compulsion except that of reason. It seems to me they're the sort of views a reasonable, intelligent person would hold. Since most journalists I meet are reasonable, intelligent people, the mystery to me is not why journalists tend to be liberals but why so many other reasonable, intelligent people are not. But it's not hard to come up with plausible theories to explain the gap, having to do with psychological disposition and so on.

The point is that there is no conspiracy going on here. People freely choose their politics and freely choose their careers. No one is forcing journalists to hold liberal political views, and no one is preventing or even discouraging conservatives from becoming journalists. If it just happens to work out that way, on average, so what?

A political preference is not itself a "bias." This basic point seems beyond the understanding of many press critics. Any journalist who has had this argument with a nonjournalist knows the frustration of being accused of "bias" by someone whose political views are of such red-hot intensity that your own pale by comparison. Many who will wave this Gannett study as proof of a press liberal "bias" will refuse to accept that their conservative views make them "biased," too.

But should journalists be different? Some media critics, and some journalists themselves, think that the press ought to function as a sort of sacred priesthood of political celibates, purged of the ideological longings that inflame ordinary folks. The executive editor of *The Washington Post* famously goes so far as to refrain from voting. Perhaps he also succeeds in having no opinion about whom he would vote for were he not scrupulous. If so, his self-discipline would do credit to any monk. Whether it is quite so admirable for a journalist is another question. In any event, it is surely rare. Journalists, by definition, are inquisitive people with an interest in public affairs. To expect them to form no conclusions about the people and policies they report on is absurd.

What do conservative media critics want? Presumably they would not favor a quota program for right-wingers, some kind of Americans with Political Disabilities Act, whereby people handicapped with conservative political opinions would get preference over better-qualified liberals for the same job. What they, and everybody else, can reasonably expect is for reporters to tell the story as straight as possible. Evidence about journalists' political preference says nothing one way or another about how they are performing that function. Most national reporters, on TV and in print, do it pretty well. Certainly of the two newspapers here in Washington, the one whose writers and editors make no effort to avoid slanting the news is the conservative *Washington Times*, not the supposedly liberal *Post*.

In Europe they do things differently. There, most newspapers are overtly ideological, and you take that into account in choosing a paper and in how you read it. There's much to be said for this system. Opinion journalism, if it's honest, can sometimes be a more efficient way of acquiring information than an American-style objective news story (in my opinion). Intelligent judgment is less paralyzed by the need for "balance," and less space is wasted on quotations from others saying things the writer dares not say herself. There are subjects on which I'd rather read a *Wall Street Journal* editorial, undoubtedly "biased" though it may be, than a *Wall Street Journal* news article.

But in this country we cling to the belief that the news, unlike editorials, should be "balanced." Thus two other silly studies, released recently, purporting to compute whether television reports and/or newspaper stories during the election campaign were pro or anti one candidate or another. One study, from the Joan Shorenstein Barone Center on the Press, Politics, and Public Policy at Harvard University's John F. Kennedy School of Government (an organization whose very name takes up half of any news story dedicated to reporting its findings), actually measured hundreds of news stories on a scale of 1 (very positive) to 5 (very negative). The study, which covered February through May, found that Bush's average score was 3.3—a full 0.9 more negative than Clinton's 2.4. The implicit premise of this pseudoscientific exercise seems to be that in a perfect world every candidate would score an exact 2.5. But at a time when Bush was presiding over a stagnant economy, running an inept campaign, and being bashed from inside and outside his own party, a perfectly "balanced" press cover-age would itself be evidence of bias.

The press brings these studies on itself. Not by displaying bias, but by its hunger for respectability and professionalization. That's what leads to the creation of things like the Freedom Forum and the Barone Blah Blah Blah, which then need to keep themselves busy by commissioning studies and heartaching over the meaning of it all. The expanding supply of solutions creates an increasing demand for problems.

Then, too, journalists have a psychological disposition—related, perhaps, to the psychological disposition that leads them to be dispropor-tionately liberal—toward public wallowing in self-doubt and self-flagellation. Conservative press critics suffer no such malady.

DEATH WARMED OVER

(*The New Republic*, DECEMBER 21, 1992)

In the past few months I've started reading the obituaries in *The New York Times*. Yes, I know, this is supposed to be a sign of age, inti-mations of morality, and so on. But the obituaries are actually somewhat reassuring on this score. Judging from the obits, one's forties seem to be a relatively safe haven. AIDS and suicide are mainly visible in the rearview mirror, while cancer and heart attacks are still mostly distant specks on the horizon.

No, what appeals to me about the obituaries is the poetry, specifically the poetry of the headlines. To some extent, this requires no art: the Ozymandias note is built in. JERROLD WEXLER, 68, CHICAGO DEVEL-OPER WHO BUILT EMPIRE. Ah, but what good did it do him, in the end? DAVID GORENSTEIN, WHO CHARTED MATH'S DENSEST FIELDS, DIES AT 69. Math's very densest fields! Would he not have settled for math's second-densest fields, in exchange for a couple of extra years?

But the art of writing obituary headlines is not to be sneered at. In-deed, the obituary is the headline writer's greatest challenge, and a great obituary headline is the highest expression of the headline writer's art. As with other forms of poetry, the key to a good headline is compression. This is hard enough when the subject is, say, a presidential pronouncement. The obituarist, though, must summarize a person's entire life—and is lucky to have five words to do it in. NATHAN APPLEMAN, 88, OILMAN AND BENEFACTOR. This hardly does full justice, I'm sure, but it sounds grand and scans well.

Not everyone is so lucky. The demands of compression can impart a sense of comic triviality to almost any lifetime endeavor, however serious or socially useful. GEORGE E. BATES, 89, INVESTMENT PROFESSOR AND EXPERT ON COINS. LILLIAN V. OPPENHEIMER, 93, INTRODUCED AMERICANS TO ORIGAMI. DR. DAVID CAPLOVITZ, AN AUTHORITY ON SPENDING HABITS. GLENN APPLEYARD, 70, EXPERT ON "DIAL IT" LINES. Would it be better, you may ask yourself as you read each day's offerings, to be forgotten completely or to be remembered for all time as JACKSON WEAVER, 72, VOICE OF SMOKEY BEAR?

Or how about DR. JOHN HOTSON, 95, UNRAVELER OF ELIZA-BETHAN LITERARY PUZZLES? Ninety-five years on earth and that's his claim? No doubt it's a greater contribution to the general welfare than most of us will make. But laid out cold on the page, it seems insufficient somehow. True, he may have bred a wonderful family or done thousands of kindnesses to others, but the *Times* does not concern itself with that sort of thing.

The obituary page does celebrate life's diversity. Professor F.S.C. Northrup, ninety-eight, who SAW CONFLICT RESOLUTION IN SCIENCE, probably never met Rudolph C. Ising, 80, A CARTOONIST AND CREATOR OF "LOONEY TUNES," and neither one would have much to say to John Bratby, "KITCHEN SINK" ARTIST AND A NOVELIST, 64. But all three are united forever by having died on the same day. Likewise PROF. ARPAD E. ELO, 89, INVENTOR OF CHESS RATINGS SYSTEM is parked for eternity next to WILLIAM HILLCOURT, A BOY SCOUT WRITER AND COLUMNIST.

Of course most of us won't make *The New York Times* at all. As with the *Times*'s famous wedding announcements, the criteria for deciding who is included, as well as the hierarchies of placement and size, are deeply mysterious. A few obits qualify for the same reason as most wedding an-nouncements: parentage. BERNARD BARUCH, JR., STOCK EXCHANGE MEMBER, 90, obviously made the cut only for the very first act of his very long life, which was being born to someone whose own *Times* obituary was undoubtedly far longer and better placed.

Almost as poignant are those whom the *Times* deems significant for some long-ago event in their own lives. CALVIN GRAHAM, 62, WHO FOUGHT IN WAR AS A 12-YEAR-OLD—and apparently did nothing of note for the next half-century. JOHN C. DANIEL, 93; ADMIRAL HAD A ROLE IN '53 KOREA TRUCE. ("Had a role" seems brutally stinting; the article itself says his was an "important role.") Saddest of all is when your demise merely revives some ancient embarrassment and stamps it forever as the defining moment of your life: G. HARROLD CARSWELL IS DEAD AT 72; WAS REJECTED FOR SUPREME COURT.

Some obituary headlines hint at the strain of having to summarize the deceased's accomplishments in a field the writer knows little or nothing about. The result is a slight sense of desperation or bluff. WILLIAM MAS-SELOS IS DEAD AT 72; A PIANIST WHO LOVED DIVERSITY. Or, HAL-LOWELL DAVIS, 96, AN EXPLORER WHO CHARTED THE INNER EAR. Or, ED BLACKWELL, 63, JAZZ DRUMMER KNOWN FOR WARM TEX-TURES.

And sometimes the headline writer just gives up. LEONARD A. RAP-PING, AUTHOR, 57; DEVELOPED AN ECONOMIC THEORY. KIMBALL C. ATWOOD III DIES AT 71; DEVELOPED WAY TO ANALYZE GENES. MARK HAWKINS, 82, HUMORIST-ESSAYIST OF THE HUMAN RACE. It's not clear whether "of the human race" is supposed to describe the deceased or his essays. But in either case the question arises: As opposed to what?

On the other hand, how about this grabber? JOHN BUETTNER-JANUSH, 67, DIES; N.Y.U. PROFESSOR POISONED CANDY. After so many professors who made the *Times* for seemingly obscure academic accom-plishments, it is refreshing to come across a deceased scholar whose note-worthy accomplishment involved taking action. In this case the action the good professor took was to send poisoned candy to a judge who was trying him for using his laboratory to make illegal drugs.

Other obit headlines signal an interesting life story more subtly. E.g., REV. TIMOTHY SHEEHAN, EX-U.S. DRUG AGENT, 53. Turns out he quit the Drug Enforcement Administration in 1973 to enter the Roman Cath-olic seminary. Died of lung cancer, by the way.

Best of all are the headlines in which death—though inevitable for all of us—is nevertheless made to seem ironic in this particular case. JIM GARRISON, 70, THEORIST ON KENNEDY DEATH, DIES. Or, RICHARD YATES, NOVELIST, 66, DIES; CHRONICLER OF DISAPPOINTED LIVES.

And what about RICHARD EELLS, 75; PROFESSOR OF BUSINESS

who—as the *Times* summarizes his life's work in two words—URGED PHILANTHROPY? Let's hope that's paying off for him. Or, GIAN CARLO WICK IS DEAD AT 82; DETECTED SYMMETRIES OF UNIVERSE. Did he indeed? Well perhaps he's now in a position to confirm them.

THE PRUNE BOOK

(*The New Republic*, JANUARY 4, 1993)

Now that our triumph over communism is complete, the next goal is to spread American-style democracy throughout the world. In a place like Somalia, to take a lively example, it is obviously no good to have the country run by nothing but a bunch of warlords. That is a recipe for anarchy. Oh, there is nothing wrong with warlords per se. But to do things right, American-style, you need Warlords, Deputy Warlords, Executive Warlords, Executive Deputy Warlords, Confidential Assistants to the Executive Deputy Warlords, etc.

My text for this sermon on the proper way to run a democracy is that Government Printing Office best-seller, *United States Government: Policy and Supporting Positions* (211 pages; $13), aka "the Plum Book." This is the publication put out every four years, right after the presidential election, listing all the jobs available for the new president to fill at his or her discretion.

At first glance, taken as literature, the Plum Book is disappointing. Job titles like "Confidential Assistant to the Executive Assistant to the Secretary of Agriculture" lack the forthright glamour of, say, "warlord" (so impressive on one's business card). At the same time, they also lack the mystery and romance of some British government sinecures such as "Lord Privy Seal" or "Chancellor of the Duchy of Lancaster." The U.S. Treasury Department has a few swashbuckling "assayers," and State has its "attachés," but by and large the American job titles don't get much more lyrical than "Commissioner, Inter-American Tropical Tuna Commission" (one of two separate tuna-related posts that are in the president's gift).

Missing, too, are all the folks who loom so large in the government as portrayed in the media. Where are all the "senior administration officials" and "aides" who fill the daily newspapers with their anonymous pronouncements?

However, the Plum Book takes on a certain incantatory power when read aloud. Repeat after me (from the Commerce Department chapter):

General Counsel
Senior Counsel to the General Counsel
Confidential Assistant
Counsellor to the General Counsel
Deputy General Counsel
Assistant General Counsel . . .
Chief Counsel . . .
Deputy Chief Counsel . . .

Subtle changes are rung as the verse moves from department to department. The equivalent passage from the Department of Health and Human Services begins:

General Counsel
Principal Deputy General Counsel
Deputy General Counsel—Legal Counsel
Special Assistant to the General Counsel
Deputy General Counsel
Chief Counsel . . .

The Plum Book may also be read as a giant literary puzzle. Hours can be spent deconstructing the text in pursuit of status codes. It's easy enough to comprehend the basic hierarchy of adjectives in which Associate trumps Assistant and Deputy trumps Associate and so on. "Executive Assistant to the Assistant Secretary" is clearly superior to "Special Assistant to the Deputy Assistant Secretary," even though the latter arguably is more euphonious.

But the rococo variations and permutations can offer challenges. Is a Special Assistant higher or lower than a Confidential Assistant? Where does an Associate Deputy Assistant Secretary—of which there are at least seven at Treasury—stand, compared with a Deputy Under Secretary/Assistant Secretary? When the same department boasts a Deputy Assistant Secretary (Policy Analysis) and a Director, Office of Policy Analysis, which one's analysis has a better chance of becoming policy?

And what do you make of Treasury, which has a Deputy Secretary and an Under Secretary and an Executive Secretary—each with the usual retinue of assistants and associates? Who lords it over whom in the Secretary's dining room?

The deeper mystery, of course, is what do all these people do. Let us not indulge in the cheap Republican presumption that anyone working in the federal bureaucracy must be a self-serving time waster. (Most of the jobs in the 1992 Plum Book, after all, are currently filled by Republicans.) But the job titles give little indication of what the holder's duties are and how much, if anything, he or she is contributing to the commonweal.

Job seekers (the Plum Book's main customers) will find this frustrating. Suppose that, inspired by Bill Clinton's campaign promises, you long to be the guy who gets to throw welfare mothers off the dole after two years. Is that person the Assistant to the President for Economic and Domestic Policy? The Counsellor to the President for Domestic Policy? The Manager of Special Initiatives of the Department of Health and Human Services? The Assistant Secretary of HHS for Children and Families? The Assistant Secretary of Labor for Employment and Training?

Would-be Clintonistas are perusing the Plum Book like a Christmas catalog, visions of sugarplums dancing in their heads. But very few of the jobs listed sound like sure fire fun. One I spotted that looked promising was Presidential Diarist (in the National Archives and Records Administration). It comes, naturally, with an Assistant to the Presidential Diarist.

At the very least, it's hard not to suspect grotesque title inflation: too many Chief Counsels and not enough Indian Counsels. One's heart goes out to the poor woman at the State Department who seems to be the only person in the entire government whose title is listed as the brutally frank "Secretary (Typing)." Are her duties so very different from the "Correspondence Officer" in her same office? Her only consolation is that in the government, unlike the private sector, "Secretary" is also an honorific. Perhaps to avoid confusion, Lawrence Eagleburger should be identified as "Secretary (No Typing)."

The government is very big on liaison. At the White House, there are two Deputy Assistants to the President for Public Liaison as well as a Special Assistant to the President for Public Liaison and another Deputy Assistant who is also Director, Office of Public Liaison. All fair enough, perhaps, in a democracy. But the Commerce Department has a ten-person office of White House Liaison—a Deputy Assistant Secretary, four Special Assistants, and five Confidential Assistants—which seems a bit much.

Why should an administration need so many people to liaise with itself?

Clinton has promised to prune the federal bureaucracy. He might well take this document as his Prune Book, though there will always be people ready to explain why we need an International Development and Cooperation Agency as well as an Agency for International Development. Indeed, Clinton's only bureaucratic foray so far has been to add a new National Economic Council to the already existing Council of Economic Advisers and Office of Management and Budget, not to mention the entire Treasury Department and economics divisions of the other Cabinet departments. Look for Confidential Assistant to the Executive Assistant to the Associate Director of the NEC in the 1996 edition.

Visiting a Place Called Hope

(*Time*, APRIL 19, 1993)

During the recent conservative era in America, circa 1980–92, liberals were often accused of hoping for things to go badly. There was some justice in this accusation. As conservatives are now discovering, the psychology of political opposition is complicated. Of course, for reasons both patriotic and selfish, you don't want calamity to befall the United States of America. On the other hand, it is hard not to relish a certain gloomy anticipation of seeing your predictions of doom come true. And as a practical matter, bad times are the usual way the out-of-power side gets back in.

But the psychology of political ascendance turns out to be complicated as well. Liberals these days are called upon to perform the novel, and surprisingly arduous, exercise of hoping for a president to succeed. Some aren't up to it. American liberals have basically been in opposition mode since around 1966, halfway through LBJ's second term (except perhaps for a week or two in 1977 at the beginning of the Carter administration). For most, that period covers their entire politically aware lives. Many are too young to have experienced firsthand the euphoria of JFK's Camelot, but are now too old and world-weary to join the twentysomethings who swoon unselfconsciously for Bill Clinton.

These pathetic souls have wandered for years in the political desert. Now they stand outside the promised land—a Place Called Hope—yet they cannot enter. What blocks their way? Four things.

First, knee-jerk iconoclasm. The habit of a lifetime is hard to break. The very phrase "the president's economic plan" starts the facial nerves twitching into the formation of a cynical sneer. As proposals for reform of everything under the sun come cascading out of the administration, the first instinct is to assume there is something wrong with each of them.

Second, there is the phenomenon known as "the narcissism of small differences." Liberals and left-wingers are enthusiastic sectarians. Some are ready to denounce Clinton for not being a "real Democrat" whenever he compromises or takes a moderate position. Others are equally quick to denounce him for not being a "new Democrat" whenever he holds firm to some traditional liberal principle they would rather see abandoned.

We all have our political hobbyhorses. One of mine, for example, has been tax reform: Eliminate loopholes and lower the rates. Clinton's tax plan undoes much of tax reform. It not only raises rates but also reintroduces a variety of (in my view) stupid tax breaks for this or that business activity. But I ask myself, Is tax reform more important than curbing the deficit and reinvigorating the government? I swallow hard and say no.

A third guardian at the gates of hope is a fear of seeming boosterish. Naked sincerity and enthusiasm can be embarrassing. One must protect one's reputation for skepticism. One doesn't want to be thought of as a cadre or a Moonie, like those absurd Reaganites of the early- to mid-1980s. Nor does one want to be associated with the real Clintonite swooners, not all of whom are youths in their twenties.

These three are all respectable motivations, up to a point. The instinct to oppose whatever those in power happen to be proposing is democratically healthy. A reluctance to compromise shows intellectual principles. The practice of jumping out of the way of bandwagons is morally superior to the practice of jumping onto them. But a fourth roadblock to hope is less admirable. That is complacency or mental laziness.

Many who are cynics about the Clinton presidency and its agenda seem to think they deserve some sort of prize for their refusal to succumb to hope, as if this were a particularly brave or difficult trick to pull off. In fact, there's nothing easier than maintaining a cynical, opposition stance. After all these years, we liberals can do that in our sleep.

It's easy to preserve your integrity in opposition, and tempting to hoard it by remaining in opposition under any circumstance. Scarier and indeed riskier is engaging your integrity by investing hope in flawed politicians operating in an imperfect world. The cheap pleasures of cynicism are always in plentiful supply. Abandoning them is like going on a diet or giving up smoking. Hope, in other words, is the thing that takes work.

It takes work, in part, because the politicians will constantly disappoint. Believing in a Place Called Hope means something different from what Bill Clinton intended in that brilliantly mawkish convention speech line. Hope is required precisely because Clinton himself is so flawed. Otherwise, we could simply swoon, and hope would be superfluous. But Clinton is a dissembler, like all (successful) politicians. He is a reckless maker of incompatible promises that destine every subgroup of his supporters to feel betrayed about something. He is wrong about some issues, cowardly about others, right on fewer than any individual supporter might wish.

But those who never invested any hope in Ronald Reagan and George Bush, and who now are withholding that investment from Bill Clinton, must start to ask themselves what hope they hold for American democracy. Are they going to spend their entire lives sneering for fear of a mistaken swoon? For liberals especially, Clinton is something of a last chance—and an unexpected chance at that. Under these circumstances, hope seems almost prudent.

A Place Called Hope. I certainly wasn't born there, and wouldn't really care to live there full-time. But it's a nice place to visit.

T HE S ERVANT P ROBLEM

(*Time*, JULY 5, 1993)

The Zoe Baird episode earlier this year revealed a deep American squeamishness on the subject of servants. We don't even have names we feel comfortable with for people who do this kind of work. "Nanny"? Okay for news headlines—nice and short—but too arch and archaic for daily use. "Child-care worker"? Too clinical. And then there's the cleaning lady. "Cleaning lady"? Please! "Maid"? "The help"?

Yuppies (or are we now "yuppies emeritus"?) find the whole subject a minefield of embarrassment, as the remains of 1960s values rub against 1990s bourgeois affluence. And leaving home is no escape. Hotels, in particular, seem intent on making you feel ridiculous, with their doormen dressed up like Nubian slaves and their insistence on having someone else carry your bag even if you're perfectly capable of carrying it yourself. You, meanwhile, follow along making desperate small talk and wondering nervously how many singles you have in your wallet. Who needs this?

It makes me wince when an older person calls me "sir." (Of course, it also makes me wince when a younger person calls me "sir"—but for different reasons.)

This squeamishness is a healthy thing. It's the tribute prosperity pays to democracy. In America we are committed to political equality and resigned, at least, to financial inequality, but uncertain and unhappy about the vast middle ground of social relations. What we want, or should want, is for financial inequality to pollute social equality as little as possible. Money should buy things, but not people. This is where the "servant problem" arises. There is no solution, but here are a few suggestions.

First, ask, Is this service valued for itself or only for the privilege of lording it over someone else? Servants are what economists call a "positional good." That means they are something that, by their nature, not everyone can have. No matter how rich a society gets, it will never be so rich that everyone can have a maid. Someone has to *be* the maid. Maids are generally valued for the work they actually do, and not for their lowly status. But the fellow standing in the restaurant bathroom to hand you a towel is a different matter.

It is too easy to say, on egalitarian grounds, that people should do their own dirty work instead of hiring someone else. Not only is this a hopeless goal in an era when few households have a spouse who stays at home full-time; it also overlooks the basic morality of free-market exchange: People work because they need the money, and denying them that opportunity in the name of equality is doing them no favor.

But this leads to a second suggestion: Make domestic service more like capitalism and less like feudalism. The relationship between customer and supplier is inherently more equal than that between employer and servant. There is no squeamishness involved in taking your clothes to the dry cleaner. If domestic service were generally provided by business firms (ideally, co-ops of the workers themselves) with all the trappings of a business relationship (monthly bills instead of cash on the kitchen table, etc.), the arrangement would be more dignified for both parties. It would also provide household workers some of the benefits— such as reliable Social Security—enjoyed by those of us who work in the grown-up economy.

Third, no adult should be expected to call any other adult "sir" or "ma'am"—outside the military, I suppose—except as a sign of respect for large differences in age. The recent trend in restaurants of young waiters who want to be on an immediate first-name basis with their customers ("Hi! I'm Courtney . . .") has been the subject of much justified mockery. But there is a comfortable balance that can be struck. Waiters shouldn't have to pretend to be your friend, but they shouldn't have to pretend to be your butler, either. What we need is an all-purpose egalitarian honorific. Not "comrade," I guess. Any suggestions?

Fourth, let's get rid of uniforms, or at least redesign them. Maybe hotels need doormen (though I'm not sure why), but why can't they wear a simple coat and tie instead of those ridiculous getups? Obviously, if someone's job is cleaning bathrooms, that can't be done in a coat and tie. But why must cleaners, in hotels and even some homes, look like they stepped out of *Upstairs, Downstairs*? You wouldn't dress that way to clean your own bathroom. It's reasonable enough to expect neatness. But neatness does not require uniformity; and even uniformity, if necessary (which I doubt), does not require a lot of status codes.

Fifth, abolish tipping. My pay for writing this essay does not depend on whether *Time* is in a generous mood on the day I turn it in. Why should waiting on tables be different? In most fields of endeavor, the economy has found plenty of ways to create incentives for good performance without making remuneration so immediately contingent on someone's whim. The real function of tipping is to make a business relationship seem more like a feudal one. Our goal in America should be exactly the opposite, and yet we are far behind Europe in replacing tips with standard service charges.

Sixth, don't stand in the way of technology. Automatic washing machines eliminated millions of domestic-service jobs. Only a Luddite would object. The more drudge work machines eliminate, the better. Someday, hotels may discover, as supermarkets did long ago, that there are machines that can open doors automatically.

Finally, if you're still feeling squeamish, try paying a bit more. That might help too.

Who Killed Vincent Foster?

(*The New Republic,* AUGUST 16, 1993)*

I have no real evidence that deputy White House counsel Vincent Foster was driven to suicide by a series of viciously unfair and hypocritical editorials in *The Wall Street Journal.* In fact, I don't even really believe it. But it would be easy enough to make the case, if one were willing to use against the *Journal* the same techniques of innuendo and demagogy that the *Journal* editorials used against Foster and his colleagues in recent weeks.

As it is, these editorials stand as a case study in editorial dishonesty. If they had appeared in, say, the Moonie-owned *Washington Times,* they could be shrugged off. But *The Wall Street Journal* is one of America's most respectable and, in its news pages, best newspapers. When its editorial writers sink so low—as they have sunk repeatedly in their hysterical response to the election of a Democratic president—it's worthy of note.

The *Journal*'s basic theme was that Foster and three other alumni of Arkansas's Rose Law Firm, including Hillary Clinton, formed some sort of sinister cabal within the Clinton administration. A subtheme was that this cabal was—is—engaged in a secret plot to subvert democracy by misusing the powers of the White House.

Keep in mind a couple of things. First, it is hardly surprising or suggestive of anything nasty that the governor of Arkansas, elected president, would bring four people from the state's leading law firm into his administration. In 1981, Ronald Reagan, with a far larger California legal establishment to choose from, gave four top administration jobs to partners in the Los Angeles firm of Gibson Dunn and Crutcher (where—full disclosure—I once worked). *The Wall Street Journal* didn't find anything suspicious about this.

Second, throughout the 1980s the *Journal*'s editorial page was the nation's loudest troubadour of untrammeled executive power. Most memo-

---

**This column is the ultimate flowering of my neurotic obsession with* The Wall Street Journal *editorial page. It was written before the reports of Foster's "suicide note," in which he did indeed blame "*WSJ *editors" for his troubles.*

rably, it defended with righteous thunderbolts the Reagan administration's alleged constitutional privilege to conduct a secret war in Nicaragua and lie about it, all in violation of explicit laws passed by Congress and signed by the president.

Yet there was the *Journal*—in a June 17 editorial titled "Who Is Vincent Foster?"—declaring that what is "most disturbing" about the Clinton administration is "its carelessness about following the law." Two examples were offered. The first involved a federal judge's accusation that the administration had "dillydallied" about preserving White House computer tapes. This from the newspaper that applauded Ollie North for his famous "shredding party" of Iran-contra documents. In the present case, there was no question of a cover-up: The tapes were from previous administrations. And the editorialists even conceded that they found the judge's order "more than a little presumptuous." But that didn't stop them from suggesting skullduggery.

Their second alleged concern was whether private meetings of Hillary Clinton's health care task force violated something called the Federal Advisory Committee Act (FACA). The editors expressed in passing their characteristically overheated view that this law is an unconstitutional intrusion on executive power. But, far from inviting Mrs. Clinton therefore to flout it, they declared that "a basic test of an administration's character and mores" is "how scrupulously it follows the law" and went on to sneer that "constitutional law may not have been the big part of the Rose firm's practice."

None of this had anything directly to do with Vincent Foster. The editorial's title—"Who Is Vincent Foster?"—referred to the White House's hesitation to supply a photograph to illustrate the predictable vilification. This, the paper implied, was all part of the administration's secret plot to . . . what? Well, not clear. But something bad. An ungracious note the next day conceded that a White House fax reporting a photo on the way had arrived before deadline time but "didn't promptly come to the attention of the responsible editors."

"Vincent Foster's Victory" (June 24) dealt with the troubling development that a federal appeals court had upheld Mrs. Clinton's right under FACA to hold her task force meetings in private. Far from apologizing for the earlier accusation that Mrs. Clinton—in cahoots with her Rose firm "cronies"—had done something improper, the editorial ironically congratulated Foster as a "movement conservative" for successfully defending executive power.

With barely a pause for breath, though, it then went on to accuse "the Clintonites, as is their wont," of allowing "hubris to smother mere principle" because "they went secret over changing the entire American health care system." Since, unlike the contra war in Nicaragua, health care reform will not be imposed without congressional approval, it's a little hard to comprehend the *Journal's* assertion that "even defenders of executive authority . . . blanch at such imperial overstretch."

"Who Is William Kennedy III?" (July 7) dealt with the official White House report on the travel office scandal. Compared, once again, with the Reagan-Bush years, this was a remarkably frank self-investigation of a fairly trivial episode. But that's not how the *Journal* saw it. The editorial began by ludicrously suggesting a cover-up. The report "would have you believe that William Kennedy III is just one of four White House aides" involved in the episode. "In fact," the editors revealed breathlessly, he "is former managing partner of Little Rock's Rose Law Firm." Dum de dum dum!

And so what? Well, Kennedy's role in travelgate "seems part of a law enforcement pattern centering on the Rose clique" (aka "the Rose firm's four-partner implant in the administration"). For example, said the editors, Vincent Foster "cut some legal corners"—unspecified—in the FACA case (though of course he turned out to be right). Furthermore, the Rose firm represented an Arkansas financial firm that once many years ago was involved in a deal with BCCI. No suggestion that the Stephens firm—let alone Rose, let alone Kennedy or Foster, let alone Bill or Hillary Clinton—had done anything wrong. Nevertheless, "the early indications of the Rose view of the law are certainly disconcerting, displaying a lot of cornercutting and casual abuse of power."

The only shred of justification for this sweeping claim is that William Kennedy was the one who called in the FBI to investigate travel office improprieties without going through Attorney General Janet Reno. That was certainly a mistake. But, in this and future editorials, the *Journal* subtly shifts to the implication that there was something nefarious about investigating the travel office at all. Outside auditors found the records a mess and $18,000 missing. I can't help feeling that if this were found at, say, the House Post Office, *The Wall Street Journal* would not repeatedly declare the investigation more heinous than the crime.

By July 14 ("FBI Director Rose?"), the *Journal* was casually referring to "the next time William Kennedy III asks the FBI to investigate some political enemy," though there was never any suggestion that the travel office was a political enemy or that the investigation was politically motivated. The theme of this editorial was that Reno had become merely "the ostensible attorney general" while real power lay with President Clinton's "legal cronies from Little Rock who are already placed at the heart of his administration." This, the *Journal* asserted, threatens "the prospects for apolitical justice."

During Waco, the editors noted with alarm, "Mr. Clinton spoke not with Ms. Reno but with his golfing pal, Webster Hubbell," the associate attorney general, another Rose alum. Thence to the usual list of Rose partners in the administration, a new list of friends of Hillary Clinton in the administration and the assertion that while "even a President (and First Lady) who used to denounce Ed Meese as a political crony of Ronald Reagan" is allowed to hire the people he wants, "cronyism is a lot more serious when it begins to involve criminal prosecution, and especially the FBI."

Of course no one ever tried to create a scandal over the mere fact that Ed Meese was a California buddy of Ronald Reagan's (Why bother, when there was so much richer material?) Yet that is precisely what the *Journal* was trying to do about Hubbell, Foster, et al. And to see the defenders of Ed Meese asserting the alleged principle of an "apolitical" Justice Department is a special laugh. Likewise watching the former zealots of executive privilege trying to raise a fuss about whether the president consults the attorney general or the associate attorney general in a crisis.

"What's the Rush?" (July 19) complained that "the gang that pulled the great travel office caper is now hell-bent on firing the head of the FBI" and asked why the "hurry." Given that the exposure of abuses by William Sessions had come from the Bush administration, and that the Clinton people had been sitting on the case for six months, it might seem a little hard to argue ulterior motives and unseemly haste on the part of the Clintonites. But *The Wall Street Journal* was up to the job. "We do not want law enforcement put at the disposal of this or that political faction," the editors unctuously opined.

The editorial offered no evidence—or even a theory—of why the "Rose Law Firm" clique should be out to get Sessions unfairly. It merely noted that "if Mr. Sessions is fired it will of course be for ostensible cause, as the travel office firings were over expense records," and that "the conventional wisdom within the Washington Beltway has certainly run against him, for whatever reason." This is apparently all it takes to create a suspicion of conspiracy in *The Wall Street Journal* editors' minds.

And thence to the last (so far) editorial in the series, "A Washington Death" (July 22). Given the *Journal's* routine use of the word "Washington" as an epithet, the title itself was tastelessly sneery. After a routine expression of sympathy for Vincent Foster's family and friends, and a defense of its past editorials on the grounds of the public's right to know, the *Journal* called for an independent "special counsel"—exactly the institution it had howled against so often during the Reagan-Bush years—to investigate Foster's death.

"We had our disagreements with Mr. Foster during his short term in Washington, but we do not think that in death he deserves to disappear into a cloud of mystery that we are somehow ordained never to understand. . . . If he was driven to take his life by purely personal despair, a serious investigation should share this conclusion so that he can be appropriately mourned."

What's most offensive about this paragraph, I think, is the notion that *The Wall Street Journal* wishes to do a favor for Vince Foster. Foster left no suicide note. If he wanted to dissipate the mystery surrounding his death, he could easily have done so. It's safe to assume he did not die counting on *The Wall Street Journal* to safeguard his memory. As for the phrase "appropriately mourned"—well, I'm afraid it defies comment.

Did the *Journal* editorials have anything to do with Foster's suicide? It's always possible that, being inexperienced in the ways of the Beltway Big Leagues, he took them more to heart than he should have. Even if so, *The Wall Street Journal* deserves no blame for his death. Public debate cannot be conducted on the assumption that public officials are overly sensitive. But the *Journal* and its editors can be blamed for trashy journalism. They tarred themselves without leaving a single real mark on Vincent Foster.

Martyr Complex

(*The New Republic,* SEPTEMBER 13, 1993)

Recently I was reading somewhere or other about an Italian curio-
dealer who attempted to sell a seventeenth-century crucifix to J. P.
Morgan. It was not at first sight a particularly interesting work of
art. But it turned out that the real point was that the crucifix took to pieces
and inside it was concealed a stiletto. What a perfect symbol of the Christian
religion.

—GEORGE ORWELL

No mainstream journal of opinion or op-ed page in America would
publish those words today, except (as here) when cited with obvious irony
and/or attributed to a secular saint like Orwell. The words are actually
from an Orwell notebook and were not published while he was alive. But
Orwell wrote often attacking not just organized religion but religious belief
itself. This, for example (from a review of T. S. Eliot):

*In theory it is still possible to be an orthodox religious believer without
being intellectually crippled in the process; but it is far from easy, and in
practice books by orthodox believers usually show the same cramped, blink-
ered outlook as books by orthodox Stalinists or others who are mentally
unfree. The reason is that the Christian churches still demand assent to
doctrines which no one seriously believes in. The most obvious case is the
immortality of the soul.*

In America, this kind of talk—once familiar, if never common—has
completely disappeared from the public discourse. Believers predominate
and nonbelievers either pretend otherwise or keep quiet about it. There is
a vast unacknowledged Church composed of those who believe in religion
rather than (or at least more than) believing in God. But the noisy village
atheist, the missionary of unbelief, is a virtually extinct social type.

In fact, the self-censorship of nonbelievers on the subject of religious
faith is far greater than that of any dissenting minority on any other subject
(including that favorite conservative example: the genetics of intelligence).

There is a virtual taboo. From the evidence of American public debate, you would guess that the premise of the existence of God is as undisputed as the premise of the existence of gravity.

For this reason, I am honestly bewildered by the frequent complaint that American culture is hostile to religion—that religious beliefs are routinely belittled and held up to scorn. That has been a familiar theme of conservatives and neocons over recent years. And it is the burden of *The Culture of Disbelief*, a new book by Yale Law professor Stephen Carter, a liberal. An excerpt from Carter's book occupied most of *The New York Times* op-ed page recently, and the book has already received favorable mention in *The Washington Post.**

What on earth are these people talking about? To be sure, the Supreme Court has made a mess of the Constitution's anathema on the "Establishment" of religion, and officials sometimes get carried away in protecting the secularism of public institutions. But are "Americans [who] take their religion seriously" consigned "to the lunatic fringe," as Carter would have it? Is there a "steady drumbeat" in American culture "that the religiously devout are less rational than more 'normal' folks"? Are those who "pray regularly" forced to keep it a "shameful secret"? Not in any America I recognize.

One problem here is of proportion. Carter's very first example of the alleged "culture of disbelief" is that a national magazine published a cover story on prayer and "a disgruntled reader" wrote in to complain that "so much space had been dedicated to such nonsense." As evidence of the state of our culture, surely a magazine cover story outweighs a single objecting letter from a reader. Likewise, Carter complains that when Hillary Clinton wore a cross to some public event, "one television commentator" asked whether this was appropriate. C'mon. These days, with TV talking heads by the dozens, any view expressed by just "one commentator" is by definition pretty marginal.

Another problem is to mistake vigorous disagreement for bias. Carter writes: "One good way to end a conversation—or start an argument—is to tell a group of well-educated professionals that you hold a political position . . . because it is required by your understanding of God's will." Well, yes: If someone asserts that his position is based, not on reason or

Shortly after this column was published, Stephen Carter and his book were ostentatiously taken up by President Clinton. So much for my influence.

logic, but on "God's will," that may be right or wrong but it does make further discussion fairly pointless. And how does Carter wish people to respond to an assertion of "God's will"? If ending the conversation is out, and so is starting an argument, this leaves nodding assent as the only permissible option. That may be some folks' view of a desirable "culture of belief," but can it be Yale professor Carter's?

Carter is right to complain about people who charge that any religiously based belief is ipso facto illegitimate in the public policy debate. But he cannot have it both ways. If religious voices want to be welcome in the debate, they must accept vigorous dissent without identifying it as antireligious prejudice.

Carter is also right to note that the culture treats oddball religions with a mockery it would never apply to the mainstream faiths. The beliefs and practices of a "cult" like the Moonies, he argues, are not inherently weirder than those of the Roman Catholic Church. Of course, if a non-believer were to make this very point—or to dismiss, Orwell-style, the Virgin Birth or the doctrine of transubstantiation—that would be taken as antireligious bias. It is the free ride enjoyed by, say, the kosher dictary rules—not the ridicule of the Reverend Moon's mass marriages—that indicates the culture's true attitude toward religious belief.

Some of those who complain of American culture's alleged contempt for religious belief are the same people who, in other contexts, complain about the politics of victimology. Blacks, women, homosexuals, and so on are accused of claiming victimhood as a way of getting special favors from society. These critics see an epidemic of victimhood spreading, through cultural developments like the self-help movement, to infect an ever-expanding share of the population. And perhaps they're right. Because what could be more absurd than religious believers—90-plus percent of the population, embracing precepts no politician or major cultural figure of any sort would dare to challenge—succumbing to the romance of victimhood?

Does anybody really think it's harder to stand up in public, in 1993 America, and say, "I believe in God," than it is to stand up and say, "I don't"?

The Free Lunch Foreign Policy

(*The New Republic*, NOVEMBER 1, 1993)

Bill Clinton is the victim of a devilish bait-and-switch on the subject of using American military force. As a Democratic candidate for president, he was told he had to prove his freedom from the taint of McGovernism and his belief in a strong foreign policy. Nasty subtext: As a man who avoided military service during Vietnam, he had to prove his courage by showing a willingness to fight. So he did it. And now the trap is sprung: He stands accused, by many of the same people, of recklessly endangering American blood and treasure in Somalia, Bosnia, Haiti. Subtext: He saved his own hide, and he doesn't care about others'.

It serves Clinton right, in a way, for not knowing his own mind. But the politics of American policy in Somalia, Bosnia, and Haiti reflect a citizenry that also does not know its own mind, and other politicians who enjoy the luxury of not being president and are happy to have it both ways on questions of war and peace.

The born-again doves say that Clinton's interventions are different from Reagan's or Bush's. They are merely humanitarian, not rooted in America's national interest. But the going definition of America's national interest used to be broader, and supporters of previous military exercises could be quite savage about lily-livered, weak-kneed appeasers who couldn't see America's vital interests at stake in Grenada or Lebanon or Nicaragua or El Salvador or Panama or Kuwait. While these former hawks did not sneer, back then, at "merely" humanitarian concerns—indeed, they played the humanitarian card for all it was worth (babies ripped from incubators, and so on)—they also lectured sternly about the crucial importance of American constancy, credibility, and so on. (The irony works both ways, of course. Vietnam-era doves now go on, Nixon-style, about "credibility" and "peace with honor.")

The former hawks used to warn against congressional encroachment on the president's authority as commander in chief. Now they warn against presidential usurpation of Congress's constitutional war powers.

They used to bemoan the way media images of war's brutality (in, say,

Vietnam) could turn a sentimental public against any use of force. Now they bemoan the way media images of human suffering (in, say, Bosnia or Somalia) can entice a sentimental public into unwise support for the use of force. They used to complain about "multilateralism" as an unnecessary restraint on the forceful assertion of American power. Now they complain about "multilateralism" drawing the United States into needless conflicts, and they transform the unlikely figure of UN Secretary General Boutros Boutros-Ghali into a bloodthirsty monster sucking America into war. They then cover their retreat by saying that this matter or that one should be left to "the United Nations"—as if UN troops come from Mars, or as if other countries should be willing to risk blood and treasure when the United States won't.

If America is of a mind to retreat from the world, leave other countries to their fate, and abandon any pretense of leadership, that is a respectable—even appealing—option. But few opponents of involvement in Bosnia, Somalia, and Haiti have the guts to put it that clearly. Instead they say they favor "preventing starvation" but not "nation building," or that some particular problem is better handled by others or that the policy is too ill-defined.

Legitimate criticisms can be made of the Clinton policy in Somalia—though many criticisms that are made smack of hindsight. But those who say they favored the American involvement there until its purpose changed are copping out. The purpose was always and remains preventing starvation. That is a more ambitious task than Presidents Bush and Clinton anticipated. The change has not been in the purpose of the intervention but in the apparent burden of achieving it. If you aren't prepared for at least a bit of "nation building," you're not really for "preventing starvation." It's fair to say, "Sorry, we now realize that burden is too great." It's not fair to say, "We accomplished our mission," or, "Don't worry—the United States is leaving but the UN will finish the job without us."

What all this suggests to me is the final triumph in foreign affairs of the free-lunch politics that have long infected domestic policy. We want all our government benefits; we just don't want to pay for them. We want to strut as the world's superpower, so long as there is no risk or cost attached.

The history of the free-lunch foreign policy actually goes back as far as the domestic version. It began with Ronald Reagan's defense buildup, paid for with borrowed dollars. America stood tall—on a pile of government debts. The so-called Reagan Doctrine—which called for the use of surrogate armies to fight guerrilla wars on our behalf—was conceived as a way for America to pursue an aggressive foreign policy while risking only foreign blood.

Then there was the Grenada Illusion. Americans had never even heard of Grenada when we awoke to learn of our magnificent victory there, purging the humiliation of Vietnam. The illusion was that real wars can be fought in hindsight and that important military victories can be virtually cost-free. A related "standing tall" myth—that America never makes deals with terrorists or hostage-takers—suffered a blow in Iran-contra, but didn't really crumble as logic might dictate.

The Gulf war might have been an exception. Although the money for that enterprise came from foreigners, President Bush did put thousands of American lives on the line for what he said was our national interest. And he got a vast majority of Americans to approve ahead of time. Whether that approval would have survived substantial American casualties was never, fortunately, put to the test.

As a result, though, the Gulf war actually enhanced the free-lunch syndrome. It encouraged both tendencies deplored by the opposing sides in the current intervention debate: on the one hand, an overeagerness to get involved in distant nations' affairs (because the Liberator of Kuwait can do anything); on the other hand, a tendency to panic and want out at the first hint of casualties (because the United States should be immune to this sort of thing).

The position of those who hold that, with the end of the cold war, America can retreat from its world responsibilities is arguable and tempting. So is the position that we are a great, bold, and compassionate country that should continue to lead the world. What is demeaning and harmful is the widespread belief that we can have it both ways.

Spin Sickness

(The New Republic, NOVEMBER 29, 1993)

On November 2 the Israeli Labor party lost mayors' races in both Jerusalem and Tel Aviv to the opposition Likud. Labor's leader, Prime Minister Yitzhak Rabin, said: "I think what has happened . . . has a negative aspect for us. I neither deny it nor hide it. It's a reality, and it's a very unpleasant one."

The next day, the Democratic party lost governorship races in Virginia and New Jersey and the mayor's race in New York City. President Clinton said: "I don't think you can draw too many conclusions from this. . . . What you can say is, the American people want change. . . . But that's not a message that strikes at either Democrats or Republicans."

Why does he do it? What does he gain from denying the obvious: that November 3 was a bad day for the Democrats? It's the great American spin, of course, practiced by politicians of every stripe. But Clinton seems to have the spin disease worse than most. And he surrounds himself with people to whom spin comes so naturally that you suspect they learned how to spin before they learned how to talk (and will, no doubt, be spinning in their graves).

Especially ludicrous spin such as Clinton's after Election Day is not merely disingenuous. It is undignified. Far from communicating strength and confidence, it communicates weakness and desperation. The image is of a cartoon character who thinks that as long as he keeps churning his legs and doesn't look down, it won't matter that he's run off the edge of a cliff. And it's connected to Clinton's larger difficulties.

Clinton's biggest image problem, I think, is that he lacks weight or gravitas (what the British call "bottom"). Even those who like him or agree with him on issues don't hold him in much awe. And something about him brings out the bully in critics and the press, far beyond any rational assessment of his success or failure. Clinton's relative youth is one unavoidable factor. And awe ultimately, I suppose, has to be earned with substantive accomplishments. But spin sickness doesn't help. Nor does the general sense he and his administration convey of frenzied eagerness to succeed. President Clinton needs to be reminded: He's already succeeded.

Bill Clinton is a lucky man. The worst thing that can happen to him for the rest of his life, careerwise, is that he won't win reelection in 1996. And how bad would that be? It would hurt for a while. But then, for the rest of his days, he would still be a former president of the United States (a fate that awaits him by the year 2000 in any event). He'd still be lionized and cosseted. His opinions would still be sought, and he could take cheap pot-shots at his successor like George Bush. He could get rich, do good, sleep late, play golf or a little of each. Jimmy Carter and Gerald Ford have both, in different ways, had a wonderful time as former presidents.

("Say, is my kingdom lost? Why, 'twas my care,/And what loss is it to be rid of care?"—*Richard II*)

Clinton is obviously a competitive fellow, passionately motivated by a desire to succeed. But in the yuppie rat race Bill Clinton has already won and, in a way, retired the crown. He was the first to make it all the way to the top. Nothing can ever take that away. The best thing Clinton could do for his presidency, as it enters yet another rough patch, is to communicate—possibly even to say outright—that it doesn't matter all that much to him whether he is reelected three years from now. Or at least that he has more important things on his mind.

At the shallowest level of political strategy, expressing indifference to reelection would appeal to the current antipolitician spirit in the land: the widespread and somewhat fatuous notion that anybody who actually wants political office is thereby morally disqualified from holding it. It would place Clinton "above politics" (and thereby, of course, improve his political chances).

Convincing the world that he doesn't live or die for reelection would also increase Clinton's bargaining leverage with Congress, Republicans, foreign leaders, and other negotiating partners. Clinton has very little leverage these days because he isn't feared. Ronald Reagan, at his peak, was feared for his political strength. Clinton, at the moment, doesn't have that advantage. But a man with no fears of his own becomes invulnerable in a different way and can be feared for that reason. In the game of chicken, the winner is the one who fears death least. Right now, Clinton's exquisite political sensitivity and defensiveness make him seem vulnerable indeed. It's one reason people find it so easy to pick on him.

A president liberated from reelection fears does not become a powerless lame duck. He becomes someone able to use the bully pulpit more boldly, to make enemies and hold them up to scorn, to cut deals or refuse to cut deals in ways that would otherwise seem politically too risky. The idea isn't to promise not to run again; it's to let people know (or at least to make them believe) that you're not living in fear of defeat.

Above all, a publicly communicated unconcern for reelection—a sense from the President that his personal ambitions, at least, have been fulfilled—would help address the gravitas problem. Clinton still often comes off as a grade-grubber, an apple-polisher, someone who is about to hit us up for a Rhodes scholarship recommendation. It's not appealing. And it helps to explain, I think, why Clinton gets not just so little respect but so little human sympathy.

He deserves more. Bill Clinton, with a minority electoral mandate, is slogging through one problem after another either not faced or willfully ignored (or, indeed, made worse) by his predecessors. You can disagree with his solution in any particular case and still sympathize. Yet few do. And it's partly Clinton's own fault.

Wouldn't it be nice if he had said, after November 3, "It was a bad day for my party, and I'm very disappointed"? Or even, "I think the voters have made a mistake"? Or if he were to say, "No, I'm not at all sure my position will prevail on NAFTA. I'm not at all sure it won't hurt me politically and I don't especially care because I think I'm right"? Truth: the ultimate spin. Well, it's worth a try.

THE PEOPLE'S CHOICE

(*The New Republic*, DECEMBER 20, 1993)

Mr. Pines said, however, that while many would call the channel's politics conservative, he prefers the term "populist." He said the channel would . . . welcome Republicans and Democrats alike who believe in "less government."

That is Burton Yale Pines, quoted in *The New York Times*. Pines is one of the founders of something called National Empowerment Television, a new cable channel being bankrolled by the Free Congress Foundation—a conservative organization by anyone's standards. The channel will feature a weekly Newt Gingrich show, among other delights of the Right.

It's heartwarming, I suppose, that conservatives now feel the need to mask their true ideological identity in euphemisms. In the 1980s, liberals often resorted to euphemisms like "progressive" to avoid being tarred with the L-word, which is still considered politically disadvantageous. In the 1930s a "progressive" was someone who didn't want to admit to being a Communist. Now it's someone who doesn't want to admit to being a liberal. Is that "progress"? I'm not sure. But at least conservatives have had to start playing the same game.

Today, "populist" is the self-label of choice across the political spectrum. Earlier associations with racist demagoguery have been forgotten. Conservatives claim it, liberals claim it. Commentators see a fearsome new "populist" coalition emerging from opposition to NAFTA. Hewlett-Packard even advertises one of its computer printers with the headline POPULIST, on the grounds that it "has brought high-quality color and black and white printing to the people." But what does the term mean?

Pines is confused if he thinks that there is any obvious connection between "populism" and "less government." The founding document of American populism—the People's Party Platform of 1892—called for a graduated income tax and government ownership of the railroads and the telegraph and telephone systems. "We believe that the powers of government—in other words, of the people—should be expanded . . . to the end that oppression, injustice and poverty shall eventually cease in the land," declared the original populists. Talk like that gets you branded a liberal elitist, or worse, these days.

The most classically populist item on any major political agenda in recent years was President Clinton's hefty tax increase on the rich. Second might be Hillary Rodham Clinton's attacks on the pharmaceutical and insurance industries. Yet many of the conservative types who preen as "populist"—Gingrich and his congressional GOP cohorts, Rush Limbaugh, *The Wall Street Journal* editorial page—not only oppose these Clinton agendas but do so in classically antipopulist terms. They accuse the Clintons of stirring up "envy," "divisiveness," "class hatred," and so on.

In today's political discourse, "populist" often means nothing more than "popular." It is a form of democratic bullying—a claim to speak for a majority of the people. As an ideology, this is pretty empty. If all you mean by calling yourself a "populist" is that you believe the will of the majority should carry the day, you are not distinguishing yourself from anyone else in this democracy. We all think that. If what you mean is that your own particular views are held by the majority, you may or may not be correct. Opponents of NAFTA, for example, never had a majority behind them.

To the extent "populism" means more than "democracy" itself, it has traditionally been associated with notions of direct majority rule, as opposed to the various filters and constraints of constitutional, representative government. But the two biggest procedural items on today's so-called populist agenda are term limits and the balanced budget amendment. Both of these would place new constraints on democratic decision-making.

Of course populism has always defined itself in opposition to some sort of "elite," which supposedly is thwarting the popular will. Self-styled conservative populists would say it's only natural, given the way power has shifted in American society over the past century, that populist ire should be directed today at Washington rather than Wall Street, at big government rather than big capital.

But today's popular animus against big government is highly qualified. People are widely opposed to taxes, but they are not opposed to the benefits those taxes—partly—pay for. And the "populist" issue du jour right now is crime, with an agenda of more cops, more prisons, more executions. This may be wise or unwise, but it is a call for more government, not less.

Today's populism, like earlier versions, deserves to be treated with both respect and caution: respect, as it is to some extent a genuine expression of pain by those who are hurting economically; caution, because like earlier versions it can curdle into ugly scapegoating of cultural outsiders—immigrants, racial minorities, "liberals." But today's populism also deserves special suspicion of its own, for three reasons.

First, there is a huge phony element. Many of the noisiest purveyors of "populist" anger are themselves chardonnay-sipping elitists. From inside the Beltway, political consultants and commentators fan the flames of rage against "Washington," and get rich at it. From downtown Manhattan, *Wall Street Journal* editors join in the chorus. Populism has always involved demagoguery, of course, but the level of cynicism among promoters of the current version is especially high.

Second, the audience for today's aggrieved populist rhetoric is different. In *Voices of Protest*, his book about Father Coughlin and Huey Long, two populists of the 1930s, Professor Alan Brinkley notes that their audience was not the desperately poor, as in the 1890s, but "those on the fringes of the middle class who had gained a foothold in the world of

bourgeois respectability." Today's populism has been ratcheted up the social scale once again. Aimed squarely at the heart of the middle class (and
led by a billionaire!), it is broad enough to embrace virtually every American short of Donald Trump, and aims its shafts of resentment downward
as much as upward.

Third, it is especially futile and self-defeating for today's American
middle class to believe that its problems are the fault of someone else.
That message may be nice to hear, but it is not the message we need to
hear. Those who spread it are doing the country no favor.

Is Democracy Losing Its Romance?

(Time, JANUARY 17, 1994)

Back in the 1980s, when hawks were hawks and doves were doves,
it used to be said that democracies don't fight each other. When
doves argued for "peace" in, say, Central America, the hawks
answered that the best assurance of peace in any region was the establishment of democracy, even by violent means if necessary. Once established,
democratically elected governments will never choose to spend the people's
blood and treasure making war against their democratically elected neigh-
bors.

It's a nice thought. Unfortunately, it's been disproved in Yugoslavia,
where the fall of communism has brought a vicious three-way war. Serbia
and Croatia, both under democratically elected presidents, intermittently
fight each other while jointly dismembering democratic Bosnia. Serbia had
a parliamentary election December 19 in which all the parties supported
Serbia's aggression—although it has left the country a basket case. The
Yugoslav mess is one reason some former hawks have become born-again
doves. They have lost their interest in promoting democracy. They look
at the postcommunist world and see that the most common cause of war
is nationalist hatred—which democracy, far from suppressing, actually
gives vent to.

Is democracy starting to lose its romance? It seems like an odd question. On the map of the world, democracy is having a great run. It has
triumphed over the Soviet empire (well, details to be worked out in some
places); it has conquered South America; it has arrived in South Africa.

And yet at the same time you can sense a certain world-weary disillusion setting in.

This can be seen, for example, in the way Western observers keep moving the goalposts for that hero of democracy, Boris Yeltsin. Democracy lovers have been remarkably understanding as Yeltsin has shut down newspapers, produced a constitution out of his hip pocket that makes him virtual czar, forbidden candidates in the recent election to criticize his constitution on television, put off for years his own need to run for re-election, and so on. This was all justified as an "interim" necessity in order to establish Russia on a democratic course. But if Yeltsin continues to govern in a style one journalist predicts will be "enlightened authoritarianism," it's a safe bet the apologias will continue.

The model here, of course, is China. While Russia—struggling to reform the economy and the political system at the same time—sinks ever deeper into poverty, China, which is trying capitalism without democracy, grows richer at an astonishing rate of 13 percent a year. China's leaders still aspire, at least, to a totalitarian regime. Dissidents are still arrested, and the government recently outlawed all satellite dishes. But it would be hard to argue honestly that China's approach has served the average citizen worse than Russia's.

The case for the Chinese model is that while democracy and capitalism may go together, democracy and the conversion of an economy to capitalism do not. Economic reform is chaotic; it makes things worse before they get better; it creates new inequalities that take getting used to. Capitalism, in short, needs an authoritarian government to push it through. Then, when widespread middle-class prosperity is securely established, democracy will naturally follow.

A less attractive version of this argument leaves out the last step. It holds that concepts like "democracy" and "individual rights" are Western notions, which (unlike, apparently, the Western concept of "capitalism") are out of place in consensual Asian cultures. Singapore and Taiwan have thrived on capitalism without democracy.

The ethnically Asian president of Peru, Alberto Fujimori, sometimes likes to imply that he is importing this Asian culture to South America. Early in 1992 he shut down the courts and the congress, abolished civil liberties, and began ruling by decree. The result? The Shining Path guerrillas, who were strangling the country, have been almost beaten; the economy is thriving; and Fujimori is highly popular. "Traditional democracies will end up in the garbage heap," he told a Peruvian magazine.

Even in the heartland of "traditional" democracy, the United States of America, there are whiffs of disenchantment. The "populism" surging through American politics these days has a certain antidemocratic flavor. Or, at least, it reflects a resentment of democratic institutions and procedures. "Washington" and politicians have replaced "Wall Street" and rich businessmen as populism's favorite targets. The favorite populist remedies—congressional term limits, a balanced budget amendment—would be new constraints on democracy. And, like earlier versions, today's populism hungers for a strong leader on a white horse. Thus Ross Perot, America's would-be Fujimori.

On the other hand, the conventional response to today's populism also has an antidemocratic tinge, as high-minded commentators bemoan democracy's incompatible demands for high benefits with low taxes, the paralyzing effects of interest groups, and so on.

As the current movie *The Remains of the Day* reminds us, there was a time not long ago, the 1930s, when openly expressed doubts about the wisdom of democracy as a system of government were positively fashionable, even in established democratic societies. These days everybody pays at least lip service to the democratic ideal. Will that change? Just asking.

Second Opinion

(*The New Republic*, FEBRUARY 14, 1994)*

In a screed against the Clinton health care plan published in these pages last week, Elizabeth McCaughey suggested that one of the horrors awaiting us if Bill and Hillary get their way is something called "utilization review." This is a system whereby doctors must get clearance from some central authority before performing a test or treatment on a patient.

McCaughey, "John M. Olin Fellow" at the right-wing Manhattan Institute, has become the leading nightmare scenarist of the Clinton plan. Her unique selling proposition is a claim to have read the whole thing,

*This is just one of my many contributions to the headachy health care debate of 1993–1994. Elizabeth McCaughey went on to become lieutenant governor of New York.

which I concede gives her an advantage over most commentators, including this one. But perhaps she has spent too much time buried in those famous 1,342 pages and not enough observing the world around her.

Take "utilization review." *TNR* readers might be interested to know that *The New Republic*'s own health care plan (of which I am a member) has extensive requirements for "utilization review." Along with health maintenance organizations, generic drug rules, and so on, "utilization review" is one of the developments rapidly spreading—for good or ill— under our current health care system. It is one reason health cost inflation has abated so dramatically, allowing Clinton's critics to engage in metaphysical arguments about whether there is or is not a health care "crisis."

Clinton's health care plan is far from perfect. But the forthcoming argument over it is not just a test of his presidency. It is a test of our capacity as a democracy to have an honest and sophisticated debate over an important public issue. In particular, it is pointless to compare the Clinton plan with some idealized version of the classic American system, in which you can go to any doctor you want, who can perform any treatment he wants, order any test she wants, prescribe any drug he wants and charge whatever she wants, all paid for by insurance. That system is disappearing, whatever we do. The important comparisons are of Clinton's system with the system as it actually works now, with the system as it will work in the future with no reform and with other reform proposals as they would actually work in practice. The Clintonites insist that their reform would reduce, not increase, cumbersome "utilization review" requirements. Could be. But it is characteristic of Clinton's sales technique that he would rather insist that his model's tires never go flat than point out that rival models get flat tires, too.

Take another example. There has been much agitation in these pages on the question of how Clinton's plan will affect medical research, especially the development of new drugs. High drug prices, high prices charged by teaching hospitals for ordinary medical services and special Medicare payments all subsidize medical research, and all will be squeezed under the Clinton plan. But all will be squeezed under any reform to control medical costs. In fact, the more "market-oriented" and less "government-mandated" a reform is, the more likely it is to efficiently root out these indirect subsidies.

Under the old system, drug companies were able to make large monopoly profits—beyond the legitimate monopoly profits their patents entitle them to—because neither price competition nor government controls imposed any restraint. Doctors prescribed, patients bought, and often insurance paid, without regard to price. These monopoly profits provided the incentive and the capital for lavish drug research. More money has gone into drug research than a properly functioning "free market" would allocate. Reform—any reform—will reduce this research. But there is no way out of that dilemma. It is a price of reform.

The Wall Street Journal editorial page fires a shot at the Clinton plan almost every day. One recent salvo, titled "Price of Managed Care," was about how HMOs harm their patients by skimping on tests. The article cited without irony a "near-dozen malpractice specialists consulted for this piece," all of whom warned that inadequate testing is rife at HMOs.

Why do I say "without irony"? Because *The Wall Street Journal* has been campaigning for years against excessive definitions of medical malpractice. Indeed, malpractice reform is a therapy urgently recommended by those, including the *Journal,* who insist that we don't need major surgery on our health care system. It has been the paper's position that—thanks to "malpractice specialists"—we give too many tests, thus driving up costs. Of course malpractice lawsuits only occur when the failure to give a test turns out badly—when an MRI for a headache would have caught that one-in-a-million brain tumor. So even under minimalist health care reform, anecdotes like those the *Journal* claims to find so alarming will increase.

The decision not to perform an MRI, even when there is a one-in-a-million chance of finding a tumor, is in effect health care rationing. Any health care system defines an appropriate standard of care, if only through the tort laws, and any such standard weighs cost against chance of success. What is more, any reform of America's system—be it "market-oriented" or otherwise—will take a more stringent view of the cost-benefit trade-off than the never-never land system we have now.

Even without reform, market forces are already driving Americans by the millions (including the employees of this magazine) into managed care arrangements. "Free market" style reforms being pushed by conservative Republicans will only speed this development. So to hold out managed care as a great bugaboo of the Clinton reform plan is absurd.

Conservatives and Republicans intone that there is "no health care crisis." Meanwhile, their own "minimalist" reform plans would constitute the biggest new social welfare program since the Great Society, and the biggest government intrusion into the workings of private industry since Richard Nixon's wage and price controls.

The coming debate is not about a "free market" versus "socialism" for health care, or about unlimited freedom to choose your own doctor and treatment versus regimentation and rationing. It is about different degrees and styles of government involvement in health care, and about the best way to impose limits on our health care appetites that are inevitable in any event.

Are we capable of having such a debate?

BACK FROM THE FUTURE

(*The New Republic*, MARCH 21, 1994)

> *he topic of the Younger Generation spread through the company like a yawn.*
>
> —EVELYN WAUGH, *VILE BODIES*

It's often said that the federal budget deficit or the Social Security system or other fiscally irresponsible arrangements are "borrowing from the future" or "burdening the next generation." (I may even have said it myself, come to think of it.) This is the political dimension of the lament of Generation X, the despairing twentysomethings portrayed in the new movie *Reality Bites.* The federal deficit doesn't actually enter into the plot of *Reality Bites* (which, as summarized by Terrence Rafferty in *The New Yorker,* is about "kids born after the baby boom, who now, as they enter adulthood, feel cheated by history"). But a few earnest, politically minded X-ers have tried to make it their generational cri de coeur—an analogy to the war in Vietnam, if you can imagine the effrontery.

Harrumph. This column bows to no one in its alarm about the federal deficit. But if the entire politics of the postboomer generation is going to rest on the premise that American society is "borrowing from the future," it gives us pleasure to point out that it's not really true. It is very difficult for whole societies, unlike individuals, to "borrow from the future." The assets consumed today must be produced today. They can't be consumed today and produced tomorrow.

Now, society can use its productive capacity in two ways: to produce consumption goods and services, or to produce things (like new factories) that increase society's future productive capacity. We are definitely producing too much of the former and too little of the latter, and we will be poorer than otherwise as a result. Federal government borrowing contributes to this tendency. But future generations have no inherent claim on any particular share of today's productive capacity.

The fact is that future Americans are almost surely going to be richer than current Americans. Among the living generations, Generation X will have a higher standard of living over the course of its life than the baby boomers, just as the boomers will do better than the postwar generation. From 1970 until today—roughly the lifetime of Generation X—America's gross domestic product has grown by 82 percent in real terms. This is considered to have been a period of alarmingly slow growth, and even so the X-er entering the work force today joins an economy almost twice the size of the one boomers were joining a generation ago.

In *The Washington Post* a few months back, a twentysomething writer named Christopher Georges published a flood of statistics debunking the notion that X-ers are suffering compared with their generational predecessors. My favorite: 30 percent of teenagers today own cars, up from 7 percent in 1968.

When I learned economics a generation ago, we were taught that the national debt didn't matter because "we owe it to ourselves." These days we owe a large chunk of it to foreigners. Because that will have to be paid back, it does amount to "borrowing from the future." But even if this costs future generations a point or two of their GDP, what's left will still be greater than what we've got now.

Likewise with Social Security. Even if it amounts to a large transfer from today's workers to today's retirees, and an even larger transfer from future workers to future retirees, so what? In both cases the younger generation will still be richer than the older one, even after the transfer takes place.

The choice America faces in issues like the federal deficit is how much present consumption we should sacrifice in order to increase our future consumption. But putting the issue in generational terms raises an interesting philosophical puzzle: Why should one group—the current generation—sacrifice anything at all so that a different group—the next generation—can be better off, when the second group will be better off than the first group in any event?

The answer to this puzzle lies less in logic than in emotions: the admirable desire of parents to see their children prosper, and of patriots to see their country thrive. This is, as I say, admirable. Less admirable is future generations demanding this as their due, and accusing the older folks of "borrowing" if they refuse to fork out sufficiently. (Douglas Coupland's clever novel *Generation X,* which popularized the term, opens with an X-er vandalizing an Oldsmobile because it has a bumper sticker that says, WE'RE SPENDING OUR CHILDREN'S INHERITANCE. Why not spend it?)

X-ers are right to suspect that boomer complaints about them are based largely on resentment. No one was ever supposed to be younger than we are. Every generation feels that way, but probably none ever milked the Young Idea as successfully as the boomers did in our time. Nevertheless, some criticism is fair. Start with originality. C'mon you guys. Generational self-pity and existential despair, which the X-ers are marketing as their own, are hardly new. Read *Vile Bodies,* Evelyn Waugh's great comic send-up of the "Bright Young Things" of London in the 1920s.

Indeed, to preen just a bit, the particular note of self-pity was relatively absent from the self-indulgent generational brooding of the boomers in their youth. The famous Port Huron Statement of 1962, founding document of SDS (Students for a Democratic Society), the premier youth activist group of the 1960s, began: "We are people of this generation, bred in at least modest comfort, housed in universities, looking uncomfortably to the world we inherit." Compare and contrast something called the Third Millennium Declaration, a conscious update of the Port Huron Statement issued last year from a twentysomething activist group: "Like Wile E. Coyote waiting for a twenty-ton Acme anvil to fall on his head, our generation labors in the expanding shadow of a monstrous national debt." Whine, whine, whine.

These kids today. They're soft. They don't know how good they have it. Not only did they never have to fight a war, like their grandparents— they never even had to dodge one.

CASTING STONES

(*The New York Times*, JULY 5, 1994)

It seems the self-proclaimed Christian Right can dish it out, but they can't take it. They have called President Clinton every name in the book. The Reverend Jerry Falwell is selling videotapes that—without a shred of evidence—accuse the president of murdering political opponents back in Arkansas. The Christian Coalition has said Mr. Clinton's inauguration was "a repudiation of our forefathers' covenant with God." They have strayed far from traditional religious issues to proclaim the "Christian" position on matters like health care reform and the gasoline tax. Yet when Clinton supporters dare to hit back, these religious warriors retreat to their cloister and piteously accuse their critics of "bigotry."

(Representative Vic Fazio, chairman of the Democratic Congressional Campaign Committee, called them "fire-breathing" and "radical." Governor Ann Richards of Texas called them "hatemongers." Dr. Joycelyn Elders, the Surgeon General, called them "un-Christian." Mr. Clinton himself, while cautiously avoiding any general denunciation of the religious Right, had some choice words about Jerry Falwell.)

Religious people have every right to be involved in politics. More than that: They have every right to argue that their political positions derive from their religious beliefs. If the Christian Coalition feels that Christ would want us to avoid universal health care, it should feel free to make that case in those terms.

But they cannot have it both ways. Having entered the political arena determined to play hardball, they cannot complain if their opponents decide to play hardball back. Labeling themselves Christians does not give them the right to complain of religious prejudice whenever anyone takes issue with them. And if they wish to declare the "Christian" position on every issue under the sun, they cannot logically scream "bigotry" when opponents call them "un-Christian" for those same positions.

The religious Right is playing the same victimization game that conservatives often accuse interest groups on the Left of playing. Its leaders are stoking the resentments of their followers, and attempting to intimidate political opponents, by striking a pose of martyrdom. Yet what could be more absurd than the idea that genuine anti-Christian prejudice is a major force in America? Mainstream Republicans preposterously insist that Democrats who dare to criticize the religious Right are exploiting or pandering to such alleged prejudice. The very fact that Bob Dole rushes to accuse the Democrats of "appealing to religious bigotry" suggests that there is more cheap political advantage to be gained from kissing Christians than dissing them.

Clearly there is a political strategy to Democrats' recent attacks on the religious Right. It is not simply the boiling over of justified indignation. The strategy might be called "marginalization"—portraying the opposition as outside the mainstream of political discourse. But it is a little late for Republicans to call this dirty pool.

Former Education Secretary William Bennett, writing in *The Washington Post,* says of the Democratic attacks: "This is not political discourse. It is argument by invective. . . . People of good will should not allow [the] vital national debate to be sidetracked by mudslingers."

Well, who remembers 1988? In the presidential campaign of that year, Republicans portrayed not just an element of the Democratic party but the party itself and its candidate, Michael Dukakis of Brookline, Massachusetts, as not merely mistaken on the issues but unpatriotic. The Christian Right participated heavily (as it participates joyously in the attempted marginalization of Bill Clinton). And Bill Bennett was there, too. He said of "that Cambridge-Brookline crowd": "These are people who don't like the Pledge of Allegiance [and] have disdain for the simple and basic patriotism of most Americans."

This was marginalization with a vengeance, and it worked. So we need no etiquette lessons from Mr. Bennett.

But the challenge is flung: Would any politician dare to attack "Jews" the way some are attacking "Christians"? The answer is that there is no group calling itself the Jewish Coalition and accusing those who disagree with it on political issues of being godless. If there were, there would be nothing anti-Semitic about attacking it by name. To be sure, many politicians might understandably hesitate. But politicians similarly hesitate to attack the "Christian" Right by the label its members are happy to apply to themselves. The Clinton party line, for example, is that one should say "extreme" or "radical" Right, and leave Christianity out of it. That may be prudent, but it is not required in order to avoid being a bigot.

As a non-Christian, I am not entitled to pass judgment on whether the political and social agenda of the religious Right reflects the true spirit of Christianity. Nor can I judge whether Jerry Falwell and Pat Robertson, with their vicious and dishonest attacks on Mr. Clinton, are good Christians (though I have my suspicions). But I do know that neither Christianity nor political decency requires Mr. Clinton, when under attack from political enemies claiming to represent the Christian point of view, to turn the other cheek.

Log Cabin Fever

(*The New Republic*, MAY 9, 1994)

The face in the photo looked familiar. It was a full-page ad for *Forbes* magazine, published in *The New York Times* on April 13. "All he ever dreamed of growing up in Detroit," intoned the copy, "was managing his own machine shop. Then one day he came to The Valley." Silicon Valley, that is. "And he had a vision." He went on, the ad explained, to found Sun Microsystems, one of the most spectacularly successful computer companies. The kicker: "Scott McNealy picked up his first copy of *Forbes* as a foreman in an auto shop in 1977."

Without stating them directly, this hilarious ad contains two implied messages. One is that the way to get rich is to subscribe to *Forbes*. That, of course, is undeniably true. The other message, however, is more questionable. It is that the founder of Sun Microsystems is a classic American up-from-the-bottom success story. There he was, working in an auto shop, when a copy of *Forbes* magazine lifted his eyes toward the heavens . . . and another glorious chapter of American capitalism was written.

Now, I know Scott McNealy, and he is indeed a classic American success story. But it's not exactly the story *Forbes* is peddling. I don't doubt that he was working in an auto shop in 1977, but I doubt it was for very long, because from 1972 to 1976 he was a student at Harvard College (where there is no major in auto mechanics), and afterward he attended Stanford Business School. Before Harvard, he was a student (as was I) at an expensive prep school in suburban Detroit called Cranbrook. While it's possible that he aspired to nothing more in those days than to manage his own machine shop, this would have been a sore disappointment to his father, who was vice chairman of American Motors Corporation.

This history is not meant to demean McNealy's remarkable achievement at Sun Microsystems. It is *Forbes,* in fact, that implicitly demeans McNealy's achievement with its ham-handed mythmaking. It is not good enough, *Forbes* is suggesting, to have gone on from Cranbrook School to found a multibillion-dollar computer giant. One must have gone on from an auto shop.

Why does the magazine wish to insult its own affluent readers in this way? It is telling them that their economic milieu is shameful and must be covered up. It is saying that anything their children may achieve in life is diminished by their own success. What point is there, one might ask, in subscribing to *Forbes* if the hollow consequence of the riches that will inevitably follow is to force your kids to fake their résumés?

It is one thing for a rock musician or a philosophy professor or a liberal columnist to be slightly embarrassed by a bourgeois background. But for *Forbes* magazine, the "Capitalist's Tool," to be promoting the idea that a triumphant capitalist needs to be ashamed of his upper-mercantile upbringing is a little strange. Is this not the kind of antisuccess attitude that poisoned our great country during the deplorable 1960s? How on earth did such an attitude penetrate into the very heart of the capitalist propaganda machine?

One lesson of *Forbes*'s own annual list of the 400 richest Americans, after all, is that the best single strategy for acquiring enormous wealth (apart, that is, from subscribing to *Forbes* magazine) is to arrange to be born into modest wealth. Numbers 1 and 2 on the most recent list, investor-genius Warren Buffett and Microsoft founder Bill Gates, both used this technique. That's not all they had going for them, obviously, but it helped.

Of those near the top of *Forbes*'s list, media magnate Sumner Redstone, publisher Rupert Murdoch, ship owner Ted Arison, and the Newhouse brothers all built up inherited businesses. Of the top dozen, only the family of the late Sam Walton and investor Kirk Kerkorian seem to have made it from scratch in one generation. Yet *Forbes* is so attached to the up-from-nothing myth that it is reduced to mentioning that various billionaires' *grandfathers* started out as poor immigrants.

Well, yes, even the Forbes family started out as invertebrates back at some point, before climbing its way up the evolutionary and financial scales (no doubt through a lot of darned hard work and gumption and a dream that wouldn't die, etc.). But how much credit does Steve Forbes, the current publisher and the third generation of Forbes in that chair, deserve that his ancestors used to be fish?

The log cabin myth—that our great figures worked their way up from scratch—is a treasured bit of Americana. It's a tribute to our egalitarian spirit. But it has its comic side. It can lead to reverse snobbery—the only kind of snobbery with any real power in America. There are people, of course, who pretend to come from snootier backgrounds than they do. But there are more, I suspect, who play the game Forbes played with Scott McNealy: shading their backgrounds down a level or three, in an attempt to appropriate some of that log cabin cachet.

More seriously, the log cabin myth helps to disguise the advantage that still comes, even in America, from having an affluent background— and the disadvantage that comes from not having one. It takes more than a subscription to *Forbes* to make up the difference.

WHY O.J. WON'T DIE

(*Time*, JUNE 27, 1994)*

They will never execute O. J. Simpson. They will never strap O. J. down in the gas chamber, seal the door, and drop the poison pellets (California's chosen method). Even putting it in these terms proves the point. It is unimaginable. We will not allow it—"we" being the same American citizenry that supports capital punishment by a wide margin in every poll, the same citizenry to which politicians promise ever more executions for an ever greater variety of crimes.

Simpson, of course, is innocent until proven guilty. He may be telling the truth when he says, through his lawyer, that he was at home two miles away when his ex-wife and her male friend were murdered. Furthermore, as a rich man, he is entitled to the true blessing of American justice— which isn't a fair trial but an unfair trial. Top criminal lawyers don't get

---

This piece, written at the very beginning of the O.J. media orgy, was partly right and partly wrong. I was right that the state of California quickly gave up on any idea of executing O. J. Simpson. But I missed a dynamic of our celebrity culture: The massive publicity finally turned O.J. from a famous football star into a famous wife murderer. In the popular mind, he became a new person—someone who probably could have been executed if he had existed at the beginning of the affair.

$500 an hour or more to supply justice no better than that sold by a run-of-the-mill public defender. Even if he's guilty, Simpson may get off, or get off lightly.

But O.J.'s real guarantee against capital punishment is his celebrity, not his wealth. Imagine that the scenario we've all had running through our heads actually happened: that O. J. Simpson drove his Ford Bronco over to his ex-wife's town house, donned a pair of gloves, confronted her and a man he at least thought was her boyfriend, inflicted "multiple sharp force injuries and stab wounds" (the coroner's report) on both and slit her throat to boot. Two deaths. Premeditated. Gruesome. No obvious complicating or mitigating circumstances.

Is that the kind of thing advocates of the death penalty have in mind when they say that some crimes are deserving of the ultimate sanction? Undoubtedly yes. Would society be able to impose it on O. J. Simpson? Undoubtedly no.

Why not? Because O. J. Simpson's celebrity means that for most Americans he is a flesh-and-blood human being. We comfortably call him "O.J.," even though we've never met him, because in our mind he's a friend. Even if convicted of murder, he'll never be an abstract symbol of evil like the typical death-penalty customer with three names—Robert Alton Harris, Rickey Ray Rector, John Wayne Gacy, et al. For once, in the competition of humanization between the murderer and his victims, the murderer would have an unbeatable edge.

O. J. Simpson is not just a famous former football star. Through his sports commentaries, his Hertz Rent-a-Car commercials, and his movie roles, he has created a persona: manly and likable, the classic good-guy jock. Whatever actually happened last week, we now know that this persona was not entirely accurate. Good guys don't beat their wives until the police have to be called, as apparently happened more than just once in the past.

But however much of our image of O. J. Simpson may have to be revised, his celebrity will continue to protect him. This is only partly because the impression of O.J.'s likability—stamped into our brain by hundreds or even thousands of media moments over the years—will never be completely destroyed, even by the most compelling of contrary facts. More important is that likable or unlikable, O. J. Simpson is and always will be a real person in other people's minds. And all but the most hardened

death-penalty enthusiasts will quaver at the thought of this real person—
O. J. Simpson!—gasping for breath as the cyanide begins to do its fatal
work.

So if it comes to the crunch, people will be understanding and compassionate. They will look for excuses: a troubled childhood, uncontrol-
lable rage, the pressures of his high-powered winner's life. They will stress
his remorse. They will point to his orphaned children. They will say the
whole thing's a complex tragedy. They will argue for mercy. They will, in
short, become liberals—at least for this one case.

As a liberal softy, I oppose the death penalty, but I'm not a sentimen-
talist about it. There are many other circumstances in which the state
sanctions the death of its citizens for policy purposes. The decision to go
to war is the most obvious example, but even the less dramatic decision
to build a major tunnel or bridge contains the statistical probability of
deaths in the process. We live with it. Furthermore, a quick and relatively
painless end strikes me as preferable to echoing decades in the typical,
miserable state prison with no hope of parole—the death-penalty opponents' favorite alternative. (Of course, most of those who actually face the
choice disagree with me about this.)

But, as retired Supreme Court Justice Lewis Powell belatedly concluded after a career of upholding death sentences, the death penalty cannot be administered fairly. Nothing illustrates that better than the thought
experiment of trying to imagine O. J. Simpson in the gas chamber. It's
just not going to happen, no matter what he may have done. And rightly
so. After all, this is a guy we've shared beers with—at least in our mind.

So, does that mean we should perhaps spare some human empathy
even for the low-powered losers who are the usual murderers in our society? Is their tragedy, perhaps, also complex? Does their remorse count
for anything? Should we hesitate to demand death for death in their cases?

Heck, no. What are you—soft on crime?

TRUE LIES

(*The New Yorker*, SEPTEMBER 26, 1994)

James Carville and Mary Matalin spin but don't lie. Or so they say in *All's Fair,* their sparring-sweethearts memoir of the 1992 presidential campaign. Carville, who ran Bill Clinton's campaign, and Matalin, who helped run George Bush's, relish their reputations as spinners. "Spin Doctors in Love" was the headline on the *Newsweek* cover story that was an excerpt from their book, and the most vivid pages in the book capture the visceral excitement of a "spin session" after one of the presidential debates. Of her mentor, the late Lee Atwater, Matalin says, with swooning admiration, "He couldn't wait to spin for his guy." The 1992 campaign was the apotheosis of spin; Carville and Matalin are its troubadours.

But lying is something else. "Cardinal rule #1: *No matter what, don't lie to the press."* So writes Matalin, and the italics are hers. Carville agrees: "The best way to develop a good relationship with a reporter is to call him or her back, fight hard, and don't lie." Thus *All's Fair* raises the vexing philosophical question: If "spinning" is good and "lying" is bad, what's the difference?

Carville and Matalin clearly have no idea, because, despite "cardinal rule #1," they blithely describe themselves lying to the press, to the public, and even to each other. Matalin writes, just three pages before issuing her anathema on lying, about her technique of floating an idea in the press without attribution, just to gauge the reaction. "If it gets shot down by pundits and colleagues, you deny your campaign said it." In the next chapter, she tells how the Bush campaign dealt with a private poll showing that Dan Quayle was a drag on the ticket. The press "had no idea actual data existed—and, in fact, we continued to insist vehemently that 'Quayle was a neutral in our polls.'"

Carville recalls his first big success as a campaign consultant: He got Robert Casey elected governor of Pennsylvania in 1986, over Republican William Scranton III. Scranton had admitted smoking marijuana in the 1960s, but Casey had promised not to make an issue of it. Carville describes with glee how he made an issue of it while seeming not to. That's just spin, I suppose. However, he also quotes himself telling a colleague, "We can't run a drug spot, but we have got to put out that we are getting ready to run a drug spot, O.K.?" Okay, what would you call that?

Matalin is amusing about the press's ludicrous multiday obsession with the question of whether she had or had not apologized to Bush for a fax attack on Clinton that was widely perceived as having gone too far. (The document began, "Sniveling Hypocritical Democrats. . . .") She recalls her heroic efforts to beat back allegations that she had apologized. Yet she also quotes herself apologizing ("Mr. President, I'm so sorry . . ."). Is she even aware that she has admitted the very thing she describes herself hectically denying? If so, she gives no sign of it. Carville, meanwhile, describes himself in the act of plotting how the Clinton campaign should respond to the fax-attack flap, and then, a few pages later, Matalin quotes Carville telling her he had nothing to do with the Clinton response. "I specifically stayed out of it," she says he said. Oh, what tangled webs we weave.

When Carville and Matalin tell us that they don't lie to the press, these statements are themselves just spin—or lies, to use the layperson's term. But you cannot win the spin game by demonstrating that Carville and Matalin are bullshitters. They will grinningly agree that they *are* bullshitters and then expect points for honesty for having said so. All the most damning arguments against *All's Fair* and the James 'n' Mary phenomenon in general—that they are "spinning their own lives," that they symbolize "the incestuousness of Washington elites, the vacuousness of campaigns and the cynicism of the handlers who run them," that they argue in public as a "shtick" because they "know it sells," that they're self-styled populists with a cellar full of fancy wine who "were created and are sustained by the establishment they claim to despise," that, in short, they're big phonies—are made in *Newsweek*'s own introduction to its excerpt from their book. But seeing through Carville and Matalin completely doesn't stop *Newsweek* from hyping them on its cover. In today's all-spin-all-the-time culture, if you actually complain about such things you look like a humorless sorehead.

Although Carville and Matalin are designated as "spin doctors," they are really more like "spin patients"—victims of spin disease, and, of course, carriers as well. James and Mary's problem is clinical: They are addicted to spin. Their book is best seen as a cry for help. In a way, it is unfair to accuse them of lying, because spin has corroded their brains to the point where they are no longer capable of distinguishing truth from that other category, whatever you choose to call it.

For example, Matalin tells of a typical campaign crisis: President Bush, campaigning in Georgia, has been booked into an Episcopal church one Sunday. She writes: "Congressman Newt Gingrich went crazy. 'We've got to go to a Baptist church!' he screamed at me. 'Twenty-four point four percent of the vote is Baptist!' " So Matalin "switched the church." But word about the switch gets out, leading to a flurry of frantic phone calls and other repercussions. All this is very funny, and well told. But then Matalin concludes the anecdote on this self-righteous note: "It's already in the papers that we're switching, so the whole point of going to the church is undermined because it looks like a political event and not what it was, George Bush doing what he does every Sunday, practicing his faith."

Now, wait a minute. If the church visit was *not* a "political event" but simply a matter of Bush "practicing his faith," then "the whole point of going to the church" was *not* undermined, since he did in fact go to church and practice his faith. To be sure, Bush was forced to go to a Baptist church, not one of his own Episcopal persuasion. But that is because it *was* a "political event," not because it "looked like" one. It was only *as a political event* that the occasion was undermined by looking like a political event. Politics was, in fact, "the whole point," as Matalin demonstrates in the very act of denying it.

Indeed, in describing a later episode, Matalin unconsciously reveals the ultimate expression of the spinmaster's creed: If a politician's statement or action is actually sincere, and not a product of the spinmaster's art, it should be treated as if it never happened. In the last, desperate days of the campaign, Bush appeared on *Larry King Live* and attacked Clinton for failing to "level with the American people . . . on whether he went to Moscow." Clinton had in fact never denied that while studying at Oxford he once visited Moscow as a tourist. What he denied, quite rightly, was that there was anything sinister about this. Matalin recalls that "the reference to Moscow created a mini press frenzy" and added to Bush's woes.

Matalin apparently agrees that bringing up the Moscow trip was a mistake. The press, she says, "played it as a red-baiting campaign strategy." Her defense: "It was absolutely not a campaign strategy. . . . No one told the president to include Moscow in his litany of Clinton evasions, and when he did . . . we knew the press would never believe this wasn't an intentional strategy, that this one came from George Bush's heart." It came from the candidate's heart, you see, and therefore it shouldn't be held against him. It wasn't "intentional"; it wasn't campaign spin; it wasn't thought up by someone else and handed to him on a platter: He *really meant it!* Therefore, under the topsy-turvy logic of spin, it doesn't count. Tragically, such genuine moments will occasionally break through the web of campaign artifice. But when they do, decent people will avert their eyes.

"There is a rule of thumb in political consulting," Carville reveals with deadpan earnestness two thirds of the way through the book. "What a candidate thinks really matters." This is good to know, but the larger burden of *All's Fair* is that Carville and Matalin don't really think it matters much. In an interesting passage Carville discusses his search for what he calls a "rationale" for Clinton's presidential campaign. This came in the late spring of 1992, when Clinton had already hired a staff, spent millions, and won many delegates. But he still needed a rationale. "It took almost three months, but finally our thinking began to crystallize," Carville recalls. "Clearly where we were was 'Putting People First.' " Carville waxes humble about this brilliant conceptual breakthrough. "Putting *something* first was an old political saw: 'Put New Jersey First,' 'Put Virginia First.' It just sort of expanded to the most universal of all universes, 'Put People First.' " As opposed to what? Putting animals first? Putting household appliances first? Oh, well. Clinton now had his "rationale."

Both Matalin and Carville (the book consists of alternating passages in her voice and his) use the Washington idiom, in which references to the campaign organization as "we" slip into references to the candidate himself as "we." When Matalin writes that "we" gave a speech, she is merely being accurate: Under modern methods of production, the actual mouthing of the words is the smallest part of political oratory. But when Carville describes the stance that emerged from an emergency spin-control meeting over the revelation of Clinton's famous draft letter of 1969—"We weren't hiding, we weren't flinching. We had convictions *and we'd had them for twenty-two years*"—it starts to get eerie. Whose life is it, anyway?

Outsiders are often surprised, and sometimes offended, to discover that people in Washington don't take politics very seriously. A friend of mine likes to tell of observing Norman Podhoretz, the New York neo-conservative intellectual, at a Washington reception some years back. Podhoretz was scandalized at the sight of his ideological allies making jovial conversation with Mary McGrory, the grande dame of Washington liberal columnists. Washingtonians live and breathe politics, as we all know, and consider the prospects for health care reform to be an adequate conversational icebreaker, the way citizens of other cities might raise the fate of the local sports team. But, partly because it is indeed the local business and the local sport, politics in Washington is drained of a lot of ideological passion.

It is easy to mock the prissy Podhoretz attitude (and I reserve the right to do so). But the worldly Washingtonian approach can also be off-putting. Of course politics shouldn't swallow up all of life, and of course in a democracy it is good for political opponents to respect or even admire each other. But surely, if politics is more than just a game or a job, it should affect how you choose to live your life, including whom you choose to befriend. Furthermore, as Meg Greenfield has pointed out, the premise that politics is "only politics"—a thing apart from real life and genuine personal relationships—liberates politics itself to be that much more cynical, nasty, and dishonest.

"Washington" is a metaphorical term, not a geographical one, and it covers most of those who sneer at "Washington" (or at "the political class," as George Will, the teacher's pet of the political class, likes to put it). A few weeks ago, for example, I got a letter from a publicist representing Ralph Reed, the head of the Christian Coalition, asking if I would supply a publicity blurb for Reed's new book, described as "the manifesto of the religious conservative movement." My only connection with Reed is that we have appeared together several times on the CNN program *Crossfire* where we have essentially called each other the Antichrist. Yet in "Washington" it was not unreasonable to suppose that our calling each other the Antichrist is a bond we share, and that I might be happy to engage in an act of mutual hype between consenting adults.

How to integrate your political values with your personal life is a difficult question, and not just in Washington. The romance of James and Mary poses this difficulty in its baldest form—"something that had never happened in the annals of presidential politics: a boyfriend and girlfriend working against each other," as Matalin theatrically puts it. She claims that the prospect made her throw up, though the both of them seem to find it mighty cute in retrospect. *All's Fair* wallows in the cuteness and contains not a drop of insight into the question of how you can love someone whose values you purport to despise.

Needless to say, love is an eternal mystery. Who can explain it? Who can tell you why? But James and Mary are also friends with each other's friends. As Carville's spouse, Matalin socializes with the Clintonites. As Matalin's husband, Carville attended the recent wedding of Rush Limbaugh, Clinton's mortal enemy. How do they do it? In *All's Fair,* the only reflection on this matter comes in passing from Matalin, in a discussion of her dealings with the press. She explains: "As a Midwesterner, I always react to people in general by liking them. . . . I always consider individuals first." Putting People First, you might say. She goes on, high-schoolishly:

> *Some of them, I know, aren't going to like me on general principles. They just have preconceived notions about conservatives. . . . For instance, I think in real life I would like liberal columnist Michael Kinsley, if I ever got to know him. But he's one of those guys who I just know is going to hate me no matter what comes up. If you know somebody's going to hate you then your first reaction is, at a minimum, to be wary. And probably not to like them before they don't like you, so you don't feel rejected. So I basically always stayed away from predictable libs.*

As a midwesterner myself, I sympathize with Matalin's distress over the way some people prejudge folks they don't know. But it is characteristic of Matalin to think that "in real life" (wherever that may be) she might even like the deplorable Kinsley. She likes everybody, by always making the crucial, if puzzling, distinction between the individual and everything he or she stands for. The one time I met Matalin, she was appearing on *Crossfire* to attack President Clinton for going Hollywood. Matalin did a fine job of inveighing against elitist showbiz liberals who disdain the values of ordinary, decent Americans, and so on. Yet she ostentatiously exempted her opponent on the program, the TV producer and Clinton friend Harry Thomason. During a commercial break she turned to him and said, "So, Harry—let's have dinner."

Matalin and Carville, despite their reputations for fierceness, seem incapable of referring to any individual, however critically, without tossing in a little valentine—especially when it comes to members of the press. *Newsweek*'s Joe Klein is "a New Paradigm kind of guy . . . very hip." NBC's Tim Russert is a "straight-up guy." Et cetera. CNN, says Carville, in the course of accusing it of bias, is "one of my favorite networks." (How many are there?) Matalin quotes a private conversation with the *Wall Street Jour-*

nal reporter John Harwood to illustrate her belief that the press was prejudiced against Bush, and then excuses Harwood himself from the general indictment of the press which she has derived from Harwood's own alleged admission. All these little valentines might be a matter of basic midwestern decency (or southern grace, in Carville's case). Or they might be something else. They might be spin.

The simple solution to the mystery of how Carville and Matalin combine their politics with their private life may be that they don't have much of either. Carville's description of how he became a left-populist Democrat by growing up in the racist South rings true enough, and his discussion of the trade-off between money and political values that he has to make in deciding which candidates to work for seems forthright and reflective. But Matalin's description of her own political journey is moronic. In high school, she was one of those "ill-informed, ridiculously naïve, liberal Flower Power hippies." In college (this is in the mid-seventies), "flower children . . . were running the joint," and when she visited her father she would "regale him with the virtues of socialism and communism, a hip thing to think at the time." Then she was assigned a term paper on the topic "Is There a Trend Toward Conservatism in the United States?" In the course of her researches, she discovered that "liberal ideas" and "big-government programs" (such as those advocated by Flower Power hippies, presumably) don't work. So she became a conservative. Really, though, Matalin is still a flower child, just floating on the zeitgeist, her conservatism as lightly worn and trivial as the "socialism and communism" of her liberal past.

Neither Carville nor Matalin even attempts to deal with the obvious conflict between their shared populist posturing and their actual roles as members of the scorned Washington elite. There are the predictable shots at "Washington insiders," and the equally predictable jacket copy touting the authors as "the ultimate insiders." Carville and Matalin self-consciously paint a picture of their lifestyle as a matter of Jeeps and down-home trash talk. Yet—and whether this is spin or the breakdown of spin I'm by now too dizzy to figure out—they also display an obsession with good tables at fashionable restaurants.

What else would you like to know about James and Mary? That James often burst into tears? That Mary's office is a heroic mess? It is already legend that during the 1990 Senate campaign for Harris Wofford, in

Pennsylvania, Carville didn't change his underwear for ten days. In *All's Fair* we learn that he "washed them but didn't change them"—a reassuring bit of corrective spin. Yes, their lives are an open book, and this is it. Their biggest self-invasion of privacy, though, concerns a matter—Matalin's recent miscarriages—that came too late for the book. But it was in time for the *Newsweek* cover story.

"James 'n' Mary: The Book" is obviously written for easy translation into "James 'n' Mary: The Movie." The he-said-she-said literary conceit strives for a Tracy-and-Hepburn effect, but the ghost-writer, Peter Knobler, falls short of Garson Kanin and Ruth Gordon. (James: "I don't know. I guess it seems like political women are not as good-looking as in other professions." Mary: "Well, I can understand that, knowing your political women.")

The back-and-forth technique also raises some ethical problems. It is peculiar enough that book publishers aren't expected to vouch for the accuracy of their products, the way newspaper and magazine publishers are. The convention is that a book publisher is just a conduit for the voice of the author, be she saint or sinner. But when you have two authors taking turns in the same book, and arguing in its pages about some factual question, the effect is especially disconcerting. Or how about when one coauthor states something that the other coauthor knows to be untrue? Matalin says, regarding a campaign controversy about how often Clinton and Bush had each raised taxes: "Carville . . . got Kinsley to write this column about what a bunch of liars we were." As Carville surely knows, Carville did nothing of the sort. Kinsley dreamed up that column all by his loathsome. Checking with the dread Kinsley might be too much to expect, but Matalin might at least have checked with her own coauthor. And what did Carville think when he read this bit of "spin" in a book with his name on it?

As a read, *All's Fair* isn't terrible. Carville has some good lines ("I was carrying all of what I owned in a garment bag that hung from me like everything I'd ever worried about"), and the gum-chewing argot that Matalin adopts has its moments of charm (she talks of "Secret Service agents in a constant state of high freak"). There are some nice war stories, too, like Matalin's tales of the Bush campaign's dealings with a heckler in a chicken costume. At moments like these, the book does convey the smell and feel of a political campaign.

What Carville and Matalin have done, cleverly, is to cut out the middleman. Why give away this rich ancedotage to some journalist, who will turn around and sell it to the public for money? Why not sell the stuff yourself? Ever since 1960, when Theodore H. White invented the presidential-campaign history, most election cycles have produced some innovative variation on the theme, reflecting innovations in the campaigns themselves. Joe McGinniss's *The Selling of the President 1968* focused on political advertising. Timothy Crouse's *The Boys on the Bus* (about the 1972 campaign) focused on the growing role of the press. And so on. *All's Fair* is this year's innovation, and a fitting one. Spin doctors have taken over the campaigns. Why shouldn't they take over the history of them as well?

To be sure, it's one thing for a journalist to point out the artifice of a modern political campaign—the issues concocted in the consultants' laboratory, the sound bites crafted by committee, the institutionalized disingenuousness of the entire process. It's another thing for the perpetrators themselves to report—and, indeed, to revel in—the artifice. It seems shameless. But at least in this one respect, Carville and Matalin are communicating a truth.

The trouble is, they're not merely mining their jobs for valuable nuggets. They are strip-mining their lives. Or, to change commercial metaphors, not only does "James 'n' Mary: The Book" come preadapted for "James 'n' Mary: The Movie"—so, it seems, does "James 'n' Mary: The Life." When you've reached the point where you're spinning your underwear, you've left the real you—if there is any—pretty naked.

THE FINANCIAL FOOD CHAIN

(*Time*, OCTOBER 24, 1994)

Recently I received a brochure in the mail from Fidelity Investments, the giant financial company, inviting me to sign up for something called "Portfolio Advisory Services." For an annual fee of 1 percent, "a dedicated account executive" will invest my money for me, spreading it among Fidelity's dozens of "equity, bond and short-term mutual funds." My "portfolio" will be "personally tailored," of course, but basically the program promises what we all want: "preservation of assets as well as . . . growth and income." This is known as a "wraparound account." It is one of the newer products invented by the financial-services industry. (Words like "product" and "industry" are intended to give "financial services" the smell of a factory, where real things are made.)

It may be worth 1 percent to have a Fidelity expert guide me through the financial maze created by Fidelity and its rivals. Nevertheless, the wraparound account is a reductio ad absurdum. "Put Fidelity's Renowned Investment Management Expertise to Work for You," blares the brochure. That is what I thought I was doing when I invested in a Fidelity mutual fund. Now I'm told I must pay someone to tell me which mutual fund I should buy. Then I pay the mutual-fund managers to put me into the right stocks and bonds.

But most big companies are glorified mutual funds themselves these days, shuffling parts as if they were stock portfolios. Like middle-class "financial services," corporate "mergers and acquisitions" have become a permanent feature of American capitalism. Any pretense that they advanced some particular theory of corporate efficiency—that small companies are better than large ones, or vice versa; that owner management is better than wide public ownership, or vice versa; that conglomerates are better than single-industry firms, or vice versa—is now passé. Firms simply unite and divide like amoebas.

So, after I pay the "portfolio adviser" to choose my mutual funds and the mutual-fund manager to choose my stocks and bonds, I pay the top corporate executives to buy and sell the right divisions—and pay the investment bankers to tell them how to do it. Eventually, way down there somewhere, I maybe pay someone to make and sell a product. I wouldn't know.

Now consider this financial-services food chain from the other end. The limited-liability corporation evolved in the nineteenth century as a way for businesses to raise large sums of money and for investors to get the benefit of professional management. It became a brilliant device for directing capital to where it could be used most efficiently. The key was the separation of ownership and management. But were they ever supposed to get this separated? Count the layers of management. There's the management of the actual business, as a nineteenth-century capitalist might have recognized it. Then there's the management of the corporate shell. Then there are the investment bankers, putting companies in and out of "play." Then there are the mutual-fund managers, buying and selling company shares. And now there are wraparound account managers, buying and selling mutual funds.

A similar layering effect happens in the pension-fund corner of the financial world. Workers entrust their savings to trustees, who hire professional managers, who allot their assets among professional investment firms, so that the investment firms can in turn allot them among various stocks and bonds. And there's a whole subindustry of pension-fund consultants who get paid to tell the managers which investment firms to allot their assets among.

Each link in the financial-services food chain may make sense, but the whole chain raises two questions. First, are we weakening the signals on which the invisible hand of capitalism relies? How many layers of decision makers are there between my decision to save a dollar and someone else's decision to put that dollar to practical use? Each layer is like a relay station along an old, predigital telephone line: It propels the message but also slightly distorts it. Cumulatively, the small distortions can add up to a lot of noise in the system.

Second, American capitalism has just gone through a tumultuous corporate restructuring, in which layers of middle management were stripped away. The result was supposed to be a leaner, more efficient economy. But is it possible that much of this middle-management fat has simply been moved from within the corporations to the "financial services" world? By the time we've paid all the financial advisers and investment bankers who stand between us and the actual productive use of our money, a large chunk has been taken out of our total return.

Well, that's capitalism's problem. I have problems of my own. Like which financial-service company's wraparound account should I sign up for? Clearly, what's needed is a "product" that will invest your money in different wraparound accounts. That would be worth another percent or so off the top, wouldn't you say?

Let Them Eat Laptops

(*The New Yorker*, JANUARY 23, 1995)

On January 5, testifying before the House Ways and Means Committee, Speaker Newt Gingrich proposed the creation of a new means-tested welfare benefit: laptop computers.

"Maybe we need a tax credit," he said, "for the poorest Americans to buy a laptop. Now, maybe that's wrong, maybe it's expensive, maybe we can't do it. But I'll tell you, any signal we can send to the poorest Americans that says, 'We're going into a twenty-first-century, third-wave information age, and so are you, and we want to carry you with us,' begins to change the game."

Gingrich himself labeled the laptop tax credit "a nutty idea," but he was using the word "nutty" in its modern, self-congratulatory sense, in which insanity is linked with creativity and freedom from convention. The Speaker was projecting his preferred image of himself as pixielike and imaginative (as opposed to his critics' preferred image of him as nasty and calculating). Also high-tech and future-oriented (as opposed to old-fashioned and backward-looking). Also, of course, full of generous feelings toward the poor (as opposed to Ebenezer Scrooge-like).

On January 10, addressing the Progress and Freedom Foundation (one of his front groups), Gingrich conceded that the laptop tax-credit idea was not merely "nutty" but "dumb," and added, "I shouldn't have said it." He even revealed that he had called up George Will to apologize—apparently what one does in such circumstances—though he did not reveal whether Will had given him absolution. Still, it's worth considering the idea, because what's wrong with it illuminates what's wrong with a lot of what comes out of the Speaker's mouth.

As a Republican, Gingrich naturally did not propose that the government should give away or subsidize laptops directly (let alone manufacture them). Instead, he proposed a "tax credit." Now, a tax credit increases the deficit exactly as much as an equivalent direct-spending program. It commandeers and directs private funds by government fiat, in the service of some purported social goal, just as direct government spending does. But in the prevailing Republican theology a tax credit is different, because it is "allowing people to keep more of their own money." By this reckoning, tax credits make the government smaller, while direct spending makes it bigger. So a laptop tax credit would bring poor folks into the computer age without enlarging the government—something that would, of course, be anathema.

One problem, though. The poor have no use for a tax credit, because the poor pay no taxes (or no income taxes, anyway). Thanks to Bill Clinton's 1993 budget deal, which cut taxes for millions of the working poor— and which Gingrich, along with every other Republican in Congress, ardently opposed—a typical family is free of the income tax until its annual income reaches around $25,000. That is well above the poverty line.

Gingrich would have two options here. He could raise taxes on the poor (which would require a three-fifths vote in the House, under rules passed last week), in order to make the tax credit useful. Or he could make the credit "refundable," meaning that if the credit is higher than your tax bill the government sends you a check for the difference. In this case, since the tax bill of virtually all poor people is zero, they would be entitled to a government check for the full amount of the credit.

And "entitled" is the word. The Republicans' welfare-reform proposal would end "entitlement" status for major welfare programs such as Aid to Families with Dependent Children. The government would allot a certain amount of money each year, and if it ran out—say, because of a recession—the poor would just have to do without. Various categories of welfare mothers, such as unmarried women under the age of eighteen, would be made ineligible for AFDC from the beginning. But no welfare mother would have to do without her laptop, because tax credits are not budgeted like normal spending programs, owing to the cherished fiction that they're different. There is even talk of ending the entitlement status of food stamps. Under compassionate Speaker Gingrich, though, "computer stamps," at least, would be safe. Let them eat laptops.

Then there's the cost. There are about forty million Americans living below the official poverty line. At, say, a thousand dollars each for a modest laptop computer—no color screens; we don't want to spoil these people— we're talking about a potential bill of $40 billion, if every poor person took up Newt's invitation to join him on the information highway.

Imagine if Bill Clinton or Hillary Clinton or Ira Magaziner* had pro-

*Architect of Clinton's health care plan, widely criticized as overambitious (both the man and the plan)

posed such a thing, even speculatively: a $40 billion welfare program to buy poor people laptop computers. Rush Limbaugh would pop his buttons. The Heritage Foundation would flood the mails with cost estimates and warnings about how computers can be misused for criminal purposes. Republican Newtoids in Congress would be lining up on C-SPAN to offer mocking sound bites about foolish liberalism.

Perhaps this is making too much of a throwaway comment. But the triumphant Republicans, having won what they claim (with some justification) was a historic referendum on "government," owe us seriousness on the question of government's proper role. Do they seriously wish to defend a vision of America where all citizens are guaranteed laptop computers but not health care?

Newt Gingrich came to his current position of power through the relentless denigration of government as an institution that can do nothing right, wastes most of the resources allocated to it, and corrupts the very beneficiaries of its misguided largesse. That he could offhandedly urge the government to start giving away laptop computers suggests that he either doesn't believe or doesn't understand his own propaganda.

Even as he retracted his endorsement of a laptop tax credit, Gingrich repeated his "passionate" commitment to seeing poor people plugged into the Internet. This is a fine sentiment. But passion is no substitute for money. Either society owes everyone a computer or it does not. Principled conservatives have the courage to say it does not. Unprincipled conservatives want moral credit for wishing everyone had a computer while sneering at any conceivable method for making that wish come true.

Gingrich seems to think he can turn various personalities on and off like a light bulb. One day he is Newt the Destroyer, out to bring down the government; the next day he is Kindly Uncle Newt, handing out government-financed computers. After sixteen years as the fiercest partisan in Washington, he declares that he wishes to put aside partisanship, and then explodes in self-righteous anger when reporters express skepticism. You could say this makes the new House Speaker complex and interesting. Or you could say it makes him a phony.

The Intellectual Free Lunch

(*The New Yorker*, FEBRUARY 6, 1995)

The weekend before President Clinton's State of the Union Address, *The Wall Street Journal* assembled a focus group of middle-class white males—the demographic group *du jour*—to plumb the depth of their proverbial anger. The results were highly satisfactory. These guys are mad as hell. They're mad at welfare, they're mad at special-interest lobbyists. "But perhaps the subject that produces the most agreement among the group," the *Journal* reports, "is the view that Washington should stop sending money abroad and instead zero in on the domestic front."

A poll released last week by the Program on International Policy Attitudes at the University of Maryland contains similar findings. According to this survey, 75 percent of Americans believe that the United States spends "too much" on foreign aid, and 64 percent want foreign-aid spending cut. Apparently, a cavalier 11 percent of Americans think it's fine to spend "too much" on foreign aid. But there is no denying the poll's larger finding that big majorities say they think the tab is too high.

Respondents were also asked, though, how big a share of the federal budget currently goes to foreign aid. The median answer was 15 percent; the average answer was 18 percent. The correct answer is less than 1 percent: The United States government spends about $14 billion a year on foreign aid (including military assistance), out of a total budget of $1.5 trillion. To a question about how much foreign-aid spending would be "appropriate," the median answer was 5 percent of the budget. A question about how much would be "too little" produced a median answer of 3 percent—more than three times the current level of foreign-aid spending.

To the International Policy folks at the University of Maryland, these results demonstrate "strong support for maintaining foreign aid at current spending levels or higher." That's just their liberal-internationalist spin, of course. You might say with equal justice that the results demonstrate a national wish to see foreign aid cut by two thirds. It's true that after the pollsters humiliated their subjects with the correct answer to the question about how much (or, rather, how little) the United States spends on foreign aid, only 35 percent of the respondents had the fortitude to say they still wanted to see it cut. But what people will say after being corrected by an authority figure with a clipboard hardly constitutes "strong support."

This poll is less interesting for what it shows about foreign aid than for what it shows about American democracy. It's not just that Americans are scandalously ignorant. It's that they seem to believe they have a democratic right to their ignorance. All over the country—at dinner tables, in focus groups, on call-in radio shows, and, no doubt, occasionally on the floor of Congress—citizens are expressing outrage about how much we spend on foreign aid, without having the faintest idea what that amount is. This is not, surely, a question of being misinformed. No one—not even Rush Limbaugh—is out there spreading the falsehood that we spend 15 percent of the federal budget ($225 billion) on foreign aid. People are forming and expressing passionate views about foreign aid on the basis of no information at all. Or perhaps they think that the amount being spent on foreign aid is a matter of opinion, like everything else.

Populism, in its latest manifestation, celebrates ignorant opinion and undifferentiated rage. As long as you're mad as hell and aren't going to take it anymore, no one will inquire very closely into what, exactly, "it" is and whether you really ought to feel that way. Pandering politicians are partly to blame, to be sure. So is the development christened "hyperdemocracy" by last week's *Time:* the way the communications revolution is eroding representative government by providing instant feedback between voters' whims and politicians' actions. But ubiquitous opinion polls are part of the problem, too.

The typical opinion poll about, say, foreign aid doesn't trouble to ask whether the respondent knows the first thing about the topic being opined upon, and no conventional poll disqualifies an answer on the ground of mere total ignorance. The premise of opinion polling is that people are, and of right ought to be, omni-opinionated—that they should have views on all subjects at all times—and that all such views are equally valid. It's always remarkable how few people say they "aren't sure" about or "don't know" the answer to some pollster's question. ("Never thought about it," "Couldn't care less," and "Let me get back to you on that after I've done some reading" aren't even options.) So, given the prominence of polls in our political culture, it's no surprise that people have come to believe that their opinions on the issues of the day need not be fettered by either facts or reflection.

Add opinions to the list of symptoms of the free-lunch disease that blights American politics. First came the fiscal free lunch: taxes can be cut without cutting middle-class government benefits. Then came the foreign-policy free lunch: America can strut as the world's superpower without putting blood or treasure at risk. Now there's the intellectual free lunch: I'm entitled to vociferous opinions on any subject, without having to know, or even think, about it.

All this may sound horribly snooty. But it isn't. It is not the argument that Walter Lippmann made in *Public Opinion,* where he advocated relying on elite "bureaus" of wise men to make crucial policy decisions. Lippmann's belief was that modern life had rendered public policy too complex for the average voter. But there is nothing especially complex about the factual question of how much the country spends on foreign aid. It may be too heavy a burden of civic responsibility to expect every citizen—what with work and family and life outside politics—to carry this number around in his or her head. But it is not asking too much to expect a citizen to recognize that he or she needs to know that number, at least roughly, in order to have a valid opinion about whether it is too large or too small. Americans are capable of making informed, reflective decisions on policy questions. But they often seem to be under the impression that they needn't bother.

We need a new form of democratic piety. It shows respect, not contempt, for "the people" to hold them to something approaching the intellectual standard you would apply to yourself or a friend. By contrast, it is contemptuous, not respectful, to excuse "the people" from all demands of intellectual rigor or honesty on the ground that their judgments are wise by definition. We honor our friends by challenging them when we think they're wrong. It shows that we take them seriously. Believers in democracy owe "the people" no less.

THE SPOILS OF VICTIMHOOD

(*The New Yorker*, MARCH 27, 1995)

Affirmative action is one of those controversies, like abortion, in which opponents have the advantage of moral clarity. They are defending a seemingly absolute principle, while supporters are defending something much more ambiguous.

If you believe that human life begins at the moment of conception, abortion is murder, plain and simple. The opposing principle—that a woman has the right to "control her own body"—can't possibly be so absolute. (It doesn't give the right to kill your Siamese twin, for example.) Few abortion opponents actually carry their morally clear principle to its logical conclusion: that women who procure abortions should be prosecuted for murder—and, in death-penalty states, executed. But the seeming moral clarity is a great rhetorical plus.

In the case of affirmative action, opponents have the further advantage that the morally clear principle they are defending is one we all profess to share. We don't all agree that human life begins at conception, but we do all agree—or, at least, fear to disagree—that the United States ought to be a society of "color-blind equal opportunity" (henceforth "CBEO"). We all "oppose on principle any counting, discriminating or allocating by race" (as one conservative columnist recently stated the anti-affirmative-action credo)—or, at least, we would like to do so. When opponents of affirmative action quote Martin Luther King, Jr., about judging people by the content of their character, not the color of their skin, who can object? You can argue about the reality, but you won't get far by challenging the ideal.

Opposition to affirmative action has a second great advantage in today's political culture: It feeds that powerful hunger for the moral prestige and political spoils of victimhood. It gives white males whining rights in the victimization bazaar, just like minorities and women. This also is an advantage not shared by opposition to abortion, which—agree with it or not—is selfless. Right-to-lifers are out to protect the interests of what they see as a powerless other person. Arguments against affirmative action, by contrast, offer a moral gloss for self-interest, which is always appealing. And the appeal cuts across economic and cultural lines. It tempts lower-middle-class workers concerned about their stagnant incomes and job security. It tempts yuppie professionals concerned about their promotions at work and their kids' college admissions. It tempts intellectuals concerned about their tenure. Republicans have decided, with almost sadistic delight, to make affirmative action their "wedge" issue for 1996—the issue that will pry various voting blocs away from the Democratic party for good. Democrats are struck dumb with terror, or reduced to pathetically disingenuous denials that affirmative action violates the sacred CBEO principle.

There's plenty to be cynical about in the current campaign against affirmative action. Conservatives, who ordinarily sneer at victim chic, embrace it in this case. Today's sanctimonious calls for color-blind equal opportunity for the benefit of whites come primarily from political elements that opposed the principle when it was enshrined, in the 1950s and 1960s, to help blacks. (Republicans as moderate as George Bush were against the 1964 Civil Rights Act.) And even today much of the political power of anti-affirmative-action rhetoric is based on its appeal to emotions that are anything but color-blind. But all that is mere irony. Most affirmative-action opponents are not racists. The issue inflames emotions that are understandable, if not logical.

Especially in our sound-bite-and-spin political culture, it is hard for logic to prevail over emotion. You cannot trump a simple and ringing principle like CBEO with "Wait a minute—it's more complicated than that." But in the case of affirmative action it *is* more complicated than that. Even as an aspiration, let alone as a description of the United States right now, "color-blind equal opportunity" is full of logical problems—problems so severe that they make any self-righteous anathema on affirmative action nonsensical.

Opponents of affirmative action have a potted history and a potted analysis that go together. The potted history is that the civil rights movement was good through about 1964, when it pushed to eliminate discrimination against blacks, and went bad after about 1969, when it started pushing for discrimination against whites. The period 1964–69 was an alleged golden age of near-unanimous agreement that there should be no discrimination either way. The potted analysis is that there is a simple spectrum of discrimination, with a zero point in the middle—the CBEO point—where discrimination against blacks stops and discrimination against whites begins. But it is not possible either historically or analytically to draw a sharp distinction between "good" civil rights and "bad" affirmative action. The two are entwined.

We needn't dwell on the obvious and boring fact that there is still plenty of racism and discrimination of the traditional white-on-black sort, which is a significant handicap to blacks trying to make it in American society. In 1990, the Urban Institute sent out young blacks and young whites with equivalent résumés and references, and who had been trained to behave identically, to apply for entry-level jobs. The whites did substantially better. You're not surprised, are you? Although affirmative action of course gives blacks an advantage in specific situations, a black face is still a net minus in the climb up the American greasy pole.

Then, there's the equally obvious fact that the typical black American does *not* run the race of life with "equal opportunity" at the starting gate. Most blacks are at a disadvantage that begins with prenatal nutrition and runs through education to almost every other factor in career success. It hardly matters whether this disadvantage is due to the legacy of past racism or the failures of the Great Society, or whatever. The fact remains.

Indeed, leave aside the racial issue and consider the alleged principle of "equal opportunity" for a moment. It is an odd one. We all pay lip service to it, but in many respects it is not even accepted, let alone realized. It is violated in ways we can all agree to deplore—e.g., nepotism—but it is also violated in ways we tolerate, or even celebrate. Elite colleges, for example, routinely seek geographical diversity in their student bodies, turning down better-qualified applicants from Brooklyn or Brookline to make room for a North Dakotan. Yet people are not tearing their hair out over that. Preferential treatment for alumni children is also fairly uncontroversial.

These are narrowly mechanical examples. More generally, consider child rearing. You cannot watch what frenzied yuppie parents do for their kids—the intelligence-nurturing toys, the infinite variety of special lessons, and so on—without concluding that either these parents are wasting a lot of money and energy or their kids are gaining a major leg up in life. I suppose the correct answer is both. Yet who would criticize these parents for wanting their best for their kids? Then, there are connections. A friend recently asked me to help her son get a summer job in journalism. And, of course, I did what I could. Should I have refused to help my friend's kid, in the name of "equal opportunity"? It wouldn't be human.

The child of a Supreme Court justice, to choose a ripe example, will enjoy vast quantities of this kind of unequal opportunity—whatever the child's race, and whatever the parent's stated views on affirmative action. Racism need not be involved. But this sort of thing does, as a practical matter, put most blacks at a real disadvantage. And it puts the whole notion of "equal opportunity" in a strange light.

It is important to distinguish two different arguments for "equal opportunity." There is the economic-efficiency argument: that the economy works best, for the good of the entire society, when an irrelevant factor like race (or connections or geography) is not allowed to interfere with selecting the best-qualified person for the job. Then there is the fairness argument: that it is unfair to a particular individual to deny him or her a job or other career opportunity because of an irrelevant factor like race (or connections or geography). The efficiency argument is valid, at least in theory. The fairness argument is much murkier. Yet it is the fairness argument that sustains opposition to affirmative action.

In *The Bell Curve*, their best-selling book on race, genes, and intelligence, Charles Murray and the late Richard Herrnstein willfully or sloppily confuse the two arguments. The authors make clear their hostility to affirmative action. Indeed, it doesn't require too much psychological over-reaching to speculate that hostility to affirmative action was a chief motivation for their project. They ask, in reference to affirmative action: "To what extent is a society fair when people of similar ability and background are treated as differently as they are now?" And they answer: "Such a society is manifestly unfair." Although they acknowledge that blacks are still behind whites in job status and pay, they argue that this is not true "after controlling for I.Q." In other words, blacks are already doing as well as they deserve to, given their lower intelligence. Therefore, Murray and Herrnstein conclude, affirmative action imposes "costs in economic efficiency and fairness."

One reviewer of *The Bell Curve*—Alan Ryan, writing in *The New York Review of Books*—labels this the "dollars per IQ point" argument, and dryly observes: "If your notion of justice is that people should be paid according to their IQs, then [affirmative action] is unjust." But, furthermore, Murray and Herrnstein have the logical connection between their factual assertions about IQ and their moral outrage about affirmative action exactly backward. The *more* ability is determined to be innate and inexorable—something you're born with and bear no moral responsibility for—the *less* sense it makes to talk about equal opportunity in moral terms as a matter of "fairness." What kind of "equal opportunity" is it to be born with a low IQ?

Whatever combination of genes and environment may be responsible, each of us plays the game of life with cards dealt by forces largely beyond our control. The content of our characters is the least of it. This makes "equal opportunity" a dubious, if not meaningless, standard of fairness. Dispensing with the fairness argument and sticking with economic efficiency would leave affirmative action opponents on a firmer logical footing (though published estimates of the cost of affirmative action—4 percent of gross national product, in one case—are highly tendentious). But abandoning the banner of "fairness" would drain the cause of most of its demagogic appeal. And, to the reasonable mind, it would raise the question of whether the social benefit was worth a certain economic cost.

After all, traditional civil rights enforcement of the kind almost everyone claims to believe in can also impose a real economic cost. Much discrimination in the economy is motivated not by irrational racism but by rational economic calculation. It is easier and cheaper to hire on the basis of group generalizations than to judge each person on individual merit. If those generalizations made no economic sense, a law would not be necessary to prevent most employers from making them. But we do have such a law, having correctly decided that social justice is worth some economic cost. In this way, among others, affirmative action is on a continuum with traditional civil rights principles, not a departure from them.

Of course, it is widely believed that the proper goal of civil rights is a society where people are judged as individuals and not as members of a group. This ideal, many people say, is what divides "good" civil rights from "bad" affirmative action. But, like "equal opportunity" and other shibboleths of the affirmative action debate, the appealing notion of "individuals, not groups" is more a slogan than a coherent principle.

What does it mean to judge people "as individuals" and not as members of a group? Does it mean that each person should be evaluated in a way that does not involve assumptions based on that person's membership in some group? In that sense, no one is ever judged as an individual. Every criterion used in the meritocratic selection process, whether for a job or a place at school, is a generalization from some group trait. Those generalizations are always approximate, and sometimes wrong. Even the most seemingly scientific and individually tailored measurement—say, a score on a medical-school entrance exam—cannot predict with perfect accuracy who will make the best doctors. People who score high on the exam are being judged, as a group, more likely than others to become good doctors, and as a generalization that may be perfectly valid. (More refined selection machinery may be impossible or too costly.) But it *is* a group generalization.

True, there are groups and groups. "People who score high on their medical-school entrance exams" are not self-identified as a group, and feel no group affinity. Other groups that get systematic group preference in our society—veterans, for example—have more of the symptoms of "groupiness." Giving veterans preference (e.g., for civil service jobs) violates the "equal opportunity" principle that a job should go to the best-qualified candidate. It does so in favor of the apparently superior principle of rewarding those who have sacrificed for their country. But that, too, is only a generalization. Some veterans may have sacrificed nothing in particular, while nonveterans who have sacrificed greatly in other ways get no preference, or may even lose out to a less deserving veteran. The point is not that giving veterans preference is a bad idea—only that, like any group generalization, it is approximate. Yet we live with it.

What is different about group generalizations based on race? Generalizations that discriminate against blacks have been outlawed for obvious historical reasons. But what of group generalizations that discriminate in favor of blacks? How are they different from the group generalizations that are the warp and woof of daily life? The answer cannot be that they are different simply because race is innate and immutable. So, according to its enthusiasts, is IQ—yet opponents of affirmative action generally wish to see the role of such innate characteristics (if not IQ, then "merit" or "talent") enhanced, not reduced. The answer must be that race is such a toxic subject in American culture that it should not enter into calculations about people's places in society—even in order to benefit racism's historic victims. That is a respectable answer. But it understandably rings hollow to many blacks, who see this sudden and ostentatious anathema on racial consciousness as a bit too convenient. Where was color blindness when they needed it?

In practice, moreover, even the most devout preachers of CBEO tolerate violations of the alleged color-blind principle, either because of a more important principle or because of some consideration more pressing than principle. The Republican party, for example, has never acted as if it regarded color blindness as a supreme moral axiom. Republicans, who were slow to approach the CBEO zero point in the 1960s, have often charged past it in the years since. If color blindness is a virtue, hypocrisy in this case is the tribute virtue pays to vice.

Like many of the supposed excesses of the Great Society, affirmative action actually got its big push under President Richard Nixon. The first official government affirmative action program was the Philadelphia Plan, designed to cure racial segregation in the construction industry by making federal contracts contingent on the racial composition of the workforce. The plan was created and then killed by the Johnson administration; Nixon not only revived it but lobbied hard to prevent Congress from killing it again.

During the Reagan years, administration officials like Clarence Thomas, the chairman of the Equal Employment Opportunity Commission, enforced racial hiring "goals." The 1988 Republican platform promised to "increase, strengthen, and reinvigorate" government programs that earmarked contracts and subsidized loans for minorities. Although the 1992 platform declared, "Promoting opportunity, we reject efforts to replace equal rights with quotas or other preferential treatment." David Frum points out in his book, *Dead Right:* "Every committee convened at the [1992] convention was required to be half composed of women and the speaking roster was filled with the names of nobodies selected only because of their sex or race." Even as the GOP plots to make racial favoritism its hot-button issue for 1996, *Newsweek* reports on a "GOP Minority Outreach Strategy" memo that calls for preferential committee assignments for minority House members and special efforts to find minorities to testify at congressional hearings.

But this kind of garden-variety political hypocrisy is less interesting than the larger, and possibly sincere, moral confusion of those who maintain that there's a good kind of affirmative action, which upholds the CBEO principle, and a bad kind, which betrays it. This is a widespread view, even among the harshest critics of affirmative action as it is practiced today. Something like it may be what House Speaker Newt Gingrich had in mind when he remarked the other day, semicoherently, "It is my belief that affirmative action programs, if done for individuals, are good, but if done by some group distinction, bad, because it is antithetical to the American dream to measure people by the genetic patterns of their great-grandmothers." In *The Bell Curve,* Murray and Herrnstein are a bit clearer. The context is a discussion of college-admissions policy, but the logic applies to affirmative action in any field:

> *Universities should cast a wide net in seeking applicants, making special efforts to seek talent wherever it lives—in the black South Bronx, Latino Los Angeles, and white Appalachia alike. In the case of two candidates who are fairly closely matched otherwise, universities should give the nod to the applicant from the disadvantaged background. This original sense of affirmative action seems to us to have been not only reasonable and fair but wise.*

Like others who take a similar line, Murray and Herrnstein claim to be asserting a prelapsarian civil rights ideal. This "good" kind of affirmative action has three elements. First, it involves only the preliminary stages of the selection process (often summarized as "recruitment and training"), not the offer of a job or other selective goody itself. Second, it is only a tiebreaker: No one of superior merit will ever be displaced by someone of inferior merit. Third, "disadvantage" is defined in nonracial terms. (This is sometimes called affirmative action by social or economic class.) Do these elements describe an effective form of affirmative action that nevertheless passes CBEO muster? Not really.

First, discrimination in recruitment and training is still discrimination. Someone in the disfavored class will not get the job who otherwise would. If the special recruitment efforts are aimed specifically at racial minorities, as affirmative action opponents less zealous than Murray and Herrnstein would allow, that means that whites who might also benefit from recruitment and training are being victimized.

Second, a tiebreaker matters only for the last available slot. If two people are equally qualified for admission to a college class of a 1,000, the solution is to admit or to reject them both, unless—by an extraordinary coincidence—they are worse qualified than exactly 999 other applicants. It is affirmative action critics—especially Murray and Herrnstein, with their IQ obsession—who seem to imagine that everyone in America can be ranked with scientific precision, from No. 1 to No. 260,000,000, in terms of his or her qualification for any desirable career opportunity. Under that assumption, or even under a less extreme version of it, tiebreaker affirmative action would be meaningless. But if you start to take a more relaxed and nuanced view of "qualifications"—that people are often equally qualified, or, at least, that the machinery for ranking people by qualifications is often crude—you undermine both the fairness case and the efficiency case against traditional affirmative action.

Third, what about affirmative action based on "disadvantage" rather than on race? In recent weeks, this has become the hottest idea in the affirmative action debate. Even President Clinton, answering a press conference question about affirmative action on March 3, said that he favors "need-based programs."

Reverse discrimination based on something other than race would indeed make affirmative action color-blind, but it would not cure affirmative action's other supposed defects. It would still be social engineering. There would still be "victims." It would still mean passing over a better-"qualified" candidate for a less "qualified" one. If that is unfair and economically costly, the injustice and the cost remain even though the color consciousness would be eliminated. The alleged stigma—to oneself and others—of having got the desirable slot through affirmative action rather than by one's own just deserts would remain as well.

Then, there is the problem of defining and comparing "disadvantage." Affirmative action opponents have justifiable fun with the puzzle of deciding, in a society of racial mongrels, who, exactly, is black—and, beyond that, what other ethnic groups should qualify for official "victim" status. Changing the standard to disadvantage in the abstract would make the puzzle a nightmare. Is it worse to be a cleaning lady's son or a coal miner's daughter? Two points if your father didn't go to college, minus one if he finished high school, plus three if you have no father? (Or will that reward illegitimacy, which we're all trying hard these days not to do?) Communist societies tried this kind of institutionalized reverse discrimination—penalizing children of the middle class—without any enviable success. Officially sanctioned affirmative action by "disadvantage" would turn today's festival of competitive victimization into an orgy.

Once you accept "disadvantage" as a legitimate ground for favoritism, moreover, the question arises of whether it is so terrible to use "black" as at least one rough-and-ready shorthand for "disadvantaged." After all, advocates of this kind of affirmative action acknowledge that many, if not most, of its beneficiaries would, in fact, be black. To be sure, not all blacks are disadvantaged, and not all disadvantaged people (however you choose to define the word) are black. But generalizations, as has been noted, are an inevitable part of any selection process. And the generalization "Black equals disadvantaged" is probably as accurate as many generalizations that go unchallenged, such as "High test score equals good doctor" or "Veteran equals sacrifice for the nation."

So opponents of today's affirmative action cannot take refuge in some ideal version of it that would avoid giving offense to their stated principles. And even today there are many situations where affirmative action opponents don't uphold the alleged principle of color blindness—or where they preach it while practicing the opposite. How much is left of the CBEO principle when all these situations are added up?

Almost everybody accepts, for example, the idea that sometimes diversity of races, or even race itself, is a valid job consideration. Hiring policemen is a common illustration. Being black is a positive job qualification for a cop patrolling a black neighborhood (or, at least, racial diversity is a valid hiring goal for a city police force). The selection of Supreme Court justices is widely accepted to be another situation where it seems to be okay to take race or sex into account. Why? Because the notion that measuring "qualifications" alone can scientifically pinpoint the best Supreme Court justice is especially absurd, and because the notion that a diverse Supreme Court has value for its own sake is especially appealing. Ronald Reagan promised outright to appoint a woman justice, and did so. George Bush swore that race had nothing to do with his selection of Clarence Thomas, but nobody believed him.

A more complicated example of acceptable reverse discrimination is the whole area of "remedies." Although there are arguments about the details, even hard-core affirmative action opponents accept the principle that racially conscious "remedies"—e.g., reverse discrimination, even quotas—may be imposed by the courts (or sometimes by lesser authorities) when an employer or an organization is found to have practiced traditional racial discrimination in the past. This is supposedly part of the "true," pre-1969 meaning of "civil rights." It's an odd exception to the alleged color-blind principle, when you think about it. Can the same civil rights precepts really forbid you to practice reverse discrimination except when they require you to do the same thing? (That is indeed how the 1964 Civil Rights Act is generally interpreted.) The idea of a judicial "remedy" is that the victim of injustice has a right to be made whole and the wrongdoer has no right to complain. But the reverse discrimination remedy usually benefits people who were not victims of the specific act of past discrimination,

and the burden falls on people who were not responsible for it or beneficiaries of it.

In a way, the "remedy" exception, if you accept its logic, swallows the
ostensible color-blindness rule. After all, a major justification for affirmative action in general is making up for past discrimination. The whole
thing is a remedy. Indeed, the "remedy" logic works better in general than
it does in the particular. Unlike past specific episodes of racial injustice,
past racial injustice in general really does have some bearing on the relative
places of random blacks and whites today. If people really could be ranked
from No. 1 to No. 260,000,000 in terms of "qualifications," past discrimination would clearly have moved blacks down the queue and moved
whites up—and affirmative action really does begin to look like rough
justice for that. Of course, in real life there is no such simple queue. So
the black person who moves up the line thanks to affirmative action may
not logically "deserve" the place he gets. But, for the same reason, the
white person who loses that place doesn't "deserve" it, either.

A third widely acknowledged exception to CBEO involves private,
voluntary efforts that favor blacks—as opposed to rules imposed by government or the courts. Of all aspects of the affirmative action debate, this
one leads to the most comic somersaults of logic by professed defenders
of the sacred CBEO principle. In 1990, the Bush administration declared
that university scholarships earmarked for minorities violated CBEO and
were against the law. A fuss ensued, and the administration retreated to
the position that the anathema on minority scholarships applied only to
scholarships financed by universities themselves. Minority scholarships financed by private individuals, corporations, and foundations were not
merely permissible but praiseworthy. "I've long been committed to them,"
George Bush said. The alleged difference was that universities are federal
contractors, and therefore semigovernmental actors. But it was never explained how racially earmarked scholarships could be immoral in the one
case and praiseworthy in the other.

Is private affirmative action good or bad? Even the right-wing Heritage Foundation has had scholarships earmarked for minorities. Private
efforts directed specifically at minorities, amounting to overt racial favoritism, are widespread, and it is unthinkable that conservatives, of all people, would want the power of the federal government used to smash them.
What's more, it is a perfectly coherent position to hold that private indi-

viduals should have more leeway to discriminate than the government has. But that doesn't solve the mystery of why the identical violation of the sacred CBEO principle should be positively evil when practiced by the government and positively good when practiced privately. After all, private, voluntary affirmative action is not "voluntary" for the victim—the white person who can't get a job or scholarship because a minority was favored. The alleged harm of affirmative action is exactly the same whether it is voluntary and private or is government-imposed.

And there's another logical problem: We do not permit—let alone glorify—private, voluntary racial discrimination *against* blacks. You cannot offer jobs or scholarships exclusively to whites. We have decided that the government can and should intrude in those circumstances. That decision, and the decision to regard private reverse discrimination differently, may be right or wrong. But, taken together, these two decisions grossly violate the principle of color blindness. Ban private racial discrimination in one case; tolerate it, and even celebrate it, in the other. Yet that represents the consensus view of most affirmative action opponents.

There are only two ways to escape from this logical box while preserving a commitment to CBEO. One would be to support a government crackdown on private efforts to help minorities—which is hardly what those plotting to make affirmative action a big political issue have in mind. (Some might favor a crackdown on brazen reverse discrimination—such as overt racial quotas—even when it is private. But few would use the civil rights laws against reverse discrimination as rigorously as we use them against discrimination of the classic sort.) The other option would be to support repeal of the 1964 Civil Rights Act, thereby allowing private, voluntary racial discrimination of all kinds. Whatever its other merits, this second option would certainly bury the notion that affirmative action opponents wish to fulfill the true meaning of the Civil Rights Act. A third option, of course, would be to abandon the pretense that CBEO is a coherent principle.

The point is that a pure, discrimination-free society is not merely a hopeless ideal; it is a logical mirage. One final example: actuarial justice. Whites live longer than blacks; women live longer than men. Actuarially, whites should have to pay more each year for the equivalent Social Security pension, and pay less for the equivalent life-insurance policy. Ditto women and men. Does race-neutral—and sex-neutral—justice require that whites and blacks, women and men, pay the same rates, or that they get the same insurance value per dollar paid? There is no logical solution to this puzzle. (That's why our real-life solutions are all over the lot.)

To be sure, affirmative action supporters have their own muddles and false distinctions, and pay their own hypocritical obeisance to CBEO. They cling to a mythical difference between affirmative action and reverse discrimination, or between goals and quotas. In the 1978 *Bakke* case, the Supreme Court's first major ruling on affirmative action, Justice Lewis Powell made much of the distinction between using race as a "factor" in the selection process and using it as the "decisive" factor. But, for any given applicant, the selection process is an all-or-nothing proposition. And a factor is not a factor unless it sometimes makes the difference. When race is the deciding factor, it might just as well have been the sole factor: Someone has gained an opportunity, and someone else has lost one, simply because of race. Likewise, there is no sensible moral distinction between a flexible goal and a rigid quota. Both are reverse discrimination. If the goal never leads to a specific advantage for a specific individual, it is meaningless. And if that advantage causes some other individual to lose out, it might as well have been a quota of one as far as he is concerned.

Good people find this hard to accept. They cling to Justice Powell's comforting belief in the ambiguity of "factors." But consider a law-school class of a hundred. Case 1: Ten places in the class are reserved for blacks. It is the "decisive" factor. This is roughly the situation that Powell found unconstitutional in *Bakke*. Case 2: In the admissions formula, whatever it may be—board scores plus grades minus parking tickets, and so on—blacks are awarded extra points. It's just a "factor"—okay by the Powell standard—but some number of extra points will produce exactly ten blacks in the class. Indeed, under the assumption that everyone, black or white, can be ranked by formula, they will be the same ten blacks who would be admitted under a rigid quota. And the same whites—some number up to ten of them—will lose their places. What, morally, is the difference?

The federal courts are currently revisiting another false distinction enshrined in their own doctrine: that between reverse discrimination in hiring and reverse discrimination in layoffs. In 1986, the courts ruled against reverse discrimination in layoffs, reasoning: "While hiring goals impose a diffuse burden . . . layoffs impose the entire burden of achieving racial equality on particular individuals." Of course, hiring goals also impose the entire burden on a particular individual—the one who would have got the job but didn't. The burden is "diffuse" only in the sense that in hirings, as opposed to layoffs, we don't know who that person is. This may make affirmative action more politically tolerable, in the way that we often impose burdens in the abstract (such as, ultimately, the burden of dying in defense of one's country) that would be unbearable to impose in the particular. But is there a real moral distinction between hirings and layoffs? I can't see it. Affirmative action defenders, like affirmative action opponents, must have the courage of their convictions—for opponents, that CBEO is an absolute principle; for defenders, that reverse racial discrimination is morally justified—or must revise them.

The current layoffs case that is drawing a lot of attention, *Taxman* v. *Piscataway,* involves two public-school teachers, one black and one white, who were equal by every available standard of CBEO, such as academic credentials and written evaluations. They were equal, as well, by seniority—a typical sort of non-CBEO standard that doesn't seem to bother anybody. If it weren't for affirmative action, the choice between them would have been made by the flip of a coin. So this is what the affirmative action debate comes down to. Is the color-blind principle so sacred, so inviolable, that the school board must flip a coin rather than decide that America might be better off with more black teachers?

Of course, what I have been arguing here has not really been the case for affirmative action—more like the case against the case against affirmative action. And I have not meant to suggest that a color-blind society—or, at least, a color-blind economy—is a meaningless or worthless goal. The point is that it's a complicated and ambiguous goal, and the notion that all other goals—including other civil rights goals—must give way before it belongs in the world of agitprop.

CBEO is not the only argument made against affirmative action. There is the stigma argument: the assumption of inferiority—by the affirmative action beneficiaries themselves as well as by others. The stigma, as critics point out, attaches even to minority-group members who are making it, or could make it, without affirmative action. There is the undeniable social tension and resentment caused by the perception that affirmative action is unfair, whether that perception is rational or not. (This argument, of course, is often advanced by the very people working to aggravate the social tension they claim to deplore.) There is the problem

of limiting the principle. What groups—women? Hispanics? Asians?—
are entitled to affirmative action, and how do you define the members of
the group?

And, as with any form of social engineering, there is the problem of
politicizing outcomes that—just or unjust—would otherwise be written
off as the workings of fate. The last thing our political culture needs is
more opportunities for people to take umbrage. By making the question
of who gets what job a matter of public policy, affirmative action opens it
up to politics. In politics, almost by definition, minority interests are at a
disadvantage. So, to some extent, affirmative action brings its current
problems on itself.

All these problems suggest that affirmative action is a social policy
that should be used with care, weighing the costs against the benefits in
each circumstance. What they do not suggest is that a ban on affirmative
action is anything like a moral imperative.

One form of affirmative action that certainly does not meet a reasonable cost-benefit test is affirmative action for businesses owned by minorities and women: preferential access to government contracts, subsidized
loans, and communication licenses. The House of Representatives recently
voted to kill one of these preferences—a fat tax break for companies that
sell broadcast and cable stations to minorities—and rightly so. Anyone in
a position to buy and operate a television station either is already affluent
or is just fronting for white males. Rich blacks undoubtedly face disadvantages compared with rich whites, but they are not disadvantages worth
incurring the real costs of affirmative action to rectify. The Federal Communications Commission's affirmative action policy has been especially
farcical. Members of favored groups who get valuable licenses, for nothing
or at a discount, are more or less free to resell them, at market rates, to
white males or anyone else. The policy amounts to the simple anointment
of black millionaires. And, because black millionaire businessmen are such
an obvious exception to the generalization that "black equals disadvantaged," these policies help to discredit affirmative action even in situations
where the generalization makes more sense.

The FCC insanity illuminates an important fact about the reverse
discrimination controversy: Reverse discrimination usually occurs in situations where someone—often the government—is allocating inequality.
Somebody gets a valuable government license; somebody else doesn't.

Somebody gets into medical school; somebody else doesn't. And, rather than obsessing about whether the inequality ought to be allocated on the basis of race, we might do better to ponder whether reducing the inequality might make more sense than arguing about the allocation.

The FCC has been anointing millionaires for decades. Most of them have been white males. Only recently has it begun auctioning off (rather than giving away) some of its valuable licenses, so that their value is shared by all of us. That change is surely a greater triumph for fairness than either applying or repealing affirmative action. An economist would look at the excess demand for medical school slots and say that this is a market out of whack. The selection process—even assuming that applicants can be ranked accurately according to their doctoring potential—excludes many who would become good doctors. Instead of arguing about the race of those who make the cut, why not try to bring the market into equilibrium? A variety of government policies—such as overrestrictive rules about what services nurses and paramedics may perform—artificially inflate the advantage of being a doctor. Reform those policies (which is starting to happen), and the market will begin to sort itself out. More of those who wish to become doctors will be able to do so. Surely that serves egalitarian principles more than a change—in either direction—in the racial composition of medical school admissions.

Affirmative action has become a scapegoat for the anxieties of the white middle class. Some of those anxieties are justified; some are self-indulgent fantasies. But the actual role of affirmative action in denying opportunities to white people is small compared with its role in the public imagination and the public debate. Black unemployment is still higher than white unemployment, and blacks still trail whites in every major prestige occupation outside sports. That reality raises many troubling questions—about affirmative action, among other things. But it also suggests that few whites have actually lost a career opportunity to a less qualified black—certainly far fewer than the number who have been whipped into a fury of resentment over affirmative action.

What is most poisonous about the campaign against affirmative action is that it invites whites to blame blacks for their problems. What is almost as poisonous, though, is the way attacks on affirmative action reinforce the 1-to-260-million myth: the myth that, in the absence of racial discrimination, we would all find our places in life according to our just deserts. Oddly, the philosophy of affirmative action itself derives from, and reinforces, the same myth. This myth nurtures frenzies of resentment that do our politics plenty of damage. American society would be healthier—and not only on the race issue—if people, black and white, would keep in mind that neither just deserts nor nefarious discrimination is as important, in determining one's lot in life, as simple luck.